"THIS MAGNETIC MAN HAD MORE SHEER ANIMAL MAGIC THAN ANYONE IN THE WORLD AND EVERY WOMAN KNEW IT."

—Joan Crawford

"What Gable had in a measure that no other star quite matched—or projected as ferociously as he did—was a true masculine personality. . . . He was consistently and stubbornly all Man."

—*The New York Times*, Editorial.

"I found myself, after all this time, stirred by memories of Gable's incredible screen presence. Watching him—and I suspect I'm no different from most Americans who first saw the light of the screen in the 30's—I learned how to smoke too much, to do without undershirts and pajama tops, to get off a wisecrack or a left jab, to hold a shot glass or a girl, to make love and war."

—Wallace Markfield,
The New York Times Book Review

Dual Selection of The Literary Guild, Main Selection of The Movie Book Club, Selected by Doubleday Book Club

More . . .

W9-CFK-180

"IT IS DOUBTFUL IF ANY MALE STAR WILL REACH THE HEIGHT OF ADULATION THAT GABLE ATTAINED."

—The Boston Herald American

"Outstanding . . . A fascinating study of the insecure, enigmatic actor who became Clark Gable. He became Gable, not by changing his name, but rather by allowing MGM Studio to fabricate his biography—and then by assiduously pursuing the lifestyle his biography described until he eventually filled its mold."

—St. Louis Post-Dispatch

"His stardom is no kind of fluke but the realest stardom on record. . . . It's a great story that has always needed to be told. The essential information here is that Lyn Tornabene has got the real Clark Gable down on paper at last."

—Philadelphia Inquirer

"Clark Gable, even in death, still reigns in Hollywood."

—United Press International

More . . .

IN HIS ARMS, QUEENS AND GODDESSES BECAME WOMEN.

Filled with rare photographs and never-before-published material, this is the first full account of the Hollywood Gable knew, of the man behind the Hollywood image, and of the many women in Gable's life: Josephine Dillon, years older than he, his mentor and the first of his five wives; socialite Ria Langham; Carole Lombard, the great love of his life, who died so tragically and so young; Lady Sylvia Ashley; and finally, Kay Spreckels, who gave him the son he always wanted, but never lived to see.

"It is, after all, Gable's private life we do not know . . . But Tornabene gets into the man's moments of cruel self-involvement, his warmth and generosity, his singleminded ambition to succeed at filmmaking, if not acting. Fascinating, even beyond its worthy subject."

—*Chicago Tribune*

Are there paperbound books you want but cannot find in your retail stores?

You can get any title in print in **POCKET BOOK** editions. Simply send retail price, local sales tax, if any, plus 35¢ per book to cover mailing and handling costs, to:

MAIL SERVICE DEPARTMENT
POCKET BOOKS • A Division of Simon & Schuster, Inc.
1230 Avenue of the Americas • New York, New York 10020

Please send check or money order. We cannot be responsible for cash.   *Catalogue sent free on request.*

Titles in this series are also available at discounts in quantity lots for industrial or sales-promotional use. For details write our Special Products Department: Department AR, POCKET BOOKS, 1230 Avenue of the Americas, New York, New York 10020.

LONG LIVE THE KING

A BIOGRAPHY OF

CLARK GABLE
BY LYN TORNABENE

A KANGAROO BOOK
PUBLISHED BY POCKET BOOKS NEW YORK

POCKET BOOKS, a Simon & Schuster division of
GULF & WESTERN CORPORATION
1230 Avenue of the Americas, New York, N.Y. 10020

Copyright © 1976 by Lyn Tornabene

Cover paintings based on a photograph from the MGM release
Gone With the Wind © 1939 Selznick International Pictures, Inc.
Copyright renewed 1967 by Metro-Goldwyn-Mayer Inc.

Published by arrangement with G. P. Putnam's Sons
Library of Congress Catalog Card Number: 76-43227

All rights reserved, including the right to reproduce
this book or portions thereof in any form whatsoever.
For information address G. P. Putnam's Sons, 200 Madison
Avenue, New York, N.Y. 10016

ISBN: 0-671-81733-7

First Pocket Books printing January, 1978

Trademarks registered in the United States and other countries.

Printed in the U.S.A.

For Norman Darer
Who should have been here

Acknowledgments

There is the risk, in trying to say thank you for the help received in producing a biography of someone who left few letters, no diaries or collected literary works, of sounding like the winner of an Academy Award for Best Director. Clearly there are endless lists of people to whom one must be grateful, including ancestors, baby-sitters, and the management of Bell Telephone. In my own case, I can't think of anyone I know whom I didn't ask a favor having direct bearing on this book.

More than a hundred people who knew Clark Gable granted interviews of varying durations, and only a few of them asked that their names be withheld. I am deeply grateful to them all. There are five of them without whose collective cooperation this book really couldn't exist: Howard Strickling, Jean Garceau, George Anna Burke, John Lee Mahin, and Z. Wayne Griffin.

I am doubly grateful to Mr. Strickling because I understand what a tormenting job it was for him to talk about a man whose confidence he never violated, and whose memory he holds sacred. Mr. Strickling was the first person I contacted about this project, and he tried to make me understand how difficult it was going to be. He would have been happier if I had abandoned it. Had he refused to see me, I would have been cut off not only from his own vital recollections, but also from many people who would not see me without his approval.

The same is true of Jean Garceau, who gave me an initial interview, then found herself answering endless queries from me by mail and phone, put me in touch with essential people, and, additionally, permitted me to use her own Gable biography, *Dear Mr. G.*, published in 1961 by Little, Brown, as a guide and reference. How is she sufficiently thanked?

Franz Dorfler, Anita Colby Flagler, Delmer Daves

ix

and Joan Blondell added special color to this book. Arthur Miller gave an instant dimension to Clark Gable that only a man with his gift of perception could offer. Richard Lang made a special contribution, which will be obvious in the text. My dear friend Ursula Theiss and her husband, Marshall Schacker, gave me moral support, comfort, and endorsement, as did Buster and Stevie Collier. Harry Belafonte stole time from a hectic schedule to talk to me, as a friend, about the nature of celebrity. Richard Kaplan of the *Ladies' Home Journal* was there whenever I said "Help!" and when I didn't, called to ask why.

My West Coast researcher, Meredith Babeaux Brucker, freed me from working in Hollywood after I had spent too many months there. She never, never failed me, not even in the last weeks of work when I confided to her that I wasn't going to make it, and she gave me the lecture that pushed me over the final hurdles. How do I thank this fellow feminist, fellow working mother, kindred spirit? My other researchers were called on less, but also came through when needed: Smae Davis and Steven Schasser in California; Roxanne Guerrero and Roz Komaroff in New York.

Major William Hansen of the United States Air Force endured and answered my persistent trivia questions. Al Newman of MGM procured for me prints of Gable films I wanted to review, as did the film department of the Museum of Modern Art.

Dr. Alice Ginott and graphologist Daniel S. Anthony made major contributions which are defined in the appendix.

Russ Tornabene of NBC (not my relative, but my friend) helped me find research contacts in major cities. The historical societies of Crawford County, Pennsylvania, and Harrison County, Ohio, provided unusual reference material, as did the Library and Museum of the Performing Arts, New York City, the Academy of Motion Picture Arts and Sciences, the Actor's Fund, the Long Beach, California, Library, and the legal department of MGM.

Belva Hall, a distant cousin of Josephine Dillon, granted me the right to quote from Miss Dillon's unpublished manuscript, "Not a Biography/A Teacher's Story" (dated 1951), and loaned me Miss Dillon's personal scrapbooks. As will be seen, Mrs. Hall's contribution was another essential one.

My typist, Michele Pastore, worked long nights for me when the pressure was on, and never mentioned how tired she must have been. Eventually she could read my handwriting and follow my chicken scratches around margins better than I could. Michele was also the first person to read this manuscript, and unfailingly said what I needed to hear to get from chapter to chapter. She is young, she is beautiful, she is dedicated to her work and her family, and I wish her all the good things she deserves.

My close and loyal friends entertained and fed me when I was in no mood to return their kindnesses. They put up with my Gable obsession, which I can compare only to major illness that obscures any other subject or event. For too long now, I have been impossible to live with. No one has told me so. I am blessed.

My editor, John Dodds, has managed to make me laugh in the midst of my worst fits of hostility, has done for me whatever I asked and more, and has been, perhaps, too patient.

My parents, my sister, and my in-laws have gone without holiday dinners, birthday gifts, and other affectionate acknowledgments of their existence without a peep. My husband and my daughter changed their life-styles to carry me through these years, which were nearly three, but feel like ten. They know why I have dedicated this book to the late Norman Darer, and know it is for them as well. I love you, Frank. I love you, Wendy-Lyn.

April, 1976

You know, this King stuff is pure bullshit. I eat and sleep and go to the bathroom just like everyone else. There's no special light that shines inside me and makes me a star. I'm just a lucky slob from Ohio. I happened to be in the right place at the right time and I had a lot of smart guys helping me—that's all.

—Clark Gable to reporter Bill Davidson
October, 1960

Contents

THE KING IS DEAD

In Hollywood, and especially at the studio of Metro-Goldwyn-Mayer, where he had been a contract player for almost a quarter of a century, Clark Gable was known informally but respectfully as The King. It was a sobriquet accepted ungrudgingly by his peers. Even among the hierarchy of great motion-picture stars, of whom there were many in the happy years of his ascendance, he was acknowledged supreme.

Perhaps he was not the most skillful and subtle in the way of technique. Perhaps he did not possess the polish of some of the latterly imported British stars. But what Gable had in a measure that no other star quite matched—or projected as ferociously as he did—was a true masculine personality.

Whether it was as Fletcher Christian, ring-leader of the mutineers in "Mutiny on the Bounty," or as the tart newspaper reporter in "It Happened One Night," or as the sententious Rhett Butler, whom he was virtually compelled to play "by popular demand" in "Gone With the Wind," Gable was as certain as the sunrise. He was consistently and stubbornly all Man.

Excerpt from a *New York Times* editorial,
November 18, 1960

Prologue

If it is possible to have an open mind about a man you have seen in perhaps fifty films, I had one about Clark Gable when I started researching his life in 1973. Clark Gable had never been my movie star. Physically, there was too much of him in the days I made scrapbooks of pages from *Photoplay*; Tyrone Power was more my type —every boy I loved looked like him (to me). I went to Clark Gable movies because I went to see nearly every movie made, not because I was his fan.

My interest in Gable as the subject of a book was rooted in my interest in celebrity, and to explain that, I'd have to have more therapy than I have time for. I have interviewed and/or written about hundreds of *film* celebrities because they have been accessible. Doctors, writers, politicians, astronauts, and the others I have probed—they have been tougher to get to, though not necessarily tougher to interview. Possibly, too, I am lured by glamor, because certainly the people I have wanted to meet have been glamorous, as opposed, say, to being weird: Alice Cooper and his snakes, or Evel Knievel and his jumps, would never be my kind of folks.

I was attracted to the idea of Clark Gable, reading about him in Gavin Lambert's *The Making of Gone With the Wind*. Finding Gable "real" on Lambert's pages, I thought it strange there was so little known about the fabric of the man who was, for nearly thirty years, the quintessential Movie Star. Superstar before the word was coined. Sex symbol supreme. Success symbol, too; simple Ohio country boy who took himself by the high-button-shoe laces and became King of Hollywood. A potentate, but hero of the people, owned and operated by them.

And yet, what was public knowledge about him? That he was Rhett Butler. That he loved and lost Carole Lombard. That in his youth he had married a drama coach many years his senior. That, as a star, he lived on a ranch. That he died of a heart attack after finishing a grueling film. That after he died, his wife gave birth to his only son.

The tapestry was known, but not the warp and woof of it, for Gable was not a flamboyant man like Errol Flynn or an exotic one like John Barrymore. He did not die at the height of public fantasies about him, as did Valentino and James Dean. He was not intrusive like Marlon Brando. He did not age in the universal television room; we didn't see him sweating out a series like James Stewart, or dolled up to do commercials like Henry Fonda. He didn't hang in there like The Duke, John Wayne, to become a freak, or a curious relic. Always the right man for each of his three public decades, Gable even died at the right time: tragically prematurely in terms of his own life, but with his images intact: glamor personified in the depressed thirties, bereaved hero in the war-shaped forties, Establishment American in the Eisenhower fifties. He wouldn't have fitted into the violent decades that followed his death. The decline and fall of grace and dignity and hope in the world would not have brought him his finest hours . . . not at all. He said himself, a few months before he died, "A man of my age has no conception of what is happening now. We are left out of society. These atom bombs, missiles, that's another world . . . one we don't know and don't understand. But there is nothing I could do to change it, and I wouldn't if I could. No matter how long I live, I would never become a part of it."

This, of course, I didn't know the day it seemed to me we should know all there was to know about Clark Gable before it was too late.

I was, in fact, too late to absorb any mood from the MGM complex in Culver City where Gable spent twenty-three years of his career—almost all as abject monarch. Though the studio still stands intact—a monument to something, I suppose—you could roll hand grenades through its streets, offices, and sound stages without hitting person or prop. It is neither a haunted ruin nor an inspiring one; it is just sad. The only thing that stands out now at this lost paradise is the Smith and Salisbury Mortuary near its Grant Street entrance, which has been there for forty years but never before seemed so noticeable, or so appropriately placed.

I was, however, just in time to see Gable's home as he knew it. The twenty-two-acre Encino ranch he bought in the late thirties for $50,000, and cherished, nurtured, and defended as a peasant would a potato patch till the day he died, was occupied by his widow, child, and step-children until late 1973. Then Mrs. Gable sold the property for $800,000 to a developer who subdivided it into thirty-seven half-acre lots; buy one for $50,000 or so and live on Tara Street or Ashley Oaks in the Gable Ranch Estates. Such is progress. Such are profit and prestige.

The Clark Gable I have come to know was a survivor, and since survivors attract me, too, learning that about him was a bonus. Fame and adulation, a notoriously destructive pair, threatened him initially, but never did diminish him. In fact, within his lifetime, he grew and expanded and mellowed until finally he blended with the man he projected on the screen. The Clark Gable of moving pictures was Clark Gable's own folk and hero, ultimately, Clark Gable himself. That character of wit and courage, virility and vulnerability, optimism and durability—that stylish persona—was what he came to be. Arthur Miller, who knew Gable in his last months, described him to me as "a real gent." There is good and sufficient evidence that he was not always thus, but "Gent" indeed was the final stage in his evolution. It was, in fact, because the Gable of the twenties was so different a man from the Gable of the fifties that re-creating him was such an adventure.

For several reasons, Gable rarely gave interviews in his lifetime, and when he did, he rarely revealed anything of the nature of his thoughts or emotions. He had a privacy threshold so low he had a reputation in some quarters of being terribly shy or a bit of a bore, or both. Commenting to me on the number of Gable myths, Anita Loos said, "They had to make up stories about him because he was so dull." "By comparison," Dore Schary said to me, "Gary Cooper talked a lot." In fact, Gable was a complex man who talked when he chose to, and only on subjects of his choice. He was once persuaded to consider writing his autobiography with the help of *Saturday Evening Post* writer Pete Martin. He considered it and rejected it, because, he said, there were too

many personal matters he wouldn't want to discuss, and
not discussing them would cheat his public. We can wish
Gable had opened up in his lifetime, but cannot blame
him for not doing so.

The frustration of this project was not pursuing an
elusive Gable, however. It was the matter of pursuing
facts, and coming up with fiction. Nonsense. Contradic-
tion. Distortion. Deception. Rumor. There was no end,
and there never will be. To be an alien journalist adrift
in Hollywood is to ski on fudge. The people programmed
in the golden days of movies believe no truth is as
interesting, or safe, as a half-truth, and certainly no
competition for a full-blown, artfully embellished myth.
To the industry-trained, no life history of a star could
be as salable as the one a publicity department could
invent for him. The alien reporter interviewing in
Hollywood inevitably gets the impression everyone is
hiding something. And everyone is, out of habit. It is
a strangely belittling experience to be begging for facts
in a place where nothing is considered as abhorrent or
as dangerous as truth.

Film folks of Gable's era were supremely skilled in the
game of manipulation. They gave the public what they
thought it would accept, and then made it accept what
they thought it wanted. In Hollywood fact became fiction
because it was based on assumptions. Fiction became
fact because the public believed what it was told. There
was no precedent for disbelief, and anyway, no one had
ever been lied to so appealingly. If the minstrels of
MGM's press department decided a product named Clark
Gable would package better as a Dutch-Irishman than
as the faintly German-American he was, that's how they
sold him, and that's how we bought him. Ironically, for
a man who tolerated so little bullshit, Gable helped prop-
agate the myths himself; it was part of the job. Would
we have rejected him (what: not gone to his films?) if
we had known that his remote ancestors migrated from
Germany? Would we have abandoned him at the box office if we had been told the fact that he never graduated
from high school, rather than the press-released myth
that he had gone to Akron U? Who knows? We were
never tested.

The test is to look at Clark Gable as a human being
and not love him less. Clearly, it will tarnish his

immortal sex appeal to know, say, that he had dentures —barely a living tooth in his mouth by the time he was forty. But we're mature enough now to think about what torture false teeth must have been for such a physical man, such an insecure actor. Aren't we? We can even find a nobility in the trivia of Gable's dentures: one day Clark Gable was strolling, toothless, through a street in La Grulla, Mexico, with a lively friend named Marie Stevens Collier. "Jesus, Clark, where are your teeth?" she asked him. "In my back pocket, biting my ass," he replied.

Sure we can. We can accept Clark Gable as a human being. Can't we?

PART ONE
KID
(1901-1924)

1

It is . . . imagine . . . July, 1960, a bucolic time in history, and Clark Gable is in central Nevada on location for a film called *The Misfits*. No ordinary film, this, in the eyes of its cast, crew, and backers. Arthur Miller has written the screenplay, his first, for his wife, Marilyn Monroe. He brings to the location his air of urbane intellectualism; she brings her own special demons. John Huston, no slouch in the living legend department himself, is directing, and brings with him the machismo of a battle-scarred ram. A gangling, energetic book publisher, Frank Taylor, is producing, and has shepherded the special, albeit touchy talents of Montgomery Clift, Eli Wallach, and Thelma Ritter. The aura created, the mystique promoted, is that this is a once-in-a-lifetime assemblage at work on the ultimate motion picture.

For his part in *The Misfits*, Clark Gable is being paid the highest advance salary anyone has earned to date in the industry: three-quarters of a million dollars against a percentage of the gross, plus $48,000 a week for overtime. Right now he is sweating it out, literally and figuratively. The desert heat on the current site aggressively mounts to 100 degrees after noon, and the workday, which too often begins hours late to accommodate Miss Monroe's psychoses, is as tedious as it is distressing for an old-line professional like Gable. In Clark Gable's lexicon, a nine A.M. shooting call means you are ready to work at three minutes to nine; he is congenitally prompt. In his contract, workdays end at five P.M., and that means he walks out at five P.M., willy-nilly.

Clark Gable, at fifty-nine, is the consummate professional film actor, and he knows it. His passion for professionalism begins in his soul. Any "pro," at any thing, is his instant kindred spirit . . . garage mechanic, egg-

3

candler, bartender, or cinematographer. "He's a real pro" is the highest compliment he can pay a man, and the only recommendation he needs to accept one.

No one alive can fault Clark Gable on his professionalism. In fact, this man, this movie star, at this time in his life, is rarely faulted at all. He is revered by fans, admired and respected by acquaintances, and nearly worshiped by the few people he considers his friends. A New York press agent on the film, Sheldon Roskin, says in an inimitable style, "You would have to be a fish not to like this man." And he adds, "Face it, you're in the presence of the Lord."

Here he stands: 6 feet, 1 inch tall, a husky man, whose girth and look of controlled power make him appear even bigger than he is. An average man wears a size 40 suit: Gable's suits are 44 long. He measures 45 around the chest, 36 around the waist; average male proportions are 44-39. He fills a doorway, seems squashed in a wing chair. He has remarkable posture and, for a man his size, remarkable grace. He sits erect even in a director's chair. If he bends as he's sitting, it's from the waist.

He wears khakis, a red cowboy shirt, cowboy boots —his costume for the film. The pants are cut looser than the jeans worn by most of the other guys around. Frank Taylor describes the mostly masculine and inevitably competitive encampment as "crotchy"; few of the men, he notes, are wearing any underwear and the morning banter is usually concerned with who's parted on which side of his zipper, and who's showing how much of what he's got. Film locations are usually horny places, like merchant ships. Gable, however, isn't crotchy. Kings don't compete in such games. Kings are kings.

He looks robust. His hair is thick for a man his age, widow's peaked, and graying appropriately (touched up for the film). His eyebrows are heavy and have to be plucked a bit. His complexion is ruddy, tanned, and he has blemishes on both his cheeks; warts, perhaps, or moles. A plain movie star would have them removed, but kings can sport warts. His skin is weather-beaten; the complexion of a man with his love of the outdoors could not be otherwise.

His hands are weathered, too. They are ham-hock hands: tough, used. He wears a wedding band on his pinky because an old break misshaped his third finger, left hand. His hands are so big he wears his shirtsleeves uncommonly long to hide their size. He does the same thing with shirt collars, wears them high or turned up to disguise the thickness of his neck. He has done this in all his films, which probably explains the fashion in men's clothing for showing a lot of linen above the collar and beneath the cuffs of a jacket. His huge hands are noticeable no matter, and so are the yellow nicotine stains on his fingers. He's a heavy smoker, Mr. Gable: Kents wedged into Dunhill filters costing three-fifty per that he wears out at an alarming rate. Sometimes he switches to custom-made Cuban cigars (four to a box labeled "Clark Gable") and consumes fifteen or more a day, inhaling them. Once his friend Z. (for Zachariah) Wayne Griffin tried to get him to stop smoking. Gable told him, "Griff old boy, you paddle your canoe and I'll paddle mine."

The same line was also intended to cover Wayne's nagging about his drinking, which he does a lot, but not publicly, and not offensively to anything except his own innards. Like the man's man he is, Gable can really put it away, drink 'em under the table, store it in a hollow leg. Scotch or vodka, champagne or brandy, or all at one sitting—he never shows the effects. When he's had enough to put an average man in the hospital, he just goes to sleep.

He isn't drinking as much now, however, as he has at other times in his life. He isn't eating as much either. To make *Misfits*, he crash-dieted from a bloated 230 pounds to 195, and he's staying with steak, tomatoes, and cottage cheese for the duration. Discipline is simple for him. He gained the weight because he didn't care, lost it as soon as he did. He had to lose the weight to be not only photogenic, but also insurable. Twice he flunked the insurance test for the film, passing only after staying in bed a few days. Twice in the last ten years he has had seizures that might have been heart attacks: once, ten years ago, while driving on a freeway he had chest pains so breath-taking he had to pull off the road and lie down on the ground. The other time he turned ash-gray and slumped in a chair in a friend's home in Palm Springs. You wouldn't know it to look at him though. He looks great. Just great.

This is his sixty-sixth talking picture (he appeared in at least six silents) and the sixth in which he will be playing a cowboy or frontiersman. In his first talking film he played a cowboy, and he couldn't ride a horse. Now he can ride and rope like the Lone Ranger. Gable likes westerns. He likes to see them, likes to appear in them. "Horse operas," he calls them. He would have been happy to have been Bill Boyd. "An actor," he has said, "feels more like a man when he has spurs on his boots and is riding across the prairie, the wind leathering his face."

With him in Nevada are his wife of five years, whom he calls Kathleen and everyone else calls Kay, and her two young children by her third husband. Kay, who was a starlet in her youth, is a glowingly beautiful Lana Turner style blonde of forty-three. She has short hair, blue eyes—transparent like an Alaskan husky's—is 5 feet, 4 inches tall, and has the clear, clean complexion of a soap model. She is curvy. She's also strong, bawdy, and smart. She calls her husband "Pa," but the relationship between them seems more sexy than folksy. Strangers to their company suspect that whenever the Gables are not in public, they're in bed; such are the vibes between them.

Clark Gable has had five wives in his lifetime, four of whom had a total of sixteen husbands in their lifetimes. He has been divorced three times, a widower once, and a lover too often either to calculate or evaluate.

He is a rich man. In the past five years of independent film-making, his acting has earned him $7 million—$2 million more than he earned in the entire twenty-three years he was under contract to MGM. Under contract, he was always on straight salary, at a peak of about $7,500 a week. It is estimated that the films he made in his MGM days made $500 million for MGM. He never saw a cent of their profits, and it bothers him mightily. Now he owns percentages of everything he makes, and his income is structured to total $1 million a year until 1976. There are richer movie stars than he; people who have earned less, but invested differently. Gable is conservative with big money, frugal with small money. The only major real estate he owns is real estate he uses—his ranch, and a house in Palm Springs. He likes cash, likes the security of $500 or $1,000 in his pocket, where he can put his hands on it. Stashing large sums of money is a quirk he copied in a small way, years ago, from Wallace Beery. When Beery was MGM's highest-paid star in the early thirties, he rarely had less than $30,000 on him, and at one point had $2 million in safe-deposit boxes. Gable, too, has kept his money in boxes over the years, but now he also has it in savings accounts and in American enterprise. There is a total of 37,783 shares of common stock in his portfolio: 200 shares of Air Reduction Co.; American Cyanamid, 200; American Home Products, 150; Bethlehem Steel, 140; Caterpillar Tractor, 400; Du Pont, 50; Florida Power and Light, 100; G.E., 125; Goodyear Tire, 312; National Lead, 100; RCA, 10; Reynolds Tobacco, 200; Standard Oil, 514; National City Bank of New York, 8; Potomac Electric Power Co., 2; House of Westmore, 200; Coal Logs Company, Inc., 30,000; Oaks Springs Ranch Co., 5,000; Hard Rock Land Co., 4; and General Motors, 68. He owns a building site in Palm Desert given him by Marion Davies, who hoped to have him as a neighbor.

He belongs to the Tamarisk Country Club in Palm Springs, the Hidden Valley Gun Club in Riverside, and the Club Patos al Vientos (Ducks on the Wing) near Ventura. These memberships make it possible for him easily to indulge his favorite sports: golf, fowl hunting, and shooting. A king, after all, can't just wade into a local blind and sit down; he would be besieged. Actually, it is hard to comprehend celebrity the likes of Clark Gable's, hard to imagine how far he must travel, or how calculating he must be to get a sense of normality, or ordinariness. He is probably one of the most familiar men in the world.

He drives a silver Mercedes-Benz SC, which has gull-wing doors that open upward instead of out, and he knows it intimately enough to be able to take it apart and put it back together, nut by bolt. In fact, he knows enough about any car to take it apart and reassemble it. Whenever he's needed on the set, and not in sight, somebody is sent to look for him under all the parked cars, and usually he's under one, with a buddy, tinkering. His former secretary, Jean Garceau, who is still his friend and fan, says that whenever she needs him she calls all the service stations on Ventura Boulevard until she finds him. He would have made a first-class mechanic, or, he says, a chauffeur. He's got so much axle grease in the pores of his hands, no amount of scrubbing will remove it.

And scrub, he does. Gable's compulsion about cleanliness has gone so far he won't take a bath because he can't sit in water he's sat in. He will only shower, and does so several times a day. At home in Encino, there is no tub in his bathroom. His bed linens must be changed every day. He shaves under his arms. He is so immaculately groomed and dressed, you could eat off him. A Palm Springs waitress, not usually given to poetry, glimpsed him in a restaurant before he left for Nevada: "I saw this man in a brown suit and a white shirt standing in the doorway. He was so gorgeous, so *clean*. He looked like chocolate melting in your mouth." By the time she realized who he was, she had turned completely incoherent.

Most people are initially struck dumb at the sight of him, and not only because he is who he is and is handsome; most people will see few men in their lives who are so exquisitely turned out. Even on the hottest California days, if he appears in public, it is in shirt, tie, and gabardine suit with a white handkerchief in the pocket. His suits and jackets are made for him at Dick Carroll's in Beverly Hills and Brooks Brothers in New York. He wears white, French-cuffed, button-down Brooks shirts, 16½-36; size 12, Farkas and Kovacs or Peal's shoes—oxfords or slip-ins à la Gucci, he started wearing way ahead of their time. He buys ten suits a year from Carroll's, at about $225 per; and a half-dozen or more sports jackets for $175 or so: tweeds, Shetlands, blazers, bold plaids, all fully lined in silk—all conservatively cut. Other men wear padded shoulders to get the Gable physique; Gable has worn no padding since 1944.

At Brooks' he orders four or five suits at a time, on an annual buying trip: navy blues, pinstripes, charcoal grays, once in a while a Glen plaid like that the Duke of Windsor wears, or a gabardine in olive or brown, or a hound's-tooth check. The jackets are three-button, only an occasional one double-breasted. The pants have cuffs, of course, and by special request, buttons on the fly. He chooses four or five sports jackets in British tweeds: heather, brown, or gray; a half-dozen pairs of gray flannel slacks; and some Shetland sweaters. He orders two dinner jackets and a set of tails, then picks out some new Locke high-crown hats. He's a little eccentric about hats. Whereas most men stand to try on hats and adjust the brim on the head, Gable sits, and rolls the brim on his lap. Once he chooses a hat, he will never have it cleaned—a fact that maddens his household staff. In his clothes closet where the vast, spotless, impeccably tailored wardrobe hangs, arranged by color, each jacket dated in a pocket—in among the cashmere and silk, Shetland and gabardine—sit row on row of felt hats with soiled sweatbands. There is no explanation for it, only a meek apology from a staff trained to be as fastidious as its boss: "Mr. Gable just loves his old hats."

He has a gun collection worth perhaps a half-million dollars; gold inlaid, beautifully tooled pistols, shotguns, and rifles. "A king's weapons," a friend calls them. He has the best, most sophisticated fishing equipment from Abercrombie and Fitch: Payne rods, Hardy reels, etc. His leather goods are so fine they seem edible, and so extensive he might save money owning a tannery. The latest addition to this collection is a set of luggage made to match the tan upholstery of his Mercedes. Kathleen has a matched set to match his matching set.

One collection he has would surprise many people who know him, and that is books. He is a voracious reader, and always has been, but is so self-conscious about his love of literature, and, in the past, so concerned it would tarnish his manly image, that only his closest friends have ever seen him with a book. There are countless witnesses to his life who claim, out loud, he doesn't read: Howard Hawks, who went hunting and rode motorcycles with him; Joan Crawford, who loved him; to name two. The *Misfits* crew will know this deepest of secrets about him, and remark on it. There are so many hours to kill on this picture, and it is so hot on location, Clark Gable just puts himself in the shade and is what he is.

With amazement, the assembly is finding him courtly, soft-spoken, dedicated, patient, modest, and a great audience for jokes. This group, not a few of whom are card-carrying cynics, is moved by his dignity and courtesy, is responsive to his scowl or frown because both appear infrequently enough to be meaningful when they do.

Arthur Miller will one day dedicate the book version of *Misfits* "To Clark Gable, who didn't know how to hate."

Frank Taylor, who is surprised by Gable's elegance, passes on the observation that "Clark Gable is a man declassed. You can't guess in any way where he came from or what he was."

Saying so, he credits Gable with achieving the essence of the American dream: not only to succeed, but to pass. Gable, millionaire movie star, now passes as Marlboro man, country squire, sage, and god, because he is all that. Perhaps, when he was what he really was, he didn't exist at all.

There are two certified records of the birth of Clark Gable, one from Cadiz, Ohio (population about 3,000), the other from Meadville, Pennsylvania, 120 miles away. Both give his date of birth as February 1, 1901. From these two documents have been woven wondrous stories —none suggesting that, indeed, Clark Gable was twice-born, but none of them plausible in the light of the rest of the meager facts. It is, perhaps, fitting that the record of the birth of a legend should be left to history wrapped in a blanket of confusion.

The families from which Clark Gable came were humble and undistinguished. There is, therefore, little known about them. William H. Gable, Clark's father, was one of nine or ten children born to Charles Gable and Nancy Stainbrook, sometime in the decade following the Civil War, in Meadville, Pennsylvania. William's paternal family, which originally migrated from Germany, was as American as corn, at least as far back as his great-grandfather, John Gable, and great-grandmother Sarah Frankfield, who were born in the nineteenth century in Pennsylvania. Writers in the 1960s "revealed" that Clark Gable's name had once been Goebel, and an official at MGM confirmed that this was so, saying that "the fact" had been kept quiet because Gable came into prominence with the rise of the Nazis, and to mention that he might have been related, however distantly, to Joseph Goebbels would have been bad business. If, however, the Gables of Pennsylvania were ever Goebels, the source of this information is no longer traceable. There is a Gable Hill near Meadville, which was once the site of a 160-acre farm owned by Charles Gable, and either his father or his brother before him. The farmhouse was sold at a sheriff's sale in 1899, one year after Charles died, and the property subdivided (Nancy died in 1927, at ninety years of age). Of Charles and Nancy's six sons, the town remembers little, except that one ran a theater in Sharon, Pennsylvania, another was a veterinarian, and a third, William, was an oil driller and wildcatter, a Methodist and a Mason, and a powerfully built and handsome man who drank too much.

The maiden name of the mother of the movie star was Hershelman: her first name was either Adeline or Adelia—both names appear variously on court records and in newspaper files. She was called Addie, she was an amateur artist, a beauty, and a Catholic. Her parents, John and Rosetta Clark Hershelman, migrated to Pennsylvania sometime before the middle nineteenth century. Both came from Germany (though Rosetta Clark was at least part Irish) and were farmers of humble circumstances and Spartan natures. They had five children; Addie had two sisters and two brothers. Her two brothers married two sisters, who were both Protestants. The religions were remembered in the town because it was unusual, at the time, for a Catholic family to absorb so many mixed marriages. How John and Rosetta felt about their sons marrying, and subsequently turning, Protestant is not known. It is known, however, that they were very upset when Addie fell in love with Will Gable, partly because of his religion, but more because of his profession. Meadville was close enough to Titusville, the center of the first American oil boom, to make the farmers wary of anyone who had anything to do with that grimy, risky, vicious business. To marry a wildcatter was to marry a poker player. And Addie was a frail lady, aesthetic, sickly: surely she was not meant to be a gambler's wife.

But Will Gable was a forceful man, so marry Addie he did, though specifically where and when (or even if) is—once again—lost to history. Predictably, soon after their marriage, Will took his wife from both their families and followed the boom-and-bust trail of the derricks to Cadiz, Ohio (pronounced CA-diz, as in CAT-is, by the locals).

These are rural Appalachian towns, Meadville and Cadiz, typical of borderline Midwestern communities, where populations grow to a few thousand, and remain, with seemingly the same number of people coming as going, dying as being born. In such towns you are considered a newcomer until you've been there twenty years. They were muddy, makeshift, foothill cities at the turn of the century, dewy in spring mornings, snowed-in all winter, muggy-hot in the summer. They were towns near lakes where kids learned to fish and swim, and groups would gather for outings: all the members of a church, or all the oilmen and their families, or the off-spring of the old sheepherders. They were square towns with good intentions, as much the heartland of America as any amber wheatfields or purple plains.

Wildcatters brought a restlessness to this part of America that it had never seen before, but would come to know well as the oil came and went and the coal came and went, and the once green hills were gouged and stripped and left naked to the rain. Some of that restlessness had to have made its way into the marrow of Clark Gable's bones.

2

Addie's life with Will Gable was short and, by and large, unhappy. In the first place, her health was bad. She was, as Will knew when he married her, frail, and she grew frailer. Her friend and doctor, John Campbell Sr., was never precise about the nature of her illness, but told Addie he thought it would be dangerous for her to have children. Addie dismissed that; there was nothing in the world she wanted as much as a child, and, anyway, she was a religious woman and to raise a family, for her, was one of the reasons she was on earth. The fact that she was not robust enough to function as a woman should distressed her deeply.

Will himself was another cause of Addie's discontent. He was rarely home because if a well was expected to come in, he had to stay with it in the field. When he did come home, he was drunk more often than not. Will was one of those men considered "very charming when sober."

Fortunately for Addie, she and Will rented an apartment in a two-family house, above good friends, Tom and Jennie Reese. Tom was that rare bird: a teetotaling tool dresser. Jennie was a gentle, hovering neighbor. While the men were away at their trade, Jennie and Addie were constantly together. They both were frugal women, and had to be, since neither knew when or if the men would be earning steady money. Will owned drilling equipment which he rented out, thus compensating somewhat for the fact that the oil leases he compulsively acquired were inevitably worthless.

Addie, of course, got pregnant, and exactly one month after celebrating the start of 1901 gave birth to a hefty, healthy boy, who had the biggest hands anyone had ever seen—just like his father's. She named the boy Clark, which was the family name of her maternal grandmother. Until 1925, various people knew Clark Gable as Bill or William C. Gable. There is, however, no publicly available evidence that William was his given name. His birth records, baptismal record, and school records all list him as Clark (or Clarke) Gable. The birth was not recorded until June 10, when the tax assessor made his annual call; Will was away at the time. Will had been home for the delivery, and had paid Dr. Campbell his ten-dollar fee right on the spot.

Clark was strong, beautiful, plump—the way babies were when expectant mothers used to eat for two—light-eyed like his mother, dark-haired and dimpled, like his father. He was, very early, able to sit up by himself and hold his bottle by himself. Will Gable bragged about that —he was proud of his husky boy. To Addie, Clark was the most wondrous creature ever born. He had an impish look that made her giggle; he often looked like a miniature Will Gable, laughing at his own intensities. The baby was a source of more joy for her than she had ever known, but in a way, a source of terrible sadness, because Addie's health grew progressively worse from the day Clark was born. She loved her boy desperately, but she wasn't able to walk him around town and show him off, or romp with him on the floor, or fuss with dressing him the way she wanted. She had to stay in bed a lot, and she would sit propped by pillows, and hold her son, promising him she would get well soon and play with him all day long. The baby, of course, didn't understand, but he knew the love and the warmth of his mother, and relaxed to the sound of her voice, the smell of her skin, and the security of her arms. He was good and he was quiet and he was happy.

Will worried because he had to be away so much and leaned heavily on the help of Jennie Reese. By April, however, Addie needed full-time care, and Will hired a practical nurse to tend her. Addie suffered the heat of the Allegheny summer, rarely going out. On July 31, when Will was away, she made one of her rare trips away from the house. With Jennie, she took Clark to her church in Dennison and had him baptized a Catholic by a priest who scolded her for waiting so long for the occasion. Soon after the trip she was so helpless Will decided to take her and "The Kid," which was what he always called his boy, to the Hershelmans' farm in Meadville. There, on November 14, Addie died, and was buried in a modest grave in St. Peter's Cemetery at Chestnut Corners in Harrison County, Pennsylvania. She was thirty-one years old.

The death of Addie Gable was recorded on January 10, 1902, in that county. (At the same time the death was recorded, probably by the local tax assessor or census taker, the surviving family, not knowing she had recorded Clark's birth in Cadiz, registered the baby's birth in Meadville, giving him his second birth certificate.) Surprisingly, the certificate specifies the cause of Addie's death as "Epilepsy," and the duration of her illness as "six months." If this is true, it was, and remains, the best-kept secret in the Appalachian Valley. Was Addie really an epileptic? Jennie Reese told her daughter Roberta, many years later, that, yes, Addie had had seizures after the baby was born. If that is so, there must have been great concern about her baby's future, for at the turn of the century doctors were convinced epilepsy was hereditary. "Epilepsy is an inherited disease. . . ." is the flat statement made in a major medical reference book published in 1899, and in the same book the question of whether epileptics should ever marry is deeply pondered, and never answered positively. Yet there was never an admission of fear for little Clark on the part of his family, nor is there convincing evidence that he grew up with anxiety about this disease. Epilepsy, in any case, is not fatal. One can choke or suffocate in an unattended seizure, but one does not die of the affliction. If Addie did die in this violent fashion, those who cared for her and her son were determined that the world would never know it.

More likely, Addie died of a debilitating disease that was complicated by childbirth and medical naïveté. One thing is certain, however: she was the first of many women who would give all they had to put life into Clark Gable.

No one in Cadiz, Ohio, or Meadville, Pennsylvania, could have known, in 1901, what an emotional wound the loss of a mother is for a ten-month-old baby. The discovery of psychoanalysis six years earlier by an Austrian named Freud, if known at all, would have been pure hocus-pocus to the stoic stock of these towns, and an affront to the religion that structured their lives. When Addie Gable died, her parents took in her child with as much tenderness as they were capable of giving, but for the baby there could be no substitute for that object that had given so much love and attention. The blow for a child of ten months is worse than it would be for a child of two or three, who might be made to understand that a mother was gone, and would never return. For the baby Clark was, there could be no understanding and no compensation. There was only a loss, a mystery, and frustration. He was wounded. He withdrew. His mother, who had satisfied all his needs, had left him before he had had a chance to learn there is satisfaction in giving as well as taking, so he would always be a taker. She left him when he was too young to grieve, so he would always be angry. She left him with a void he would always be seeking to fill.

Such was the baby, the Kid, that Will Gable turned over to his in-laws for care. But no one could fault Will for that. A wandering man—a gruff, tough, wildcatting man's man—can't tend a tiny baby. And Will didn't abandon the Kid; he merely left him in Meadville until someday. Because someday Will would have a home and a wife, and then he'd reclaim his son. Furthermore, the case of Clark Gable, parentless child, was certainly no rarity. Women often died in childbirth or thereabouts, and men were really obliged to see the children had a woman around.

Families had obligations, too. No one would be abandoned. The most able would take in the needy.

Clark stayed briefly with his mother's sister, Aunt Josie. Then, as Will Gable would tell a reporter many years later, "His Uncle Tom Hershelman and his wife took charge of him for a hundred dollars a year." These Hershelmans had no children of their own at that time, and though they led a harsh, American Gothic life on their farm, they did as much as they could for the little boy, and grew to love him in their fashion.

If Will felt grief at the loss of his wife, whom he had termed "a real woman," he had no time to indulge it. He was off on his quest for the gusher that would make him rich, and, not at all incidentally, for a woman who would make a suitable mother for his son. He found that woman in Hopedale, Ohio, seven miles east of Cadiz, living in a home where he was boarding. Her name was Jennie Dunlap. She was one of five children of Henry and Mariah Richards Dunlap, only one other of whom (Oscar) ever married. John, Ella, and Edison, the other three, also lived in the Dunlap house. The two men were coal miners. Lucille Kyle Taggart, who was a classmate of Clark's and still lives in Hopedale, remembers the Dunlaps as "ordinary people, not bad people . . . but a very peculiar family." No one ever went to their home, Mrs. Taggart reports, and that was odd in Hopedale. Mother Dunlap was a stern woman, and the whole family was, well, "distant."

Jennie was the most outgoing of the group. She was at least thirty when Will met her. ("She fibbed about her age," Mrs. Taggart claims; "said she was twenty-nine.") She was a milliner and a dressmaker, not beautiful, but striking in that town because she was tall, stately, and always dressed in the latest fashion. She was an old maid in the eyes of the town, but not a spinster type, in that she was lively and well informed. She read books and would gladly put up ten cents a month for, say, the *Ladies' Home Journal*. She would send to L. Shaw, in New York City, for their illustrated catalogue of "Half-Wigs, Pompadours, Wavy Switches, etc." She would spend five cents for a single cake of Fairy Soap—"each cake wrapped and packed in a separate carton." She knew about the latest "Erect Form" corset ($4.00 for the best model), and the Ferris Good Sense Waist "made in shapes to suit every

form and size." She could copy the illustrations for twenty-
dollar blouse suits shown in the magazine, and would turn
up in one long before the other Hopedale ladies even
knew what it was.

Jennie was, in Will's eyes, another "real woman" and
he married her on April 16, 1903. He bought four acres
of land on the edge of Hopedale, and got plans for a six-
room house. Then he went to Meadville for Clark.

He ran into trouble. The Hershelmans didn't want to
relinquish the dark-haired toddler with the family eyes.
And surely the little boy didn't want to go away with a
man who was almost a stranger to him. There was a scene,
and then there were tears, as Clark and his belongings
were packed into his father's wagon and taken away. Indeed, Will promised he would bring the Kid back to visit,
which, indeed, he did, but the relationship between the
boy and his aunt and uncle was over. And they all knew
it.

3

Clark Gable, the famous movie star, never referred to his
stepmother as "mother." When he talked about her at all,
which was neither often nor in depth, he called her "Jennie
Dunlap." She was his father's wife, and a wonderful, patient woman; he admitted no more. He never discussed
what must have been so: that she nurtured, single-
handedly, the sensitive, aesthetic side of his nature that
clashed head-on with the chauvinistic male image he (like
his father) considered "normal."

Clark Gable always considered himself a man without a
family. Yet he grew up with a stepmother, a father, three
grandparents, a host of true-blood aunts, uncles, and
cousins, and Jennie's doting relatives. Apparently unim-
pressed by any of their efforts at warmth, once he matured
he blotted them all out of his life, lopping off his roots
with a bitter finality. He had no happy memories of his

past; therefore he had no past at all. To all intents and
purposes, Clark Gable the movie star sprang full-grown
from a film projector.

"He was just an ordinary, unassuming boy." That's
what the people of Hopedale have been saying about
Clark Gable for forty-five years. Funny how often that's
said about people who become great achievers or celebrities, or both; and also about people who turn out to be
murderers or revolutionaries or suicides. "I remember
Clark Gable real well," says a high school mate of his
named Norman Shilliday. "He caught, on the baseball team.
He also pitched occasionally. He was a nicely built, good-
looking, quiet boy. I also remember my surprise when I
read that he was in the movies. As I remember, he mostly
stood around with his arms folded."

The infant Gable boy was as much a joy to Jennie Dunlap as he had been to Addie Gable. He was the
only child she would ever have, and she basked in him.
She called him "Clarkie" and, usually, "Clarkie dear." She
stopped working to care for him. No more hat making, no
more dress making. She had a full-time mothering job, and
it gave her a lot more status in the town than sewing ever
did. Many of the children Clark grew up with never knew
Jennie was not his real mother. She was Mrs. Gable, and
she was a nice lady. Maybe she hovered too much, but it
was fun to go to her house; she played with the kids, and
made them good things to eat, and never raised her voice.
Her house was a nice house, in fact; two-story, with three
bedrooms upstairs. Not luxurious, but fully furnished with
pleasant-enough things.

The house took Will two years to build, and in
the meantime he and his family stayed with the Dunlaps,
all of whom were enchanted with Clark, the only child in
the family. Even when the Gables moved into their own
house, Clark spent many hours with Jennie's folks. All the
time he was growing up, he went there as often as possible.
He would say, later, that they spoiled him as a child. Certainly they tried. Aunt Ella herself described some of their
efforts:

"He was a cute, smart little fellow, and John and I did
what we could. We never had much to do *with,* but a body
don't really need much to mind the Lord and live a decent
life. We just couldn't get him the toys and pretty clothes,
or even the warm things that most children had. I'll never

forget how John and I saved almost all one winter to get him a toy horse he had seen in the store window, and wanted so much that he kept hankering after it, and wouldn't be coaxed to eat or play, just said he wanted the horse.

"Well, we got it for him, saving here and there, even doing without a bit more, but he loved it and John and I were glad we got it, he was such a cute one. I used to sit on the porch and wait for him to come down the hill from school, and he would tell me about what he had done that day and the other happenings in the school and he would ask me about things that he couldn't think out just yet for himself."

Little Clark kept his hobby horse tied to his bedpost, covered with a shawl. He was afraid of the dark, and the horse protected him. When the horse was afraid, too, Jennie let Clark keep a lighted lantern in his room.

Will was rarely home. He worked in the Scio oil fields, which were only about eight miles from Hopedale, but too far, in those days, for daily commuting. There was no public transportation, and there were still very few cars. Monday mornings, so early it was still dark, Will and some other oilers would get into a shared wagon and go off to Scio. Sometime on Saturday they all came home with the smell of the fields—the gases and the tar—still on their clothes, the red-neck language still on their tongues.

Into the domestic tranquillity of his home would come Will Gable, to check on the growth and activities of his son. "Hi, Kid, how'ya doin'? Mother, how's he doin'?"

Well, the Kid was in a spotless Buster Brown outfit and a neatly knotted little tie and, though only five, was borrowing crayons from Miss Thompson, the first-grade teacher, and drawing really fine pictures. ("Gotta get the Kid some crayons of his own," Will would note, and remember.)

Then Will would rough-house with his son, just a little, to make sure Clark wasn't turning out to be a momma's boy, and then he would lean into the task of getting good and clean for Sunday morning. Jennie had gotten him the job of Sunday school superintendent, you see, and the family showed up *every* Sunday at Hopedale Methodist Church.

Being home a day and a half a week didn't give Will much time to establish his authority in his own house, but

he managed. Will learned that the quickest way to make
Clark behave was to call him a sissy. Clark learned that
when his father was home it was best to be as inconspic-
uous as possible, and Jennie learned, very early, that a
big part of her role in life was to be a buffer between
her husband and stepson.

Jennie had dreams for little Clark. He was different
from the Hopedale men she knew, gentler, finer, more vulnerable. He wouldn't be a miner, or a gambler, or a tool
dresser. He wouldn't spend his life forcing a living out of
the mud, not her Clarkie. He would be a doctor, a minister, or maybe a musician.

See him in his first long pants, going off to the Hopedale
Grade School across from the Dunlap house. Just see that
fine young man, his thick hair (like Addie's, his father
said) parted neatly on the side, his shirt collar clean and
stiff up under his chin, his jacket fully buttoned. That was
no wildcatter. So he wasn't a scholar; he didn't do really
badly in school. He would have done better if he had applied himself. He was just bored, that's all. But Jennie
made up for that when he got home. She read to him,
honed his manners, taught him to sing and play the piano,
showed him pictures, in magazines, of the world beyond
Hopedale.

Every now and then, Will would latch onto some extra
money, and when he did, Clark got some special treat.
One bonanza brought him a bicycle; another, a pool table,
something Will enjoyed as much as Clark did. None of the
other kids Clark knew had a pool table—or a bike, for
that matter. Under Jennie's influence, a later bonanza secured the Library of the World's Best Literature in
seventy-two volumes, the complete works of Shakespeare
in thirteen volumes, and the History of the Bible in sixteen
volumes. The outlay for the books always irritated Will.
Some twenty-five years after they were paid for, he would
say to a reporter, "They were all in a bookcase right before him but I never saw him open a single volume." Indeed, if there was one thing Clark wouldn't do in front of
his father, it was read.

Will was happier about the activities of his son that he
could control. One day, for instance, he decided Clark
should learn to swim. That day he took him to a swimming
hole, and that day Clark swam. "When I got through with
him, he knew how," Will bragged. He also bragged that

Clark was "a real he-boy and no sissy," but of that, he wasn't really certain.

Jennie sent Clark to a music teacher when he was twelve, who taught him to play the French horn. The boy was so adept with the horn that by the time he was thirteen he was invited to join the town band—the only child so honored. Not that you would have noticed he was a child when the band marched; he was as big as most of the men in it. If there was one thing everyone in town noticed about young Clark Gable, it was his size. "He was a big fella," Lucille Taggart says, typically, "very broad-shouldered, big bones, big feet." At fourteen, he was nearly six feet tall and weighed 150 pounds. When he marched with the band he could wear a full, man-sized uniform, and fit right in it. Well, to tell the truth, none of the uniforms hung exactly perfectly. They had to be passed along, you know. The town couldn't afford for them to be custom-fitted.

Clark was not shy about performing for an audience. As he grew older, and with Jennie always present to cheer him on, he happily joined the parades, competed in the annual track meet at the Cadiz fairgrounds (100-yard dash and shot-put), and performed in high school programs, held at the opera house because the school had no auditorium. Only if Will showed up would the climate change. Once, for instance, Will watched Clark in a town play in which he sang "Silver Threads Among the Gold" in a duet with a female classmate. Ever after, whenever Dad wanted to put the Kid in his place he would hum the song, and laugh when Clark blushed. Will could get the same reaction just saying it: "Hey, Kid, Silver Threads Among the Gold." If the purpose of the needling was to get Clark to stop singing, it failed. He didn't sing particularly well, but he sang loud, and he sang often, not as a budding thespian, but as a young fellow who took real pleasure in the great big sounds he could make.

Outside his home, life for young Clark Gable was the saccharine one of small-town boys all across America in the early twentieth century. He even got the measles right on schedule. About the most unusual thing he did was to make a best friend of a boy three years his senior. Andy Means was his name, and he was the son of the owner of the only hotel in Hopedale. He and Andy went fishing together, and shot frogs together, and dared each other to go

faster and farther taking turns on Clark's bike. They went
to Jolly's Drug Store, where "everybody" went; Jolly's had
round tables, where you could sit and have sodas. They
went to Charlie Houghton's for haircuts once a week or so.
They hung around the Means Hotel, enjoying the piano
player—the best in town, they thought. They went to
church socials. And they went to parties with the gang:

There was Lucille Kyle; Thelma Lewis and her brother,
Tom; Marjorie Miller (she was two years younger than the
other girls) and her brother, Francis; Bill Henry, Mable
Bell, and Daphne Reed. Clark had a girl for a while,
Marie Winland, but she wasn't one of the gang and wasn't
invited to the parties. What she missed was a gathering in
one house or another (not Mable Bell's or Daphne Reed's
because they were farm girls who stayed in town with relatives during the school week). There was always at least
one parent present. There was no card playing, because
nice girls didn't play cards; and little dancing, because the
boys didn't dance very well. There was piano playing and
singing ("I sang like a cow," reports Lucille Kyle Taggart), teasing and feasting. Yes, the girls knew they were
different from the boys, but there was no exploring as to
the extent of the difference—not at *those* parties.

The townspeople of Hopedale remember Clark Gable
as being quite girl shy. It doesn't seem to be any wonder
at all.

In high school Thelma Lewis sometimes helped him
with his homework. That is to say, she let him copy hers.
Such methods couldn't have gone unnoticed; there were
only eight pupils in his entire class, and they took all their
courses together; math, science, English, Latin, history,
and spelling. In their sophomore year they were also
graded in "Self Control," a judgment in which Clark was
never graded higher than 80.

He was a student who did well when the spirit moved
him, and miserably when it didn't. An exasperating creature to his teachers, he would go a whole school year without missing a day, be tardy only once (by eight minutes),
and then just not bother to apply himself. In his freshman
year of high school he consistently made grades in the
seventies. In his sophomore year, however (years 1916–
17), he would go from a 72 in one month in math, to a 90
the next, then down to 80, then 70, and then up to a 93.
In English he averaged an 80, with a low of 66 and a high

of 88, with grades above 80 in six out of ten months. In
Latin he made a high of 75 and a low of 48. And history
—two months he ignored the whole subject and made a
40, followed by a 20. Then the fear of the Lord got into
him, and he went to a 95, a 98, an 85, and a 94. But
in spelling, he stayed in the 90s, going as high as 99 and
averaging 95 for the year. He liked spelling, and always
would. He was at home with the sound of words and
pleased with the way the look of them would stay in his
head.

Clark was, in fact, a very verbal fellow. His friend
Andy Means stayed impressed all his life with the way
"Billy" could talk himself out of trouble: "He never had
one fistfight while he was growing up. If there was an
argument and it looked like another kid was going to belt
him, he could always talk his way out of it." Will Gable
couldn't understand why Clark never got into scuffles, and
never stopped trying to convince his son the quickest way
to end a fight was with a right to the jaw. But Clark wasn't
interested in physical violence—not as a kid, and not ever.
Being so big so early, taller than his own father when he
was still an adolescent, he never had a physical fear of
other men. What he did fear about fighting was that with
the power he had in his arms, and the size of his hands,
he might kill someone. Someone he feared enough, and
therefore hated enough, and therefore feared enough—in
the classic cyclical way that fear breeds repressed anger
breeds hate breeds fear of reprisal—to hit and maybe
kill. That someone was his father. So he didn't hit anyone.
He charmed, instead.

"The Kid was brought up to depend on himself," Will
told a reporter. "When I bought our first Ford he, of
course, wanted to drive it. We went out where the road
was wide and there wasn't much traffic and I put him behind the wheel. I put my arm around him to help drive,
but there was no need of that. He drove right off and that
was the only lesson in driving he ever had."

Will didn't know how carefully he had been watched
when he drove. That was a trick of Clark's: watching sur-
reptitiously; he learned a lot by watching, and he stored
what he learned.

One thing he learned at a precocious age was that
money had a magic power. So in the summer of his twelfth
year, Clark got his first paying job as a delivery boy at the

local flour mill. He earned fifty cents a week, which he considered not bad, but not enough. He would work, from then on, all the summers of his life, until, in the final weeks of his final summer, he was earning $48,000 a week, and that, at last, was enough. That was the kind of money a man could earn if a gusher came in and flowed three thousand barrels a day, and he owned a hunk of it. That was the kind of money Will Gable saw in his head every time he got a lease in his hand. That was the kind of money that could free a man to hunt for more oil all over the earth. A man was a man, and got freedom in varying amounts, depending on how much money he had. Even a boy could see that.

So life had a pattern for young Clark Gable. School and friends, work and play, a woman to cater to him, a man to prod him. And he grew tall, and strong, and sort of funny-looking because it became fashionable to slick down your hair and part it in the middle—and he followed the fashion; and because his teeth were too small and they parted in the middle, too, and because his ears were too big and they stuck out beyond the brim of the hats he liked to wear way down over his forehead. But he was a personable fellow, young Clark. If not admirable, at the least likable.

There was a war on in Europe when Clark was in his teens, but that didn't seem to have any bearing on his life, except maybe to put a whiff of prosperity in the air, and make a fellow wish he was old enough to get in on the industrial boom. So much of the outside world passed you by in Hopedale. For instance, all over America, people of all means and ages were finding themselves hooked on a miraculous new pastime. They were going off to theaters to watch something called moving pictures. They were going to theaters so often that they were floating a whole new industry and, more than that, making gods and goddesses of the people they were watching. Fortunes were being made in this new industry; tycoons were being formed who would have more power one day than oil barons and railroad barons put together, because their product was aimed not at human necessity, but human fantasy. America was being inexorably bound by railroad ties, telephone cables, and oil pipelines, yes, but it was also being tied together by strings of theaters in which people sat in the dark and responded and related to images moving, more dreamlike than lifelike, on a large screen.

Hopedale, however, had no theater. The teenaged Clark Gable had never seen a "movie." He had never even heard of a man named Arthur Johnson, who was, in 1913, the first movie matinee idol, and who, by 1915, was somewhere drinking himself to death because the public which had made him an instant success had whimsically, and just as instantly, rejected him. Arthur Johnson was setting a precedent of fear that many an actor would follow, but Gable didn't know that then. Gable didn't know about the machinations of a New York movie company called Metro that would one day own him, or the manipulations in Boston of one of its officers, a pint-sized man named Louis Burt Mayer, who would pull the strings on nearly half his life. Gable didn't share the national excitement about an epic called *The Birth of a Nation,* or the national passion for a fair-haired child-woman named Mary Pickford, a young comic named Charlie Chaplin. He didn't know that a flamboyant jock named Francis X. Bushman was making so much money being a "movie star," he gave $100 tips to busboys, drove a lavender Rolls-Royce, and had cigarettes dyed to match. Young Clark couldn't have imagined that the hottest new consumer item about to appear on the American market was people, who would perform in front of a camera, be deified on the screen, and be packaged and sold as living legends. He wasn't in on this new path to fame and fortune.

Clark Gable's mind, when he was sixteen, was on the actions of only one person: his father. For, in the summer of 1917, inexplicably to Gable historians, Will Gable decided to abandon the search for oil and become a farmer. Gable biographies have maintained, simply, that Will Gable turned to farming at that time because Jennie's health was bad. Such reasoning doesn't make any sense; one did not take up a back-breaking rural life for one's health. Will Gable wouldn't be a gentleman farmer, he would be a dirt farmer, and he'd need Jennie to help with the sixteen hours a day of farming chores. Will himself explained his move like this: "I had a chance to sell my outfit and my home at a good price, so I bought a farm and we all moved out there." He didn't say that the oil wells were drying up in Harrison County—but they were, and that may have had something to do with his decision.

Possibly he sold his house and his rig because Jennie had finally had her fill of being an oil-widow, and demanded a more stable existence. The fact remains that Will Gable bought a farm near Ravenna, about sixty miles from Hopedale, and that his doing so changed the course of Clark Gable's life.

Suddenly Clark had a full-time father and the full-time responsibility of working a farm. The old order—whatever its worth—was gone, and the new order was devastating. Gone were the friends he grew up with, the socials, the sodas at Jolly's. No more fishing with Andy Means, no more sitting on the porch swing with Aunt Ella, no more outsinging Lucille Kyle. The sixty miles between him and what was, if not dear, at least familiar, may as well have been a thousand.

In the fall, Clark started his third year of high school at Edinburgh High, where he stood around a lot with his arms folded, and learned how to smoke. He went there only until November. "One day," Will said many years later, "I found Clark loafing around the place, so I asked him if he wasn't going to school. 'No, I'm not going to ride with a bunch of kids half my size,' he said, and that settled it. There was a consolidated high school about five miles away and a bus hauled the pupils to and from school. Perhaps some of them were as old as Clark but none of them was a big, full-grown man like him."

Clark would be self-conscious about his lack of formal education for many, many years. When he quit school he knew he was doing the wrong thing, but he simply hated everyone at Edinburgh High. Telling this in his thirties, he said, "Youth is so extreme in its emotions."

Will tolerated his son's quitting school because he needed him on the farm, but Jennie was deeply distressed. Her hopes for Clark were shattered. If he would have no formal education, he would have no chance for the position in life for which she had been preparing him. If he would ever amount to anything, it would be out of common labor, and what good would all his fine manners, his fine style, do him then? Jennie was resigned to her own life; her strong religious faith answered all the questions she needed answered. But Clarkie—what would become of him?

One thing he knew for sure: he wouldn't be a farmer. Work was one thing; he never minded doing it. Hardly a celebrated man in America would have as rigid a work ethic as Clark Gable. But toiling—warring with nature—that was different. He was not prepared to battle the seasons, struggle with the earth, cater to the boundless capacity of farm animals to eat and get sick and make dirt.

He didn't stay long on the farm. At Christmas time he went to Hopedale to see the Dunlaps and his friends. He returned home, but stayed only long enough to pack his clothes. Within a few days he was back in Hopedale and on his own. Will Gable let him go, but he wouldn't support him. Such a minor threat, however, wouldn't make a farmer out of Clark. Recalling those days, later in his life, he said:

"Working on that farm meant getting up at four in the morning every day in the year, spring, summer, fall and winter, and the winters were sure cold. I fed the hogs, the rest of the stock, plowed in the spring until every muscle ached, forked hay in the hot sun until I was sweating a crop of calluses. I did what I was expected to do on the farm, but it takes a certain knack for farming in the old-fashioned way. I just didn't have what it takes."

He got a job carrying water for a mine crew. It paid $5 a day. Clark saved every penny he could. He had a goal: he wanted to buy his father's car. He'd written Will and asked if he would sell it for what he had paid for it: $175. Will accepted the deal. In April, Clark went home with the money and became sole owner of the Ford his father called "the roadster." If Will thought the car would keep Clark down on the farm, he was wrong. The boy did his chores, but he had plans. Andy Means and some of the other guys in Hopedale were going to take off, in the fall, for Akron, and Clark was going to go with them, one way or another. Akron was an industrial boomtown, pressed to turn out essentials for the war effort, and responding in the great American way. Goodyear, Firestone, Miller, and Goodrich ran day and night, producing the tires, other rubber goods, and dirigibles needed by American armies fighting in Europe. The companies were devouring labor as fast as they were turning out goods, and were scouring the country for workers. A fellow could make a fortune in Akron—guaranteed.

Will said no. There were only two honest ways for a man to make a living: drilling for oil or working the land. Clark said neither was for him, and withdrew. The man and the kid who towered over him were stalemated. "I thought my father cruel," Clark would say later. "His stubbornness increased mine." But there was Jennie to reckon with, and Jennie was on Clark's side. She couldn't stand to see him sulking around the farm, and she believed the time had come for him to go to the big city. At least he had chosen a place that was only sixty miles away, a place she could reach without too much trouble. She entered the battle, and swung the tide of it; Clark would go to Akron. At the height of his fame, Clark was able to appreciate what she had done. "If it hadn't been for Jennie Dunlap," he said, "I'd probably be on a farm in Ohio."

Clark was off to Akron, acting out what might have been a scene from any of a dozen dramas of Middle America: big, rawboned farm boy arrives in wicked city, straw suitcase in hand, home-made sandwiches in suitcase.

Wow!

It was hardly an unusual move for that time—or any other. Andy Means did the same, after all. But Andy would go home one day. Clark never would. Though he stayed in touch with various members of his scattered families, and would go back to Pennsylvania and Ohio for specific reasons over the next few years, he never did really return to the places he was raised. Charlie Houghton, the Hopedale barber, never would get the fifty cents Clark left town owing him for his last boyhood haircut. In the future, his past would become for him mostly a collection of horror stories, and his childhood a mean and bitter time. "I was certainly not a very nice little boy," he would tell reporters in his later life. Anyone who thought otherwise was simply abandoned. Hear Aunt Ella in 1935:

"Of course, the girls noticed him when he was pretty young, and he began running around with them, and that meant he wanted money to spend, and John and I just didn't have it. So he went to the city pretty young, and got a job just like a grown man, and we didn't see much of him after that. When John got so sick I tried to get word to him, but nothing happened, so the church and the neighbors had to tend to John's burying, and then take care of me. I've been sick just about ever since John went. Clark should have answered, with his own folks that brought him up needing him so much."

A boy pretending to be an adult in the big city needs to cut the cords that hold him to his youth, and make him different from the city folks. He needs a lot of courage to leave home and if he's going to make it in this rough, tough, frightening new world, he's got to act as though he cares for no one, and forget that anyone cares for him. Jennie's CARE packages, sometimes mailed, sometimes delivered in person, were appreciated, but not fussed over. As far as Jennie was to know, Clarkie was doing just fine, and needed nothing. If, in truth, he was calling his own bluff, that was strictly his own affair.

Clark got a job as a clerk in the timekeeping department of Firestone, then moved over to the Miller Rubber Company as a timekeeper, earning nearly $100 a month. He boarded with a pharmacist and Andy Means boarded next door. For Andy, the biggest attraction in Akron was girls. Not for Clark. For him, Akron offered fantasies too alluring to compete with anything. There were movies to see: westerns, particularly. And something even better than that: THEATER. He would tell Bill Davidson in 1960:

"One day I wandered down to the Music Hall on Exchange Street, where a stock company was doing a play called *Bird of Paradise*. It was about the South Sea islands and I had never seen anything so wonderful in my life, which, I guess, had been pretty drab until then."

One of the most frequently told tales about Clark Gable —one he himself told over and over—was that his first screen test, supposedly sponsored by Lionel Barrymore, was for a film version of that same *Bird of Paradise*. This, from an Ed Sullivan column in 1937, is the way the anecdote went, "told" by Clark, released through the MGM publicity department:

I arrived at the studio and they sent me to a dressing room and told me to get undressed. Then a guy came in from the make-up department and daubed my whole body black. Another fellow came in from the wardrobe department and handed me a leopard skin, a big dagger and a rose, so I looked at him and said: "What's the idea of the rose?" He said to stick it behind my ear. I sneaked out of the dressing room in that outfit with a rose behind my ear and every electrician on the lot yoo-hooed and whistled at me as I slunk along. It was in that get-up that I was screentested. Lionel brought me and the test in to Irving

Thalberg. "I've got a find for you, Mr. Thalberg," he said. Irving took one look at the test and chased us right out of the office.

In an article by Jess Stearn, years later, Gable talked about the legendary screen test: "They put me in some kind of leotard, gave me a knife, put a hibiscus over my ear and turned me loose. I must have been wondrous to behold. King Vidor, the director, took one look and yelled, 'Get that thing out of here!' "

In her book *Dear Mr. G.*, Jean Garceau quotes Clark as saying of his being screen-tested in a scene from *Bird of Paradise:* "I was sure this was good luck for me, because it was the first play I'd ever seen, years ago in Akron . . . . They covered my entire body with some sort of dark goop . . . ." etc.

Then from Hollis Alpert:

One of the more minor mysteries of Hollywood is why Lionel Barrymore had Gable take the test made up as an Indian warrior. . . . "Lionel was fidgety as a cat," Gable remembered. "He insisted on supervising the make-up job in his own office. As an Indian warrior, of course, I wore a minimum of clothing. . . . I was never so embarrassed in my life. I whispered to Lionel, "Let me go back to the dressing room and get a top coat." "The hell with all of them," Lionel said. "Haven't they ever seen feathers before?"

Feathers or loincloth, Indian or native, rose or hibiscus —Gable's first agent, Minna Wallis, in a taped interview in her home in Palm Springs in 1974, said that, to her knowledge, Clark Gable was never screen-tested at all— doing a scene from *Bird of Paradise* or any other bird.

The Akron stock company was called the Pauline Mac-Lean Players, and all its members would get to know the face—if not the name—of Clark Gable terribly well. So stage-struck he was punchy, young Clark started to hang out at the Music Hall stage door, and at the restaurant where the actors ate. He claims he became a call boy, "for which I was paid a salary of zero . . . but I loved it." The man ger of the troupe, Ed Lilley, when interviewed for an Akron paper many years later, didn't remember Clark

Gable, the happy call boy. "He just hung around the theater all the time," Mr. Lilley said. "I did let him go on
once. It was carrying a spear or something like that."

Once on stage was all Clark needed: "I thought I'd die
as I waited to go on. When I didn't fall on my face,
I thought I was an actor. It was all over then."

Clark Gable, at eighteen, finally found out what he
wanted to be when he grew up, and no amount of adversity, hardship, or negative opinion would ever change his
mind. When Will Gable learned about his son's ambition
he was appalled, and he stayed that way until he died.
Nothing Clark would accomplish in his career would ever
impress him; when the Kid became the idol of millions he
was still a prodigal son. A real man wouldn't put paint on
his face and act, according to Will, so Clark would spend a
lifetime trying to prove his manliness to his father in other
ways. An actor he wanted to be, and an actor he would be,
suffering self-doubt every inch of his climb. Nothing could
have dissuaded him, any more than being told there was
no oil in ground he had leased could have made Will Gable
stop drilling for it. Rigid as mules on glue, those Gables
were. But the Muses were watching and would be moved;
they would see to it that one of them would one day strike
it rich.

4

In November, 1919, eighteen years to the month after his
mother's death, Clark Gable learned that Jennie Dunlap
was fatally ill. He and his father had taken her to the hospital when she "took sick," and then borne her sadly home
when they were told her sickness was incurable. Clark did
not stay home, but he came to see Jennie nearly every
week. On one of those visits, she told the men she wanted
her pastor from Hopedale to conduct her funeral service.
When she died, in January, Clark went to Hopedale for
the minister, Aunt Ella, Uncle John, and Uncle Edison.

He took them all back to Hopedale, and from there, went to Akron. Clearly, whatever loss he and his father shared, they were no consolation to each other.

It has been suggested, for years, that Clark Gable had an abiding attraction for women older than he because he was looking for a replacement for his stepmother. In the light of how he felt about her, such speculation is unsound. She was not a mother to him. "When she died, I felt I had lost the greatest friend I ever had," he said. On another occasion: "Jennie Dunlap was a wonderful woman, though I didn't realize it until later. She used real adult thinking in figuring out what a kid without a mother needed."

"A kid without a mother"—that's what he was despite Jennie. Surely, her death must have upset him; if nothing else, his only champion was gone. But the blow of her death was nothing like the one he had felt when Addie died. The relationship he had with Addie was symbiotic. She was his other half. Indeed, in his lifetime, he would replace Addie, not Jennie, and not with an "older" woman. Carole Lombard, the mother he would finally have, the glamorous wife he called "Mother" or "Ma," was five years his junior. And the woman who would replace Carole, Kay Williams, another exquisite "Ma," was sixteen years his junior.

Jennie Dunlap, however, made it possible for Clark to be comfortable with women all his life. Clark Gable would have female friends whom he trusted as much, and maybe more, than any man he would ever meet.

With Jennie gone and the Kid away, Will Gable had no reason to keep his farm. One can imagine that in the winter of 1920 Will spent many long, lonely nights, and that he drank himself through a lot of them. When spring finally came, he sold the farm—in April, the month he had married Jennie Dunlap, fourteen years before.

With money in his pocket and no responsibilities to gnaw at him, Will returned, quite naturally, to the oil fields. The place to go was Oklahoma, where the oil was fairly bubbling out of the ground, and that was his destination. On the way, he stopped off in Akron to see his son. He had interesting news for him. Grandfather Hershelman, who died in 1919 at age eighty-seven, had left Clark $300. Unfortunately, Clark couldn't get it until he was twenty-one; Will was guardian of it until then. Even so, the news must have seemed like a miracle to Clark. Death had never been kind to him before.

Will stayed in Akron only two days "running around with Clark." They played pool, bought some clothes, and had their picture taken together. The photograph is an interesting one. They both wear dark suits, vests, and ties. Will's white shirt collar is high and round, Clark's is pointed, and he wears a wider tie than his father. Clark has a white handkerchief in his pocket; Will does not. They are both so broad that only one shoulder of each fits in the portrait. Will's shoulder doesn't reach his son's—Clark is probably three or four inches taller. Will's hair is parted on the right; Clark's is darker and parted in the middle. Both have protruding ears. Both look troubled; Will's brows are knit, his eyes stare coldly, his mouth turns down sternly. He looks like a classic Victorian. Clark is trying to smile, but the effect is wistful because his eyes—so much bigger and rounder than his father's—are sad. Will has a more aquiline nose than Clark. Clark has a fuller mouth, a wider jaw and neck. They are both handsome, but they really don't look like each other at all.

Will asked Clark to come with him to Oklahoma. Clark turned him down. So Will went alone to Tulsa, and a little later, to a place called Big Heart, which was too small to be listed in an atlas.

Though the roaring twenties had begun, they were not roaring for Clark, nor would they, ever. No flappers would kick their heels for him, no parties would burn all night on hijacked booze. What Clark knew about the first meek growls of the twenties was that a postwar depression was turning Akron into a mass breadline. Andy Means lost his job and went home, so Clark spent more and more time with the friends he had made in the stock company. He ran errands for them, held mirrors for them, and sometimes slept in the theater. But hard times were affecting the theater, too, and sometime in midsummer the stock company folded and moved to Canton, Ohio. Clark prayed he would be invited along. He wasn't.

There are two versions of what happened to get him by September to Big Heart. The circumstances of that move, as told by father and by son, are very different. According to Clark, in an interview with Joe Hyams in 1956:

I quit my job as a time-keeper so I could work nights in the theater. Foolishly, I wrote my father that I wanted to be an actor. . . . He wrote and said if I wanted to be an actor I should go out there and he'd get me a job. So I went and he did get me a job—as a student tool dresser on the business end of a sixteen-pound sledge, twelve hours on and twelve off.

According to Will:

In August the Kid wrote me that he was coming to see me. One day in September he surprised me by dropping in on me unexpectedly. He wanted to go to work with me, dressing tools as a driller's helper. I got him a job, but not dressing tools. He worked around the outfit at odd jobs. And that was when times were getting slow.

Clark's lodgings were a tent, where the beds were used in shifts around the clock. He worked twelve hours a day for a dollar an hour. The food he ate came from a cook tent set in the mud. His days were foul-smelling, evil-sounding, physically brutalizing. He weighed 165 pounds when he started his "odd jobs." He weighed nearly 200 when he finished that siege, and the weight gain was all muscle. Recalling the building of that muscle forty years later, he said:

I had to chop wood to keep up steam in the boilers which were some distance away, because if we hit gas or oil, the fire would ignite it and we'd all be blown to bits. From time to time I had to "dress" the seven-hundred-pound bit which was drilling the hole. My job was to get the fire going, and then, after the driller heated the bit to a white heat with a bellows, he'd tell me he was ready—a dresser wasn't supposed to know anything—and I'd have to swing at it with a sledge hammer to sharpen the cutting edges. I worked like this seven days a week, eight or nine weeks at a time. I'd get up at midnight and in the freezing cold, I'd have to climb a rickety eighty-foot wooden tower in the driving wind, to oil the bearings on the rig. There was no light and it was pitch black, and even in World War II, I was never so scared.

The men of the fields relieved their tensions with camp-following whores, bootlegged and almost toxic alcohol, violent bullying. Every two or three months they'd go into town to bathe and get into trouble. For Clark, who did not drink and showed no interest in women—at least when his father was around—going into town was almost as bad as staying in the camp. He loathed the planked, muddy streets, and he was embarrassed by the open hostility of the townspeople toward the oilmen. He hated the dirt everywhere and the dark and the cold. He had to get away.

He got a job as a garage mechanic for $50 a week; the garage went out of business. He went to Tulsa and worked as a bookkeeper for a haberdashery called Curtis and Brown's for $35 a week. Within five weeks he was laid off. His father wrote him to come back to Big Heart; he would get them a house, and he would get Clark a job far from the oil fields.

Will got Clark a job in an oil refinery, cleaning stills. As Clark remembered it, it was another trip to Dante's Inferno:

A terrific heat is created inside those stills. There is a certain amount of deposit, like asphalt, that settles in the bottom of those stills. You have to go in there and take that out. They let the boilers cool for twelve hours. You can stay in there for about two minutes. In two minutes, if you don't come out, they go in and drag you out. In a gang of eight men you start work every sixteen minutes. We cleaned out storage tanks, too. You go in with a pick and shovel and they tie a rope around you. One man would go in at a time. I don't know how they work it now but then we'd work until we felt faint. It was a very small manhole—very small. I saw lots of them in there get a little hysterical. They'd start to laugh. Then they'd haul them out.

Why didn't he go mad? Surely there was no respite in going home to the shanty his father was renting. There was no place to cook in the shack; they ate out. They had a woman come in to clean and do the laundry. They were stuck together in their exhaustion, and yet, only one of them saw any need to escape. It was insane. Will was so proud of his manly son he thought their companionship ideal. "One day," he would recall, "I was at the refinery and one of the fellows asked me if I had seen the baseball game that afternoon. I told him that I hadn't been around. He said, 'Well, that boy of yours played and when he came to bat he almost killed a cow a half a mile away.'"

Yes sir. Quite a kid.

In the final days of January, 1922, Clark told his father he was leaving to pick up his legacy. Will told him he couldn't quit his job; he'd never get it back. Clark told him he didn't want the job, or any other that had anything to do with Will's oil habit. They went the limit in what they said to each other; they may have fought physically as well. Neither would ever say precisely what happened, but the moment had to have been an ugly one.

On February 1, 1922, Clark's twenty-first birthday, he showed up at the county courthouse in Meadville, Pennsylvania, and collected his $300. It wouldn't take him far, but any place away from the smell of oil was far enough.

Clark did not see his father again for ten years. Once, when he was sick and so broke he couldn't pay his doctor bills, he wrote Will for money. Will didn't reply, but he was traveling so much he may never have received the letter. Once, in 1928, when the remains of the Hershelman estate was divided, Will wrote his son in care of Actor's Equity in New York. Will said he got an answer with photographs inside; Clark said there was no return address on the letter, and it went unanswered.

In 1932, Will told a reporter, "As for our not seeing each other or writing much for the last ten years, that is nothing. We are both independent and it has just happened that our paths have gone in different directions. He has never asked nor expected anything from me and I never ask nor expect anything from him. But we think a lot of each other."

In 1939, when Will was living in a house in Encino Clark bought for him, being completely supported by him, and their relationship was amicable, Clark gave his father tickets for the black-tie Los Angeles premiere of *Gone With the Wind*. Will went to the opening, but he refused to wear a tuxedo.

5

The young man who went to Meadville in 1922 as Clark
Gable left Pennsylvania and started west calling himself
Billy Gable, or W. C. Gable, or William Gable. Adolescent for his age, for some reason he considered "Billy" a
more manly name than the effete, almost British-sounding
"Clark," a name the oilers doubtless thought sissified, and
might even have teased him about. (Letters and notes he
wrote in his Billy years bear two signatures giving both
names: "Billy" first, then "Clark Gable.") Clark Gable
would not be heard from again for several years, and the
next time he would show up he would be living in the heart
of Los Angeles, with the citrus groves and movie industry
blossoming all around, but not for him.

In 1922, Billy Gable was starting a long, indirect jour-
ney to Hollywood, but he didn't know it. Frantic to flee the
outposts in Oklahoma which were such an assault on his
senses, he surely wouldn't have headed directly for the
official sin city Hollywood was considered in 1922—and it
had to be really bad to be singled out in the morally loos-
ening America of those early Prohibition, postwar years.
Indeed, to outraged church groups and women's clubs, the
film colony was evil incarnate. Bad enough theaters were
filled with those sexy movies starring a Vamp named
Clara Bow and a Sheik named Rudolph Valentino. Bad
enough all those newly franchised movie-going ladies
wanted It, and wanted to enjoy it, too. Now the news
spreading from the movie colony was nothing but shock
on shock. Marvelous reading, you understand, but utterly
scandalous. For instance:

There was a report of the drug death of the delicately
beautiful actress Olive Thomas, Mary Pickford's sister-in-
law. Found in a Paris hotel room, was lovely Olive
Thomas. Wearing only a sable coat. *Awful!*

One hardly had time to finish the run-over on that story,

when there was a terrible party (orgy?) in San Francisco
where a starlet (call girl?) was raped and fatally injured.
And who should be charged with her manslaughter but
"Fatty" (Roscoe) Arbuckle, the country's favorite overweight movie clown. How disgusting. And how peculiar
that the girl's name would be Virginia Rappe. Something
very odd about that, wouldn't you say?

And Wallace Reid a drug addict. Dead in an asylum?
Impossible. No matinee idol was ever more wholesome,
more prairie-clean, more admirable. They say it was the
movie company's fault—that he was sick and they made
him work anyway, and gave him morphine so he wouldn't
feel any pain. Is that what they do in Hollywood? Is it?

And who shot that strange director, William Desmond
Taylor, as though anyone really wanted to know, what
with everything else going on out there? But was it precious little Mabel Normand? She *was* the last one to see
him alive. And she *was* having an affair with him. While
she was married, too, to that nice actor, Lew Cody.

And would Charlie Chaplin marry Pola Negri (that
foreigner) or wouldn't he? Whatever happened, anyway,
to the child-actress he married a few years ago!

They were all too rich in Hollywood, and crazy with
success: everybody knew *that*. They were building houses
bigger than castles, swimming pools bigger than lakes
(Mary Pickford and Douglas Fairbanks rowed a *boat*
around theirs), and tooling around in lavender roadsters.
Outrageous!

Hollywood, sin city of 1922, said why pick on *us?* The
whole world's crazy.

Billy Gable's small world in 1922 was not exactly crazy.
Unreal would be a better word for it. Unreal to him then,
and unreal now to anyone who knows what Clark Gable
came to mean. How totally incredible to hear him invoked
at the 1975 Academy Award presentations fifteen years
after his death—still the glorious symbol of manliness and
stardom—knowing where he was and what he was at
twenty-one. That the crude boy would become one of the
ultimate heroes of modern American history is nearly un-
imaginable.

It is not illogical to wonder if Billy Gable didn't have
some notion of his ultimate fate. An unconscious one, or a
mystical one. "We didn't know we were going to become
legends," Myrna Loy, still enchantingly lovely and im-

pressively bright, says today. Unlike contemporary stars, all she and her peers knew in the embryonic days of their careers was that they were working their asses off, being paid better than any laborers in the world, and that their strange good fortune could disappear without a day's warning.

Nevertheless, Gable's inexhaustible resilience, his determination to keep moving forward, his active rather than passive reaction to hardship, makes for wonder: did he, perhaps, have some feeling about his destiny? Did he know, perhaps, that his fate hinged on being in the right time at the right place, and thus perhaps keep moving until the time and the place finally merged?

To know the early life and times of Clark Gable is to ponder, again, what Churchill called "Divine Discontent" —that mysterious element in human nature which makes one person say, "This is not enough for me"—and another say, "This will do." In so many stories of celebrity and/or success there is the early, unexplained nudge: "I am different from these people" or "different from my father, my brother, my mother. . . . What was good enough for them is not enough for me." Ohio was enough for Andy Means but not for Clark Gable. Nothing he knew how to do was worth doing. Nothing familiar was worth having. And so he kept moving—kept running—and always, closer to his fate.

In July, 1922, Billy Gable was in Portland, Oregon, and in love at last with a complete charmer who would love him in return. Unknowingly, he was holding a strand of the braid of his destiny, for this first lady love of his—her name: Franz Dorfler—would eventually send him to the woman who would start the creation of the movie star named Clark Gable.

He was in Portland by chance. In fact, everywhere he'd been since he picked up his legacy in February, he had been by chance. He was a drifter, without roots, without direction. Once he left his father, he was like dandelion fuzz blown on somebody's wish into the air. Every now and then he'd alight, then take off again, when and where the wind blew him. His course, as it happened, was due west.

From Meadville he had gone to Akron, looking for his theatrical friends, who were nowhere to be found. A waiter in the restaurant where the players used to eat told

him to try Kansas City, Kansas; they were hiring anybody
and everybody there, the waiter had heard, for traveling
tent shows. So Billy went to Kansas. He didn't find his
friends, but he did latch onto a traveling tent show. For
$10 a week, he hawked plays on street corners by day,
and performed at night. He would say later that he was
probably hired for his brawn rather than talent, because
he spent a lot of time either hoisting the tent or taking it
down. In any case, the job didn't last long; in March the
show was snowed into Butte, Montana, and when the thaw
came, simply melted away. The players who had enough
money, or family to wire for some, got out of town as fast
as possible. Billy had neither money nor family but he had
a friend, Phil, the company pianist, who had an uncle in
Bend, Oregon, about three hundred miles away. This being the closest source of help around, the two of them
hopped a freight, jumped off at Bend, and holed up in a
flophouse to await rescue. Unfortunately, Phil's uncle was
no longer in Bend, and so Billy found himself, once again,
cold, broke, stranded, and job hunting.

He found work as a lumberjack, and had yet another
physically brutal experience he would recall often when
his fortunes changed. This description, from a 1940 *Saturday Evening Post* article, is consistent with what he told
reporters and friends over a period of about twenty-five
years:

> I got a job piling green logs. All the fellows worked
> by the foot. They worked hard. They made me work
> hard, too. Probably the toughest work I ever did. The
> logs were rough, of course, and heavy, and I had no
> gloves. They all wore leather gloves or a leather palm.
> I'd tie into that lumber and it was like grabbing hold
> of sandpaper. I used to soak my hands; they had cuts
> in them and would be all stiff and crack open. I'd
> soak them in salt water and vinegar to toughen them.
> Alum, too. I had hands like a prize fighter until I got
> my first pay check and got my gloves, but I didn't use
> them before I got my hands all hardened up and
> toughened.

He was sick and he was tired, but he piled logs until late
spring, when finally he had enough money to escape to the
nearest big city, which was Portland. There he got a job

selling ties at Meir and Frank's Department Store, and there he met a young man who would lead him back into the clean and civilized theatrical world he feared he had lost forever.

It was fate, or, as Gable termed it later, it was luck that placed Billy at a counter next to Earle Larimore, an Oregon State graduate with theatrical aspirations and promise. Larimore, twenty-three, slim and aristocratically handsome, came from a family entrenched in the theater for generations. (He was, for one thing, the nephew of Laura Hope Crews, the Broadway character actress who would become a screen immortal playing Aunt Pittypat in *Gone With the Wind*.) At the time he and Billy met in the department store, he was already performing with, and directing, a local theater group called the Red Lantern Players. In short order, Billy became Earle's little lamb; everywhere he went, Billy was sure to go. Earle went to the Red Lantern every night; Billy followed. It was only natural that when Earle accepted an offer to become leading actor in a touring stock company he would try to take Billy with him. More than likely, the only way he could have stopped Billy from tagging along would have been to shoot him.

At the auditions for the Astoria Players Stock Company, Billy met Franz Dorfler and began his first love story. It was right that he should fall in love (and in love with love) in the summer; he always felt better about himself and the world when he was warm. In the summer of 1922, love could mean so much to him that nothing mattered more, not even money. There would be very few such summers, in his life.

6

Franz Dorfler came to light as a party to Clark Gable's life in 1937. At that time, he was the defendant in a paternity suit and Franz was a witness in his behalf. Had she not been at the trial, chances are the public would never have known she existed. But once the newspaper stories appeared: Ex-Sweetheart Aids Film Star, etc., etc., Franz's role in popular history was indelibly inscribed: she would forever be known as the love of Gable's life; the one sweetheart who talked in detail about him; the jilted, stoic innocent who loved him When, and then could never love another. Franz Dorfler was doomed to be followed into her sunset years by her gift of nearly total recall. She never married. Today she lives among friends in Southern California, at peace with herself—as, indeed, she always seems to have been—lucid as creek water about the events and emotions of half a century ago. She even remembers the first time they met.

For the occasion of the Astoria Stock Company auditions, Billy had bought a $90 tweed suit (on credit and an employee's discount at Meir and Frank's) and a white Brooks-style shirt with French cuffs. "He always wore French cuffs," Franz says, "even when he was penniless." If, in fact, there was anything at all that attracted her the first time she met Billy Gable, it was his immaculateness. It was part of her continuing attraction to him, that he was always clean, refined, and loved "nice things."

In no other way was Billy impressive at the tryouts. Despite his new clothes and immense size, he didn't look healthy. His color was bad—sallow, jaundiced. Billy's "yellow complexion" was noticed so often over such an extended period of time that it seems safe to guess he had hepatitis, or some related disease, and had had it at least since his days piling lumber. That vulnerable look of illness got to the women around him in those years. He was their homeless pup—the irresistible mongrel of their lives, like the canine ones (usually yellow or spotted) that managed to crawl into the life stories, or press releases, of any number of film stars. Gable himself supposedly had such a puppy. As Will Gable described it to a reporter, it was "a little yellow cur" that followed him into a railroad station. It tried to follow him onto a train, Will said, but couldn't climb the stairs. "I picked him up and took him home on the train," Will reported. He then turned the puppy over to his son.

"How the Kid took to that dog. I almost believe he had more confidence in that yellow cur than he had in me. He had the dog four years and then a neighbor shot him because he was always fighting the neighbor's dog. That upset the Kid terribly and he said that when he was big enough he was going to lick that fellow, who was about twenty-five years old."

Judy Garland's canine affair had more class: she had a pair of German shepherds that were, when she was a teenager, allegedly her only friends in the whole world. Eventually she would be torn from them, but at least the dogs had their pedigree.

Marilyn Monroe's legendary puppy had a history more like Will Gable's kid's. It supposedly arrived in her life when she was five, was black and white, and got to her by following her sort of foster-uncle home from the trolley. She named the mutt Tippy. It went with her to kindergarten every day, and then waited in the school yard to walk her home. Tippy's fate, alas, was to be shot by a neighbor one year later. If the span of time and distance were not quite so large (Gable cur, dead in Hopedale before 1912; Monroe cur, dead in Hollywood in 1932) one might wonder if the same neighbor had shot both dogs.

A very large mongrel puppy—that was Billy Gable to Franz Dorfler the first evening they met. Indeed, he even followed her home, as puppies will, after she refused to let him walk her there. She had turned him down because he was too aggressive for her taste, and a bad actor, besides. Billy Gable had read so badly he was completely ignored, and Franz figured she would never see him again. Billy, however, had decided to win Franz, and that being his goal, he saw to it that she could no more ignore him than she could a St. Bernard with its paw in her face.

She was tiny (five feet two), pale-eyed, chestnut-haired, and piquant. Convent-schooled, one of seven children of a prosperous farm family, refined and chaste, Franz, at twenty-two, had an interesting personality—dichotomous. She was unusually ambitious for a young lady of the early twenties—very forward and headstrong when it came to the theater. In her personal relationships, however, she was terribly naïve. Billy was her first beau, though hardly her first suitor. Until she met him she was interested only in acting. It had taken all her energies and all her wiles to convince her family to let her stop teaching high school and pursue a stage career. Nothing she could do would ever persuade them that Billy Gable was right for her.

Rex Jewell, the director of the Astoria Stock Company, felt that Billy was not right for *him,* either. He rejected him the first night of tryouts, and years later reported: "I had not the slightest desire to add him to the company. He seemed to me to lack the slightest gift for the stage with nothing, absolutely nothing to offer then or in the future."

Rex Jewell didn't know about the Gable determination, either. Billy stayed with the tryouts to the bitter end, watching every night, pouncing on Franz at every opportunity, and sulking as, one by one, the company was assembled. Among the chosen were Earle's girl, pretty Peggy Martin; Rex Jewell's wife, Rita Cordero; Lucille Schumann, who was to be the female lead; two barely experienced carnies named Silvey and Chinn; and Franz Dorfler, who, upon reading only three lines, was made ingenue lead.

From the first night Billy walked Franz home he took territorial possession of her. Franz was bewildered and annoyed with his aggressiveness, but she didn't know how to escape it. It wasn't that Billy was rude, or offensive, he was just pushy. Well, pushy in a nice way, she began to think. And he was always well mannered and clean, and respectful, and quite charming, and funny. Certainly no one had ever found her quite so irresistible before. And even though he was awfully juvenile, telling everyone how much he loved her when they hardly even knew each other, underneath it all he was just sort of sad. Sad-eyed. And undernourished. Not handsome, surely, though it was fun to see his dimples break all over his face when he smiled. And when he looked straight at her, she couldn't hide from his eyes and the need in them. He was just, really, overpowering.

And in no time at all, Franz couldn't bear to be anywhere Billy wasn't. Particularly, she could not live with the idea of touring without him, particularly since he insisted he would die (suicide perhaps) if she left him.

Franz and Earle formed a committee of two and prevailed upon Rex Jewell to take Billy along, at least to give him a chance. The director capitulated: Billy could join the tour, with the understanding, however, that he would get a chance to perform only in an emergency. Franz and Billy and Earle and Peggy rejoiced, and prepared for the great adventure ahead. For Billy, preparations were simple; he had only one suit to pack.

The troupe's destination was Astoria, about fifty miles from Portland as the goose flies, but twice the distance the way Rex Jewell made the travel arrangements. The troupe was booked on a paddle-wheeler which would wend its way up the Columbia River, perhaps to give the group time to rehearse, perhaps to have a chance to congeal. Going to Astoria at all seems inexplicable, at least to anyone except troupers. Though the town boasted a legitimate theater, its population of about 15,000—mostly lumber- or fishermen—had never given it any genuine support.

Theater folks, we know, are never ones to bet on a sure thing.

The company's repertoire included such spellbinders as *It Can't Be Done, Are You a Mason?, Dregs, The Villain Still Pursued Her,* and *Corinne of the Circus,* the latter really *Polly of the Circus* with the title changed to avoid royalty payments.

Billy, not knowing whether he would appear in any or all of the plays, in any or all of the parts, studied them all as the paddle boat headed for Astoria. He got Franz to read with him, and their evening rehearsals on the deck proved to be among their giddiest moments together. During one night's acting games, Billy was so overcome with the joy of his new life and love that he seized Franz and kissed her, thereby changing their puppy love to the regular kind. Franz would never forget the moment. "It shocked me," she reported many years later. "For a while I just sat there because I wasn't accustomed to it. But then I thought, how wonderful this is. I've met somebody who lives to be an actor and so do I, and wouldn't this be fun."

Clark Gable never told how Billy felt at the time (he never talked about Franz at all), but he must have been equally delighted because, according to Franz, he was given to grabbing and kissing her, publicly, all through their relationship.

What a blessing she must have been for him. How lonely he must have been before he found her. With her, his emotions behaved as though they had been unexpectedly paroled from a lifetime sentence. He had vaulting highs, subterranean lows. Franz never criticized him, never judged him. Though the man she describes was wildly moody, she never termed him that. She tells how close they grew on the way to Astoria: "He began to depend on me. He seemed insecure because of past hardships, financial troubles, and had to be reassured that he was liked. . . . Normally, he was jovial and outgoing." He told her often that no one had ever loved him: not the aunt who took him when his mother died, not Jennie, not his father. He said he had never had a family, and envied Franz hers. He asked her to tell him about her family and their life on the farm, over and over and over. "I am alone in the world," he would say, "absolutely alone."

Franz mentions his "fits of depression." And yet, she claims, it was usually easy to cheer him up. No matter what else he was, he was "the nicest boy you ever saw," and "always tender, affectionate, and demonstrative." He clowned for her, sang for her, and bought her banana cream pie. If Billy had any faults, she was blind to them, and would remain so for more than a decade.

In Astoria, Franz and Billy shared every offstage moment, as moonstruck lovers. They earned only a few dollars a week, but their room and board was paid for, so what else mattered? Billy would have liked to have been needed on stage, but until the company's first crisis, he didn't get in front of the curtains. That crisis was only a few weeks into the tour; one of the managers took off with the company's cash (a fairly common occurrence on the road), and one of the actors departed soon after, refusing to go on limited rations with the rest of the group. Billy got his break, but it was short-lived and ill-fated.

Suffering acute stage fright, Billy fairly staggered around the stage, bumping into props, tripping, dropping his hat or knocking off someone else's. Each time he appeared in a role, Jewell reacted by threatening to fire him.

These failures were one of the causes of the "fits of depression" Franz recalled. The only thing Billy did well was comedy; the more burlesque, the better. The audience (however meager) loved him as the baby in *And the Villain Still Pursued Her;* it laughed and applauded his silly, satirical antics, and Billy loved the sound of that laughter. What he couldn't stand was that he got laughs all the time, and few of his parts were meant to be funny.

One word characterized him: clumsy. But he couldn't be replaced because who would join a group earning about a dollar a week, up to its fright wigs in debt, and playing to a steadily shrinking crowd? In time, hardly anyone in the company was eating more than two meals a day, at least one of which usually included stolen canned goods. No one had anywhere to go.

Rex Jewell had to dissolve the company, but he did so optimistically. He asked his players to stay in the area, give him a few weeks. He was going to try to organize another tour, this one a traveling show that would go back down the Columbia River to Portland and play all the towns along the river. Everyone agreed to wait except one man; now, if they ever reorganized, Billy would be indispensable. Chances are, he would perform every night. With such an opportunity within his grasp, he could endure anything. Many years after his lean ones, he told a journalist: "You're always scared the first few times you find yourself broke. Later you just feel interested in what is going to lift you out of it *this* time."

He was over being scared, he was certain Rex Jewell would come through with some backing, and he had Franz. He also had an identity; he was a starving actor. This time being homeless and hungry would be different. It would have drama; it might even be fun. He would be with his love. They would share *La Vie Bohème.* As it happened, they shared it on a beach. A few decades too early to be hippies, their temporary life-style was very much like that of our much younger contemporary kids dropped out and flaked out on coastlines all over the world.

Lucille Schumann's mother had a beach house in a resort town called Seaside, about twenty miles from Astoria. Lucille planned to wait there for Jewell's dispatch. She took with her Franz, Billy, and Earle, whom Mrs. Schumann welcomed, but could not house. The trio took turns sleeping on the beach, huddled around a fire that would inevitably go out sometime in the night, leaving the beachcombers exposed to the cold and the dampness of Oregon's early fall.

Soon Mrs. Schumann found she couldn't afford to feed her daughter's friends. She let them buy groceries on her credit for a few days, and then that became impossible for her, too. Billy and Earle dug for clams, Franz stretched the few dollars she had saved as far as they would go. But there wasn't enough to eat, and the constant hunger began to irritate the young men's normally obscure tempers. Billy was often openly belligerent, and Earle could set him off just by breathing too hard. One day they fought over the weather, Earle saying the day was misty, Billy insisting there was no mist, only rain. Billy became critical of what he considered Earle's vanity. "Larimore is always running around looking for mirrors," he complained to Franz.

Nothing dampened the lovers' relationship, however. Neither Franz nor Billy had ever spent time at an ocean resort before, and both found simple joy in the sound of the sea, the sight of boats leaving the harbor, the smell of the tide. They liked to walk, holding hands, through the curio shops; they liked to stand at the wharf and watch fishermen unload their catch. With no symbol exchanged between them, they considered themselves engaged, and Franz wrote that exciting news home to her family. They would marry, she said; she wasn't sure when. They would wait to hear from Rex Jewell, finish their tour, and then she would bring her actor fiancé to the farm in Silverton for everyone to meet.

Early in September, Rex Jewell summoned his troupers to Astoria to rehearse for the river tour he had finally scheduled. The group would use their old repertoire, and would criss-cross the river, playing Waluski, Clatskanie, Ilwaso, Cathlamet, and Kelso, maybe a few other towns as well. There was no guarantee of pay; salaries would depend on the goodwill (and draw) of local managers. Billy and Franz accepted with a shrug. "It seemed better than starving," Franz reports. Earle Larimore had a better offer. His Aunt Laura had placed him with a well-known actors' training troupe, the Jessie Bonstelle Stock Company; he was to leave for New York at once. (He eventually became a distinguished performer with the Theatre Guild, was married to and divorced from actress Selena

Royle. In October, 1947, at age forty-eight, he died a penniless alcoholic. His funeral expenses were paid by the Actors Fund of America.) Earle's departure meant that Billy would assume several leading roles—either that or no tour. Once again, the company took to the river, in worse shape than ever.

This time, the actors were shipped around on milk boats, the cheapest transportation available. There were no cabins; passengers slept on the open deck, no matter what the weather. There was little to eat, and the nights were raw. Audiences were scarce and difficult in most of the towns. But it was show biz, and the troupe went on. Billy's health declined, and so did his limited acting talent. He was oafish, his voice was too high-pitched, his timing was terrible, and he invariably drew laughs for the wrong reasons. By the time the limping tour was over, even Franz doubted that Billy would ever be an actor, and wondered where his next acting job would come from.

The only acting he would do in the next year was convincing the Dorflers he was an indispensable part of their family. Like a circus acrobat he vaulted into every corner of their lives, spinning them around trying to keep up with him. Here he is, and here, and here. In the kitchen, in the garden, up a tree, in the woods, in a haystack, at the piano. Mrs. Dorfler immediately became "Mom," or a more affected "Mater." Sister and aunt were "Hon" or "Sweetheart"; Mr. Dorfler, "Dad" or "Martin." There was Brother Fritz, whose jeans Billy borrowed for romping around (he still had only one suit, plus a jodhpur costume pruned from *Corinne of the Circus*). Grabbing Franz for a crazy kiss, or doing imitations, or singing "Who Put the Overalls in Mrs. Murphy's Chowder," he was a giggle a minute. Franz remarks on his "high spirits" and "infectious laughter." She says, together, she and Billy were like ten-year-olds. She says he lit up every inch of the farm.

There was love and laughter, but there was no money. Billy didn't care; he wanted to get married, and asked Franz to set a date. Franz cared; she refused. "To marry a penniless actor was out of the question" . . . and "I still had my career to think of." Initially, her family objected even more than she did. "Mother learned to love him, although she did more than anyone else in preventing me from marrying him when we first came out home. It was she and the aunts and others who had never known

an actor—or how difficult it is to save money in that profession."

But Mom and the aunts could not resist the way Billy's
eyes stayed sad no matter how explosively he smiled, and
soon they fretted about his sallow complexion and his obvious undernourishment. They began to cook especially
for him, and to pamper him generally. They were always
rewarded because he made his appreciation deeply felt. He
was, after all, a thoughtful and well-mannered young man.
He did not drink, he was never disrespectful, unless one
would take offense at his ebullient displays of affection
for Franz. The Dorflers decided not to be offended.

In mid-autumn, Franz, Billy, and a couple of aunts went
north to earn some money hop picking. It was a miserable
dawn-to-dusk job usually done by women, but Billy would
do anything to earn a dime. They lived in tents and endured the rain and the gnats for three weeks. Well-
chaperoned, Billy and Franz spent their free time studying
grammar from books that Franz had carefully packed. He
left her only to sleep, and flared into jealous rages if she so
much as talked to anyone male. Franz was always intimidated by this jealousy. Billy had shown it from their first
meeting, and it grew worse as time went on. If she made
friends with a man, no matter who, Billy "would get mad"
or "furious," then sulk. Eventually they would be separated
by their work, and when they were, he wrote her two or
three letters a day. At one time, Franz had a collection of
two to three hundred love letters from him—written in less
than a year.

After the hop picking ended, Billy and brother Fritz
got jobs clearing brush for a surveying crew near Portland.
This was more back-breaking labor, but never soul-breaking
for Billy. He traveled nearly forty miles on weekends to
see Franz, and he made jokes about the rain and the bugs.
But he was sick, and he was weary, and he was hungry
again. Franz, meanwhile, began to brood about her career.
She had had enough of rest and the farm and decided to
go to Portland to take singing lessons. She made plans to
live with a married brother. Billy was struck dumb. He
had just taken a $3-a-day job with a lumber company
seven miles from Silverton, just gotten a room in a boarding house, and just consolidated his plans for marriage.

Franz was not to be dissuaded. She told him it was easier
for him to get a ride to Portland weekends than it was for
him to walk the seven miles to the farm. And off she
went.

Three weeks later Rex Jewell asked Franz to be in a
new musical he was taking on tour. Incredibly to Billy,
she accepted and departed, leaving him to huddle close to
her family, who by this time must have shifted its senti-
ments to the lonesome lover. He spent Christmas with
them, and they tried, futilely, to cheer him. When the re-
lentless snowstorms kept mail from moving regularly, Billy
was sure Franz was abandoning him. He became incon-
solably forlorn. Late in January, he quit the lumber company and went to Portland. Franz, by this time, was settled
in her show in Seattle.

Billy got a job soliciting want ads for *The Oregonian*,
stayed with it about six weeks, then worked as a telephone
lineman, then as a garage mechanic. A few hundred
miles away, Franz worried that Billy was drifting away
from "the theater." It is logical to speculate that she fretted
because marrying a job-hopper was not in her plans. She
had never had the slightest interest in the hometown boys
who tried to court her, at the time other girls her age
were either marrying or trying to marry, because their
ordinary jobs and ambitions bored her. What had tied her
to Billy, by her own admission, was the career they would
share. She urged him to take singing lessons, hoping this
would get him back into the groove, and sent him to her
Portland singing teacher, Lawrence Woodfrin.

For Billy, the devil that had to be coped with was poverty. He could earn enough money to pay for singing lessons and occasional meals, but he couldn't save any, and
without money, he couldn't marry Franz. This is the sentiment printed on the Valentine he sent her in February,
1923:

> *Valentine Greetings*
> I'm yearning for you today
> and if my *earning* capacity
> equalled my *yearning* capacity
> I'd ask you to be my Valentine.

He signed it, "More truth than poetry. Billy." He must
have looked through a thousand Valentines to find it; most

of the Valentines of that time were strictly hearts, flowers, and doilies. This one was "comic," with a colorful cartoon on the front of a man alone on a park bench staring at a pair of cuddlers on a bench behind him. He is reading a newspaper with a headline, "WEDDING BELLS." Near his feet is a squirrel with a question mark over its head and the word "NUT" coming out of its mouth. "I AM YEARNING FOR YOU!" shouts the legend under the park bench.

The winter passed. There is no record of how Billy spent its dreary months, but they couldn't have been happy ones for him, yearning to earn, and yearning for Franz. In the spring, however, the days began to have more meaning. Billy was doing well with his singing and would have a recital in early June. Franz's sister, Bertha, was getting married in Portland about the same time, and Franz would appear for the wedding. Love and ambition would merge once again.

Franz attended the wedding and the recital, noting "His voice wasn't outstanding but I felt like I was going to burst with pride." Franz and Billy had a few days of bliss in Portland, and when Franz returned to Seattle she left Billy with the promise that she would marry him before the year ended.

Later that summer, Franz heard that a distinguished Broadway actress and teacher named Josephine Dillon was starting a theater group in Portland. She wrote Billy the news, urging him to get in touch with Miss Dillon. He did just that, and nothing in his life was ever the same again.

Josephine Dillon was the first person to tell Billy Gable that he could be an actor, and how it would happen. It would not be easy, or quick—she made that clear. But if he made a total commitment, if he would be her disciple, his career was assured. For him her faith was better than money. He was, in essence, being born before his own eyes. Life, for the first time, had a direction. At last there was a core to him, a reason to wake up every day and attack the hours, forcing them to his will. No longer a temporary this or part-time that, he was an apprentice with much to learn. When the apprenticeship was over, he would be an actor and a man. He would not be back where he started; he would never be back where he started. Now, each day he would be a day ahead of where he was the day before. What had been deprivation would become willing sacrifice. Billy was going somewhere.

Billy wrote Franz excitedly about his plans to study with Miss Dillon. Then, when that study began, he wrote her less and less frequently. His usual two or three letters a day became two or three a week, two or three a month. Concerned, but not discouraged, Franz wrote Billy that she would be in Portland for Christmas, and would marry him then, as she had promised.

That there was no holiday marriage was, this time, Billy's fault. The lovers' reunion was awkward and distressing to them both. Franz bubbled with wedding plans she immediately sensed were not welcome. Billy had the difficult task of making Franz understand that everything had changed. He told her he was going to spend the next few years studying. He told her that was the only way he would ever amount to anything. He even told her a doctor advised him never to get married, about which, Franz says, "I was frightfully ignorant, but I sensed a ruse. He had never mentioned such a thing until Josephine Dillon had him well in hand."

Franz and Billy continued to see each other, but their relationship cooled. Being together was physically easier because Franz got work with a stock company in Portland, but emotionally, there was a strain. Billy did, however, stay in close touch with her family. After her mother sent him a birthday present in February, 1924, he wrote his thanks to Mrs. Dorfler ("Dear Mater") on Portland Hotel stationery. The letter was adolescent but touched on all his concerns: seeing Franz, being broke, staying warm.

He signed the letter "Billy," and, underneath, "Clark Gable, that is"; at the time of his twenty-third birthday, he still didn't know who he wanted to be. In the summer of that year he appeared in two stock company plays, billing himself as "W. C. Gable." Paychecks made out to him the year before by the Silverton Lumber Company were also billed "W. C. Gable."

From all available evidence, it is clear that Billy's life was evolving into one long acting lesson, into which, plans of marriage, a love nest, and a passel of little girls who looked like Franz no longer fitted. Franz broke their engagement but continued to see Billy whenever he had the time and inclination. The relationship continued that way for many years—until, as Franz puts it, "Bill began making money and success."

In the summer of 1924, Josephine Dillon left Portland for Hollywood, and within a few months Billy followed her. Soon after—"one Sunday afternoon, a sad lonely afternoon"—Franz took her packet of love letters and threw them into the fireplace. "Did I love Bill Gable?" she asks rhetorically. "I have never been a crying person, but I bawled every night for five years when I realized he had gone to California and there was never any letter for me."

In the summer of 1924 the first films ever to bear the stamp "Produced by the Metro-Goldwyn-Mayer Corp." were going into production. About the time W. C. Gable was appearing without salary in a Dillon Stock Company production called *Miss Lulu Betts,* L. B. Mayer was earning $1,500 a week, plus a percentage of the profits of MGM. One day Mr. Gable would contribute heavily to the profits Mr. Mayer shared. No one who knew Billy would have thought it possible that he would ever cross the street on the same green light with Louis B. Mayer, much less help to make him rich as Midas.

Except Josephine Dillon.

Now there was a *real* wildcatter. She sensed something in Billy Gable that could be dredged and drilled and refined. And she took a lease on him when no one else would. Unfortunately, by the time the Gable gusher came in, Josephine's lease had expired. But a real wildcatter kind of expects that.

PART TWO

PROTÉGÉ

(1924-1928)

7

The *Misfits* scene to be shot on September 10, 1960, around a Dayton, Nevada, saloon, includes the entire cast of the film and has attracted a crowd of spectators. Though actors, crew, and most of the population have been hanging around the Dayton bar since early morning (sipping grapefruit juice), shooting does not begin until after Marilyn Monroe is on the set with her entourage shortly after noon. Most conspicuous among the actors, spectators, et al, is Marilyn's small and bulky acting coach, Paula Strasberg, who is dressed today, as every day, in black, from the tips of her sandals to the pointed top of her brimmed black straw hat. "Black Bart" the crew calls her. Reporters, who have moved in and out of the Nevada locations like mice looking for peanut butter, usually note that she looks like a character in a Charles Addams cartoon.

Gable is costumed in his Stetson with the stained sweatband, the red cowboy shirt, a silver tooled cowboy belt, and the khakis over the cowboy boots. The focus of the scene is on him. He is supposed to be drunk. Previously, in the crowded bar, as the part is written, he sighted his grown children and wants to show them to his girl, Marilyn, and friends, Clift, Wallach, and Ritter. But the children have left the area, trying to avoid him. In the scene about to be shot he pursues them, shouting in drunken despair to bring them back. He must climb on the hood of a car, pound on it desperately, shout in anguish, and then fall off the car in a drunken stupor. There are mattresses where he will fall, but the action is still hazardous and demanding.

Gable knows what he must give to the scene. He has had a script of the film for nearly a year, and he rereads it every day. Frank Taylor, the producer, and Arthur Miller, the creator, feel Clark understands the story better than anyone else on the picture. Taylor has been very moved by Gable's telling him: "I'll know more about it tomorrow than today, and more today than yesterday."

Today, as always, the star is totally prepared for his work, and approaches it casually, sitting in the sun talking to reporters about acting—or standing in the bar signing autographs. About the time shooting will begin, Kay Gable appears and sits quietly near the camera. This is a rare visit for her. She is pregnant, and spends most of her time with her children, away from the pressures of the production.

With the assistant director's "Quiet please, take one," the shooting begins. Take two, take three, take four . . . Gable seems to be perfect in every one, but is not satisfying John Huston. During take ten, there are tears in the eyes of some of the spectators—do they cry because they are moved, or because they are afraid for this huge man who must spill his guts for them all? Finally, on the twelfth take, John Huston calls out: "Perfect. Print it." And the crowd bursts into applause. It is the first time any of the Misfits has been applauded, and it will not happen again.

Later Paula Strasberg makes a statement to the press that amazes Gable detractors. She says: "Gable is a magnificent actor. . . . He is truly wonderful, and I want to find some way to tell him."

If only Josephine Dillon had been there, how proud she would have been. She, the great teacher of the old school of acting, winning the approval from Paula, the oracle of "method" acting. Not that Josephine didn't have a thousand moments of pride in what she made of a raw youth named Billy Gable, it was just that they all happened in the dark. Reports Belva Hall, "She watched every picture he made and would say how proud she was and how hard she had worked to make 'that big lug' picture material for the world to enjoy."

Sadly for Josephine, when she tried to tell anyone else how proud she was, she found the world deaf in one ear and hard-of-hearing in the other. Josephine Dillon had a tough time, fully half her life, coping with the bitterness she felt at having lost her identity to something known as the first Mrs. Gable. Though Josephine was an intractable martyr, she was, as were all Gable's wives, a real person with real needs and real sensitivities. Like most martyrs,

Josephine needed recognition (would Joan of Arc have been so willing a live torch if no one had been watching?), but no matter how she tried, she couldn't get through to the press, which ultimately dehumanized her, as it did all the Gable wives except Carole Lombard.

Mr. Gable didn't help matters any. He never denied Josephine's contribution to his career, he simply ignored it, possibly out of his own bitterness at being considered Josephine's creation. People who were close to him have claimed he was grateful to Josephine, but one wonders how they knew. In the interviews he gave early in his career, and then again toward the end of it, Gable talked glibly and proudly about his early struggles, never mentioning Josephine. Indeed, he didn't talk about any of his ex-wives (perhaps out of gallantry), but Josephine was more than his wife, she was his coach. Maybe that made her less than his wife. Maybe being her pupil made him less of a man.

The clues are all in a book Josephine tried to write—a "fictionalized" account of her relationship with Clark, in which she stays close to known events but disguises most names and some places. It is interesting to note that she did not try to publish the manuscript although she did publish a work of nonfiction, entitled *Modern Acting*, in 1940, in which she refers to Clark Gable as one of her many famous students. But the book that was revealing of herself she kept and guarded like money in a mattress. In 1964 she gave it to Belva Hall, a distant cousin, as her prize possession. Mrs. Hall had taken Josephine into her home to care for her; she had been living alone, was ill, and suffering from malnutrition. When she left the Halls to go to a sanitarium, she handed them the manuscript. Mrs. Hall reports, "Josephine had slept with it under her pillow at night and carried it with her wherever she went." The manuscript, though crudely written and often inadvertently comic, gives the only intimate view available of the reverse-Pygmalion relationship between Clark and his first wife.

Josephine never did make up her mind whether she should protect Clark Gable or damn him to hell. And she was even more ambivalent about her own ego. On the one hand, she was desperate to establish her existence as a person; on the other, she believed in the nobility of silent suffering and self-sacrifice. In a moment of overt self-pity, she writes in her book about the ex-wife of the famous movie star: "Had Mark Craven let her put her life into making him a star, and then forgotten her? The old Hollywood pattern over and over again." She then reasons:

> Could it be that every top person is the sum total of the tremendous outpouring of love and sacrifice and training and protection they have received from those who guided and influenced their growth? and that the sum of that outpouring is given back into the world through them as entertainers, statesmen, artists, preachers, or fighters. Could be. . . . Nothing is lost that is given.

She never asked her husband for anything, yet she would tell her post-Gable pupils, bitterly, that in five years of marriage, Clark gave her only two presents: a pair of shoes ("I suppose I needed them to walk from studio to studio getting him jobs") and an alarm clock ("to wake me early so I could get up and iron his shirt and wash the egg off his tie").

She talked and wrote constantly of her desperate efforts to support herself and her husband, yet, once Clark plunged into his acting studies, she wouldn't let him take any job that wasn't related to his career.

The first time the heroine of her book actually speaks, she says:

> How eager the world is to pry into our privacies. I can understand the curiosity of the public concerning the celebrities, but no one escapes. The burden of publicity is sometimes heavy for us little people. We have no compensations to soften the hurts.

Josephine agonized, but how she hated to complain.

Her choices of fictional names for herself and Clark are surely symptoms of her conflict. She is "Julia Hood" (her mother's maiden name, but covering what?); he is "Mark Craven" (cowardly Mark); and she becomes "Mrs. Craven."

She begins the book with an immediate assertion of self,

writing from the point of view of a reporter* looking for
a story on Mark Craven. She abandons the reporter device
early, and then writes in the first person. While he exists,
her reporter can say more modestly what Josephine really
believes: that Julia is a much better story than Mark.

Josephine also used the reporter figure to express for her
in the manuscript her concern with her public image. She
has him approach his assignment mulling what he had
read about "Mark Craven's ex-wife":

> I remembered that some stories spoke of her as a
> frustrated, love-sick old-maidish creature, who had
> snatched at a late happiness and lost; some had
> spoken of her as a bookish person, who could not pos-
> sibly understand the vigorous, sparkling gaiety of the
> man she had married and brought into Hollywood's
> limelight; some spoke of her as an entirely unfit per-
> son socially and intellectually to be the wife of this
> new star who was now properly married into the top
> social circle of the moving-picture colony. And by the
> way, what was her name? She must have one, she
> must have some name besides Mark Craven's ex-
> wife.

The "reporter" finds the name "Julia Hood" on the
mailbox, and then wonders why it's *just* Julia Hood. "Might
be a story there . . ." he suggests, and indeed there is, but
it isn't in the manuscript. According to newspaper reports
in the thirties, after her divorce, Josephine was adamant
about remaining Mrs. Gable, saying, "The name's Gable,
and always will be. . . . It came to me in a roundabout
way that someone preferred that I drop the Gable. But
it's my name and I intend to keep it." Within a few years,
however, she had her maiden name legally restored,

---

* Miss Dillon described her reporter as a young newspaper man who
became one of the "greats in the publicity field of Hollywood." She
wrote, "Later he would meet his death in a plane crash, protecting
another of Mark Craven's wives. . . ." The MGM publicity man who
died in the plane crash with Carole Lombard, Otto Winkler, originally
met Clark Gable when he was a young reporter covering the trial at
which Franz Dorfler testified. Gable was so impressed with Winkler
that he got him a job at MGM. If, indeed, Josephine Dillon knew
Otto Winkler, and made him her confidant, his part in Gable's life
was much more involved than was ever known by the public, or
possibly by Gable himself.

"to be free from the constant attempts to inveigle me into various deals."

Initially, the reporter in Josephine's story finds Julia Hood downtrodden. That impression is instantly dispelled. Julia goes to "her tiny kitchen" to prepare tea, and while she's out of the room, the reporter thinks:

> Could this woman that I had just met ever have been the elderly, helpless, frustrated, sex-starved, broken-hearted, love-sick or old-maidish person described in various fan magazine stories? Never! Here was a vigorous, forward-looking woman, with the speech and manner of good family background.

Her manuscript aside, these are the facts of Josephine's life: She was born in Denver in 1884, one of six children, and lived in Long Beach, California, from 1889 to 1906, when the Dillons moved to Los Angeles. She was educated first by a tutor, then in Long Beach public schools, then in Europe, and finally, at Stanford University. She graduated from Stanford in 1908, one of the few females to be admitted to the university in those Victorian years, much less to learn her way out of it.

Her father was a fighting Irish lawyer, legislator, and district attorney who is credited, among many things, with helping to save California's missions (the Pope awarded him a private audience for this), and helping to shape the state laws protecting property rights of women. Her mother, Florence Hood Dillon, was of pioneer stock, and extremely active in Southern California cultural activities. The Dillon ranch covered forty acres. The main house was square, had eighteen rooms, all with fireplaces, and a rococo veranda on all sides. Long after the Dillons sold it, it was turned into a boarding house for oil workers. Eventually, it burned to the ground.

Josephine, who was called "Joe" as a child, had one brother, James, who became a lawyer, and four sisters: Florence, who became an opera singer in Italy and changed her name to Enrica Clay Dillon; Fannie Charles Dillon, a composer and teacher; Anna Hood Dillon, Fannie's twin, and the only other Dillon girl who married; and Viva, who studied painting, but also became an opera singer.

Josephine, before becoming a drama coach, was an

actress who reached Broadway, and had a promising career, with no distractions. She never expressed an interest in boys or men, except academically. In her manuscript she insists she had had a great love in her life who died a few years after World War I, just before they were to be married. (Miss Dillon did lose a great love about this time; her father, Judge Henry Clay Dillon, died in 1922.) She also told this dramatic tale to reporters much later, but it is doubtful anyone ever believed it was more than a pride-protecting tale, including Belva Hall. Says Mrs. Hall, "Josephine really loved Clark Gable. She carried a torch up to her dying day for him. That was her one and only real love. She always kept the very young picture of Clark in front of her and she loved that until she passed away."

Josephine's early life was as different from Clark Gable's as Henry Higgins's must have been from Liza Doolittle's. Josephine—Julia—grew up on a farm,

> . . . not a real farm at all. We call them estates now. It was one of those show places that tired professional men involve themselves in when they have worked too long without rest.
> Father did everything the romantic way. He bought each of us a horse, and hired a riding master. He bought us musical instruments and hired teachers. . . . And because we were too far from any town to go to a public school, he bought us an English tutor. That meant we were trained in Latin and the classics.
> . . . Our mother was a musician, a pianist. So we had a piano in the nursery, and absorbed Mozart and Bach and Beethoven instead of bedside stories every evening before going to sleep. We did our story telling and reading earlier in the evening before the library fire, with Father and Mother taking turns with Dickens or Louisa Alcott, or sometimes shivery Poe.

Sounding more and more as if she's narrating a scene from *Gone With the Wind,* Josephine elaborates on this splendid childhood. Since it is known that Henry Dillon spent nearly every cent he had on the education of his daughters, we can believe that Josephine's memories are real ones. The Dillon girls were prepared as youngsters to be anything they wanted to be in life—except housewives.

Later in the manuscript Josephine—Julia—admits her esoteric education was a handicap in her marriage: "It was hard for Mark to understand that any woman could be ignorant of the various chores that had to do with caring for the welfare of her man. [He thought] it must have been carelessness." Though this is a rare insight for Josephine, it is one taken too lightly, for what her husband required from a woman was complete care, complete mothering, with nothing demanded of him in return. Such was the nature of the object he had lost, and he couldn't endure for long any unmatching substitute. Josephine may have looked like an Earth Mother, but she turned out to be a Stage Mother. How could she replace Addie Gable?

The Dillon girls were raised the normal way women were in those days, Josephine writes, "until we developed a career 'bug.' My sisters had announced that they were going to be great artists, in opera, on the piano, and one, a painter. I had to be something, and announced that I was going to be a great actress."

She pursued an acting career for probably a dozen years before she decided she didn't have the personality for performing and would do better teaching those "who could stride out before an audience full of self and the thrill of exhibiting that self." She went back to Europe to study teaching, and then to New York, where she met a singing teacher who had a studio in Portland, a woman she calls "Madam Beaurien" in her manuscript. Meeting the woman, she dispatches her fate on its way to its sealing:

I've always been grateful to Madam Beaurien for persuading me to go to Portland. That is, I am almost always able to make myself think that I am grateful to her for that. For that is where I met Mark Craven. Should I be grateful for that? I don't know, and probably I will never know. We only know what our lives have been, never what they might, or should have been.

Julia and Mark were two of the strangest bedfellows in the history of Hollywood.

8

People have long wondered what Clark Gable ever saw in Josephine Dillon, a slight, sad-eyed, thin-lipped, didactic woman, seventeen years his senior. Reading her manuscript, however, one wonders what she saw in him as well. As a husband, he emerges from her pages a selfish, ambitious, unfaithful bumpkin; as a student, a plain bumpkin. But from the first moment she sees him she is drawn to him like a cobra to a flute.

Recalling the young Gable in her book *Modern Acting*, she wrote: "Clark Gable had the furrowed forehead of a man who is overworked and under-nourished. He had the straight-lipped, set mouth of the do-it-or-die character. He had the narrow slit-eyed expression of the man who has had to fight things through alone, and who tells nothing."

This is Josephine's account in her manuscript of her first meeting in Portland, late in 1923, with Billy Gable:

> I organized a study group in my new studio, to delve into early American plays, for evening sessions. And Mark Craven came, and Mark Craven joined that group.
>
> I was glad to have a big, stalwart, eager young man among the professors, writers, ex-actors, society daughters, artists and others. The typical little theatre group that assembles when a new dramatic venture offers.
>
> He had a wonderful smile. He was physically awkward, but full of assurance, and with the look of the man who makes easy conquests in an easy circle. He had a girl with him, young, pretty, a little theatrical in make-up and manner, with a tiny little face, and great mops of hair hanging around her shoulders. She said she was just visiting and would wait for Mark—gave me the once-over, the cold shoulder, the

toss of the hair, and sat down at the back of the room by the old wood stove reading a movie magazine, and paying no attention at all to the rest of us. I never saw her again, at least I think that I never saw that particular girl again—there were so many.

That night the group started to read the old play that is known as the first play ever to have been written, acted and produced by Americans, in America. You know it, of course—"The Contrast" by Royall Tyler.

As I told the group about those days in our theatre, I could not help but notice that Mark Craven was entirely absorbed, drinking in every bit of information, making no comment, no smiles of recognition when the humorous side of those shows was explained, just intense interest. I knew he had never heard of these things before, and that he was seizing clearly and soundly on the information about theatre and acting that he had been hungry for.

"Well, we'd better get into the reading of the play," I said, and Mark heaved a great sigh, and said, like one stirring from a dream: "That's what I've been looking for all these years!" And I looked at him then, really looked at him, for the first time, and thought, "I will help him. I will give him my book-learning, and acting knowledge, and speech and a voice. This is the one!"

When the group broke up for the evening, it was quite late. Mark waited until the rest had gone, and he asked me if he could come by and talk to me a few minutes next afternoon on his way home from the office where he worked. And I said I would like it very much.

Josephine struggles through the next day wondering if Clark will show up. He does. And they plunge into his career the way some couples leap into bed:

. . . the door burst open—no knock or ring— just the door flung open, and in strode Mark, coat-tails flying, lock across his forehead under an old pushed-back, snap-brim hat. He didn't say "Hello," or "Good evening" or anything at all, just began walking up and down the studio with his hands in his pockets, talking. About acting, of course. The act-ing he had not had a chance to do yet.

Mark Craven told me nothing at all about himself that evening, and he told me everything about him-self. He told me no chronicles—where he was born and when, where he went to school, and who he was, none of those things. But he told me the whole of his longing to be a good actor; of his dreams of suc-cess, of being a top guy on the screen; of having bigger and bigger chances to do things the way he wanted to do them, and had dreamed of doing them.

I don't remember his saying anything about going somewhere for dinner, but automatically I put on my hat and went with him to a little place down by the river front, where they served soup in great bowls for you to ladle out, and salad the same way, and then some sort of fish. We sat there a very long time, talk-ing.

His objective was Hollywood, and his questions were about Hollywood. "What is it like? Who gets into the movies, and why? Who tries to get in and don't make it, and why? What's the best way to go at it? What do you have to know? How do you learn it?" And a stream of other questions, all so eager, and strong. That is the word for him, strong. There was force and strength in this man.

She responds to his strength the only way she seems to know how: with a lecture. Such is the pattern of their re-lationship: he asks the question, and she makes a speech. Like many a teacher, Josephine settles for a listener in lieu of a lover. How she does go on, and how he does pay attention:

I told him that Hollywood as I knew it, was a different one from that pictured in the "fan" maga-zines, and the gossip columns, pictured as a checker-board of shifting love affairs, favorite cooking receipts, maneuvers for starring positions, frantic pub-licity stunts, flashing millions, and struggling poverty. Different too, from the stories of Hollywood that present it as a magic city sternly walled against all would-be entrants. Stories that would tell that anyone attempting to scale those walls, or to batter them through, must end in failure, unless they decided to pave their way with panderings to various forms of whispered degeneracies and sensuality. And the tales of failure always picturing tragic and broken people, facing a life hopelessly ruined and unredeemable.

People are defeated in Hollywood, of course, many, many of them, and there are many hearts broken there, and many lives broken. It takes strong people, that's all. The others should stay in their own home towns, or scurry back there at the first tough going.

Josephine has found the best listener in America. But just in case that isn't enough, he leaves her smitten that very night with more than the sound of her own voice:

As I unlocked the door, Mark turned to me and said suddenly, "Say, you know, you're a darn fine looking gal!" And off he went, with his long stride, whistling, and giving the brim of his hat a tilt, like a knight raising his visor before charging the windmill.

I went through the studio and up the stairs to my apartment, wondering. I was wondering at the amazing courage that true acting has, and the endurance; and I was wondering at the warmth around my heart, and the curiosity that the impulsive remark had brought me.

The "romance" progresses, with Clark absorbed in his work, and Josephine absorbed in him. Meanwhile, one of his special talents is emerging: attracting women.

The acting group put on a rough cut of "The Contrast" and Mark did the comedy "hick" part. He was funny, but not really good, too nervous and tense, and he tried too hard.

He memorized a long dramatic poem about a starving poet, that ended with a touching line about the poet, on the verge of suicide, worrying about the probable fate of his dog—and recited it to music at the Women's Club, and got away with it to a startling success.* That was something to put over a sentimen-

---

* A Portland newspaper notice of this "special programme" carried a picture of "William Gable . . . who will be presented at the Mac-

tal poem for a big rugged guy without romantic long hair. But he was good, and the ladies were delighted. So was I. The leap from the "hick" comedy to sentimental poetry spoken to music might have stopped a lesser talent, but Mark took it in his big stride, and had fun.

The women of the club became interested, and began appearing around my studio and asking casually about him. One of them—she had a big car, and a big house, and a big income—let him drive her through the beautiful moonlight roads around Portland and encouraged him in his art. She helped him. Besides raising his taste in cigarettes, she roused his curiosity about Shakespeare, and he asked me about it. He drank down the tragedies in great gulps, and did some Romeo and Hamlet and Macbeth with the prettiest girl in the studio; and did it extraordinarily well.

Months go by. (Months in which Billy Gable was still seeing Franz Dorfler and having jealous tantrums if she had another male friend.) Months in which Josephine Dillon tries to concentrate on her many classes and activities, but is too distracted. Suddenly, it seems to her, there is no one to teach except Clark. "Why, where are the others?" she asks herself, and answers, "I don't know when they dropped out." All she knows is that she is molding an actor who will do anything she says. "Check?" he asks, meaning "Does this please you?" "Check," she replies, even when he is his most sophomoric.

Long talks in the studio, or in the little French restaurants. Never about the past, always about the future, and about acting—acting in its relation to Mark—Mark the actor. It never occurred to either of us that he might not be an actor. That was never even mentioned.

We started the analysis of character, using great plays, and I was astonished at the sureness of his judgment. I would expect, of course, that he would know

---

Dowell Club Tuesday." "William" looks every inch "the poet," in an open-necked white shirt, his black hair parted in the center, his eyes sad, his nostrils taut, and mouth sensitive.

many of the modern types, because of his varied experiences, but I was not prepared for the directness with which he understood the fundamentals of the great classics.

He was not bringing in any more library books, so I surmised that the little Librarian was off the list. The expensive blue-boxed cigarettes were prominent, however, and there were frequent telephone conversations during class, with much talk of "I'll pick up the car and get you—eleven? Oke!" I knew it wasn't just the cigarettes or the car, but that he was learning things about big cities and theater and rich living and money.

One evening Mark came in just as he had that other time when he was bursting with the need to spill out his thoughts. No door bell, no knock, just the door flung open, and the plunging into talk.

He pulled the Shakespeare volume out of his coat pocket. "Now these fellows. Take this Romeo, well, any young fellow will be about like that at his age, whether he's a Duke's son, or the kid of the garage man. He gets conscious of the girls and goes from one to another, fast, if he's a good normal sort. Not the love 'em and leave 'em like an older man who's got the habit of playing around with girls just to feel young, but experimenting like a kid. When he saw the girl he wanted, he knew it fast enough, and nothing could ever have shaken him—he never in the world would ever have wanted anyone else, if he and Juliet had lived. Great guy, that Romeo, don't you think so?"

"Yes, I think so."

"I'd like to learn it. I like that chase at the end, crashing into the tomb, and finding her over there in the corner, where they tossed her cousin. Just like a Mack Sennett chase. Exciting, and young. Kiddish! Older man would have found out for sure that she was dead before he kicked himself off."

"Yes, I guess he would."

Mark shoved his hat on the back of his head, and sprawled out his long legs, and went on with his discovery of Shakespeare.

"This Macbeth guy! There are lots of men like that, you can see them almost anywhere you go. They can think out what they should do, or what they shouldn't do, but they let their wives run them. Macbeth would have waited to be king the natural way, but he let his wife talk him into killing. Pretty dumb! Don't you think so? He should have slapped her down. Check?"

"Check."

"But this Hamlet! Now there was a guy!"

Mark was up on his feet now, striding around the studio—expansive—excited. "Here's this kid, sent away to school for the first time, a prince, and everything, sent with a companion to look after him—so he must be pretty young. Then when he's hardly got used to the college, he gets word to come home, his father is dead, and he has to get back and be king. He gets off the boat at the harbor—like coming home here to Portland, from school in San Francisco —and he is met at the dock by some more men from the court, telling him to hurry along back to the castle, his mother has just got married to his uncle, and to come along to the wedding party. His uncle is king.

"Now wouldn't that upset anyone? Came too fast for him. What do you think?"

What Josephine thinks is that it is time for Clark to move onward and upward, to a place where his career, or, at least, his ego, can let out its spinnaker and go full ahead with the wind.

. . . it was time for him to be in the center of acting, where everyone was interested in one thing— the entertainment business; where in every garage, and market, and bowling alley, and drive-in . . . everyone was talking acting, and movies, and acting, and movies, and me, me, ME!

I knew it was time to get Mark to Hollywood!

In the past, writers have said that Clark Gable and Josephine Dillon ran into each other in Hollywood quite by accident. That is not Josephine's story:

Things in my studio were not too busy anyway. I had not paid much attention to the opportunities that were constantly presenting themselves to spread out

and increase the activities of my work. So I announced
a date for closing, and for returning to Hollywood.
And I arranged with Mark to let him know when to
join me there.

It didn't occur to either of us that he would not follow me . . .

It was taken for granted that we would be together.

9

Before leaving for Los Angeles, Josephine got Clark, who
was still called Billy, settled with a stock company in
Portland. She must have been feeling very sure of him;
it was the same stock company Franz had been performing with for several months. And for once in his young
life, Billy showed no conflict of interests. He stayed as
far away from Franz as two people can get in one
theater, cutting her off from his affection and his thoughts.
Franz had no idea how excited Billy was at the idea
of going to Hollywood, how thoroughly Josephine had
managed to transfer her own passion for films to him.
Those last weeks in Portland, Billy ceased existing in the
present. He lived in his head, where projections of his
future were going off like fireworks.

He was one of hundreds of thousands of people for
whom Hollywood had become the Fourth of July. The
population of the movie-manufacturing town had tripled
since 1920; there were one hundred people waiting for
every single available extra's job. One hundred thousand
people were registered with Screen Service, the industry's
largest employment agency. If it was a loony time everywhere, nowhere was it as loony as in the town where
$10,000-a-week employees of film factories were driven
by liveried chauffeurs to see their swamis, or hear Aimee
Semple McPherson, or would jump, fully clothed, into a
friend's gardenia-filled swimming pool—cheered on by

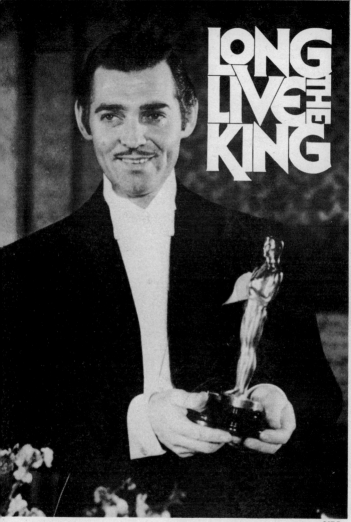

LONG LIVE THE KING

UPI

Clark with the Oscar he won for *It Happened One Night*, 1934.

Who's This? He's Clark Gable!

The shy boy shown above holding a close reign on the hobby
poised for a daring gallop down the lane and over the Hope-
Ohio, hills bears little resemblance to the nation's current pro-
ype of the compelling lover.

Nevertheless it is Clark Gable at the mature age of 3 years

With his beloved hobby horse; a love story exposed
in 1932

HE WAS RAISED IN HOPEDALE, OHIO
The house his father built

At a wedding, baby Clark (bottom left) with his father
(William, seated second row, left) and stepmother (Jennie
Dunlap, next to William)

With his stepmother, whom he always called Jennie Dunlap

The student body of Hopedale Elementary School; Clark in center of top row

The Hopedale Band; its youngest member, Master Gable, behind the drum

Courtesy of Harrison County Historical Society

Be-muffed and clowning with best friend, Andy Means

Visiting the old gang; Clark is the teenaged dandy with gloves and cigarette

Museum of Modern Art/Film Stills Archive

CLARK, THE ASPIRING ACTOR OF THE ROARING
TWENTIES

UPI

UPI

He was engaged to aspiring actress Franz Dorfler (as she looked in the thirties, opposite top), who sent him to drama coach Josephine Dillon (opposite bottom). Josephine married him, groomed him, and lost him when his theatrical career began on Broadway in 1928 with Zita Johann in *Machinal* (below left). Miss Dillon struggled as a teacher (in her studio in 1962, below right) until she died in a sanitarium in 1971.

Courtesy of Belva Hall

Museum of Modern Art/Film Stills Archive

Clark, the MGM movie star, with second wife, Ria, strolling in Beverly Hills

Museum of Modern Art/Film Stills Archive

At Big Bear

Museum of Modern Art/Film Stills Archive

Ria, seventeen years his senior, provided a ready-made family; daughter, George Anna Lucas (far left) and son, Al Lucas (far right).

Clark's skyrocketing career provided the means for a Dusen-
berg one foot longer than Gary Cooper's and the studio's
explanation for a troubled marriage.

Courtesy of George Anna Burke

Clark and Ria had essentially separated when he attended George Anna's Houston, Texas, wedding to give her away. Ria never married again. She stayed in Hollywood a few years, then moved to Houston where she died in 1966.

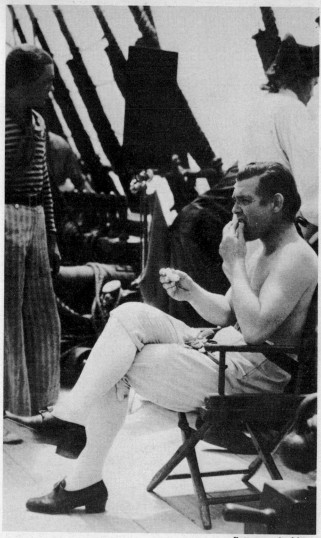

Bettmann Archive

Clark feared that his role in *Mutiny on the Bounty* (1935) would undo his man's-man image; *Bounty* earned him an Oscar nomination.

Bettmann Archive

With Jean Harlow, who became a special friend, Mary Astor and Donald Crisp, on the set of *Red Dust,* 1932

Bettmann Archive

Though he was MGM's leading luminary, his relationship with studio head Louis B. Mayer was never any better than it looks here (at a luncheon for George Bernard Shaw, far left, with Mayer and Marion Davies).

UPI

Clark's father, William, a wild-catter who never struck oil, believed acting was only for sissies. Nothing Clark did impressed old Bill, not even his winning an Oscar for *It Happened One Night*.

Bettmann Archive

THEN THERE WAS CAROLE . . .

They met co-starring in *No Man of Her Own* in 1932, but their affair didn't begin until '35 when she was the ex-Mrs. William Powell and he was separated from Ria. He called her Ma. She called him Pa. Shortly before they were married, they bought Raoul Walsh's Encino hideaway for $50,000. The last Mrs. Gable sold it in 1973 for $800,000.

UPI

Carole had the approval of Clark's trusted friend, Howard Strickling, head of MGM publicity. Carole's secretary-business manager, Jean Garceau, became Clark's as well, and worked for him for twenty years. She says the "dictating picture" is a joke; Clark hated dictating and she couldn't read her own shorthand.

Courtesy of Jean Garceau

Copyright © 1939 MGM Inc. Reprinted by permission

Rhett and Scarlett

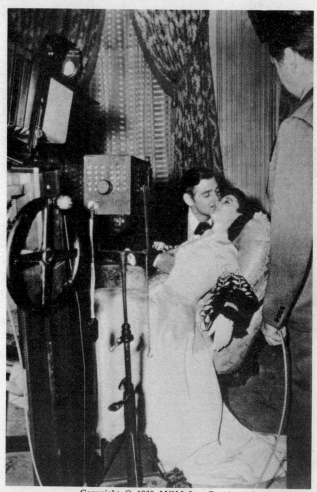

Copyright © 1939 MGM Inc. Reprinted by permission

Courtesy of Mervin LeRoy

Clark Gable and Vivien Leigh

Copyright © 1939 MGM Inc. Reprinted by permission

Victor Fleming was Clark's friend and the man he chose to replace George Cukor as director of *Gone With The Wind*.

Copyright © 1939 MGM Inc. Reprinted by permission

Clark and Carole and Marion Davies and Raoul Walsh at the Hollywood premiere of *Gone With The Wind.* The fifth of the group was Scotch, which was guzzled in the manager's office for the duration of the film.

AND MARRIED BLISS . . .

Hunting ducks in La Grulla, Mexico, with Buster and Stevie Collier and Liz and Tuffy Goff.

Clark and Carole

A tent party at home: Clark and a flute.

Courtesy of Buster and Stevie Collier

Clark on the drums, Buster Collier on bass, and Fred Peters on percussion

Courtesy of Buster and Stevie Collier

Carole, her mother behind her, Stevie Collier, and two other guests

masses of people who didn't have two dimes to rub together.

The smog had not yet started to screen out the sun in
Hollywood, and the palm-lined streets were bathed with
a golden dust all day, and a pale rose hue at dusk. Evenings smelled of citrus, and the night sky was rhinestone
clear. What a gorgeous boomtown Hollywood was, if you
knew nothing of the grubs on its underbelly. How glorious
a promise it held, if you didn't know that an unknown
actor had about as much chance of being discovered there
as a tick in a deer's ear.

No one could have been more kinetically charged than
Billy, in Portland, awaiting his next move. And that's because no one could have been more intoxicated with the
idea of Hollywood than Josephine Dillon. "So, here I am
in Hollywood, back again in Hollywood, bringing grist to
the picture mill," she wrote in her manuscript. Such an
innocent. She had no defenses at all for the time her
beloved Hollywood would laugh at her, belittle her,
accept her offering, and burn her for a witch.

She was forty.

She was pregnant with a great white hope for which
she was going to build a nest in a battleground she remembered as a wonderland.

Her first concern is to find the nesting spot for Billy.
She finds a twenty-dollar-a-month cottage—a shack, she
calls it—on a street where Tom Mix lived, and where
there were "movie people all around—the whole pano-
rama of little Hollywood folk." She is terribly busy, so
busy it takes her weeks to face her own motivations.

I had opened a studio and things started to roll
without much trouble. Except the same trouble I had
in Portland, the difficulty of keeping my mind on the
students and their needs, when every thought was
racing with plans for getting Mark settled and started
in his work.

I raided the family storerooms and furnished the
little cottage. I found mirrors and lined the walls of
one of the rooms. I found a tiny piano, and the
kitchen things and good old rugs, and window drapes
that were still beautiful and were once in the music
room of the old farm home. The furnishings were
sparse, and rather severe. But that was good, that

meant work. But it was comfortable, and there were lots of books . . . good books that work along with you.

I was living in a hotel not far from the studio where I taught, and spending my spare time on the little cottage. I painted the walls and the floors, and a gay front door and planted geraniums on both sides of it.

Then the little house was ready.

I turned the key in the door, the night that the job was finished, and looked around me at the old garden, and up at the stars, and across the street to the great Star's Mansion, and I thought, "This little cottage will house a bigger star than that great mansion. Tom Mix is mighty big, and he's got to top him."

Then it struck me. So suddenly that I sat down on the bench there beside the door, astounded and confused. Was I preparing this little home for him, or for us? Was that what had really been in my mind all this time, and I not mindful of it? Did I intend to occupy this little place with Mark? What was this going to be? If a twosome, what sort of a twosome? There was only one answer to that, marriage. I knew my Hollywood. No other relationship would be possible; everything else is tawdry and stupid. Then I laughed, and thought, "Ridiculous!"

And I went back to the hotel, sure that I had forgotten the whole startling thought, and went to sleep and dreamed of playing house in a little cottage on Movie Street.

In short order she sends her protégé $50 for his trip south, and in short order "there was Mark dashing across the lobby."

He was dirty, shaggy, almost ragged, dusty, no hat, hair over his eyes, open shirt, sagging belt, faded gray plaid baggy trousers, dusty white socks, old brown shoes, but his personality banged through all that and struck with the same impact that has since become famous throughout the world.

He grinned about his appearance, and said that he and his companion had gone off the road, and rolled over into a ditch. But he had another suit in the suitcase, and anyhow, here he was in Hollywood. Gosh!

I knew of a little eating place, and we went there, and talked and talked through dinner, and then late into the night in the room I had engaged for him in the hotel. Talked about acting, of course, and Hollywood, and acting and Hollywood, just as though he had become one of them already.

"Mark" makes the key statement, "If I can count on being close to you, Julia, perhaps I'll get in and get away with it, but I'll never make it alone."

I left early next morning for my studio. I had thought of cancelling that day's appointments, but they needed my work, and I needed their money. So I chopped away at little actors all day, and rushed home. Mark was not in the lobby, nor in his room. I didn't go out to dinner, for fear I would miss him, but stayed right there, and about ten he tapped on the door.

"Hey, honey, I've got a job, in a garage, only one I found so far." He came in and flung himself in a chair, looking fierce and confused. "Do you know, honey, I've been thinking, and if it didn't sound so crazy, the thing to do would be for us to get married. That would be the way to do it."

Josephine accepts immediately and then self-consciously writes the one romantic event of the manuscript (and, perhaps, the relationship):

"Listen. You don't love me, and I don't love you, but we like each other a lot and it looks pretty much as though we need each other. At least, we are both interested in getting you somewhere, and proving that you can go places here. I can't see love affairs— what Hollywood calls 'engagements,' they're too messy. So if you really mean that, Mark, I'll do it."

He was standing leaning against the door, his hat on the back of his head, his overcoat hanging loose, his face very serious. I was standing by the chair I had been reading in when he came, and was probably looking pretty serious too. Not a very romantic love scene. You couldn't sell that in the movies. Suddenly

Mark grinned, "Well, I'll be getting along, good-night." He turned and reached for the doorknob, then stood there looking at me again seriously, his hand back of him was fumbling for the doorknob and catching in his overcoat. I stepped to him and started to reach for the doorknob myself, putting my hand through the bend of his elbow. And suddenly I was in his arms, held very closely.

"You may not be in love with me, or I with you, as you say, perhaps not, but I think you are the grandest person I've ever known, and I shall love you as long as I live. You'll see." And he kissed me, and then opened the door and went out quickly.

I opened the door swiftly and called him back: "Mark, I want to show you something. Wait for me in the lobby, I'll meet you right away." He nodded okay. I closed the door again, put on my coat quickly, and joined him there in the lobby, hurried him out of there, and over to the little cottage a few blocks away.

The electricity and gas had been connected, so there was light and warmth—it was a home.

In all of the pictures I have seen Mark in since, I have never seen such an expression on his face as was there when he looked around the cottage that was to be his home. Deeply touched by all that it meant to work and thought, and by the realization of security and a home, and a friend in this strange Hollywood. There was peace here.

The only outside door the place had entered into the kitchen, so I had painted it bright blue on the outside and inside both, made the tiny kitchen a light blue, and the floor a dark blue, and put blue and white checks at the windows—both of them, on the kitchen table, and even made covers for the two kitchen chairs. Dutchy. He liked that kitchen. The ridiculous bathroom opened off the kitchen, and I had painted it bright yellow, floor, walls, ceiling, everything, and there were more blue checks at that window. When I painted it, I wondered how in heaven a man as big as Mark Craven would use such a small space. He would just have to content himself with large singing and splashing, and very small gestures. Perhaps it would be good training for opera acting.

There was another room, larger than the kitchen, about twelve by fourteen, I should say, and that was the "settin'" room. Mark roared with laughter at the tiny bathroom, then went through the "hallway," perhaps four by four, into the sitting room. It really did look attractive with its old, good furniture, its soft-colored drapes, the old piano and comfortable settee and lamps. He just said, "Well, what do you know," and stood there looking around, then went over and sat at the piano on the old turn-style stool, touched a few keys, then began swinging around on the stool, like a youngster, and tossing his old hat up and catching it.

There was a coat closet off that room, utilizing the space under the narrow stairway, and there was a telephone, that essential life-line in all Hollywood activities.

"What's up the stairs?"

"You go up and look."

And a few moments later I could hear him stepping carefully around up there—carefully because of the sloping roofs that left only a small central space where he could stand erect.

We decided to be married right away, and face Hollywood together, barriered snugly in the cottage with the blue floors and checked curtains.

10

Josephine wanted the world to believe that she and Clark Gable were married within days of his appearance in Los Angeles. In truth, five months elapsed before they wed, during which Billy lived in a hotel, and Josephine paid his bills. (They were married quietly in the church office of a Reverend Meadows on December 18, 1924.

For the occasion, they narrowed their age difference. Clark claimed he was twenty-four; Josephine said she was thirty-four.) It was enough time for Billy to realize how tough it was going to be to break into films, how much he had to learn, and how impossible it was going to be to support himself. Often there were such mob scenes at casting offices he visited that they became news events; a call for thirty-five extras would go out, and three to four thousand people would respond, ready to do battle for the $3-a-day jobs. He couldn't get an agent to help. Agents, what few there were in the mid-twenties, took only the choicest Eastern or European talent, and in any case, had little clout at the studios. Whatever else Billy Gable may have felt for Josephine Dillon, he certainly was aware that she could mean the difference between his swimming or sinking in Hollywood.

What existed between them physically, we will never know. Josephine told any reporter who would listen in her later years that her marriage had been "in name only." That may have been true, but her manuscript shows her more than sufficiently jealous of him to be his lover. Though she never writes a pure and simple statement about finding him appealing, she never stops writing that other women did. Chances are, that just as Josephine was too embarrassed to confront the age difference between herself and her pupil, she was too Victorian to admit, even to herself after a while, that she went to bed with him. Furthermore, to have been Gable's real wife would have detracted from her role of martyred saint. In the mind of the public that considered Clark Gable one of the most desirable men in the world, a woman who'd had him in bed even for ten minutes had had more than her share of goodies in life.

Friends of Gable's shrug off the notion of the loveless first marriage. They believe Clark married Josephine because he was ambitious, but that he paid with whatever service he could provide. Says John Lee Mahin, who was with Gable in the Air Corps and constantly baffled by the star's choice of homely bed partners, "Physically, one woman was the same as any other to him."

If we were to believe Josephine, she had a husband who did only two things: studied or played around. And his flirtations begin when they would have been honeymooners, had they had a honeymoon, at a party given in their honor ("What a good party that was," she writes. *Good?*):

One of America's famous sculptresses gave us a kitchen shower when she found that we had set up housekeeping with practically nothing to cook with . . . Ella's huge studio, full of guests that might have met together at a party in Greenwich Village or on the Left Bank in Paris, or most anywhere else where people study and make a profession of the arts.

Painters, poets, noted camera artists, newspaper folk, no stars, no movie executives, but brilliant people from all over the world. Good food, fun and laughter, and the shower of housekeeping presents! Those pots and pans were very very precious.

I was terribly impressed, and so happy, and so at home. These people I was used to, the people I had always known and been with. I understood them, and what they were doing, and what they were trying to do, and they understood me, and we were all friends.

I had not paid much attention to Mark, he seemed to be constantly surrounded by people and having a very good time, and I was busy helping Ella with the supper. Ella came in and said: "Julia, I don't want to start anything. But I also do not know who that creature is—someone brought her here, but if you want your new husband, you'd better go and drag him away."

Through the big arch between the dining room and the studio we could see the dancers, and Mark's dark head and big shoulders stood up above the shorter men. His old gray coat would have marked him out in that group of evening clothes, even if the slow, almost imperceptible movement of their dancing had not made them conspicuous among the artists happily bouncing around to the lovely old waltz music. Yes, "them!" A tall, sleek slender woman, with a huge nob of smooth red hair on a very white neck, long jade earrings, jade coronet, beautiful alive body sheathed in gold cloth, green slippers, jade bracelets, her head on Mark's shoulder, Mark's cheek on hers, lips whispering, oblivious of others dancing, or of others who might be watching, or waiting.

I didn't take Ella's advice to go out and cut in, I just stood there with a wooden spoon in one hand and the beautiful frying pan in the other, in amazement.

The party Josephine describes breaks up instantly, and the newlyweds go home. There is a short, mindless exchange of dialogue between the bride and groom, and the night ends thus:

"Gosh, honey, hope I don't have to take much of those long-haired artistic nuts, they get me down."

"We needed the things. They will come in very handy."

"The old gal I was dancing with said to drop around; said she would wise me up to the Hollywood racket."

"I wouldn't be surprised if she could."

"Yeah. She looked rich, notice the bracelets, got a lot of dough. Goodnight."

And with his good pair of shoes in his hand, Mark grinned at me, and started up the narrow stairs to the slope-roofed little bedroom, placing his stockinged feet carefully sideways on the narrow stairs, and whistling the old waltz tune.

I stood a moment looking around the tiny little sitting room, with its gallant pretensions—and with a long happy sigh I tossed ART and Culture into the cobwebs of my educated past, and whistling the waltz, ran cheerfully up the golden stairs.

The marriage takes on a tempo, the rhythm of it established by Josephine's droning lectures and Clark's dogged efforts to learn his trade. Josephine flourished in the tempo and probably could have gone on with it forever. Her husband rejected it as soon as he sensed its aggressions. Eventually, when she criticized his acting, he would become furious, "would slam out of the tiny house and rage off—I never knew where." Clark would one day tell Franz Dorfler, "She can't stop playing teacher. She is just too domineering. Sometimes she acts like she's Mrs. God." This is Josephine's description of the early, "idyllic" days:

Breakfast: Cereal, eggs, toast with butter, milk.

Lunch: Salad of raw vegetables with olive oil dressing.

Dinner: Whatever we could afford to buy, except no pastry.

Mornings: Speech voice, breathing and diction and quality and pitch.

Afternoons: Theory of acting and theory of dialogue.

Evenings: Before and after dinner—what ever you please.

But of course we pleased to talk about acting.

There is a bee buzzing around this love nest: poverty. The Gables are so broke only one of them can go to the movies at a time, and only with considerable sacrifice. Of course it is the protégé who goes, and of course, teacher never complains. Everything is for the future star.

Clark got a couple of used golf clubs, and he played golf on the public course at Griffith Park, with a couple of men friends (Stuart Irwin, Stanley Smith, Paul Fix) whom Josephine never mentions in her story. When she writes about the many hours he was missing—afternoons, evenings, nights—she implies he is with some woman or other, and usually, a rich one.

What is clear in the manuscript is that Josephine committed the unforgivable sin in her marriage: she fell in love with her husband and wanted him to respond. Because this wasn't part of the deal, she suffered as much anguish as Dr. Frankenstein would have had he fallen in love with his monster. From the start she knows the only thing that matters to Billy Gable is becoming an actor, but—just like a woman—the one thing she can't bear is that the only thing binding them is his acting. "After all," she once wrote, "one must sometimes want to talk about something else than acting, or theater, or movies, or even the husband's career! What went on in Clark's mind that did not concern acting, I don't know, have never known, and will never know. What did I think about when we were not talking about acting or his career? He never knew. And I have never known whether he even wondered or cared."

Her repressed resentment probably became an attempt at more and more discipline for her budding star, which he could only resent because he didn't know her true feelings. The manuscript shows him becoming inwardly petulant. She writes this scene that transpired after one of his frequent one-way trips to the golf course:

Mark did not come home for dinner.

Mark did not come home.

This was Tuesday.

He came home Friday . . . was practicing putts in the yard when I came in from the office about half after five.

"Hello."

"Hello, there, honey. Lookit, I can roll this thing right into the little hole there by the geraniums three out of five. Pretty good, eh?"

"Fine. You ought to make it every time on turf. I'll take these things into the house. Have some dinner ready pretty quick."

And I went in into the kitchen with the parcels from the market, and on into the typewriter table and left the typewriting work there, and on into the bathroom, and closed the door softly, feeling very, very sick.

There was plenty of food in the house, because I had not been eating much, and it didn't take long to get it onto the table, although it would be impossible to remember what it was.

Mark came in, put his sticks in the bag, and the ball carefully in its pocket, and joined me at the table. But just before he pulled out his chair, he said:

"You know, honey, why men tell lies to their wives?"

"No."

"It's because the wives ask questions. The way to be sure that a man doesn't lie to you, is not to ask him anything." And he pulled his chair out, seated himself, and drank down his glass of milk while I served.

"Okay?"

"Okay. It's not important."

It is not important. It is not important. It is not important.

What is important?

Becoming an actor. Being a success. A Star! That is important. All right, if that's the way you want it. If that is what you want, it is important I suppose.

Josephine has gotten to a point where she can only suppose something she once didn't doubt for a moment. How touchingly she sees him go one afternoon, "out to the golf links, probably":

> I watched him running up the garden path and out onto the sidewalk, with pride in the improvement of his stride and body carriage, appreciation of his fine acting talent. But underneath it all, I watched him go with the woman-wish in my heart that my man might have everything in the world he wanted.

11

Sometime in his first year with Josephine, Billy disappeared and was permanently replaced by Clark Gable. Legend has it that Josephine decided Clark was a more suitable stage name than Billy, but the young Gable's choice of names was so dependent on how he felt about himself that he had to be ready to be Clark, or he wouldn't have been, no matter what Josephine said. Clark was a better specimen than Billy, he fitted better into his body.

Billy's voice, when Josephine first knew it, was "nervous and hard in quality and much too high in pitch, as is true with many big men." He had to sit for hours, daily, at a piano, working his voice down, a half-step at a time, until Josephine was satisfied that "the register of his speech was proper for his big man type"—proper for Clark. Clark would always have to work at voice control, however. As late as 1952, director Delmer Daves asked the star to lower his pitch. They were making a film called *Never Let Me Go*. Daves felt Clark's part called for a lower-ranged voice, and told him so. As Daves recalls, "Clark said, 'Hell, this is my style.' I said, 'Oh forget style, Clark. I can talk like a tenor, or a second tenor, or I can talk like a baritone, and you have to do exactly the same thing. By God, if I want to I can talk a bass, but each one is honest.' I said, 'Clark, don't think you're being dishonest if you lower your voice range. You're a gutsy guy doing a gutsy part and you have to talk with a gutsy voice.' So Clark, in this film, lowered his voice range."

While Billy was training his voice, he was also getting rid of the tension in his face. Josephine observed: "As the muscles of his face relaxed in the assumption of correct speech habits, the forehead smoothed, the eyes opened, the lips began to be flexible, and his [Clark's] now famous smile was born."

Billy's clumsiness turned into Clark's muscular grace, mostly on forced marches: long walks necessitated by lack of transportation, and repeated trips up and down the cottage stairs under Josephine's supervision. Billy was so disciplined he did breathing exercises even when playing golf. It is hard to imagine his degree of self-absorption unless you have known a young, aspiring actor, and it is a tribute to Gable that he was able to outgrow his narcissism; too many actors never do. The weary joke about the actor who says to his friend, "Let's talk about *you*. What did you think of my last picture?" has become a classic for good reason. And young Billy Gable was the worst kind of all: untried, overeager, with a sleep-in audience.

Billy Gable looked half-heartedly for a way to try his new talent: he made the rounds only as far as he could walk. Clark Gable went looking for work like a starving lion stalking prey, as far and wide as a newly purchased second-hand car would take him. (Typically, when he was able to buy his first car in Hollywood, he chose an open Roamer that could pass for a Rolls-Royce.) He was lucky immediately, getting a $15-a-day bit part in a silent film called *White Man*. There couldn't have been more excitement in "the little cottage" had he been asked to do a remake of *The Sheik:*

A job in the movies for Mark! A good bit in a picture for Mark! A car coming for him. A car for Mark!
Shirts, ties, socks, shoes, shaving soap, hair brushes in every direction! Rushing back and forth, or stand-

ing absorbed at the mirror, for the shaving, for the hair a thousand ways, the toothbrush, the smile . . . the walk . . . then up the garden path with great strides, into the waiting car from the studio. How important! This was it, this was the starting of a career. Now things would happen!

Money! He would need money. His coat was hanging on a chair, and I emptied my coin purse into a pocket, and the bills from my billfold. Six dollars and some. Not much for a career, but enough to start. . . . That would be a good joke to tell one of these days, a story of starting off to be an actor with six dollars and thirty-two cents—and a grin.

"One of these days" was a long way off. Work on the film lasted ten frantically busy, supremely happy, fourteen-hour days. Then there were none; just weeks of looking and hoping, Josephine forever optimistic, Clark in deep, silent despair. He could get work, when there was a call for tall men, as an extra, but he hated the thought. Extras weren't actors, they weren't even human, they were movable props. Actors and actresses were protected from the rigors of film-making; extras were dispensable. If they passed out from the heat of the high, hissing arc lights, or went half-blind from the lower Kleigs, or threw up from the nauseating green glow of the Cooper-Hewitts used for full illumination—oops, replacement, please, and roll 'em. Extras never got near the director, only one of his assistants. They didn't talk to the principals. They weren't addressed as people; "atmosphere" or "background" the a.d. would call when he wanted his extras' attention. (Which is still true, by the way. A guild protects extras today, but their working conditions, not their egos.) Extras stood around all day, many a tedious day, waiting for some kind of action. Actors lounged in canvas chairs, at a discreet distance from the peasants, made jokes, talked dirty, had a drink brought on a tray, got a neck rub, called everyone endearing names. An actor was what Clark wanted to be, not a prop.

But Josephine believed in working, not waiting, so Clark worked, and fairly steadily, too, appearing as an extra in at least five films released in 1925, the most famous of which was MGM's *The Merry Widow*, directed by Erich von Stroheim, starring Mae Murray and John Gilbert. Clark was originally slated for a bit part in *Widow*, but von Stroheim, referred to as "the great" by his admirers, "the Hun," by everyone else, didn't like him. However, even being an extra on that film had to have been what the film colony calls a living experience.

Von Stroheim and Miss Murray loathed each other from the first day of shooting and fought openly nearly every day thereafter. Von Stroheim regularly turned his back on his star and stage-whispered an insult or two. Miss Murray constantly made temperamental demands and complained to the bosses, Louis B. Mayer and Irving Thalberg. Not getting anywhere, finally, in a fit of frustration, she called von Stroheim "a dirty Hun," whereupon he walked off the picture. Mayer, who never minded losing a director whose contract gave him a share of the profits, replaced him with a director named Monta Bell. This caused an immediate mutiny among the stagehands and extras, who refused to work unless von Stroheim was reinstated. Bosley Crowther, in his book *The Lion's Share*, described what happened next:

> . . . Mayer was hurriedly summoned. . . . Whereupon Eddie Mannix, a former bouncer at the Schenck brothers' Palisades Park who had just been sent out to the studio to serve as an aide to Mayer, clipped the nearest insurgent on the jaw. The exercise sobered the gathering and cooler heads prevailed. Miss Murray was persuaded to apologize to von Stroheim and they finished the film.

The occasional excitement, fun, and games were not enough to keep Clark phoning all over town for extra jobs which led nowhere. Silents, it seemed, weren't for him, nor he for them. Josephine's coaching, particularly in speech, prepared him in no way for the exaggerated performance required of a voiceless actor, and, in any case, he was too big to fit into the mold of five-foot-six-inch heroes. Clark gave up waving his arms at casting directors and looked once again to the theater, which, in the mid-twenties, was burgeoning in Los Angeles. Every major road company made a stop there; there were as many as thirteen plays running simultaneously in some weeks.

In the spring of 1925, a husband-wife producing-directing team, Louis MacLoon and Lillian Albertson, announced they would present Jane Cowl in *Romeo and Juliet*—fresh from her triumphant tour (or as fresh as she could be at thirty-nine, playing the teenaged Juliet). Clark and Josephine rejoiced. If there was one thing Clark was ready for—they were both sure—it was Shakespeare; could he not recite, by heart, all of *Hamlet*, *Macbeth*, and *Romeo and Juliet*?

He was the first on line at the first call for the ensemble, and one of the first chosen . . . for spear carrier. He didn't care. He was so eager to get on the stage he would have volunteered to be a turret. The job paid $30 a week, it offered status, and had infinite possibilities. What he didn't know, for about a day, was that Jane Cowl, the female Don Juan of the legitimate theater, had hand-picked him. His principal job at the start of the production turned out to be in Miss Cowl's dressing room; within one week after the play opened, he replaced a departing Mercutio, and was asked to complete Miss Cowl's tour of Portland, Seattle, and Vancouver. On tour, his pay went to $40 a week.

Miss Albertson, who directed the Los Angeles production, was not nearly as impressed with him as was Jane Cowl. She found him clumsy, thought his voice too high-pitched, and his acting amateurish. Mrs. Gable thought that if there was anything wrong with Clark's acting, it was the direction he was getting, and she worried that her protégé was being ruined forever. Clark didn't care what any of them thought; all that mattered was that he was playing Shakespeare in a fine Los Angeles theater.

He was so happy he was irresistible. As once his ebullience lit up the Dorflers' farm, so did it now brighten the lives of his troupe. He clowned and he teased and he was thoughtful and kind. Enthusiasm often makes up for a lack of talent among jaded professionals, and Clark couldn't have been brighter-eyed or bushier-tailed. And with it all, he was appealingly vulnerable and self-mocking. He couldn't help being courtly; if Miss Cowl dropped something on the floor, he instinctively went to pick it up, but he'd drop to one knee and swoop it, like a gallant knight, and teasingly return it. He really loved to have fun, and—damn it—life with Josephine was so deadly serious.

He did the tour as though he'd never seen the North-west before, full of a tourist's excitement. But he wrote Josephine only about his work and the weather.

When he returned from his tour, and his leading lady, he went into the MacLoons' production of *What Price Glory?*, staying in it nearly four months, and working himself up to one of the major roles. Lillian Albertson had begun to be impressed with him. She was not, however, impressed with his wife, who came once too often to the theater to coach Clark, and got herself banned from rehearsals.

Clark worked in at least four more MacLoon productions, the next one, *Lullaby*, taking him to San Francisco, where he ran into Franz and put her into yet another tailspin. She was teaching dancing in a studio across from his theater. After hours, she went with friends to a café nearby. "One night," she says, "Bill Gable and a stage manager came there—to our surprise. He asked me where I worked, and came to call on me every time he came to San Francisco after that." They'd kiss goodnight, nothing more, but it was enough to make Franz realize he was still the love of her life. Franz dated often, but it seemed that whenever she found someone she could care for, her Bill would show up and spoil her relationship. She couldn't fight his possessiveness. "Once," she says, "in San Francisco, I asked him to walk with me to my singing lesson. We met my teacher, and chatted. I could see it made Bill mad. We had a luncheon engagement the next day—he didn't show up."

He wasn't showing up much at home, either. Nor was he sending any money to his wife. Josephine one day would tell reporters that after Clark started working she moved out of their cottage into a studio loaned her by a friend. At least one writer has claimed that Gable moved out and left Josephine the cottage. Josephine mentions neither move in her manuscript; she just drops Clark out of it for many pages in which she writes only about her experiences with other pupils, all female. When Clark reappears, it is via a letter from somewhere, in which he ominously says of an actress, "She is really wonderful. Gives a fellow a build-up, makes you feel important, sort of, instead of like a little boy trying to learn something too big for him."

On the heels of this letter, Josephine gets a bag of laundry Clark sends ahead of his return so he'll have a

clean shirt to wear to the theater. Josephine finds it more
ominous than the letter:

> Dumping everything together onto the kitchen floor
> I saw—white silk shirts, three of them, blue silk
> shirts, three of them, blue silk shorts and under shirts,
> two sets, and two of blue and white stripes, and socks,
> the old beloved and preciously cared for woolens,
> and then blue, gray, tan, solid, striped, checkered,
> beautiful silk socks, twelve pairs. I knew how to
> wash silk, I had always had silk until now.
> My first reaction was astonishment, then the
> thought that surely the expressman had left the wrong
> bag. No, those other things were all too familiar.
> Well, anyway, they all needed washing, and I must
> do them myself, or hire them done. Okay, I must do
> them myself.

She figures a woman has bought Mark the shirts, but,
as usual, rationalizes rather than acts:

> Later, upstairs, lying in bed waiting for sleep, I
> thought, "Thank God I'm not in love with him. . . .
> You have taken on a job, Julia, finish it."

Josephine tried to finish it. She sent Clark to a dentist
who plucked the two widely spaced front teeth from his
mouth, and relaced them with closely fitting gold ones.

She followed Clark on some tours, even after they had
separated, showing up at rehearsals—like Paula Strasberg
—to coach her actor, and give him strength.

She hung on for at least two more years after that
laundry bag arrived, believing every day that Clark
needed her and would return; that she could go on wash-
ing his dirty laundry and all would be well.

In her manuscript, she has only one scene with her husband after the silk shirts are hung up to dry. One of his
trips has ended, and he calls her on the phone:

> "Hello, honey, Mark. At the bus station here in
> Hollywood. How'r'ya? Be right home. Got any
> chow?"
> Food? Yes, of course, lots of it. Soon the salad was
> on ice, the eggs ready to pour into the pan, the table

set, then a rushing to put away the newly ironed shirts, and socks and undies. They were really ironed well. A clean dress, hair swapped at, hands? Well the hands would have to do. Down the tumbling stairs, eggs in the pan, milk and jam on the table, steps on the walk—he is walking right—the door thrown open and Mark was back.

"Lookit my tan, honey, good, eh? Real stuff, no lotions—and whiskers—feel 'em? Tough guy, eh? Gotta shave right away." And he was pounding up the steep steps with his bag, was banging around up in the little room, was plunging down the steps into the bathroom with his hands full of shaving things. Then the familiar sounds of a male prettying up.

I put on the eggs to scramble with bits of bacon and tomato, put the salad on the table, and the new apricot jam the neighbor woman had given me. "Don't ask any questions, don't ask any questions. This will pass, the main objective is bigger than any of its incidents—marriage is an institution and is more important than any of those concerned in it— don't ask—let him talk."

Mark talked rapidly, contentedly. About the director's approval, and the grand wonderful thing it is to be an actor. At last, a professional actor along with established professionals, and finding that what he did was secure, and good and right, and that what he had been studying all worked. His lunch was gulped down, his story told—he must go.

Mark jumped up, and with one of his rare moments of tenderness stood behind my chair with his hands on my shoulders and said:

"Thanks for everything. I couldn't have done it without your help, or without what you have pounded into me. Thanks." And he tipped my head back and kissed me lightly. Then at the door, "Thanks for the laundry. I'll tell you about that." And he was gone.

Josephine knows it will be a long time before she sees Mark again. She faces life, in her fashion.

12

Even if the first Gable marriage had been what the world considered an ordinary one, it probably would have had slim chance for survival. Clark's single priority was his career, and his career put him on the road and out of reach, unpredictably, for long stretches of time. Other wives in other years would travel with him. Josephine could not because there was no money for such luxury. Other wives would at least have a chance to fend off carnivorous ladies who found Clark Gable appetizing. Josephine was too far away to fight, didn't have the weapons, and was more possessive of his talent than his body, anyway. For Clark, fidelity was never a critical issue. If there was a woman around the right place at the right time, and she was overtly interested, fine. In the early years, if he could profit by the relationship, all the better.

His fourth play for the MacLoons, *Madame X,* brought him his first really big-league affair. The star of the show was a fabled film and stage actress (and courtesan-class beauty) named Pauline Frederick who lived in a mansion on Sunset Boulevard. When Clark encountered Pauline in 1926, she was forty-four and still active on all fronts. She had had three husbands, a lover who hanged himself when she rejected him, and a great number of divorcées who blamed her for their wrecked homes. All of her talents drew vast audiences wherever she appeared.

Clark's part in her play was minor; his part in her backstage soap operetta, major. Like Jane Cowl, Pauline took an immediate fancy to the curiously attractive, gaunt young man Clark was at twenty-five. Also like Miss Cowl, she was in the best possible position to have Clark respond: top of the cast. Since 1960, writers have described Pauline as sexually insatiable, her romance with Clark exhausting for the reluctant lover. "That woman acts as though she's never going to see another man," Clark supposedly sighed into history.

But star she was, this remarkable lady. Opening night of *Madame X* in San Francisco, she received thirty-one curtain calls, and on the last, wept with joy and gratitude. When Pauline broke into tears, the audience joined her; it was an unusually damp night, even for San Francisco.

We can wonder what the sound of that applause did to Clark, standing behind the curtain with the rest of the cast. The cheering, the whistling, the echo of the raised, clapping hands—did it all make him willing to bleed to hear it for himself?

Pauline left Clark at the close of the play, and went on to conquer London. Clark returned to Los Angeles with a gold cigarette case inscribed from Pauline, and got a small part in a Lionel Barrymore *tour de force, The Copperhead,* also a MacLoon production. Clark admired Barrymore (for years he had been cutting his shirt collars to look like Barrymore's) and, as was his custom with people he admired, followed him around soulfully. Barrymore thought the young actor looked like Jack Dempsey, had some potential, and needed more experience. He also thought Clark should be working in films rather than the theater, but the two men were worlds apart on that. Clark had a new goal now that he'd worked behind real footlights: not just acting, not just "theater," but Broadway. Josephine was in on the goal. Though she and Clark were emotionally divorced, she had promised she would get him to Broadway, and to Josephine, a promise was as much a *fait accompli* as a goal was to Clark.

In fallow periods between plays, Clark hung around the golf course with actor friends, or around Ray Scovell's service station on Hollywood Boulevard with mechanic friends. When he had first gotten a car, he and Josephine used to drive to a mountain cabin of a friend for weekends. Those little pleasure jaunts were over. He was not yet drinking because liquor was, to him, a rich man's indulgence. Drinking still had to be done in speakeasies, or with friends who had enough money to get illegal alcohol. It would have been uncharacteristic of Clark to spend his hard-earned cash on something that evaporated so quickly.

The most significant play he did for the MacLoons in this time period (1926–1928) was *Chicago,* in which he played a reporter. Clark Gable would play a journalist in nine films in his career. The prototype for all of them was his characterization of "Jake" in *Chicago*. Gable's Jake wore his hat on the back of his head, and his coat collar up. He walked with shoulders and arms forward, a bit ape-like. When he stood still he had at least one arm akimbo, and an impudent, wiseacre grin on his face. All of these tricks isolated him on stage, and drew the audience's attention, particularly when they shouldn't have. They were successful bits of upstaging that he used regularly in his career, never having been given a good reason to discard them.

Chicago got him his first notices and widened the field open to him. When the show closed, its star, Nancy Carroll, signed a contract with Paramount Pictures. MGM scouts came sniffing around Clark, but he would have nothing to do with them. In mid-1927, movie attendance was at such an ebb studios were cutting salaries and running into their first labor crisis. The public was bored with silents. Radio was the new diversion, and you didn't have to leave home to enjoy it. If people were going to go out to be entertained they didn't want to read subtitles anymore; they had gotten used to the sound of voices making drama. Legitimate theater was booming all over the country, and actors with any kind of experience could count on having fairly steady work. Gable felt that, if nothing else, the momentum would carry him right where he wanted to go. He might have felt differently had he been aware of the tidal wave about to overtake the motion picture industry.

On October 6, 1927, the first major talking picture premiered at the Warner Theater in Manhattan. It was called *The Jazz Singer,* and it starred Al Jolson *singing* (not mouthing) two gut-tearing numbers: "My Mammy," and the lament *Kol Nidre.* It was a smash, not in the trade, but in the movie houses. Audiences loved it and begged for more.

On May 15, 1928, Paramount, United Artists, and MGM would sign contracts to have sound equipment installed in their studios.

On July 31, 1928, MGM would release its first sound picture, introduced by a roaring lion named Leo.

By December, 1929, the United States would be experiencing the most devastating financial disaster in its history. The film industry, unknowingly, would be equipped to fill a genuine, universal need for entertainment.

And Clark Gable would be ready, unknowingly, to fill a genuine need in the resurging film industry.

13

When *Chicago* completed its run, Clark had a number of options open to him. One, to join the Houston stock company of a man named Gene Lewis, did not interest him. Another, to make personal appearances with a film actress named Dorothy Davenport, did. However, he wound up in Houston, and the way that happened spelled the end of his marriage to Josephine. Josephine wrote in the early thirties: "I thought he needed some stock experience, and I must confess that I forced him to accept an offer to go to Houston, Texas, with a stock company instead of working in an act with Dorothy Davenport by lying to Miss Davenport over the phone saying he had signed with someone else. I don't think Clark ever forgave me that."

Worse yet, she turned out to be right again.

Clark became a huge success in Houston, a local celebrity who was stopped for autographs on the street, lionized in the best social circles, and recognized in shops and restaurants. The stock company put on a different play every week in the Palace Theater. For three months Clark was the second lead, earning $75 a week. Then the leading man left, and for the next twenty-five weeks Clark took over his roles and upped his salary to $200 a week. The first of them, "Matt Burke" in O'Neill's *Anna Christie*, he did so impressively he could do no wrong for Houston audiences ever after. He became the city's personal matinee idol, and had a steady following of teenaged girls who adored him so much they could do little besides giggle when he walked on stage. Grown women hung out in his dressing room or sent him mash notes. The kids stayed a respectful distance and sighed.

One of those kids was a porcelain-complexioned, red-headed fourteen-year-old named George Anna Lucas, who looked just like her socialite mother, Ria Franklin Prentiss Lucas Langham. Jana, as George Anna is called, was very close to her mother, but didn't tell her about going to see Clark every Saturday because she and her best friend had a crush on him and didn't want anyone to know. It is unfortunate that Jana, now a gracious Texas lady with beautiful children and grandchildren, didn't share her secret with her mother because she is the only person alive who would know whether Ria Langham, the second Mrs. Gable, fell in love with Clark in Houston and followed him to New York, or met him in New York. Says Jana, "If she met Clark in Houston I was completely unaware of it. It could have been that mother did meet him in those years, but I feel, had he been in my home I would have known it."

Josephine, who pursued her husband to Houston (thereby infuriating him), often implied that he and Ria were involved there. For instance, in a letter to Jim Tully in 1936, she wrote:

> I went down to Houston to see how Gable's acting was developing. I had made him a promise to get him through to New York—and although we were not particularly happy together by then, I made keeping my promises a religion. In Houston he had met people who are now in his life—I was asked to step out—and I went to New York to finish my promise, saying I would give him his divorce when he had accomplished what we had set out to do—make a good actor of him.

In New York, Josephine made the rounds of producers she knew, beating the drum for Clark. One of the producers was Arthur Hopkins, who had a property called *Machinal* he wanted to open in the fall. He had signed his leading lady, Zita Johann, an enchanting, much-respected actress, who chose to do his play rather than sign a five-year contract with Universal. "I was worried over the part," Miss Johann remembers. "It was a heavy part and I needed men to support me—big names. I told Arthur, and he said, 'Don't worry. I'll get you the proper

men.' Then he came and told me 'I've got you a Woolworth Romeo.' "

The Woolworth Romeo was Clark Gable, whom Miss
Johann, along with everyone else in New York theater,
had never heard of. It was the best of all possible Clark
Gables, the happiest, most self-assured, most optimistic
so far. He had gone to New York not only with the path
trimmed for him by Josephine, but also with the recom-
mendations of the MacLoons, and the blessings of theater-
goers in Houston. He looked good, he felt well. He told
the late Elza Schaller of the Los Angeles *Times* in 1932:

> All my life I had been waiting for the chance, just
> to plant my feet on the sidewalks that all actors have
> walked at some time. I entered New York with money
> in my pockets and some good clothes. I didn't feel
> like a beggar. My Houston engagement had given
> me a barrel of confidence. And a little money and
> wardrobe had done the rest.

Even the idea of facing The Critics challenged him:

> I had heard a lot, and read a lot about the New
> York critics and how they could make or break an
> actor. I sure wanted to meet them, from the other
> side of the footlights . . . scared to death, you under-
> stand, but anxious just the same. I wanted to see
> exactly what they would do to me.

Within two weeks of his arrival in New York he was
signed with a major agent, Chamberlain Brown, and in
rehearsal for *Machinal*. Josephine was also in New York,
standing by to assist her protégé. She would not see Clark
in his Broadway debut. As soon as he signed with Hopkins,
Josephine claimed, "Clark phoned me to keep out of his
life, said he was through with me. I said I was going to
California and that he had better become the best actor he
could as he could never be a man." Josephine went home.
Clark started four weeks of rehearsals.

Zita Johann was pleased with Clark. "He was very
good in the part," she says, "gave me complete support.
He didn't have ups and downs; he knew his lines and
didn't make mistakes." Unlike previous leading ladies,
she was not attracted to him at all. Her most vivid off-

stage memory of him is seeing him sitting in front of his dressing-room mirror painting his two gold teeth white before every performance. She says, "He did have impact, but no impact for me. We were on good terms. I liked him. Sometimes he walked me home, but to the door. I didn't even go out to supper with him. But he was genial. He was affable, lovable. Nice." With further thought Miss Johann adds, "Bemused is the word for him. Bemused."

One of the actors in the play, Hal K. Dawson, roomed with Clark during the tryouts in New Haven and remembers him as "a swell egg, a really swell guy." According to Dawson, Clark was never in the room they shared, he was out with women all the time. "He was a handsome brute. If he was in the room you knew it. He could take anyone on with that smile. Had a commanding voice. Nice personality. He was always immaculately dressed."

Machinal opened at the Plymouth Theater on September 7, 1928, much admired by the New York critics. Clark's first major notices were also good, but brief. The New York *Times* observed that Gable "didn't have a hackneyed gesture," and the *World-Telegraph* termed him "vigorous and brutally masculine." Zita Johann took up the rest of their reports, as *Machinal* was unquestionably her play. She had a run-of-the-play contract. Gable had been signed on a five-day basis, but he, too, stayed the run of the play, which was three months, and probably would have been longer, except that another play, *Holiday*, was scheduled into the theater.

There were so many shows available for production in the late twenties that few had long runs. And there were so many available because there was so much big money around to support them. Not only did nearly every man who made a killing in the stock market want to become an angel (even if you lost money you gained culture); producers also were putting their own money into their shows. In 1928, Florenz Ziegfeld had three musicals going simultaneously. All of The Greats were active: the Shuberts, George M. Cohan, Sam Harris, David Belasco. Gable planted his feet on Broadway at a beautiful time in its history. But it was a gigantic field for the little frog he still was, regardless of his charm, and when *Machinal* ended he was in for another rough time.

During the run of *Machinal,* however, Clark was introduced to a life-style to which, as the saying goes, he would

like to have become accustomed. That was Ria Langham's
self-made version of aristocratic, which was so smooth,
cool, and refined it was just as good—if not better—than
the real thing.

Ria was a strong woman with precise tastes and an in-
stinctive sense of propriety. One of her grandchildren
characterizes her like this: "My grandmother—we called
her 'Nannaw'—was the kind of woman . . . if she saw you
with chipped nail polish, she would shake her head and
say, 'Dear, either you wear nail polish or you don't.' "
Another Ria-ism was "You can't spoil the right kind of
people; they don't spoil." Ria, if she hadn't been so
family-oriented, would have made a perfect *Vogue* editor.

She was petite—five-foot-two—had auburn hair always stylishly groomed; soft, pale, flawless skin; and dark
eyes that spoke volumes. She was beautiful, but not photogenic. She dressed modishly, but understated, and had a
genuine flare for picking just the right hats in the days
hats were a woman's most dramatic accessory. She always
looked distinctly Eastern. Typically, one society columnist
reported, in the early thirties, that at a Hollywood premiere
Ria attended with Clark, "in a sea of silk, satin, and velvet, she was the only woman in a wool gown."

Ria was born in Kentucky on January 17, 1884. She
was raised in Macomb, Illinois, as Maria Franklin, and
married there at seventeen to William Prentiss. She lived
with him four years, and had one son. At the time the
marriage ended, her father, George, was living on a ranch
in Pecos, Texas, for his health; he had tuberculosis. Her
mother, Anna, was dead. Ria needed help caring for her
son, and went to Pecos, where she stayed with her father
and his new wife. After one year, she moved to Houston,
to the home of an aunt and uncle, who acted as baby-
sitters while she worked in a jewelry store. When she had
enough money, she went to night school to learn book-
keeping.

Four years after she moved to Houston, she chose to
marry, from many suitors, a wealthy widower, Alfred
Thomas Lucas, who was twenty-two years her senior.
(One of his two children was only five years younger
than she.) Mr. Lucas was, as Jana puts it, "a very successful contractor." He had two brick companies, the first
started when he couldn't find the kind of brick he liked.
Jana points out that many of the old buildings and streets

in Houston are made of "Daddy's brick," as is her own handsome, sturdy house.

Three years after Ria married Mr. Lucas, she gave birth to George Anna, and, six years after that, to a son, Alfred, Jr. They all led a life Jana terms "perfectly marvelous." She says with a soft Texas drawl, "Of course, Mother was foremost a mother, and a marvelous homemaker. She was an excellent cook, and a marvelous hostess. She sewed beautifully; she made everything I wore until I was twelve." Ria was that much-admired anachronistic being: an accomplished housewife.

Alfred Lucas died in 1922, leaving Ria what was considered by folks in Houston a sizable fortune. Three years later she married Denzil Langham, but must have had someone else in mind because Jana believes her mother married on the rebound. "Mr. Langham was a very fine person," she says, "but I think it was a mistake." Two years later, in 1927, Ria left Mr. Langham. A year later Jana graduated from school ("it had just nine grades in those years"). At the same time, Ria's son by Mr. Prentiss, who was going to school in Hartford, Connecticut, and working for Aetna Life Insurance, became very ill. Jana says, "Mother decided it was a very, very good idea to go East and take an apartment in New York City." She registered Jana with her best friend, Nellie Green, at Miss Mason's School for Girls in Westchester County, and got an apartment on Eighty-first Street and Park Avenue where "the swells" lived, and still live in Manhattan. Al, who was nine, was sent to Riverdale Country Day School; he lived at home.

And so Ria was ensconced and available in New York when Clark opened in *Machinal*. Jana describes the way she believes Ria and Clark met, and the way she learned they were courting:

"Nellie and I would come to New York once a month to see Mother. And one of the weekends when we came in, we were looking at the theater page to see where we wanted to go to the matinee, and she said to me, 'Look, Clark Gable is in New York.' We decided that was great, and we would go see Clark Gable in whatever [it was *Machinal*]. Now, my mother's half-brother, Booth Franklin, was an actor, and he said, 'I have met Mr. Gable, and I'll take you girls to the matinee, and if you want, I'll take you backstage and introduce you.' Well, we were beside ourselves. And this is what we did, and Mother was with us.

"When we came in about a month later, Mother looked at us and said, 'Guess who I've been seeing a lot of?' And Nellie sort of shrieked, 'CLARK GABLE!' (I'll never forget it.) And Mother said, 'That's right.' Nellie and I were extremely impressed and thought it was great, and we could tell that Mother was happy, too."

In fact, Ria Langham was very quickly very deeply in love with Clark. And in many a note to her he wrote, "I love you, my dear, and always will."

Josephine Dillon couldn't bear to think Clark had any feeling for Ria whatsoever. For her, Clark's relationship with Ria was a case history, something she referred to near the end of her manuscript as a Step-Up Marriage.

To Josephine, Ria was a buyer, and Clark sold out. Hollywood, too, preferred this explanation of the Ria and Clark merger. It was a tidy, simple way to explain why the sex symbol married yet another matron. Perhaps it was true.

PART THREE

HE-GUY

(1928-1935)

14

He strolled up Fifth Avenue, those crisp early autumn days when New York is its most seductive, Ria's leather-gloved hand delicately holding his arm, the fur collar of her wool-crepe suit brushing his sleeve. After lunch at the right French restaurant, where Ria taught him to order the right food with the right accent—food he would never really develop a taste for—they would take a walk and he would sneak a look or two at their reflection in the shop windows. He would try not to smile too openly, try to look as though he'd been doing this all his life—and try to record the image he caught of himself in case he'd ever need it for a part.

They'd stop in some of the shops, and Ria would choose for Clark the stylish clothes she thought he should wear. It was his choice, though, to add a derby and a gold-headed cane as finishing touches. It was the only time in his life he chose to look like a dandy, and he took the costume all the way. With just a slight change in the cut of his pinstriped suits, he would have been ready for a walk-on as Diamond Jim.

Lounging on the brocades in Ria's apartment, he wore a smoking jacket—very appropriate. He also found that a perfect accessory for his jacket and his cigarette was gin, chilled and poured over ice, with a twist of lemon. For a day off in the country—Ria had good friends with estates in Connecticut—he had leisure clothes; for conversations with the bankers and stockbrokers Ria knew, he had a little money he wanted to invest. And for the occasional suspicion he had that people might think him a gigolo, he had the assurance that he and Ria would marry as soon as he could get a divorce. He didn't know when he could go to the Coast to talk to Josephine, but when the time was clear and right, he would take care of it.

Clark fell into step with Ria's life so easily because he

still had no strong tastes of his own. Whatever security he might have felt in his career destructed when *Machinal* ended, because he couldn't get another job. That fact sent him reeling. Publicly, he maintained his high-spirited, affable personality. With Ria, he indulged in depression. He would never amount to anything, he would never be anyone. His father's contempt echoed in his head, and added to it were Josephine's well-aimed words: "You'd better be an actor, because you'll never be a man." With Ria on his arm, he could feel like a man—feel the sensuality of her pride in him, and her trust. But alone, in his agent's office, waiting and waiting and waiting for work, he didn't know what he was, and suspected the worst.

He told Ria he thought he should forget the theater, once and for all, and open a haberdashery shop. In extreme moments he said the shop should be in Ohio. Whether he ever really meant to follow through his threat to send himself to that Siberia is doubtful. But he needed to say it all, needed to hear Ria repeat that all would be well, that he was a fine actor, that everyone had setbacks, and that the theater needed him, which it didn't. Broadway had, among its promising newcomers, James Cagney, Cary Grant, George Brent, Humphrey Bogart, and Spencer Tracy, to name only a few. Clark's old buddy, Earle Larimore, was the toast of the intellectuals, starring, as he was then, in Eugene O'Neill's Pulitzer-prize-winning *Strange Interlude*. There was plenty of theater to study, and he and Ria were regular playgoers, but he couldn't get work. The year 1928 ended as a mud-slide for him— all the more upsetting because it had held such promise.

Ria didn't care. She had had in her life a man who took care of her paternally, who needed nothing from her, who had met his challenges before she was born. At this stage in her life she needed to give, and she adored this moody, beautiful young man with whom, as she envisoned it, life could never be dull because it could never be easy. She knew that one day the difference in their ages would be a problem. Friends told her Clark was nothing but a fortune hunter. She didn't care. She wanted to marry him.

Clark could not get rid of the wife he already had. Josephine did not believe in divorce, and she wouldn't make a move. So Clark went to a Park Avenue lawyer, who promised he could get him a Mexican divorce for the astronomical fee of $100.

In February, Clark headed west in a drawing room on the Twentieth Century Limited. When he arrived in Los Angeles, he went almost directly to Josephine. She later wrote: "He had one of those Mexican divorce papers that he wanted me to sign before a notary. I refused to enter into any such affair, knowing that the next woman he married would find herself in a legal mess if she trusted herself to Mexican marriages and divorces." Josephine did her own investigating, getting advice from a judge who had known her father. On March 30, 1929, she filed for divorce on the grounds of desertion ("I could have added all the other things but I was protecting Clark"). Typically, she asked for nothing: no settlement, no alimony. It would take a year for the divorce to be finalized.

Clark returned to Ria and two months of making the rounds. Then his agent came up with a part for him that, in retrospect, should have been the making of him. It was the lead in George M. Cohan's *Gambling,* a subject about which Clark knew more than he cared to. The part was good guy playing bad guy to solve a murder—certainly, a shoo-in for Clark Gable, movie star. But for Clark Gable, aspiring Broadway actor, something went terribly wrong. He opened in the play in Philadelphia. A few weeks later, in Atlantic City, he was fired by Cohan, who decided to rewrite the play and cast himself in the lead.

Ria had gone to Philadelphia for the opening, and the evidence of this is frustratingly mysterious. In a note to Ria on Warwick Hotel stationery, Clark said he would leave her ticket at the box office "in the name of Mrs. Clark Gable." The envelope was addressed "Mrs. Clark Gable." Yet it seems unlikely they were married at the time. There has always been a cloud of dust over the exact date of the Langham-Gable marriage; even Jana is vague about when the event may have taken place. "I think they were married by a judge or something, in the East," she says, noting that it was not a ceremony she would have attended. We can speculate that Clark did get the Mexican divorce, considered it sufficient, and married Ria in 1929; or, as has been reported elsewhere, that he waited a year, and married Ria in 1930.

In any case, Ria was on hand to console him about failing in *Gambling,* on hand to listen with him to the news of the stock market crash that took with it his modest investments, and there to say, "See, I told you everything would be all right," when he was cast in a play called *Hawk Island*. Clark had no illusions about that one; during its terminal four weeks, he made the rounds even on matinee days. One former producer remembers him coming by the Cort Theater on Saturday, before matinee, "wearing most of his make-up and white paint on his teeth." That producer, Charles Abramson, had never heard of Gable at that time, and was not impressed with his background because, he thought, stock actors got bad habits they could never break. He did not consider Clark for a part in *Veneer*, which he produced, thus joining the ranks of producers who told him don't call us, we'll call you—and never did.

From *Hawk Island*, Clark went into a Belasco play that closed out of town. Then he settled for a minor part (wearing a villain's mustache) in an Alice Brady vehicle called *Love, Honor, and Betray*, produced by A. H. Woods, which opened on March 12, 1930, at the Eltinge Theater, and ran for less than eight weeks.

During the run of the Brady play, Clark heard from his old friends the MacLoons. Lillian Albertson, still Mrs. MacLoon, had remained a firm believer in Clark's potential and had kept him in mind when considering New York properties to take to the Coast. The property she decided Clark was suited for was a Broadway success callled *The Last Mile*, a disturbing account of prisoners on Death Row who make an eleventh-hour attempt to break out. The part available for Clark was Killer Mears, hostile leader of the attempt, being played on Broadway by Spencer Tracy.

Clark and Ria went to see *The Last Mile*, and Clark came away completely undone by Tracy's performance. He didn't want to go near the play. Killer was a different role from anything he'd done—stronger, meaner—and even if he hadn't been intimidated by Tracy's interpretation, he didn't feel up to it. Ria urged him to try. The MacLoons urged him to try. And, cutting a stencil for behavior he would repeat often in his career, he reluctantly signed to play a role that would turn out to be a milestone for him.

Ria couldn't leave with Clark for the Coast because her children were still in school (Jana had gone from Miss Mason's to Monroe Junior College, which many of her Houston friends attended). Though by now they were surely married—Josephine's divorce was final on March 30, 1930—Ria and Clark would have to be separated for a while. The understanding was that Clark would return to New York, and he urged his agents to line up something for him for the fall season. He left New York with just four weeks to prepare for the prophetically titled *Last Mile*.

15

His world became a locomotive that had puffed and struggled up one side of a mountain, then careened full-speed down the other. *The Last Mile* opened and closed in San Francisco with as much notice as a breeze blowing in from the Bay. Then, on June 7, 1930, it opened at the Belasco Theater in Los Angeles, and Clark Gable became the epicenter of the city which, a year and a half before, seemed to make a business of ignoring him. Everyone wanted to see the show the critics termed stark and stunning (everyone in Hollywood did see it, if the survivors of that era are to be believed), and everyone went away talking about the stark, stunning actor who, as Killer Mears, was equal parts man and animal. His stage cell seemed to be a cage, with his huge hands around the bars. The glaring top light on him cast shadows under every bone in his skull and trapped his eyes deep in his head. He looked, more than one observer noted, primeval; and his voice fairly snarled with the aggression he felt toward this audience, which had once too often rejected him.

Not that the events that followed were the classic overnight success story; Clark Gable as Killer Mears was still not Marlon Brando as Stanley Kowalski. But for Clark, compared to what he had known, and with no way to compare with what he would know, all the signs pointed to his arrival. A large sign was that he acquired an agent who was clearly devoted to him: Minna Wallis, unmar-

ried sister of Hal Wallis, and partner of more noted agent
Ruth Collier. Minna was still fairly new to flesh peddling;
Myron Selznick and Leland Hayward, top agents, had
financed her first year in business to the tune of $10,000.
But Minna knew everyone who mattered in the film business, and was a hustler. She was just what Clark needed,
and from the start, knew just how to handle him.

His New York agent was also hustling for him, and lined
up several important shows for him to consider when he
could get back to New York. There was no question in
Clark's mind that he would do one of them. He simply
didn't care that Hollywood was frantically searching for
talent to fit into talking pictures, or that MGM, having
finished its last silent film eight months earlier (*The Kiss*,
with Garbo), was scrambling to complete its soundproof
stages, or that economically shocked people all over the
world were so hungry for diversion they would have gone
to see the telephone book had it been made into a movie.

Then Clark was offered a part in a Bill Boyd western
for $750 a week and filed his longing to return to Broad-
way. Minna Wallis had taken him to Pathé, where
Painted Desert was in the works. Clark was examined,
found suitable, and asked if he could ride a horse. He
stared, dumbfounded. Minna stepped forward and said,
as only an agent would, "Of course he can," and the deal
was made—one picture, option on long-term contract.
Later, outside the office, Clark, who had not spoken in
some time, grabbed Minna's arm in panic. "Minna," he
said, "you've got to be out of your mind. I've never been
near a horse, let alone on one." Minna said, "Well, we're
going to start right now," drove them to Griffith Park,
got Clark an instructor, and for two weeks he rode every
day, until he sat a horse like a wrangler.

It's hard to comprehend in these days of flying, leaping,
loping, hairy actors, but that story of how Clark learned
to ride a horse made him a hero all over town. It was
and is repeated so often by Gable devotees it could easily
qualify as a chapter of *Beowulf*. What's so great about
learning to ride a horse (western, yet) in two weeks? one
might logically ask. If there is any answer, it is knowing
how much stunt men and stand-ins were doing for actors
in silents, and what contempt was felt for those actors
by the people who worked with them. By and large,
male stars of the silents, with the exception, perhaps, of

Douglas Fairbanks, were considered effete, or temperamental, or absurd, or helpless, or all four. They were treated like mental patients, or, more specifically—since they were royalty—like the retarded Dauphin of France. Indeed, look at the ledger: Lou Tellegen, one of the first movie matinee idols, rarely spoke a word of truth in his lifetime and stabbed himself to death with rusty scissors when his career declined. Francis X. Bushman, an exhibitionist and wife-beater, was black-balled by Louis B. Mayer for upstaging Ramon Novarro in *Ben Hur,* lost his great fortune in the Crash, and publicly offered to marry any woman who would support him (no one volunteered). Rudolph Valentino died of a ruptured ulcer, trying to prove he wasn't the "powder puff" he had been called by the press. Ramon Novarro, a recluse, left films to practice yoga (he was beaten to death with his own cane in 1968). Wallace Reid, as mentioned earlier, was a drug addict. John Gilbert and John Barrymore were alcoholics who flaunted their degeneracies publicly before they died of them. And William Haines quit movies when he was told by Mayer to give up his boyfriend or else. Though Haines wasn't the first (and hardly the last) film he-man who was an overt homosexual, he seems to have been the first whose proclivities made the papers.

Small wonder, then, that when cool journalist, sophisticated lady Adela Rogers St. Johns met Clark Gable, after *Painted Desert* was released, she lost her objectivity.* Small wonder she would take the time to probe Clark's first riding instructor (apparently one-eyed) for the details of their experience together. She wrote what she learned like this:

> Out at the Griffith Park Riding Academy, where the picture stars and social world learn to walk, trot, and canter, is an ex-cowboy from Montana named Art Wilson. He had the cold, mosaic-blue eye of the born daredevil. I have seen that eye in great racing

---

* Mrs. St. Johns became one of Clark's most trusted friends. She wrote about him extensively, for which Gable biographers must be eternally grateful, and still speaks of him with awe and affection. One of Hollywood's favorite rumors is that she had a child by him in the thirties. When asked about this on a Merv Griffin television show in March, 1975, she answered, enigmatically, "What woman would deny Clark Gable was the father of her child?"

drivers, in stunt men, in a famous bank robber I once knew well.

Art taught Clark Gable to ride.

Rather wistfully, his cold eye fixed upon the distant hills, Art said, "If I could get that guy away from pictures, I'd make a top hand out of him."

Allow me to tell you that the admiration of a man like Art Wilson is something of which to be very proud. Money won't buy it, fame won't command it. Art's comments upon some other movie idols whom he has instructed are biting and slightly profane. In most cases, Art feels that the horse is the better man.

Of Gable he speaks with reverence.

"First day he come out here," said Art, "I took a look at him, and I says to myself, 'Art, he's a big devil and he ought to make a rider, but, hell—he's an actor. Chances are he'll be thinking about his face.' Anyhow, he says to me, 'I got to learn to ride so's I can play a part in a picture, and I ain't ever been nearer a horse than when I was plowin'.' So I says, 'How much time can you give me every day?' He grins and says, 'Art, I ain't got a thing in the world to do. Write your own ticket.'

"Well, about then I'm beginning to weaken, what with his admittin' about plowin' and that grin; and then, I'm a little runt myself and he was sure built for horses, same as Gary Cooper. But I says to myself, 'Art, don't get excited. Lots of folks are O.K. when they got both feet on the ground, but they turn yellow when they see how far down it is from the back of a horse.'

"Well, anyhow, I took a good safe cow pony I had, that I knowed had more sense than most men. Gable gets on top of him. An' I took 'em up on top of a hill in Griffith Park. I knowed that hill and I knowed that pony. But Gable didn't. So I says, 'Now come on down after me.' I wanted to find out, right off, if he had guts. I started down lickity-cut and I yells at Gable, 'Come on brother!' And he come! Right down that hill just as fast as that pony could carry him. Never been on a horse before that day. Say, when he got to the bottom he was laughing like a kid. 'I'm still on top,' he says.

"Le'me tell you something. I know, and a horse

knows, when a man's afraid. Maybe he don't show
it. Maybe he acts O.K. But there's little things you
can tell. That Gable don't no more know the meaning
of fear than a mountain lion. I give him the works,
too. At the end of two weeks he could pick up a
handkerchief going full tilt. He could get on and off
a big horse running. There's western stars around
can't do that yet. He's got a body that's just about
perfect—balance, strength, everything."*

In the weeks before *Painted Desert* got under way,
Clark ate dinner with his agent at the apartment she shared
with her mother "pridnearly every night," as Miss Wallis
puts it. Then he left for Arizona, where the film was to
be made. (Though Hollywood has always had the greatest facilities in the world for making films, directors have
always been a little embarrassed about using them, and
producers have taken pride primarily in films made away
from them.) Within a few days after he started work,
Clark sent Art Wilson a telegram reading, "The first thing
I had to do was ride down a hill fast. Got away with it
O.K. Thanks, kid."

All was well.

Having made it down the hill, there was nowhere to go
except up.

16

By the time *Painted Desert* was finished, Ria Gable and
her two youngest children had settled quietly and modestly
in Hollywood, in two flats in the Ravenswood Apartments.
Clark and Ria lived in one, the children in another. The
reason Ria gave for this arrangement was that neither
apartment was big enough for the whole family; space
was hard to find in the crowded, crowding movie colony.
Chances are, however, Ria wanted some time alone with

* *Liberty*, March 12, 1932.

her new husband, and wanted time to ease him into being the father of a seventeen-year-old daughter and an eleven-year-old son. In any case, she certainly didn't enter Hollywood waving a Texas heiress banner.

Jana never thought of Clark as a father, or even a stepfather. She called him Clark; he called her Sister. He was her mother's husband, an attractive man of whom she was extremely fond. Jana was a sensible, sensitive youngster (friends always said she should have been the mother, Ria the daughter) and kept her distance from the lovers. She attended business school at UCLA, visited friends in Houston, led her own life. When she was home, she relaxed and enjoyed her new stepfather. She says, "Clark could charm everyone, regardless of age or station in life. And for a person who had not had any more education than he had, he was very smart. He could listen to your conversation and the next day repeat exactly what you had said. He was a very handsome man, but even more handsome, say, five years later."

Al adored Clark, and did think of him as a father. He and Clark had a special relationship, one that would hurt when it ended. Clark took Al to ballgames and the races and picnics at the beach. He teased him and loved him and guided him—when he had time. But there was so much Clark had to do.

Minna wanted to keep him working even more than he wanted to work. He had not come back from Arizona in high spirits, to say the least. No one had paid much attention to him on the set and he had found himself, as he often did, a stranger in a strange land. There had been a terrible accident in which one extra got killed and many were injured—something had gone wrong in the timing of a scene in which Clark was the principal, and a whole group of men had ridden into a dynamite charge. When the film ended, Pathé decided not to pick up his option. And finally, the picture opened with the scenery getting the only good reviews.

In the same time span, director Mervyn LeRoy wanted Clark for a part in *Little Caesar*, which was to be made at Warner Brothers, home of crime movies and actors getting famous playing gangsters. America was enjoying its Prohibition mob wars so much that becoming a movie mobster was almost as secure as becoming that other folk hero, a cowboy star. But Clark didn't get the part because Jack Warner thought his ears were too big. Or because Darryl Zanuck thought his ears were too big. Or because both of them thought that his ears made him look like a big ape. No one had noticed Clark's ears in *Painted Desert* because he wore his hair long. No one, in fact, noticed Gable's ears until he became famous, and then all sorts of people remembered remarking about Gable's ears. Some people even remembered that Gable remarked about Gable's ears. In the late forties, Gene Tierney danced with Clark at the Macombo one night and teasingly said to him, "You and I are freaks; people like me for my teeth, and you for your ears." Clark didn't like it at all. He had heard enough about his ears to last him two lifetimes. Some collector's items:

Irving Thalberg, allegedly rejecting Gable: "Look at his big, batlike ears."

Milton Berle at an Academy Awards dinner: "Clark should get an award for The Best Ears of Our Lives."

Agent Myron Selznick describing Gable to a friend: "He had ears like two spoons."

Ben Piazza, MGM casting director in the early thirties: "With those ears he looks like a giant sugar bowl."

Actor Paul Fix, who worked in MacLoon plays with Gable: "His ears stuck out and he got them fixed. Christ almighty, they stuck out like barn doors and he was sensitive about them. They did it after he was established at Metro."

Minna Wallis: "He never had anything done to his ears, never. I remember one night Jack Warner had a print of *Dancing Daughters,* and after it was over he said, 'My God, who's that guy?' I said, 'That's the guy with the big ears that you wouldn't see.' He said, 'I don't believe it. He had his ears fixed?' I said, 'No. He didn't.' "

Photographer Clarence Bull: "The only thing Clark was ever anxious about were his ears. During one sitting after the studio had made a big thing about his ears, he asked, 'What am I going to do with these flops?' I told him to forget them. 'In their prominence, they're a bit like Valentino's nostrils. If nostrils can become sex symbols, so can ears.' "

MGM publicist Larry Barbier to Jean Garceau re director Clarance Brown: "When Brown saw him, he said, 'We've got to do something with those ears.' He told the

make-up man to tape Clark's ears close to his head. Clark
shot a few minutes this way and then tore the tape off. He
said, 'I'm not going to use this stuff. Either you take me
as I am or I will go back to New York.' That ended the
business about his ears."

Douglas Fairbanks Jr. got the Gable-type part in *Little
Caesar*. Gable got a part in a B-minus Warner Brothers
film called *Night Nurse* with starlets Barbara Stanwyck
and Joan Blondell. In this opus, Clark was a really rotten
egg, a mean family chauffeur. So mean he slapped poor
Barbara in the kisser—something he would do again twenty
years later in their other film together, *To Please a Lady*.
The slap in *Lady* is erotic; the slap in *Night Nurse,* brutal,
but coming from Clark, costumed in black, and made up
so pasty-faced only his eyebrows seemed alive, it could
just as well have been a fang-bite on the neck. In 1930,
film make-up had advanced only microscopically over the
greasepaint of the silents. Women were made up like
clowns. A heavy stick base was rubbed over every inch
of the face, then covered with a heavy coat of powder.
When that was over, there were no eyebrows, eyelashes,
or lips; each had to be painted back on. The deep red
lipstick which was used blackened on film, but anything
lighter showed up white. Eyelashes were mascaraed and
beaded. Men wore less make-up, but the net effect was
to make both sexes look embalmed. Clark hated the make-
up, and just as soon as lighting improved technically wore
very little of it. From 1936 on, he had his own make-up
men, first Stan Campbell and then Don Roberson, whose
primary function was to pluck a few of his eyebrows.
    Another handicap in the early talkies was that micro-
phones were not mobile. They were strategically placed
in a vase of flowers, or some such, around which the actors
had to cluster if they were to be heard. In Gable's case,
this was potentially disastrous because he wasn't free to
move his ears out of camera range. In films where he had
to wear his hair fashionably clipped, he did, indeed, look
like a sugar bowl. Fortunately, he had the vanity of a
person who never thought of himself as attractive, which
is to say, none at all. But he was sensitive to the constant
criticism he heard, and the way it was delivered: as though
he weren't there. He was used to the personal involvement stage directors have with their actors, not the in-

structions film directors dispatched by way of underlings around them. In time, he would favor the directors who worked with him one-to-one and showed some sensitivity. In time, some of his best friends would be directors. In 1930, however, he had no friends. He had Ria and he had Minna, and he was dependent on them both. Both did everything possible to see that he was exposed to the people who could help him in his career.

It was through Minna's machinations, both socially and commercially, that Clark met Irving Thalberg, and it was Irving Thalberg, with the encouragement of Eddie Mannix, Benny Thau, and Mayer's secretary, Ida Koverman, who signed him to his first MGM contract.* Pandro Berman at RKO had been negotiating to sign Gable at the same time, and stopped speaking to Minna Wallis for a year when his long-term contract was refused. Clark's choices being the theater, RKO, or MGM, his decision should have been an easier one than it was. Clearly MGM was the place to be, the prestige house, with little competition for a man with Clark's distinctions. Though the studio aspired to MORE STARS THAN THERE ARE IN HEAVEN, a slogan coined by advertising and publicity director Howard Dietz, its most glittering personalities in the transition from silents to talkies were female: Garbo, Joan Crawford, and Norma Shearer. Its highest paid male stars were Wallace Beery, obviously not a romantic figure, and John Gilbert, whose falsetto voice and belligerence to Mayer were turning him into the most dramatic casualty of talking pictures.

The fourteen-page, double-spaced contract Thalberg offered was for one year, at $650 a week. That meant that should Gable prove to be a bad investment, the studio could end its losses at $33,800, which, if they kept him working all year, could in no way be a total loss. In short, the contract was not exactly a magnificent, fearless gesture on the part of MGM.†

---

* Louis B. Mayer would wallow in Gable's stardom in later years, but had nothing to do with the start of his career. Mayer, who was earning about a million dollars a year, was away from the studio more often than in it in 1930 and 1931. Thalberg had Gable lined up for a battery of films before Mayer really knew who he was.

† The most interesting thing about the contract was the standard morals clause, which read: "The artist agrees to conduct himself with due regard to public conventions and morals and agrees that he will not do

For Clark, a guarantee of $33,800 for a year's work was manna. He signed the contract on December 4, 1930, and was cast in an adaptation of a Broadway melodrama entitled *The Easiest Way*. Constance Bennett, willowy blonde of silents fame, had the lead role of a slum child who grows up to be what the Depression era considered worse than cancer-ridden: a kept woman. In time her keeper, Adolphe Menjou, rejects her, as does the love of her life, land baron Robert Montgomery. She does what any tainted woman would do: becomes a prostitute. At one point she might have been saved by her sister, Anita Page, but our hero, Clark, the sister's earnest, trustworthy, laundry-man husband, refuses to let her darken their door.

The Easiest Way was the one film in his career in which Clark Gable looked young, and he was totally enchanting. Irresistible. Even adorable, in the best sense of the word. The dimpled, boyish charm of him is irrepressible in this plastic role, and must have been seen and nurtured by director Jack Conway, who could have thrown the movie to Montgomery, but didn't. Though Clark was too self-absorbed to realize it at the time, Conway was his kind of man—hard-drinking, lady-killing, fun-loving, and fair. They would make a total of six films together. Montgomery, archetype of the social register school of actors cutting a swath in the talkies, was essentially Gable's only rival at MGM. He had come in earlier, was three years younger, and was a full step ahead in rank: he had a five-year contract. It was a stroke of good luck for Clark that he had Conway as a director when he needed him most. It was also a stroke of luck that he was cast as the Common Man, in contrast to Montgomery's Privileged Man, at a time when moviegoers were commoner than they were privileged. Gable, in his first MGM film, was a glorified laborer with sex appeal. Audiences loved him instantly. In the days talking pictures were aborning, studios solicited audience reaction at sneak previews, and responded to it, posthaste. Studio heads also responded to vibrations around the office, and at MGM, the new guy, whats-is-name in *The Easiest Way*, was

---

or commit any act or thing that will tend to degrade him in society, or bring him into public hatred, contempt, scorn, or ridicule, or that will tend to shock, insult, or offend the community or ridicule public morals or decency or prejudice the producer or the motion picture industry in general."

causing an unusual amount of blushing, giggling, and whispering among secretaries and file clerks.

Without Clark's knowing it, MGM brass set the machinery in motion for his exposure and exploitation. The studio's incredible master plan for 1931 included the production of fifty-two films and Clark would appear in nine of them. There would, in fact, be twelve Gable films released in 1931—including one made on loan-out, *The Painted Desert*, and *Night Nurse*—and by January, 1932, he would be the hottest mass aglow in that much-abused firmament. This fact of life, and all its ramifications, would come as more of a shock to him than D'Artagnan's learning his king had a twin brother. Despite the awesome energy he had put, for so many years, into becoming a successful actor, Gable never believed he would be one, and then never believed he would stay on. Security—and peace—would elude him through the best years of his life.

17

When he was thirty, he was molded clay, ready for a glaze and the kiln. Whatever MGM wanted of Clark Gable, that would he be. It was partly this, his pliability, that secured for him the best friend he would ever have, MGM publicity man Howard Strickling. "If it weren't for Howard," Gable said often, "I'd probably be driving a truck." There was more to it than that. If it weren't for Howard, Clark probably would not have survived his own success. Certainly the relationship was mutually beneficial; Howard made life smooth for Clark, and Clark's dependence on him made Howard indispensable to MGM. Over the years, however, that ceased to be the point. Their mutual friend, Z. Wayne Griffin, declares what is known by everyone connected with Gable: "If ever a man had a close alliance, had a real love of another man—an admiration for him—Clark had that for Howard." Griffin

points out another indisputable fact: "Howard is a significant man himself. A real well-knit personality you can't
poke holes in. In his own very individual way, he was
trusted by everyone."

That is a rare tribute, indeed, in a business where the
word "trust" is understood only if it is followed by "fund."
What makes it rarer still is that Howard, who still declares
himself a company man, though he was retired in 1969,*
could be loyal, simultaneously, to Mayer and to everyone
who worked for him. Being a company man never made
him a rat fink. He was a vindictive, hypercritical boss
whose department vibrated with fear, but he was also the
company priest who knew all and told nothing. Clark's
occasional message to Mayer via Strickling, to shove something or other up his ass, would be transmitted by
Howard as "Clark thinks it's a great idea, but he wants
some time to mull it over." Mayer's occasional message to
Gable via Strickling that he made him and he could
break him, and tell that big ape to get on the set or else,
would come out equally softened and diplomatized. To
Howard, even now, Mayer could never be wrong, only
misunderstood.

Actors, on the other hand, tended to be naughty, but
certain of them were irreplaceable, and vital to the success
of the company, than which, to him, nothing mattered
more. Howard decided, from the start, that his job was
"to keep things together, not tear them apart." It was not
his job, he says, "to throw gas on the fire." Repeatedly,
he says, "I was a company man. Somebody has to be for
the company, you know." It was like this, he explains:

"The success of Mayer and Thalberg was that Mr.
Mayer said, 'Talent is like a precious stone. Like a diamond or a ruby. You take care of it. You put it in a safe,
you clean it, polish it, look after it. Who knows the value
of a star?'

"What Queen Elizabeth is to the British government,
Gable and Taylor and Shearer were to MGM—like the
Signal oil field, you know. But it was the only organiza-
tion in the world where all the assets walked out the gate

---

* Strickling is today a gentleman farmer, living with his wife on a
120-acre farm in Southern California. Once he retired, he never returned
to the studio and never will. He says, "My fifty years in the entertainment business were wonderful but as Irving Berlin said, 'You can't
live there.'"

every night. In other businesses it's different, like if an editor gets drunk too often you hire another one. Well, if you've got John Barrymore in a picture you can't say throw the bum out. Okay, you've got Gable and Taylor and Garbo, but there's only one of each so you work things out. You give and take. You try to influence the bosses to use reason, and try to get the stars to be reasonable, also.

"You see, when I started out I discovered that everybody needs help and particularly actors and other people in our business. I was a company man. I found if I could help Gable or Taylor or Harlow, I became important to them. And in that way I could get them to do things. But, well, my relationship with Clark, and Bob Taylor—maybe Jean Harlow and Norma Shearer—was different, because I was closer to them than to some of the others."

Howard never wanted to admit, even to himself, that he did, indeed, favor these four of his many wards. All the stars there were in heaven weren't the same to him, though his loyalty to them was. Howard loved Clark Gable, not much more than Taylor, perhaps, but longer, and misses him very much. He still believes that had he been tending him—"helping" him—in his last years, he never would have died when he did. Howard feels he could have saved Clark had he been allowed to, such was the intensity of his devotion, and the degree of his certainty that he knew what was best for him.

They first met, very casually, at Minna Wallis's apartment, in November, 1930. For Gable, the meeting was just short of meaningless, another occasion when he was trotted out and examined—the latest addition to the stable. He thought the tall, sparkling guy with the distracting stutter seemed nice enough, but so what? Minna said he was important to know; Clark accepted that, though Strickling—called Strick by equals—was third man down in the fifteen-man MGM publicity department. Howard Dietz, based mostly in New York, was executive head of the department, Pete Smith was director, and Strickling was Smith's assistant. He was about Clark's age, though certainly more seasoned. He had been a publicist since 1919 when Adela Rogers St. Johns started him in his career, in the inbred way things happened in a fiefdom like Hollywood. She had spotted Howard when he was a struggling office boy on a Los Angeles paper and recommended him to director Rex Ingram, who was looking for a press agent. ("I couldn't ask a grown man to take such a job," Mrs. St. Johns explained.) The first actor Strickling worked with was Valentino, an Ingram discovery, so he really hadn't needed Mayer to tell him stars were different from other people. By the time he met Gable, Strickling had developed such a paternal tolerance for MGM's mobile assets that Gilbert's hysteria, Barrymore's vulgarities, and Garbo's xenophobia didn't strike him as being the least bit strange. When Pete Smith was moved into the production of his now classic short subjects, Howard moved into his job without a ripple.

Meeting Gable was so special for Strickling he remembers it still. He recalls Miss Wallis saying, "I want you to meet a young actor I just signed." He recalls "a guy in a turtle-neck sweater" walking into the room. "He was the biggest man I ever saw. His hands were tremendous. His feet were tremendous. He had a tremendous big head. His ears were tremendous. He was the biggest guy I ever knew, and I would say one of the most powerful. One of his great fears, I learned as I got to know him, was that he would hurt somebody. Physically. He never did. He always knew he had this tremendous strength, but he never used it.

"I thought, gee whiz, what a tremendous guy. What a hell of a man. There was nothing effeminate about him. Nothing actorish. He came in, you know, sat down in a chair, and right away you could see he knew how to handle people. When Gable gave an interview, he would know more about you than you would know about him. If you walked in and started talking to him, before you knew it you were talking about yourself and liking it. From the very first time he talked to me he was interested in me."

It's called turning on the charm, and it was something Clark found as easy to do as sliding under a stalled car. Unlike the ability to fix a motor, however, the ability to charm gave him no sense of accomplishment. Like many charmers, he distrusted this mysterious power to woo and win on command, and distrusted those who were won by it. They had to be tested further, and so did he. Okay, he was charming, what else was Clark Gable? Strickling passed his test much easier than he did himself.

After *The Easiest Way* was screened, he was a name on interoffice memos, none of which he saw. Messages went up the company tree from the casting office to Billy Grady, who was in charge of talent, to Benny Thau, who was the stop-gap between all creative departments and the top, then back to Thau to Grady, and out through the branches. The word was out that the new guy who'd been signed up, Clark Gable, was about to be processed in the Mayer method. He would be made into a product, like a Baby Ruth. He would become *a* Clark Gable, and then, when the studio (or another studio) needed a certain flavor for a picture, somebody could say, "This calls for a Clark Gable," and be understood. Under the Mayer method, new products evolved out of their relationships to old products. It was what has become known as the Star System, and as simplified by Howard Strickling, it worked like this:

"You've got this great creative talent signed up: Norma Shearer, John Gilbert, Greta Garbo, Joan Crawford. Well, along comes a Bob Montgomery. You put him with a Norma Shearer, then with Greta Garbo, and you've got a star. Along comes a Clark Gable. You put him first with a Joan Crawford, then with a Norma Shearer, then Greta Garbo. Along comes a Bob Taylor. You put him with a Garbo and then with Irene Dunne, and you've got a star. Along comes Myrna Loy, and you put her with a Tracy or a Gable, and *she's* a star. A Rosalind Russell . . . the same. Then you have a thing like the Hardy Family, you know, and you bring in an Esther Williams and give her a little part, and you bring in a June Allyson.

"This is how Mayer built his dream. More stars than there are in heaven."

And while the Clark Gables and the Myrna Loys were being established through their screen roles, the publicity department busied itself with their packaging and display racks. A product with some sense of its value, a Garbo, for instance, might balk at being packaged, and require special handling. An insecure product, a Gable, specifically, did whatever it was told. And furthermore, a person with as vague a self-image as Clark Gable could find some of the elements of a Clark Gable extremely comforting. Surprising, but comforting.

What Clark did, and probably without any conscious

knowledge, was fit right into Howard Strickling's first indelible impression of him. "Gable you visualized as a real he-guy." And when the biography collected by one of his staff was shown him, he was overjoyed. Hardly a thing had to be changed: there existed, in truth, Clark the lumberman, Clark the oiler, Clark the telephone linesman (well, almost). The only thing missing was Clark the sportsman, and that the department could supply with the press of a button.

The first time Clark posed for publicity pictures he found himself right back at Griffith Park astride a horse. Soon he would be photographed half-buried in fishing equipment, then leaning against a fireplace cleaning guns, then resting on the fender of a roadster.

Sports clothes became part of his wardrobe; Minna saw to that. She'd always hated his "New York actor" duds. "They had to *go*," she says. And within a remarkably short time, the horse, the fishing rods, the guns, and the roadster became a part of his life. "He liked the image and fit into it," says Strickling. "He was willing to be molded. He wanted to be a star. He wanted to be a success."

As far as Clark could see, Howard's plans for him (and therefore, the company's) were flawless, so he did what he was told. His days were shaped by the disciplines of his work. He was at the studio fourteen hours a day, six days a week. He went dutifully to the gym and worked out—as Mr. Mayer commanded. He was on time for photo sessions, charming to journalists, patient with wardrobe, a buddy to the grips. He got his teeth capped.* A Clark Gable was, in fact, a model of cooperation, and why not, when there was everything to gain, and nothing to lose.

---

* The subject of Gable's teeth is as overworked as Gable's ears; no one involved with him can escape it. In the beginning, there is the question of who paid for the reconstruction. Choose one:

"Even after he was with the other Mrs. Gable, I was still paying installments for work done on his teeth. Of course I feel repaid, when I see him smile in his pictures."—Josephine Dillon

"He had his teeth recapped . . . it was Pauline Fredericks who paid for most of it."—Paul Fix

"I recall that Mother did have his teeth fixed. And she paid for that, as I recall."—George Anna Burke

"L. B. Mayer paid."—Clark Gable

18

Strickling saw him as a "he-guy," MGM as a gangster, which was really the same thing in the days when the world was divided into good guys and bad ones. A man couldn't be both good and overtly masculine—there was no such animal. Gable would be cast in six consecutive bad-guy roles, in films calculated to compete with the rash of meanies being produced at Warner Brothers. The collective works did little for MGM; that studio rarely triumphed with nasty movies, largely because Mayer was pathologically sentimental about things like motherhood and chicken soup. To be treated sympathetically in an MGM film, a woman had to be a potential mother. And mean men had to be so mean they were repugnant. Occasionally, however, audiences didn't respond the way they were supposed to, and a bad girl became a heroine, as did Harlow; or a bad guy a hero, as did Gable.

With barely a breather after *The Easiest Way*, Clark was cast as a mobster in *Dance, Fools, Dance* with Joan Crawford. The film had a concave, Depression era plot in which Joan starts out rich, is plunged into poverty, becomes a journalist, poses as a kingpin's moll (Gable's), learns her brother is the kingpin's henchman, and survives their slaughtering each other. The film was another hype to Gable's onrushing career, partly because the film was a fair success, but mostly because a Joan Crawford thought a Clark Gable was the sexiest man ever to walk on a sound stage; and said so to anyone who would listen. Only a few years ago, in a David Frost television interview, Miss Crawford was bleeped off the air, still touting Gable. In answer to Frost's query about who was the most exciting actor of them all, she replied, as though Frost were feeble-minded, "Clark Gable, of course."

"Why Gable?" asked Frost innocently.

"Because he had balls," declared Miss Crawford.

In her autobiography she says that in a scene in *Dance, Fools, Dance,* in which Gable grabbed her and threatened to kill her brother, "his nearness had such impact, my knees buckled." She further says that if he hadn't been holding her by the shoulders, she would have dropped to the floor. "This magnetic man had more sheer animal magic than anyone in the world and every woman knew it," she said.

Today, Miss Crawford reiterates what she wrote. "I adored him. Just adored him. I don't believe any woman is telling the truth if she ever worked with Gable and did not feel twinges of a sexual urge beyond belief. I would call her a liar." She also discovered early what many other people perceived about Gable later: that he had a presence. Way back in *Dance, Fools* days she says, "I knew when this man walked on the set and I didn't know which door he came in, but I knew he was there. That's how great he was."

She claims the attraction was not only instant, but also mutual: "I had the kind of chemistry that wanted what he had, and he had the kind of chemistry that wanted what I had. And you look at any picture we made together . . . there's something going on on that screen that is alive and can walk right out at you."

Indeed, the Crawford-Gable relationship would soon become complex, but at the time of his second MGM film, Clark just let the lady rave on. A., he was too busy. B., Joan Crawford was married to Douglas Fairbanks Jr., and C., as one of the queens of the studio, she was still off-limits to the likes of him. It is interesting to note, in regard to item B., that Gable, to all available knowledge, never did more than flirt with seriously married women. He was not a home wrecker, either on film or off it. (In *Red Dust,* for instance, he sends Mary Astor back to her husband despite his love for her, and he does the same with Grace Kelly in the remake of the film, *Mogambo,* twenty years later.) It was one of the reasons Gable had as many male admirers as he had female; he was enviable but not threatening.

From being cast with Joan Crawford, Clark was blended with Wallace Beery in a predominantly male film called *The Secret Six,* in which he is the journalist passing in the mob, and so convincing he would have been fired by any rational city editor. The one noticeable female part in the

film is played by Jean Harlow, who was under contract
to Howard Hughes and also at the start of her processing.
The film was chock full of gang killings and kidnappings
and crooked lawmen, but done well, the critics said, so it
was an important one for Clark, a fact he didn't have time
to ponder as he moved from picture to picture. In the
few weeks before *Secret Six* had gone into production, he
had been loaned to First National for the role of "gangland
czar" in *The Finger Points,* a vehicle for Richard Barth-
elmess, whose career was floundering. It was a minor film,
best forgotten, about a journalist on the payroll of the mob
who is executed by it, as audiences felt he deserved. (One
could understand a vicious gangster, but not a rotten
journalist.)

As soon as *Secret Six* ended, Miss Crawford requested
Clark for another film, a penny dreadful called *Laughing
Sinners.* Plot: fallen woman saved by Salvation Army
captain. Joan was the fallen woman, of course, Clark the
captain, and if ever there was a capital miscarriage of
packaging, it was putting him in a Salvation Army uniform.
Clearly, he did anything he was told, and clearly, Joan
Crawford had a lot of clout in the front office. Most of the
film had been shot earlier with John Mack Brown as
Crawford's savior. When somebody up there didn't like
Brown, his footage was clipped and then reshot with Gable.
They shouldn't have bothered. There were enough Crawford fans around to support the film, but not enough
scenes between the potential lovers to ignite their relationship. The film did nothing for Clark, and if romance was
what she had in mind, less for Joan.

Behaving as though Gable might melt if left outside
the gates overnight, the studio then assigned him to
Norma Shearer for the villain's role in Adela Rogers
St. Johns's *A Free Soul.* As far as Clark knew, this was
another routine job, only more tense than usual because
the lady he had to romance was the boss's wife, and
Norma Shearer Thalberg didn't wear any underwear. In
fact, though everything seemed the same old thing for
him, nothing was. In *A Free Soul* Gable is more than
another gangster named Ace, he is a new kind of rough,
tough lover. And his woman is not fallen, poor, or misguided. She's rich, independent, and in heat. Norma lusts
for him, gets him, and telegraphs the audience a shocking

message: I have broken all the rules and the orgasms are incredible.

As the story goes, Norma is the loving daughter of an eccentric, alcoholic criminal lawyer, played by Clark's old mentor, Lionel Barrymore. Through Daddy, she meets ruthless gambler Gable, and becomes his mistress as fast as possible, leaving in the dust a crestfallen proper fiancé played by Leslie Howard, as who could be more proper? Daddy is so appalled he makes a deal with his daughter: he will stop drinking if she will stop rutting. Okay. But Daddy can't stop drinking. Ruthless turns Sadistic, Fiancé turns Hero, Daddy turns Noble. Then Sadistic and Noble get killed, and the proper couple gets married and lives happily, and probably platonically, ever after.

A good moral film, thought the studio. In its infinite insulation from reality, it couldn't have been more wrong. Nobody connected with *Free Soul* anticipated the agitated response it got in theaters. Particularly did Thalberg lapse from his alleged genius in angling the story. It was he who insisted the Gable character, clearly appealing early in the movie, be made thoroughly cruel by the end. The change in Ace is so drastic one wonders if the gambler had a brain tumor, but Mr. Thalberg believed this would make audiences respond better to Mrs. Thalberg. What he didn't know was that sexually repressed women would be thrilled by the suggestion of emotionless, brutalized sex, and that their righteous men could be hostile to the lady who had stepped out of class to get laid. In *A Free Soul* the rich girl was teasing the hard-working, self-made racketeer; she was playing with him, using him. As far as moviegoers were concerned, she didn't deserve to be transported to ecstasy by him on a velvet couch. She did deserve to be manhandled, just the way Clark did it.

In retrospect, *A Free Soul* looks like it was created to make Gable a hero. Clark meets Norma at a party, to which Daddy drags him, in the family's Park Avenue penthouse. Clark is wearing his best gambler's checked suit and spats. The stuffed shirts at the party are in white tie and tails. Norma and her skinny, blond fiancé with the British accent are playing backgammon. Norma is in a see-through satin gown that a respectable woman wouldn't sleep in. She has a voice like an affected Minnie Mouse. When Clark enters the room, filling it, as it were, she gives him a very uncivilized look; he doesn't make a wrong gesture. The swells in the room behave like cannibals—roasting Clark alive because he's not one of their kind. When Norma leaves with Daddy and the guy who's supposed to be bad, she drapes herself in an ermine cape with sable trim. People in the audience were *poor*.

Next time Norma appears she's in chinchilla. And her great big bad guy, now in gambler's tux, picks her up in his arms so easily she's a feather. What a fantasy—to have a man who makes a woman weightless. There couldn't have been a normal woman viewing that film who wouldn't have given her homemade coconut cake to be Norma Shearer in Gable's arms. "Come on, put 'em around me," she purrs at her lover when he is angry at her harping on their class difference. And he does what she asks.

She wants him only for one thing: sex; now there's a therapeutic reversal for the ladies watching in the dark. And for the men, there's Gable turned "mongrel," as Barrymore notes, pushing Norma into a chair when she's finally gone too far, shoving her back into her chair when she gets up to protest. "Sit down and take it and like it," he snarls. Relief. "You're an idiot—a spoiled, silly brat that needs a hairbrush now and then." More relief. That high-falootin' dame who's been gettin' all that stuff she loves now gets somethin' she didn't bargain for. The stud strikes back, not by slapping Shearer, as legend now has it, but by shoving her around. And audiences loved him for it.

Clark Gable was the man the world was waiting for. At just the right moment he stepped out of a telephone-booth-sized dressing room and appeared on the screen, unrealized superman of a transitional era. He was a guy who'd made it the hard way, knew the rich for the heartless fools they were, could be pushed so far and no farther, had no illusions about himself. In his arms, queens and goddesses became women. Cocksure, but not arrogant, he was the man every woman wanted, and every man wanted to be. As Fairbanks was assumed to be a real swashbuckler and Chaplin really a sad clown, when movies absorbed logic like a sponge, so audiences assumed Gable was really Gable.

When, in June, 1931, *A Free Soul* was released, critics completely overlooked this mythical creature. Their only praise went to Barrymore, who got an Oscar for his

role in the film. The public, however, organized behind
the new idol, writing thousands of fan letters to him, and
thousands to MGM demanding more Gable. Those who
could make it crowded around the gates of the studio
waiting for him to enter and to leave.

Suddenly Clark Gable had a discernible, audible body
of followers, and therefore, a powerful champion in the
front office. Word went around: Thalberg is very fond of
Gable. "Thalberg was fond of anybody who made
money," says Howard Dietz. Yes indeed.

With five months still to go on his first MGM contract,
Clark watched as it was torn up, and a new one written
for $1,150 a week. Five hundred dollars of that was to
be put in trust each week, to assure the studio Gable
would stay a while; the rest handed him every Tuesday
for fifty-two weeks.

The five hundred words Strickling had released on
Clark in seven months turned into a thousand a day,
maybe more. And the next film he was assigned, *Sporting Blood,* had not one candy bar in it—except him.
Granted, it wasn't much of a production—Gable as a
crooked gambler, for a change, only this time with
horses. Nevertheless, the film *starred* Clark Gable.

He had arrived, but he still didn't believe he was anything more than temporarily lucky. That, perhaps, was
wiser than it was neurotic. He was, really, the first major
screen personality exclusively created in talkies. What was
the career span of a talking picture actor? How long
could talkies last, for that matter? How many stars could
talkies support: could a Clark Gable co-exist with a
Gary Cooper? The industry was too young for any of the
answers to be known.

19

With the public panting for information about its new idol, it was inevitable that what MGM considered Clark's cans of worms would be opened by the press. Specifically, there was Ria. Until the release of *Free Soul* she had managed to go almost unnoticed, and Clark, for a short time, actually denied being married to her or anyone else. The studio didn't support him in this pose; it stayed neutral. No releases were sent out saying he was a bachelor but none said he was married, either.

Sometime in June of 1931, someone—an MGM lawyer, or a reporter—discovered that Clark's New York marriage to Ria wasn't legal in California and told him so. In a panic, on June 13, Clark applied for a marriage license, under the name of "William C. Gable," to a bureau in Santa Ana, Hollywood's favorite marrying ground. It was a misguided move. Because so many screen celebrities married there, Santa Ana was staked out like a war zone. Reporters learned of the application and contacted Clark to ask him if he was getting married. He said no, William was his brother, and planned a trip to Santa Ana within the week.

Howard Strickling fretted, but Clark went blithely along with his plans. Still naïve about his position in the heavens, he couldn't imagine anyone bothering to stay with the story after he had so cleverly thrown reporters off his track. Howard knew better, and worried that if Clark and Ria were besieged when they went to marry, both would go into shock over the aggressions of the press. He feared that the Gables' remarriage was going to be a fox hunt, and if found, Mr. and Mrs. Gable would be torn apart by the hounds.

Nevertheless, on June 19, Clark and Ria and a man named Joe Sherman, of the MGM publicity department, were at the Santa Ana courthouse at 9:20 in the morning. At 9:30, when the courthouse opened, they hurried into the judge's chambers, where Ria and Clark were married once again. When they emerged at 9:40, the worst happened. A pack of reporters surrounded them at once. Their questions were predictable: Was this the couple's second marriage and why? Was she the rich Mrs. Langham of New York and Houston? What did she think of Clark's success? How did it feel marrying a great screen lover? Etc., etc.

Joe Sherman threw himself to the hounds. He told them to let the newlyweds go, and he would answer their questions at the studio. Clark stayed cool and silent. But Ria went to pieces. She begged the reporters to leave, pleaded with them not to print anything about the wedding, and fell on their mercy as a mother. Clark and Joe managed to get her into a car and off the scene before photographers arrived, thus sparing the studio of having to deal with pictures of the tearful Mrs. Gable. When she found her composure, she ached from the loss of her normal dignity. She would never again be surprised by the press, and she would never again knowingly be its victim. She would give no interviews and make no public statements about her marriage or her husband. She would, however, appear at premieres and parties as Mrs. Gable and she would, as it turned out, glory in that role. She was the wife of the star, and as she saw it, that was a privileged position in life. But she wasn't the star. She was a smart woman, and she set a precedent followed by the next two Mrs. Gables. Quite possibly, her posture was dictated (or "suggested") by Howard Strickling because the precedent was broken by Josephine Dillon and Kay Gable, neither of whom was married to Clark when he was under contract to the studio.

Clark simply couldn't get used to the fact that he had become public property. It had happened too quickly. Even Howard had not anticipated the extent of the interest in this new property; his department couldn't fill requests for material fast enough. How to handle Gable's public image was the problem. After the batches of "life stories" went out, then what? There would be no layouts of Clark and Ria at home, because Ria was not glamorous enough, and anyway, the public saw Clark as a lover, not a husband.

Fan magazines pressed to interview Clark about women

and marriage; he wouldn't talk. So they filled their pages with hokey stories of his early "loves": "She was seven and I was eight. She was short . . . dark . . . beautiful . . . and brown-eyed. Her name was Treela." When that phase passed, there was a rash of stories comparing Gable to Valentino: "CLARK GABLE, Don Juan by Popular Demand"; "The Great American Male Has Hit the Screen at Last!" Then came, "What a Man, Gable!" stories declaring him to be a lover like no other. When Clark still insisted his appeal was in a certain type of role rather than himself, and wouldn't talk, the Hollywood reporters got mad, and their stories were laced with rumors of his having had three or four wives, at least one son, and most certainly, a speckled past.

The press then found just what it wanted: a local drama coach who billed herself "Josephine Dillon (Gable)"— "a woman alone and poor and therefore easily dealt with," as one reporter noted. According to Josephine, she was "threatened and bullied, terrified and insulted." For a short time, she saw all reporters who called her, only to find that her "mild little reminiscences" were not wanted. They wanted "dirt," she claimed. She wouldn't give. She said "they" threatened to ruin her and to find ways to take away her pupils.

The Josephine matter attached itself to everyone concerned like a tick. The press used her to bludgeon Clark, printing items like this one from a fan magazine which described the Gables' luxurious life-style and then said, "The first Mrs. Gable lives in actual want. She has a tiny voice culture studio, none too well patronized in these days of depression. Often she is not sure where the next few dollars are coming from."

It finally dawned on Josephine where she might get her next few dollars. On August 2, 1931, she wrote this letter to Louis Mayer:

My dear Mr. Mayer:

I have received a number of offers for a story of my experiences as the wife and coach of Clark Gable. I have prepared such a story and have it ready for mailing to a publication which has made me an offer for it. It begins with our meeting when he came to my studio in Portland Oregon, when he was an em-

ployee of the telephone company there, and gives
the intimate details of our life and the way I made it
possible for him to arrive at his present prominence,
and it tells of his treatment of me.

My reason for being willing to sell such a story of
the sorrow and disappointment Clark Gable caused
me is that he has made no attempt to repay me in
any way for the hours and years of careful instruction
and coaching that he received from me and the
money he cost me, nor has he shown the slightest
concern for the heartaches and humiliations he
brought into my life. Even so, I would not have considered the publication of my intimate life were it
not for the fact that his attitude has made it extremely
difficult for me to earn even a modest living as a
coach. The paragraph recently printed in the Hollywood Reporter, in which it commented on his rise to
prosperity while the wife who made it possible is living in poverty in a backyard in Hollywood is only
too true.

Mr. Gable has given me no cause to be concerned
for his welfare, but your company has never done
me any harm and this story will probably damage
one of your properties. If you would rather buy this
story from me than have me sell it for publication, I
am willing to agree not to give out any information
concerning Gable while he is in your employ except
through your office. I should, of course, consider any
such agreement voided upon hearing any further
denials from him that he was ever coached by me, or
received help from me or was married to me, or
any more stories to the effect that he has offered me
help which I refused. In fact, there must be an acknowledgement of my help and instruction in the publicity concerning him which your department places,
in order to counteract in some degree the great harm
done me and my business by the false stories already
circulated.

I have constant calls from local newspaper and
magazine people asking for gossip for their chatter
columns, but have refrained from that sort of vulgar-
ity. But my present position forces me to sell this
story as I am in desperate need. If you would like to
discuss the story with me and my offer to sell it to

you, you can reach me at the above address or at
HE: 1372.

Yours very truly
(MRS.) JOSEPHINE DILLON GABLE

On August 31, Josephine wrote to Mayer:

This is an acknowledgement of my gratitude to
you for your great kindness. The world looks much
brighter than it did, and there is a chance to go on.
I wish I might do something for you in return. I really
am a very fine coach and have an uncanny success
with men's voices for microphone. I wish I could do
something about John Gilbert's voice for you. I know
it can be done and just how to go at it. That would
help and show my sincerity and appreciation. . . .

To this, Mayer's secretary sent a polite "no thanks."
The next Dillon paper was an interoffice note, with no
names on it, dated 7/25/32:

Josephine Dillon called and asked me to give you the
following message: said she is all upset about the fact
that they have stopped her checks—they are behind
on the last two checks and today she called to Mr.
Swartz of Loeb, Walker and Loeb and had been advised that Mr. Gable was very angry because of an
interview she is supposed to have given out. She
does not know what they are referring to because she
has not given any out. Said she hates to do so but
supposes this will have to come through Mr. Mayer as
it did the last time.

The last memo, dated 7/30/32, to a "Miss Nelson"
from "M. E. Greenwood" read:

Following our telephone conversation a couple of
days ago I talked to Clark Gable with relation to the
Josephine Dillon matter. His understanding and feeling is briefly as follows. That his payment of $200 a
month to her could be discontinued by him at any
time without cause. That she had agreed not to give
any interviews during the time he was paying her,
that she has not kept this agreement and he is send-

ing her copies of her alleged interviews, together with a check for $200 accompanied by a notice that this payment will be the last. Boiled down, his position was that it was senseless on his part to continue making the payments when they did not accomplish the purpose for which they were intended.

Clark's payments ceased and Josephine then opened up to the press, writing stories about her days in Hollywood with Clark. The stories were meant to be kind and loving, she insisted, but the space between the lines read, "I made him what he is today." Writers picked up on the inference, declaring Josephine the woman who had created Clark Gable. Then Clark Gable defenders attacked Josephine, which was easy because she was hypersensitive. "If anyone made Clark a good actor," wrote Adela Rogers St. Johns, "it wasn't Josephine Dillon." Josephine hurt from that line, but not nearly as much as she did from Mrs. St. Johns's ambiguous description of her: "You remember your elocution teacher in high school." That made her bleed.

Josephine counterattacked, telling yet another writer that Adela had written what she did because Josephine had refused to see her, referring her, instead, to the studio. "I am a well-known writer," Josephine claimed Adela said. "You are making a mistake not talking to me."

On and on it all went, until Howard Strickling decided the best thing to do was turn Clark over to the press. Reporters would discover what a regular guy he was, and lay off. Clark was made available, anytime, anyplace. He and Ria and her children moved into a fancy apartment in a fancy apartment house, and a reporter followed right behind, but not to talk to the wife and kids. The deal was, you can have Clark if you leave out his family. So the reporter wrote about Clark's hundred-dollar silk robe, his fifty-cent cigars, and his luxurious surroundings. "Not much like the dump I lived in a few years ago this time in Hollywood," said Clark, on the record.

Howard winced, but worse was yet to come. Clark was so regular the studio couldn't stand it. Stopped by a reporter on a set and asked what he thought of the roles he was playing, he answered, "I just work here. I try to work well and hard. They have an investment in me. They've spent money on me. It's my business to work; not to think." Another reporter, from a fan magazine, asked him how to become a star. He got one dilly of an answer:

> . . . It isn't looks. It isn't experience. It isn't ability, because everyone knows there are stars who can't act worth a damn.
>
> . . . the public is the only thing that makes stars; and the public wants one thing one week and something else the next. It doesn't know what it wants nor why it wants it, and neither does anyone else. . . . You can't explain *anything*, in this movie business.
>
> It's a chain of accidents. When you step into Hollywood, you wind yourself into thousands and thousands of chains of accidents. If all of the thousands happen to come out just exactly right—and the chance of that figures out to something like one in eight million—then you'll be a star.
>
> If you're enough of a gambler or enough of a jackass to figure everything will come out right just for you, then trot ahead to Hollywood. You want to be a movie star. You think you'd like it. Maybe you would and maybe you wouldn't. You might turn out to be not so happy as you think you'd be.

It didn't take long for MGM to throw a net over the head of this blabbing myna bird and whisk it out of sight. The public didn't want to hear the sort of things Gable had to say, said the publicity department, meaning, MGM wanted people to read only what it wanted them to read. Gable was kept away from the press while he was working, and as soon as he was finished with a film, he was sent to some remote body of water to fish, or to some field to hunt. He went with Larry Keith, the head of wardrobe, or Bunny Doll, an assistant director, and occasionally, with Ria. And in no time at all, he found out he could relax on these trips as he never did before.

In no time at all, hunting, fishing, and shooting were genuine passions for him. As Howard says, "We encouraged these pursuits, yes. But he took to them and did them well. After all, he had never played in his life."

For the rest of his life, Clark would disappear after every film he made, going hunting, fishing, or shooting.

For the duration of his contracts with MGM, he would not give a single significant interview.

He said it himself, "You might not turn out to be so happy as you think you'd be." No one can be happy living with the fear he had: that one false step and he'd be back on all fours, sniffing for a lost bone. At the end of a studio day of watching his step, on camera and off, Clark was a brooding, unpredictable, volcanic, weary man who often found being a husband and father two burdens too many.

He left home around five A.M. and returned after seven in the evening, six days a week. In the early months of 1931, he also worked fourteen straight Sundays, and lost fifteen pounds. The family waited to have dinner with him—since he studied his lines at night, it was the only time they saw him—but that wasn't always a pleasant hour. Jana says, "I can remember so well sitting at the table and Clark not wanting to visit or talk, and just didn't. The rest of us would just carry on with sort of light conversation which he would never enter into. Mother would say, 'He's so tired.' And he would shove his chair back before we were through and excuse himself. He was moody. Maybe for several days at a time."

He was unsure of his tastes; the uncertainty made him extravagant, and the extravagance made him anxious. He bought expensive clothes, and when he wore them searched faces around him for reactions. If he sensed a negative vibration, he would discard what he had been wearing, and replace it. Ria couldn't stand the waste and sent his suits and jackets to her friend Ferris White, who was temporarily down on his luck, big enough to fit into Clark's clothes, and good-natured enough to enjoy showing off the name "Clark Gable" stitched into his jacket pocket.

Before Clark bought his first sportscar, he called Ria to get her approval. The first day he was teased about the flashy machine, he sold it, for hundreds less than he'd paid for it.

He took more riding lessons, then took up polo, which was the chic thing to do, then bought a polo pony and wardrobe, then was forbidden to play polo by the studio because it was too dangerous.

He became a photography buff and compulsive camera buyer. He enjoyed making home movies, which, at least,

brought pleasure to everyone in the family. Jana says,
'He'd always get me coming out of the bathroom wearing
a long robe or something. I'd shriek and say 'Please, no'
and he thought it was terribly funny, to catch any of us
off-guard."

He loved dogs and indulged in some pedigreed chows.
He upped the quality and quantity of his gin. He acquired
fishing and hunting equipment and clothes that went with
them. Then, it seemed, the Gables were bursting out of
their apartment so they rented a house on San Ysidro, not
far from Pickfair. Then Clark began to complain about
expenses, because his soul couldn't afford the fling his body
had earned.

Success in his lap, he wasn't sure whether he had
seduced it, or it him. Or was there some reason to suspect rape? If he was so successful, why did he have to
work so hard? If he was a star, why had he no control
over his career? Years ago he had rebelled against his
father and had gotten away with it. Now he had a
mightier parent to deal with: a whole bloody studio; and
every kid on the block ready to squeal on him if he
misbehaved.

"There are no complexes, no inhibitions, no fixations,
no phobias about Clark," wrote his friendly neighborhood
scribe Adela. He had hidden at least one can of worms
from the press: the one in his head.

20

There was never any time for him to catch his breath or
to pull back and get a perspective on the events of his
life. In the summer of 1931, when the year should have
been beginning to coast, it had only begun to roll. There
was no way he could slow it down.

He was on a hunting trip designed to get him out of
town after *Sporting Blood* was finished when he read in
a trade paper that he would play the male lead in the

next Garbo vehicle, *Susan Lenox, Her Fall and Rise.*
Though the announcement was big news in terms of his
career, the surprise of it infuriated him. Unfortunately,
there was nothing positive he could do with his anger.
He could rant at Minna Wallis, because she hadn't consulted him, he could tell Strickling what he thought of
MGM's moving him around like a pinch-hitter, but he
most assuredly could not refuse to do a film whose ad
campaign would shout, "Don't miss the one and only
Garbo in the arms of Clark Gable!"

Gable went into the film as its stepchild, a position he
thought he had advanced beyond. The studio's only concern was that Gable be the right foil for Garbo; no one,
observed Gable, gave a hoot what the film would do for
him. Great minds brooded about the possibility that his
rough, tough image would tear Garbo's pure silk gauzi-
ness to shreds. She wanted Gable for the picture, however, and her whim amounted to a demand. So the object
was to turn Gable into a Robert Montgomery-Leslie
Howard figure of chaste sophistication, yet retain enough
of Gable to satisfy his fans. It was an impossible task.
Before the film was finished (in forty-nine shooting days
instead of the average thirty-five) twenty-two writers
worked on it, and Garbo walked out six times.

In the film Gable and Garbo relate only in clinches.
The rest of the time the pair seems as ridiculously mated
as they would have been had they paired off-screen.
Garbo, through most of the film, seems so out of touch
with reality as to be certifiably insane. Gable switches
from looking scared, to puzzled, to silly. Even his voice
is unusual; he has no control of it and it is sometimes
smoky, sometimes high-pitched. It is one of the few films
in his entire career in which he tried to be high class,
and his discomfort is obvious. In time, when his roles will
be tailored for him, writers will be handed a formula, as
was Frances Marion: "He's tough, uneducated, got a hell
of a temper, can fight his weight in wildcats—you know,
Frances, typical Gable stuff, with sex that drives the
women crazy." The formula will frustrate Clark's drive
to be a versatile actor, but any time he deviates from it,
he will suffer, either internally or at the box office.

Susan Lenox was the only film Clark would make with
Garbo, much to his pleasure. It was an experience for
the record, and not a waste of time by any means. Being

in a poor Garbo film was better than not being in any; the picture made money, therefore friends. And there was a lot to be learned just watching the elusive lady wend through a workday. Nobody pushed Garbo around; there was even a clause in her contract permitting her to work no more than eight hours a day. Gable stored that, and, when he was in a position to make demands, had it written into his contracts as well. Once a boy who drove a car without a formal lesson, he was still a keen observer.

For his next epic he was cast again with Joan Crawford. The film was called *Possessed*, and it seems they certainly were. "In the picture we were madly in love," wrote Joan. "When the scenes ended, the emotion didn't." Within two weeks into the film's production, rumors ricocheted around Hollywood about Crawford and Gable, and local gamblers were giving odds on the match. In Hollywood's eyes, Gable was available, married or not.

The rumors got to Ria, whose theory was that there was always a little truth in every story. In this case, she also had clues. Clark was leaving home earlier and earlier, returning later and later. Where he was occasionally moody before, now he didn't talk at all. No more complaints about the studio or how tired he was. Evidently, he had once again found a woman whose mind was on the same single track as his own: acting. As Miss Crawford explained it, "We had a great deal to talk about. His job, like mine, was the most serious thing in the world to him." Though Ria catered to Clark's ambition, she had other interests as well.

Ria and Joan saw each other socially and seemed to like each other. Chances are, this heightened the affair in the strange way that impossible situations become appealing for their impossibility. Crawford and Gable were star-crossed stars, and the melodrama of that position probably appealed to the performer in both of them. Wrote Miss Crawford:

Occasionally we'd break away early, go for a quiet ride along the sea. And all day long we'd seek each other's eyes. It was glorious and hopeless. There seemed nothing we would do about it. There was no chance for us. . . .

We talked of marriage, of course. But I dared not

ruin the dreams. I'd rather live with them unfulfilled than have them broken. . . .

It was like living over a lighted powder keg, but it was worth it. . . .

The only time I could be with Clark was on the set, and I was disconsolate that I was cast in *Letty Lynton* without him. Clarence Brown, who also directed *Letty*, knew. He came up to me one day just before a big scene and said, sotto voce, "I understand, Joan, I know who you're missing." I threw my arms around his dear professorial neck and went right into my crying scene, my own unhappy tears for unhappy Letty. . . .

Unhappy Ria was not about to shed tears for anyone. She wouldn't be a patsy and she wouldn't sit in the Brown Derby accepting condolences. She had the studio arrange a whistle-stop tour for her, and took off for New York with the children. On that tour, as on several others, she established full well who Mrs. Gable really was. Jana describes the trip like this:

"Al and I, we sort of felt like bottles of ink, sometimes, you know? Like, what are we doing here? We were on the train going from California to New York with our mother, and when we would stop at these various little stations along the way there would be maybe one thousand people to see Ria Gable. We would sort of hide in the background, you know. We'd stay in the drawing room because we didn't feel that they wanted to see us particularly. But Mother loved it. She'd go out and wave and sign autographs.

"We never waited in line for anything. Mother would go right up to the box office and say, 'I'm Mrs. Clark Gable and I would like three tickets for such and such or so and so. Al and I would be cringing in the background, and she would say, 'Come along, children.' We never went into a restaurant and had the maître d' tell us we had to wait. Mother would march right in and we'd get a good table. She loved it, just loved it."

For a change, Ria had MGM on her side. The studio didn't like the smell of this potential scandal. There was nothing new about marriages falling apart on a sound stage, but the publicity department assumed the public

would consider this case unfair. Ria didn't appear to be
any match for the glamorous, aggressive Miss Crawford.
Clark had just married his "older woman" for the second
time; it was too soon for him to discard her without
emerging public heel number one. The pressure was on
Clark to get his wife home and appear in public with her.
Whether he responded to the pressure, or acted for reasons of his own, he did just that, and Joan went into
Hollywood lore as the heroine who had sacrificed the one
true love of her life for the sake of preserving a hearth
and family. Like many of Clark's relationships with
women, this one didn't end when it ended. Crawford
and Gable would be an item of one sort or another for
the next fifteen years.

 Possessed in the can in a record twenty-seven shooting
days, Clark was put to work immediately in "a man's
movie" called *Hell Divers,* with Wallace Beery. The
film was a saga of naval aviators, their triumphs and ri-
valries, with Beery the more triumphant, even in death.
Critics didn't like the film, and neither did Gable. He did
learn a new trick making it, however. The naval pilots he
met never put a twist in their gin-on-the-rocks. They took
their gin straight, with half a lemon on the side. For the
next year Clark bit on lemon between sips of gin, noting
to any observer, "Something I picked up from some Navy
guys."

Clark finished *Hell Divers* in a feisty mood. More than
likely, anything next assigned him would have annoyed
him; he was ready to blow. The returns were coming in
on the films he had stacked up all year, and he hadn't
made a picture that lost money. Still, he felt, he was
being treated like a basic accessory, the decent pair of
shoes to go with a custom-made suit. Beery made ten
times his salary, and even though he was the industry's
top box office draw, Gable thought the disparity insulting.
Clark wanted more money, and he wanted a choice of
pictures. He also wanted a rest. His mood was not a secret, but Ria was the only one who paid attention to it.
As quickly as Monday follows Sunday, he was handed a
script for another film and told to report to work on it.
This time William Randolph Hearst had pulled the
string; his love, Marion Davies, wanted Clark to work
with her. Hearst's production company, Cosmopolitan
Pictures, maintained for Miss Davies, distributed through

MGM. W. R. Hearst was L. B. Mayer's idol. Marion had a two-story fourteen-room bungalow on the studio grounds; her "dressing room." The facts added up to a command performance, and might have been, if the property involved were more palatable.

Incredibly to Clark, the picture Hearst wanted him for was the old tent-show chestnut *Polly of the Circus,* with Gable assigned to play a priest. That did it. Minna Wallis remembers, "Clark called me up in a terrible mood and said, 'I don't want to do this bloody thing.' I went to the studio immediately, met Clark there. We stayed till two in the morning, with L. B. hammering at him. Finally Hearst said, 'I'll buy him the best car . . . there's a new car out, ten thousand dollars . . . I'll give him a present of the car.' Clark was right in the room. He said, 'I'm not interested. I don't like that picture. I don't want to do it. Rewrite it. Do something to it. Maybe then . . .' Finally they did, and he started the picture without the ten-thousand-dollar car."

They turned the priest into a preacher, and the movie was still bad. After the first day's shooting Clark refused to continue working. Minna hid him in Palm Springs, where all film actors went to have temperamental fits (and where a lot of them ended their careers) and waited for someone to make the next move. Mayer did. He told Minna to return Clark to the set, or he'd suspend him, permanently. Clark wouldn't budge. Now Marion's feelings were hurt. She wanted to get on with her movie and insisted W. R. make everything well again. So he did. He got Clark a new contract, which Hearst thought he deserved anyway. It was for two years at $2,000 a week, $500 withheld, and it would go into effect January 22, 1932. Clark went back to work a contented man. He had waged his first power battle and won, made friends of Marion and Will, and even survived the fizzle of the small bomb *Polly* turned out to be when it was released in late February, 1932.

The year 1931 wound up a remarkable one—in terms of his career, the most significant of his life. MGM had fallen nine short of its projected fifty-two films for the year. The total of forty-three pictures was also six less than the studio turned out in 1930, and its profits were off by a million dollars as a result (from $6,260,000 in 1930 to $5,209,000 in '31). Gable had become an MGM

asset at a time the studio genuinely needed him, a fact he
grasped sooner than the moguls did. When the time would
come to reckon with Gable's position at the studio,
it would have to be realized that he triumphed in the
worst of the bad years. Within another year, a year in
which he would make only three films, Clark Gable would
be more than a movie star. He would be an event. To
see him "in person," even once, no matter at what distance, would be as memorable as being there when Lind-
bergh landed, or the *Normandie* listed, or the Mets won
the Series. Clark Gable would be the rock festival of his
lifetime.

21

Gable often said he didn't believe in working at marriage.
In fact, he didn't work at any kind of relationship, and
when he did, he ultimately rebelled against what he considered his submission to someone else's needs. He was a
man who couldn't abide being dominated, yet he was
attracted to strong people on whom he would lean for limited periods of time. Being leaned on by him gave a person no rights at all—and that oblique fact caused both
parties a lot of trouble. Says Wayne Griffin, "He was one
to seek advice. He'd ask, 'What do you think of this, or
this, or that?' Now that's difficult, because if someone
seems to rely on you and ask what you think, pretty soon,
if you're not careful, you're telling him how to live. And
Gable didn't want to be taken over by anybody. He wanted
his life to be free, and to live it the way he liked."

Three of his five wives got caught in the trap. One of
them was Ria. In the beginning, Clark had given her reasons to believe he needed and cared for her ("I believe
Clark liked me, but never loved me," she told a Houston
friend). When she went over some boundary line only he
defined, he made her life miserable. "He seemed to love to
devil Mother about things," Jana says. She is being kind.
Living with him was like living on the San Andreas Fault;

tremors occurred without warning, and the big break was inevitable. Ria told the same Houston friend, "I knew when I met Clark that the difference in our ages would count against me, but I wanted him, even if just for a short while." As it turned out, their age difference seemed to be the least of their problems.

After their post-Crawford reconciliation, Ria and Clark began an active social and public life. Ria was a choice hostess, and entertained all who were who at small dinner parties and large ones. The Thalbergs, Mary Pickford, Gloria Swanson, the Goldwyns, were frequent guests. She also welcomed Clark's old friends, though she didn't mix the castes. In time the old friends grew uncomfortable with Clark's success, and as such things happen, the friendships died.

Hollywood's elite were not Clark's style, and he balked at seeing them, either in his own home or theirs. Eulalia Chapin, a Hollywood socialite in the thirties, remembers one of Ria's Sunday galas for fifty or more guests, during which Clark, typically, spent all his time with the parking attendants. "He was terribly nice, and polite, and charming," says Eulalia, "but I only saw him when I arrived and when I left. Juggling the cars around was quite a job, I'll admit, but he really didn't have to see to it himself."

Clark didn't mingle with big shots at the studio, and didn't see why he should at home. At work he was happiest with underdogs, not only in the early thirties when he identified with them, but throughout his career. He wooed and was loved by all the hired hands, by extras, by the guards at the gate. Hal Dawson remembers Clark fondly from *Machinal*, but more so from working around him in films. He says, "I remember one time when there were thirty extras on one of his pictures at MGM. He'd been talking to them all, and asked them if they were coming back the next day. They weren't, and he knew they all needed money. So he fluffed his lines, just fluffed them and fluffed them. He knew those lines, but the director had to give in and the scene was reshot the next day, and the extras got their checks.

"That's 'a Clark Gable,' " Dawson says. "What I mean is, he did that kind of thing so often the trick got named for him. On another of his films, I had a small part, with a two-week guarantee. Any delays, I could get three weeks' work. So Clark came back for added dialogue, and I got another week's salary.

"I was in *Teacher's Pet,* which he made with Doris Day . . . well, only for a week and a half, for one scene. He asked me to lunch, so we had a bite, and talked about old times. He said, 'Look here, Hal, when you want work, have your agent come and see me, not the producer or the director.' You know, I would have done it, but he died not too long after that. Usually, I don't like to get work that way; I don't like to be beholden if something goes wrong. But I would have done it with Gable. He would always have been on my side."

He wanted to make his own friends and have them on his own terms. Take, for instance, the case of Leo Martin, a vice-president of Abercrombie and Fitch in Manhattan. Mr. Martin was a $30-a-week salesman in the store's fishing department when he first met Gable, about forty years ago. He remembers the meeting, he says, as though it happened yesterday:

"I had come into the store around nine A.M., the time it opened in those days. As I walked into the fishing department, I noticed a man sitting in a leather chair, holding his head with his hands. I thought he was one of the other salesmen, but when he looked up, I saw this unshaven guy whose first words were, 'Hey, son. Any place I can get a cup of coffee?' I realized right away that he was Clark Gable, and I told him I would get him some coffee. As I went off, he said, 'Black, by the way.'

"He was really hung over. He said that the night before he had done a really stupid thing, but he never told me what, and I didn't ask him. It was apparent that he had gotten soused. I asked him if he'd been in the store all night. He said he had just come in. When I brought back the container of coffee, he said, 'You're a nice guy. What's your name? When I get all cleaned up, I'll be back to see you.'

"He came back a few hours later and asked if I could have lunch with him. First I said I couldn't, and then I said, 'Why not?' He took me to Twenty-one. He didn't buy anything at Abercrombie's that day. He probably had come in for fishing equipment, but in his state had forgotten. He did say he'd always call me when he was in New York, and hoped we could have lunch together.

"I must have eaten with him ten to fifteen times over

the years, mostly at Twenty-one. Throughout all those years, I could never understand why a man of such stature would bother with a poor schnook like me. In the beginning I said to myself, 'Hey, Martin, maybe he's queer. What are you getting yourself into?' Of course it was clear that this wasn't so. Quite the contrary. He was a real ladies' man. He always had an eye for the girls. At lunch he was always looking at the 'broads' passing by. He didn't miss one.

"He was all man. He was always polite and proper. He looked, talked, walked, exactly the same as on the screen. He was always impeccably dressed, even on that day I first met him. I never did see him again in that unshaven state.

"His mood was not always consistent. If he was troubled or something was depressing him, he showed it; he would drink a lot. Other times, he seemed loose, an 'I don't give a damn' attitude. He never talked about his problems or anything personal in his life. It was the strangest relationship because he only wanted to know about my life. I wish now that I had become involved in his life, but I never wanted to pry into his business. I felt that if he wanted to tell me anything, he would."

Leo Martin made Gable an ideal friend; none of Gable's other friends knew he existed, he didn't encroach, and he wasn't easily available. Either of the latter could have aborted the friendship before the third lunch. Jana says, "Clark would tire of people and things. This was always very embarrassing to Mother. He would rush a couple and see a lot of them—be with them all the time, take them hunting and all—then suddenly he wouldn't want to see them anymore. If he would run into them he would be perfectly charming. But he didn't want to see them. This was his disposition, always."

Jana describes Clark as a man who did things on the spur of the moment. This, too, was "his disposition," she says, and the family used to laugh about it. "I remember, for instance, when they were having a dinner party (Mother had decided they should have a dinner party), she'd say, 'This chair looks just awful,' and she wanted the chair done over, but Clark didn't want to spend the money. Weeks later he'd say, 'We'll get the chair done over before the party. When is it?' And she'd say, 'Well, next Friday.' And he'd say, 'Well, get someone out here and get it done.' This was the sort of thing he did. He wanted everything fine for the party, but he'd put off for months getting the house in shape, and then when the party was on top of us, he wanted it all done right away."

Ria may have laughed, but she had to have been exasperated. "Mother was a very methodical person," Jana notes. "Very orderly and very fastidious. Extremely so."

Jana feels that Clark was unhappy having such big stepchildren in his first days of being a matinee idol, but there is evidence that he did try to relate to them both. With Jana he was so overprotective he was like a Sicilian brother. She had her portrait painted when she was seventeen, and Clark went with her to every sitting. "He didn't think the artist was the type I should be left with alone," says Jana. Her first serious beau was someone neither Clark nor Ria approved of, and Clark came just short of murdering the fellow to break up the romance. Jana says, "He was very definite about that," and smiles gently. What Clark did one night was pick up a poker from the fireplace and brandish it at the head of her boyfriend. The young man ran from the house, Clark ran after him, followed by Ria, Jana, and Al. It took all three of them to restrain Clark and recover the weapon.

He gave Jana an allowance of $100 a month, and bought her a two-door Ford. He also made her his secretary, and paid her another hundred a month for that. Jana was supposed to use the money to buy her clothes and gas for her car. "I thought I was so well off," she says. "It was a lot of money in those days." She was also proud of her secretarial duties, which she took quite seriously. She learned how to forge Clark's signature so well she could handle all his mail for him. Jana says, "A lot of this was to give me something to do, now that I think about it. I didn't think so at the time. Clark disliked that young man I dated so much, he hoped to get me interested in different things." He discussed with Ria the possibility of sending Jana on a prolonged trip to distract her, but Ria vetoed that. "Mother wouldn't allow it," Jana says. "She wanted me near her warm side."

Jana had other "jobs" in the household; there was an obvious attempt by either Clark or Ria or both to make her feel a vital part of the family. When Clark and Ria traveled—and on most of their trips the children were not included—Jana packed for them both. At Christmas time, it was Jana who wrapped all the gifts and stayed up Christmas Eve decorating the tree.

Ria was the kind of woman who somehow was always busy. Youthfully energetic, she rose early and never sat down until she went to sleep. She played cards, she lunched out, she went to the races, she shopped, and she kept a chain of phone calls going with her friends and the people she felt she should cultivate for Clark's career. When Clark was working, she had a lot of time on her hands, and she involved herself in many lives. She was forever arranging screen tests for actors she thought had promise; friends often brought young hopefuls to her before they approached a studio. She promoted designers she admired, who, in turn, gave her samples to wear so their clothes could be showcased. She rarely bought anything retail; getting things free or wholesale was a game for her. She enjoyed the thrift of it, and she enjoyed seeing her suppliers' merchandise move rapidly into the homes of her friends.

Clark shared few of her pleasures. He went to the races and the parties, the yachting trips and the elaborate weekend outings (at San Simeon, for instance), but reluctantly and infrequently. When he had free time, he wanted to hunt, fish, or shoot, and the undemanding companionship of kindred spirits. Ria went with him on many sporting trips, but mostly as a spectator. She would sleep in the sleeping bags and cook over an open fire, but she wasn't one to get into a pair of waders and submerge. Clark had been introduced to the magnificent Rogue River in Oregon, and a lodge there called We Ask U Inn, owned by "Rainbow" Gibson, a legendary guide and fisherman, and his wife. Over the years, the Gibsons were as much a family to him as any he'd ever known, the inn a faithful refuge. When he first went to the inn, he was charmed by the Gibson children: three daughters, ages ten to fourteen. Many years later, he dated (or courted, or befriended) the middle daughter, Carol. For close to three decades, Clark challenged Rogue River salmon every spring, steelheads every fall. It would take a world war to keep him from his seasons on the river; such was his love and need for it. And if his spectacular career gave him no primary satisfaction, it did, at least, give him the mobility and freedom to be on the Rogue when the fish were running.

Clark Gable, movie star, could never really fathom people who didn't share his passion for the outdoors, nor they him. At the studio, his friends were men who would shoot or fish with him; the rest were potential enemies. He didn't walk the same ground with MGM's stable of brilliant, quip-a-minute writers, or the mini-rajahs of the pressure-filled executive bungalow. He also had a low tolerance for homosexuals. As Strickling puts it, "When there was some nance or fluff around him, he'd say, 'Get that guy out of here.' He had an obsession about pretty boys." Since the studio was heavily populated by literati, gray-faced moguls, and "fluffs," Clark's workdays were not exactly fraternity parties. He withdrew and became the man nobody really knew, and the man on whom no one intruded. "Very few people were close to him," Strickling says. "He was friendly and kind, but there were very few people that he really talked to."

He told Minna Wallis at the start of his celebrity, "Look, Minnie, before I did this, I was shoveling. It's no different from any other job. I start at seven in the morning, when I finish at the end of the day, that's that. I want my own life at home. No pictures, no talk, no nothing. It's a job that I do; I try to do the best I can . . . when I come home, it's finished."

He was, and would be the rest of his life, an odd sort to make it big in Hollywood.

22

Red Dust lay around the MGM shelves for nearly a year in various stages of development. Originally, the play by Wilson Collison had been purchased for John Gilbert, whose contract for four pictures a year for a million dollars, signed in his zenith year, 1929, didn't expire until 1934. Hunt Stromberg was the film's supervisor (the title "producer" wasn't used as yet; Thalberg didn't believe in it). A handsome, young, red-headed journalist named John Lee Mahin was the writer. A Frenchman named Jacques Feyder was scheduled to direct ("A sweet, delicate old-timer who didn't know too much," Mahin says).

The hot item of the film was Jean Harlow, the $1,250-dollar-a-week white hope Mayer had recently purchased from Howard Hughes for $60,000. Says Mahin, "Harlow was supposed to help Gilbert's fading image. Gilbert had a high, squeaky voice, and was too thin from drinking and everything else, and nervous because he was unsure of himself. If she liked him, maybe it would help. The banns were posted. We were starting the picture with about ten pages of script and were going to spitball it as we went along. Then I saw a screening of a new Gable film —I don't remember which one. I went to Hunt and said, 'There's this guy, my God, he's got the eyes of a woman and the build of a bull. He is really going to be something.' Hunt looked at me; I guess he thought I was queer or something. I was raving. I said, 'He and Harlow will be a natural,' and Hunt said, 'By God, you're right.'"

This, so the story goes, is how Gable was cast in *Red Dust* and this, it also can be interpreted, is how Gable helped push Gilbert into oblivion, and how Gable knew oblivion was always just a screening away, million-dollar contract or no million-dollar contract.

Once the working group of Stromberg, Mahin, and Gable, all men's men and a half, was established, Feyder had to go. He was replaced by Victor Fleming, man's man and three-quarters. This virile group guaranteed Clark comfortable working conditions, but he wasn't happy with the story line; he found it vulgar. Stromberg decided Mahin should complete a shooting script, and tailor it for Gable, so the film was delayed, and didn't start until late in the summer of 1932. The star still didn't like the story of the plantation manager, the whore, and the lady, but he was locked into it.

Mahin realized what few people in the trade recognized about Gable: that he was at his best when not taken seriously, and when his sense of the absurd was written between the lines. Mahin says, "When I'd write things like *Red Dust* I'd give the girl the cracks because Gable was funniest when he reacted. And he'd say, 'Gees, John, those lines are not particularly funny.' I'd tell him, 'But your expression when we cut to you—that's the funny thing. The audience doesn't really start to laugh—doesn't get it—until that big kisser of yours comes on and you're terribly uncomfortable or sore.' Clark accepted that." Mary Astor, the good-girl foil to Harlow's bad-girl in the film, also perceived this quality about Gable. "Clark's own native wry humor saved him from the unreality of being too good-looking, too manly and strong," she noted. It would take three years, and a loan-out film, to make MGM as aware of Clark's innate sense of comedy.

Gable and Harlow, who had no rapport whatsoever making *The Secret Six*, got along like a pair of bear cubs on *Red Dust*, causing the usual rumors around the colony. Clark's friends say today they don't believe the two were ever lovers, only playmates who understood every nuance of each other. Portraitist Clarence Bull reported that at their sittings, "They'd kid around and wrestle until I'd say, 'Let's heat up the negative.' And they almost burned it clear through. I've never seen two actors make love so convincingly without being in love. How they enjoyed those embraces. And the jokes and laughter."

Whatever the Harlow-Gable relationship, it was strong enough to survive an affair, had they had one. They both had an earthy and often self-deprecating wit. Both were aware of their physical appeal. Both were essentially frightened and lonely people.

Clark's attitude toward "Baby" was primarily protective. She was, when the film was made, only twenty-one. She had just been married to Paul Bern,* Thalberg's favorite studio sophisticate, but the marriage was already ominously unhappy. Near the end of the production, Bern killed himself, and the suicide set off a raging sex scandal, the only one of its nature in MGM history. At the time of Bern's suicide (Labor Day weekend, 1932), Clark was on a hunting trip with Harlow's stepfather, a fact Strickling hid to keep Gable from being dragged into the fetid mess. Five years later, when Harlow tragically would die of some mysterious illness, it would be in the midst of the sixth Gable-Harlow film.

---

* Bern was Harlow's second husband. At sixteen she married a twenty-one-year-old Chicago lad named Charles McGrew from whom she was immediately separated by her parents and his. In September, 1933, she married cinematographer Harold Rossen and was divorced from him eight months later.

It seems safe to guess that when Gable was cast with Marilyn Monroe in *The Misfits,* he had a feeling of *déjà vu.* Says Arthur Miller, "[He] was always understanding and full with Marilyn, who seemed to stand in the foreground of a painting whose depths went back into his own past and all the actors and actresses who had killed themselves for the illusory victories of the business." If Miller is right in his literary license, surely one of those actresses was Jean Harlow.

By the time Clark worked with her on *Red Dust,* he had become accustomed to the dishy ladies of the silver screen who swore like Army sergeants, wore no underwear, and iced their nipples to make them show through their silks and satins. After his first year at MGM, he called them all "Baby," though Harlow was the only official "Baby" on the lot. In fact, if there was anything that could well have put that all-knowing grin on the face of actor Clark Gable, it was the attitude about women around the studio. They were really so much meat on a hook—you want one, cut off a piece. If you got a bad slice, somebody would tout you onto a good one; there were pimps in all the woodwork. Howard Dietz, in telling a story about Carole Lombard, starts out: "I said, 'Get me a date for tomorrow night,' and they got me Carole Lombard." Whom did he order "Get me a date"? "Someone in the department, I don't remember," says Mr. Dietz.

Actresses' menstrual periods were tracked on a posted chart. "You could take off two days a month for cramps," explains Joan Blondell, "and everybody knew which days they should be." The wardrobe department had a shelf bearing a row of falsies (actually perfect replicas of bosoms) with labels on them. Whose boobs were real and whose weren't was public knowledge at the studio, as was who was a real blonde and who wasn't (both Harlow and Lombard reportedly bleached their pubic hair—were they not blondes, after all?). But which new starlet was whose latest lay, was a game to learn. Frances Marion wrote in *Off with Their Heads:*

> . . . we called the silver-platter girls "Moos" when they became the bosses' sacred cows. Often we would tip each other off: "Might be smart to write in a juicy part for So-and-So, she's L.B.'s latest Moo." Once, a male scenario writer, with a few drinks

under his belt, walked up to a luscious redhead sporting a diamond bracelet and a year's contract. "Who's Moo is oo?" he asked. She snapped back, "Don't get fresh with me or I'll tell Sam Katz on you!" And that's how we kept in touch with the transient love affairs on the Metro lot."

There was no way, however, to keep accurate track of the random humping. Once a man reached a certain level in the movie business—whether actor, writer, director, etc.—he was expected to screw everything that moved. If he didn't, his masculinity was in question, so sure as hell nobody was going to admit he wasn't getting his share, or worse, wasn't interested in his share. Clark Gable had to be a stud, just as Gary Cooper had to be, and Warren Beatty has to be today, and Jack Nicholson does, and Burt Reynolds does. Rumors of an affair between Gable and Harlow, like rumors of affairs between Gable and nearly every other leading lady in his career, had to circulate because no ordinary mortal could imagine that the sex god and sex goddess would not couple—to the accompaniment of lightning, thunder, and shrieking stallions, of course. But maybe—just maybe —each knowing how much the other had to prove and how often—Clark and Baby did each other a favor and declined. Gable, for certain, avoided sex goddesses in his early career. In the days, for instance, when Lupe Velez was the in-group's favorite tootsy, Gable rejected a third party's offer of her services. "She'll be all over town telling everybody I'm a lousy lay," he said. He preferred females who wouldn't be demanding, and who would be grateful rather than critical. (His rival stud, Gary Cooper, was not so shy; he accepted Lupe, and got rave notices. Gable got back at him, however. As soon as he could afford it, he bought a Duesenberg and ordered it be made one foot longer than Cooper's . . . Duesenberg.)

Rumors never did circulate about Gable and Mary Astor, despite what audiences considered their steaming screen clinches.

The kisses still seem convincing today, but they don't steam by any current standards because the Hays Office wouldn't let them. Though the Motion Picture Production Code formulated in 1930 by the Association of Motion Picture Producers didn't specifically prohibit open-mouth

kissing until it was revised in 1954, directors knew that a
kiss scene was subject to cutting if either kisser's lips
were even faintly parted. Gable kisses, throughout his
career, were so tight-lipped audiences could well have
wondered whether he was afraid his teeth would fall out.
He probably was conscious of this himself, because he
developed a technique—obvious in many of his films—
that involved holding his partner and subtly turning her
away from the camera so that their kiss wasn't seen head-
on.

This kissing taboo, which helped a whole generation
of women believe being "soul-kissed" was tantamount to
losing virginity, is one of many handicaps pros like Gable
learned to act around. Since reality was potentially dirty,
sex symbols were caricatures, sex scenes were fairy tales,
and human relationships were absurd—all products of a
censorship which, good or bad, funny or sad, was awe-
somely hypocritical. No industry has ever been so pre-
occupied with sex within its walls, while so concerned
that everybody outside those walls stay clean. "Pictures
shall not infer that low forms of sex relationship are the
accepted or common thing," the Code ordained. "In general,
passion should be treated in such a manner as not to
stimulate the lower and baser emotions." A sampling of
the specifics:

Children's sex organs are never to be exposed.

Obscenity in word, gesture, reference, song, joke,
or by suggestion (even when likely to be understood
only by part of the audience) is forbidden.

Pointed profanity and every other profane or vulgar expression, however used, are forbidden.

No approval by the Production Code Administra-
tion shall be given to the use of words and phrases
in motion pictures including, but not limited to, the
following:

Bronx cheer (the sound); chippie; God, Lord,
Jesus, Christ (unless used reverently); cripes; fairy
(in a vulgar sense); hot (applied to a woman); "in
your hat"; Madam (relating to prostitution); nance;
nuts (except when meaning crazy); pansy; razzberry
(the sound); S.O.B.; son-of-a; tart; toilet gags; whore.

Undressing scenes should be avoided, and never
used save where essential to the plot.

Dances which emphasize indecent movements are to be regarded as obscene.

The treatment of bedrooms must be governed by good taste and delicacy.

Red Dust sneaked by the Hays Office because it broke no specific rules. It was, however, an erotic film for its time—because of the overt Mae West-ness of Harlow and Gable's pleasure in it. "Whatcha been eatin'—cement?" Harlow asks a parrot, as she looks in its cage. The humor is like that.

Really another class-war movie, with the slobs far more lovable than the swells and infinitely smarter, *Red Dust* was one of MGM's three big profit-makers of the year. (*Tugboat Annie* and *Grand Hotel* were the other two.) The picture, rushed into release to cash in on the Harlow-Bern news, was good for everyone concerned with it, and did wonders for Gable's manly image. Throughout most of the film he is damp and unshaven, with shirt collar turned up and shirtsleeves rolled above his elbows. In one uncharacteristic scene he is naked to the waist, displaying his beautiful, hairless torso (hairy chests were considered obscene, and it was as routine for male stars to have their chests shaved as it was for females to shave their eyebrows). In the climactic scene, when he rejects Mary Astor and she shoots him in passionate fury, he emerges the ultimate Gable. He snarls at her, "I'm not a one-woman man. I never have been and I never will be. If you want to take your turn . . ." Bang goes Mary's revolver. He clutches his side and snarls, "All right, if it makes you feel any better."

What a man.

In his next film he was instantly divested of his raunchiness, and given to Norma Shearer for stud. The picture was Eugene O'Neill's *Strange Interlude,* and strange it was. Thalberg supervised it himself, as part of his personal master plan to upgrade the level of MGM films, but the property was just too bizarre to be a digestible movie. The actors speak constantly; they have normal dialogue, plus they narrate their thoughts in voice-overs. The net effect is of people standing around twitching their eyebrows; in a word, awful. Clark, however, was pleased to be playing in an O'Neill opus, even though his role was simply to make a baby with Norma Shearer which she could pass off as her husband's. He and Shearer age during the film (there were eighteen tests made for make-up, costing $200 each), and the aging brings the first glimpse of Clark in a mustache. It soon became a permanent fixture, taking him once and for all out of the "pretty boy" class.

For his last film of 1932, Clark was loaned to Paramount in exchange for Bing Crosby, whom Hearst wanted for a film with Miss Davies (or Miss Davies wanted, as was rumored). The Gable picture was a slight, entertaining, typically thirties bit of romantic nonsense called *No Man of Her Own* about a big-city card shark who marries a small-town beauty on a bet. Miriam Hopkins was scheduled to be the lady of the picture, but she tricked out, and was replaced by Carole Lombard, a new acquisition for Paramount, and still an unknown quantity for that studio. The film was made swiftly and painlessly under Wesley Ruggles's direction, it got good notices, and it no doubt would have passed quietly into the archives if, four years later, Lombard and Gable had not become lovers.

There is no evidence of anything but an admirable professional relationship existing between the two when the picture was made. The twenty-four-year-old Miss Lombard was, as far as Gable could see, a young lady with a lot of preoccupations, none of which engaged him. She was the wife of William Powell, which took some concentration on her part; and a very ambitious actress. A pedigreed publicity hound, she put excessive energy into practical jokes that would have seemed sadistic if they so obviously hadn't been done to attract attention. At the conclusion of the film she gave Gable a gift of a large ham; nothing personal, she gave the same to countless other actors, always in the presence of a photographer. It was a typical Lombard gift; she specialized in ego-deflating.

Her campiness attracted a crowd of male homosexuals, her tomboyishness made her an easy friend for lesbians, of whom there were many more in the movie colony than has ever been discussed. She swore profusely, she kept a black dildo in her dressing room, she had a retinue of servants and sycophants fussing over her from head to toe. Her doting mother practiced the Bahai religion and kept two astrologers on retainer.

Fan magazines told more than anyone cared to know about her. The 1932 issues contained the details of her Jell-O diet; the fact that she had reduced from a size sixteen to a twelve with the help of a studio masseuse whose fees were deducted from her salary; and her vital statistics: 109 pounds, 34B-28-38, 6¼ glove, 4C shoe, leaving no alternative but to assume she was a skinny woman with a wide waist, big hips, and short, fat feet. In fact, she was gorgeous and had an incredible bone structure. She had once been overweight and was dedicated to seeing that never happened again. Reputedly a forerunner of the no-underwear school, she actually was one of the first American ladies to wear a nonporous rubber girdle that melted away fat—or, perhaps, strangled it. In short, she was a self-absorbed, interesting, but not fully formed human being.

And Clark was busy elsewhere.

23

Franklin Roosevelt was the new President, bankruptcies and unemployment were at a historic high, and Depression anxiety was so bad MGM asked all its employees to take a 50 percent salary cut, which they did, unnecessarily, for six weeks. Irving Thalberg was ill and off to Europe for his health. L. B. Mayer reigned unhindered, and brought in his son-in-law, David Selznick, as a producer. Double features and giveaways were offered as a last-straw come-on to dwindling movie audiences, and the repeal of Prohibition was imminent.

Times were changing.

Clark and Ria posed regally at premieres—he in white tie and tails, she in silk and mink—and went about living up to the public image of a matinee idol who was not an eccentric, only a god. They rented a new two-story colonial-style house in Brentwood—nothing "Hollywood," but something better suited to Clark's station in the colony.

There was more to the move than a status step. The public had learned where Clark was to be found on San Ysidro, and women gathered in packs outside the house like male dogs waiting for a bitch in heat. Women fought to get near him wherever he went, and the Gables had to be fast and clever to have any privacy whatsoever.

Strickling's role in their lives grew stronger and stronger. "You must remember that these people were in great demand for everything they did," he says. "They lived in a fishbowl. There were twenty Hollywood columnists, there were fifteen fan magazines, there were all kinds of photographers. There was such a great demand for the stars. Somebody had to channel all that, you know? Otherwise they'd get themselves in jams and things. Everything they did was news. There were so many demands on their time. So many requests for them to go to parties. Clark would talk to me and say, 'What'll I do; so and so wants me to go to so and so?' You would try to help them duck things."

The Gables also learned to appreciate the fleet-footed MGM police department, which, at its peak, had eighty-seven policemen, four captains, two plainclothesmen, one inspector, and one chief, Whitey Hendry—in all, a larger force than that of Culver City, where the studio was located. Each member of the force was trained to recognize all contract players. Each was required to salute when passed by a star.

Obviously, the MGM army was supposed to protect the company's priceless galaxy from the public. But Hendry's twenty-four-hour-a-day job was to protect the stars from themselves. If they committed murder, rape, or ran over a cat, Hendry had to beat the local police to the scene, where he would be met by Strickling or Ralph Wheelright, who would beat off the press. He had informants in the local police department, and friends in police departments of major cities all over the country.

Ria depended on Hendry and company to keep the new house free from gawkers and to return her husband intact should he get drunk and into trouble. The cook and maid the Gables had hired also knew to rely on the family cops. Should anything happen, the help was instructed, studio police were to be called—no one else. Thus buffered from a percentage of realities, the Gable household functioned as though it were a normal one. Clark complained about family finances, Ria spent freely anyway, to keep up with the rapidly expanding Hollywood social set.

The family itself expanded, in a most unpredictable way. William Gable joined it. The circumstances of that event are mysterious. One source claims Clark spent years trying to locate his father and then, finding him, months trying to persuade him to come to Hollywood. Reporters seem to have found him with no trouble at all, however. One newspaperman, early in Clark's stardom, located Will and wrote that he ran a gas station in North Dakota. Later, fan magazine writers published long personal interviews with him, mentioning that father and son had not seen each other in ten years.

Certainly it was easier for William to find his son than vice versa. Once Clark became famous, he was found by a whole tribe of relatives, some of whom were authentic Gables living in the Los Angeles area.

Jana believes that the man she called Grandpa Gable showed up in California under his own steam, and was reconciled with his son by Ria. She says, "Mother was a great family person and she believed in family ties. She thought that Clark's father should be welcomed and have a place in her home, and that's the way we operated and that's what happened. He didn't have any money at all, as I recall; that's why he moved in with us. They built another bath and gave him my younger brother's room. Then they made the sewing room into a bedroom for my brother and he shared a bath with me. Grandpa wasn't a bit well when he came to live with us. Mother also fixed him up with clothes—I mean, she probably didn't pay for them but she went with him to buy. He lived with us fully a year, possibly longer. He gained weight and looked fine. He was sweet; we all liked him. I don't think Clark thought about it much one way or the other. I don't think he had much closeness there. But he accepted it."

What Clark "accepted" was his father's consistent contempt for the way he earned his living, and his pressure to buy oil leases. What he no doubt told his father was what he would tell anyone who passed by: that he was going to make his bundle and run before the balloon burst. Once his father was on the scene, he said more often than ever to Ria that he wasn't an actor, he was a personality, and he couldn't last. If only he could be Walter Huston, he said—to Strickling as well as to Ria. "You are

an actor," Ria assured him. Strickling took a different tack.
"They line up to see you out there, not Huston."

His father's appearance was the landing of Clark's al-
batross. Almost from the moment William arrived, nothing
went right, and a lot went wrong, It couldn't have been
a worse year for Clark to be cast in a series of numbing
films, but that's precisely what was happening. With Thalberg away, he was fully available to David Selznick, and
Selznick didn't grasp the Gable character in any way at
all.

His first move with Clark was to pair him with Helen
Hayes, whom MGM had just acquired, in a melodrama
called *The White Sister*. Where Garbo seemed in danger
of being shredded by the force and size of Gable, Miss
Hayes seemed in danger of being squashed by him. Miss
Hayes also had a peculiar effect on many men around
her; they didn't know whether to treat her like a grandmother or an infant. Eric Portman once remarked that
working with her was like walking barefoot on mice. Gable
became hopelessly self-conscious in her presence. She
remembered thirty-five years after they worked together
that Clark was always trying to hide "his big, scarred
hands" from her. In *White Sister*, he looks as if he's trying not to step on her. It was nothing that carried over
socially. Ria liked Helen as a friend and a dinner guest and
met no objections from Clark. But Gable and Hayes as
screen lovers—that was something too implausible even
for fans to accept. The picture was released in late February, 1933, and died at the box office.

Clark escaped Selznick briefly, to work in a Sam Wood
production with Harlow, *Hold Your Man*, but that was a
mixed consolation. The picture started out tough and
sexy, with Gable a con man and Harlow his female
counterpart, but it was forced into a maudlin ending and
wound up a lily-livered film that frustrated both stars.
Mayer's fine hand had made the unfortunate twist.

Clark was turned over to Selznick again and assigned
to a stock company exercise called *Night Flight*. Multi-star
films were becoming important to MGM. They were popular with audiences looking for the most they could get for
their money, they were a good place to try out new talent,
and they kept loose actors off the streets. This film, unfortunately, had none of the *éclat* of *Grand Hotel* and
Dinner at Eight, though it had no less than two Barrymores

in it: John and Lionel. There were cameos, also, for Robert Montgomery, Myrna Loy, and William Gargan. Incredibly, Clark was paired again, in his minor role, with Helen Hayes, which may explain why in most of his scenes in the film he is sitting in a mocked-up airplane cockpit. The film was just short of a fiasco and by the time it was finished, Gable had developed a distrust of Selznick that would metastasize with slow but deadly progress over the years.

Clark carried home his anger at the way his career was going, but found no solace there. Father Gable responded to his complaints with nagging: "Kid, why don't you get out of this silly business and do a man's work?" Ria, according to some observers, began to treat Clark like a little boy who'd eaten too many toll house cookies. Though as Jana points out, "She believed in his talent, and pushed him and encouraged him when he was terribly depressed and upset," she had tired of his chronic anxiety and became condescending. Mary Astor's husband, Franklyn Thorpe, told Charles Samuels about hearing Ria give Clark instructions for a dinner party. "Honey, please try to greet our guests as though you were glad to see them," Thorpe claimed Ria said. "Clark told her wearily, 'Ria, you should know these people care nothing for me. They do not come to see me. They come to see a label. The day I lose my popularity you won't be able to get them to our house without a police warrant.' She listened to him all right. But as one does to a child."

Clark's general distress was compounded by the fact that he didn't feel good. In early spring he had an attack of appendicitis which he chose to ignore. He could not, however, ignore the persistent pain in his teeth and gums that frequently was so bad he couldn't eat. He could not ignore it, that is, when he was sober. So he increased his daily intake of gin. The more he drank, the more he and Ria fought. Minna Wallis recalls, "They came down the hill from Jack Gilbert's house one night and they had a big quarrel because he drove badly and she said he shouldn't have been drinking. It was an awful scene and I thought surely they were going to separate afterward."

Separation from Ria was not imminent. Separation from Minna Wallis was. In his sour mood, Clark was a perfect target for the sweet talk of a smart agent, and one of the smartest was cruising him, a man named Bert Allenberg. Allenberg's powerful agency, Berg-Allenberg, handled both Wallace Beery, whom Clark envied for his salary, and Walter Huston, whom Clark envied for his versatility. The agency also handled directors Jack Conway and Wesley Ruggles, whom Clark liked, and Sam Wood, who had been his recent refuge from David Selznick. Berg-Allenberg had, in fact, most of MGM's talent as clients and was watching the growth of Gable very carefully. "We were rather predatory," says Phil Berg today. When the agency was ready, it would have Clark Gable. For the moment, it didn't like some of the things he was doing, and neither did he.

To add embarrassment to his discomfort, Josephine surfaced with another right to the ego. Having exhausted all fan magazine publishing possibilities on the agonies and ecstasies of being the ex-Mrs. Gable, there was but one obvious angle open to her by-line: critiques of Clark's acting. In July, in *Motion Picture*, appeared two "Open Letters to Clark Gable from his Former Wife" beginning "Dear Clark." The first, about his "screen voice," included these paragraphs:

> The other day a very pretty woman remarked to me that you should never try to play the polished gentlemen parts, only "the rough-guy" things; for although you could look the gentleman, you hadn't the voice.
> So, as soon as I had time, I found the picture . . . and watched it to see why she had said that. I watched it carefully, through all those reels of silly story, beautiful photography, handsome people, and unconvincing dialogue; and as I watched, I thought many things.
> . . . I am afraid that what the pretty lady said is true. I am afraid you have less variety of tone quality in your later pictures than you were using when the public discovered you and demanded you. And you are using a hard, brittle quality.
> . . . don't let the microphone and its demands fool you. Don't let that machine's need for a front resonance fool you into getting careless in your study of the characters you play. Don't forget what you learned so well about voice. Make that man you are

playing talk the way that man would in real life. You can. You used to. . . .

In the second letter, "About Clark's Acting":

. . . Are you on that screen to make a show yourself, merely letting the girls look you over, or are you there to make an entertaining show of the story?

. . . You remember, don't you, that fine old definition of acting?—"To act is to arouse in your audience the same emotions you are supposed to be feeling in the part you are playing." If people in the audience are not included in the varying emotions of the story, they don't get their money's worth, and they soon cool off. . . . Just sitting in silent admiration doesn't last.

I haven't seen *The White Sister* yet, but I've been told that although you have one or two very fine scenes, you are still doing those funny things with your mouth to make your dimples show, and that the audience is distracted away from the story in watching your mannerisms.

Aside from these growing mannerisms, your technique is excellent. You have never forgotten that technique, have you? You can still make a better entrance than anyone on the screen, and you make every move count, because your moves are right.

. . . Will you ever forget all those thousands of times you went in and out, and in and out, and in and out, until the right habit was established? And the foot positions, and the walks, and the turns, and the sitting, and the standing, and kneeling, and rising, and the exercises in holding attention and in reproducing emotion? And the hand studies? Those were hard for you. But no one would guess it now. . . .

. . . Personally, I think you should go back to the simple, straight-forward, fine acting of your earlier pictures. I think you should go back to a keen interest in presenting the man in the story, instead of presenting Gable. I think you should avoid acquiring facial mannerisms, and that you should "give a show," instead of "being the show."

. . . I remember so well how furious you used to be when I criticized you. And you would slam out of the tiny house and go off in the old car (I never knew where). . . .

So if you should come across this letter, and should slam out of your lovely home and race off in your beautiful car to wherever you go—perhaps later, you will really think carefully over your recent pictures and realize that perhaps you may be a bit on the wrong road, and will think deeply of your next roles and of what sort of men they are and will give us the truly fine work you are so well able to do. . . .

There was no way to escape Josephine, and no way to deny the truth in her assaults. But Clark didn't need her to tell him he was a personality, not an actor; that was his abiding self-assessment. Josephine had learned well, in her years with Clark, where he was most vulnerable. Ria, who read everything written about Clark from the time they met until the day she died, tried to screen this kind of material from him, but she couldn't always do it. When the "letters" were published, Clark was at work on another film, and surrounded by friendly studio folk who couldn't wait to tell him how *dreadful* they considered Josephine's behavior.

He was, once again, making a picture he had fought against doing: a Selznick production, *Dancing Lady,* which, with Nelson Eddy and Fred Astaire in their film debuts, was one of the biggest profit-makers of 1933. Joan Crawford was his leading lady, but even the glow of her adoration didn't help. Clark considered his part "a gigolo role" and griped about it loudly. He was tired of playing prince consort to studio queens, and tired of being billed beneath them. He did his job in the film, but kept aloof from it in his fashion. Shooting lasted sixty-five workdays. When it was finally over, on June 20, Clark was hospitalized.

The official report was that he had an appendectomy, a tonsillectomy, and exhaustion. He may, indeed, have suffered all three. There is strong evidence, however, that it was his teeth that leveled him. Mrs. George Hollenbach Jr., widow of the renowned Los Angeles dentist Clark used all his Hollywood life, says today that Clark first visited her late husband in the early thirties. Her husband told her, she says, that Clark's teeth had rotted, and his gums "were very, very bad—almost malignant."

She says, further, "He [Dr. Hollenbach] advised him to have his teeth extracted and then wait a month because his gums were so bad. They had to heal before they would put his new dentures in." As Mrs. Hollenbach recalls hearing from her husband, he removed all of Gable's teeth in one siege. He may, however, have left a few natural teeth which were capped and removed later. Jean Garceau, whose close association with Clark began in 1939 and lasted until he died, says, "It was my understanding that C. G. had a partial denture, as I can remember that he still went to Hollenbach every once in a while to keep some back teeth that the denture was attached to." Mrs. Hollenbach also mentions Clark's regular visits to his dentist over the years, some of them purely social, as dentist and patient shared a passion for sports cars, and Clark would tool over to George's whenever he got some dandy new specimen. Mrs. Hollenbach remembers, particularly, Clark's coming by with a super Jaguar. She also remembers Clark's flying back from Africa, while making *Mogambo*, because he needed work on his teeth (real or unreal or both) and wouldn't let anyone else do it.

Whatever the case may have been (and it has become nearly federal over the years), Clark didn't work for ten weeks, an unprecedented event at MGM, and one that put him on Mayer's delinquents list. Mayer suspended him without pay from June 20 to August 27.

Clark resigned himself to his physical condition in those weeks, but didn't retire from his personal interests. He made one move, in particular, that had to have taken some groundwork: he joined the Masons. Becoming a Mason is not a simple commitment. Even understanding it is not simple. "Freemasonry," as defined in a Masonic encyclopedia,

is an oath-bound fraternal order . . . deriving from the medieval fraternity of operative Freemasons; adhering to many of their ancient charges, laws, customs and legends; . . . inculcating moral and social virtues by symbolic application of the working tools of the stonemasons and by allegories, lectures, and charges; the members of which are obligated to observe principles of brotherly love, equality, mutual aid and assistance, secrecy, and confidence; have secret modes of recognizing one another as Masons when abroad in the world; and meet in lodges, each governed somewhat autocratically by a Master, assisted by Wardens, where petitioners, after enquiry into their mental, moral, and physical qualifications, are formally admitted into the Society in secret ceremonies based in part on old legends of the Craft.

No one is invited to become a Mason. A man who wants to join must request a petition from someone already in the society. Clark did not have to look farther than his guest room to find a petitioner; Will Gable was a Mason, and darn proud of it. Joining the Masons was one of the few things Clark did in his life with his father's help.

Considering his affinity for pursuits considered manly, it is easy to see how Clark could be attracted to a ritualistic organization whch boasts thirteen United States Presidents as past members. And it must have been the actor in his soul that allowed him to participate wholeheartedly in ceremonies for which otherwise gray-suited men donned satin robes, fake beards, and ornate crowns. With requisite pomp and ceremony, in the Beverly Hills Lodge, he became an Entered Apprentice on September 19, moved up to Fellow Craft on October 17, and to Master Mason on October 31. He then chose to "continue his education in a variety of additional degrees and/or fraternal orders" as a Masonic pamphlet puts it, and within a year, received (or achieved) degrees of the York Rite: Royal Arch, and Knights Templar. Still later he became a shriner, joining the Al Malaikah Temple of the Ancient and Arabic Order of the Nobles of the Mystic Shrine.

Participating in these initiations had to be like appearing in a D. W. Griffith spectacular. For instance, a Masonic handbook describes a Royal Arch chapter room as "representative of the Tabernacle erected by Prince Zerubbabel and his associate near the ruins of King Solomon's Temple preparatory to the erection of The Second Temple." There is also the information that "Masters of the Veils are guardians of the approaches to the Council sitting in The East and work of the veils is an important part of Chapter ceremonies which include passing the veils, and the reception of the three sojourners from Babylon." Clark was a "sojourner," wearing a full dress suit and a white apron framed with scarlet braid.

It could be supposed that he went through these incantations to advance his career in some way, but that is not consistent with the way he chose his male companionship. It is more likely that he took his membership seriously, and that ideals, like the Mason's "kindness in the home, honesty in business, courtesy in society, fairness in work, understanding and concern for the unfortunate, etc.," genuinely moved him.

John Lee Mahin had an enlightening experience with Clark when they were in the Air Force together:

"We got a three-day pass just before going overseas, and we went to the Colorado Springs Hotel. We were just going to have some comfortable beds, and some drinks, and if there were any females around, boy, we're going to have three days, you *know*. We were sitting in the bar and we saw a very attractive girl, around twenty-five, and another very attractive older woman (around thirty-eight, forty; she had gray in her hair). With them was a dog—you know, glasses, sensible shoes, and a bun. Eventually we said, 'Come on, girls, have a drink,' and the next thing, we went up to our rooms. They knew who *he* was, of course.

"They were getting awfully giddy. The young, pretty one, he had his eye on, and he was sitting on the couch with her. I got the older one, nice girl. Every now and then he'd turn from his girl (he had his arm around her) and he'd say, 'How you doin', honey? Is John giving you enough to drink?'—to the dog. Suddenly, he stands up and says, 'Okay, sorry, the party's over.' We all looked at him like he was out of his mind. His girl says, '. . . but that doesn't make any difference,' and he says, 'Sorry, Honey, out you go.' They left.

"I asked him, 'What in the name of God? . . . we could have had a lot of fun.'

"He said, 'Her husband's a Mason.'

"I said, 'Her husband's a *Mason?*'

"He said, 'Yup.' And he went to bed."

William Gable never did know how much his own values meant to his son.

24

Frank Capra, gentle man and one of the first creative directors in the history of cinema, believes that "a film about the making of *It Happened One Night* would have been much funnier than the picture itself," and film buffs could well wish he had chosen to make it before his lamentable retirement in the mid-sixties. The saga began long before Gable entered it in November, 1933, with the purchase of a magazine short story by Samuel Hopkins Adams called "Night Bus." Capra and his writer-man-Friday, Robert Riskin, had read it, and requested that their studio—Harry Cohn's lowly, struggling Columbia Pictures—buy it, which it did, for $5,000. The property was shelved so long before Capra could get to it that when he reread it he forgot what he had liked about it. The moment he chose to go to Palm Springs to work on it the farce went into action. Capra remembers it all today, but defers for details to the version he wrote himself—and reasonably; people have been asking him about *It Happened One Night* for more than four decades.

"Like hell you're going to Palm Springs!" roared Cohn between flailing his riding crop and barking into telephones for the benefit of his captive audience. "You're going to Culver City—to MGM. . . ."

"Not unless I can produce my own show, as I do here."

"That's not in your contract."

"I don't read contracts. Besides, what about *Night Bus?*"

"Forget bus pictures. People don't want 'em. MGM and Universal just made two bus operas and they both stink."

. . . I went to MGM; this time not as a scared "B"

director, but as a protégé of Vice President Irving Thalberg. . . .

But, protégé or not, MGM always gave me the queasy, uneasy feeling I had entered a strange world that denied rationality. . . .

I didn't envy or scorn Irving Thalberg. Like everybody else I fell in love with him—and he with me. From the dozens of scripts he had me read I chose *Soviet,* a strong melodrama. . . . Thalberg promised me a "dream" cast: Wally Beery, Marie Dressler, Joan Crawford, and Clark Gable—wow!

Nearing *Soviet's* starting date, frail Thalberg had to go to Europe for health reasons. Left in sole command, Mayer couldn't wait to harpoon Thalberg's pet projects. He canceled *Soviet,* sent me packing back to Columbia, but he still honored the loan-out of one of MGM's stars. Without Mayer's hatred there would have been no *It Happened One Night.*

Capra returned to his studio determined to make a comedy called *Night Bus* "trends or no trends," and took off for Palm Springs with Riskin. They laughed themselves through the gags they scripted, changed the story's title, and went back to Cohn.

There followed several executive conferences, much politicking and wrench throwing, until Cohn finally gave the okay to cast the picture—over the dire predictions of all his executives.

"Who can play the girl?" Cohn asked.

Capra reminded him that MGM owed him a star, and suggested Myrna Loy. She turned it down with Mayer's blessing: "I never ask one of my little girls to play a part she don't want." Margaret Sullavan, Miriam Hopkins, and Constance Bennett also turned it down.

Capra and Riskin then made key revisions in the script. *Night Bus* had been the story of a spoiled heiress and a bohemian painter. It became the story of a bored heiress and rebellious reporter. (Heiress, running away from home, boards a bus to New York. Reporter, having just been fired, boards the same bus. They pool their meager funds, share motel rooms, wind up broke and hitchhiking. Reporter turns in heiress, but love and humor conquer all.) The hero and heroine now infinitely more sympathetic, Capra started casting again, and this time decided to try for a male star, figuring a top male would lure in the right female. The script was sent to Robert Montgomery, and contracts drafted for his loan-out. Suddenly, however, Montgomery was withdrawn and Gable named as the "star" (later, "co-star") of Capra's film. It was a Mayer maneuver.

Clark had reported back to the studio after his illness in fighting form about his suspension. He would not play any more gigolo roles, and he would not play anything at all unless he got a raise. He didn't shout it to Minna this time, he went to Strickling, Eddie Mannix, and Ben Thau; who went to Mayer, who had an Olympian fit. Almost simultaneously, the gods and Harry Cohn provided Mayer with the perfect punishment for his house ingrate. He would send Clark Gable to Columbia (e.g., from Abercrombie and Fitch to Klein's) to appear in Cohn's lousy bus picture. Screw Gable, screw Cohn, screw Capra, screw Thalberg. Fantastic.

When Cohn called Mayer to weep about the loss of Montgomery, Capra reports, the conversation went like this:

"But, Harry, Montgomery says there are too many bus pictures. And Herschel, no offense, stars don't like changing their address from MGM to Gower Street. But, Herschel, you caught me in a good mood. I got an actor here who's being a bad boy. Wants more money. And I'd like to spank him. You can have Clark Gable."

"Louie, 'spose he don't like the script?"

"Herschel, this is Louis Mayer talking. I'm *telling* you to take Gable."

Cohn informed Capra it was Gable or nothing, and Capra understood. "Whenever Mayer sneezed, Cohn took aspirin. Cohn *had* to make *It Happened One Night* now because Mayer wanted to punish 'bad boy' Gable by forcing him into a Poverty Row picture—exile to Siberia for hoity-toity MGM stars."

Clark knew nothing of the comedy behind the comedy. How could he, when no one was laughing? He had been shafted. He was humiliated and he was blindly angry. In a luxurious rage at home, he told Ria he wanted to quit MGM. She pointed out that he was under contract, and would never get another job in films if he breached it. He said he didn't care. Tired of his petulance, she then said that perhaps it was time for him to open his little shop

in Ohio. That remark ended all conversation with him for
several days, during which he did little except drink.

At his first meeting with Capra, he was both inexcus-
ably drunk and unforgivably rude. He said, for instance,
"I always wanted to see Siberia, but damn me—I never
thought it would *smell* like this. Blech-h-h!" ("It stinks
like a flicker's nest" was a favorite expression of Gable's,
but he was probably too drunk to be poetic.)

Capra was steaming himself. He said, picking up a
script, "Mr. Gable, you and I are supposed to make a
picture out of this. Shall I tell you the story, or would you
rather read the script yourself?"

"Buddy," Clark replied, "I don't give a fuck *what* you
do with it."

Capra tucked the script under Gable's arm, watched
him careen out the door, and hoped he would never see
him again. There was no way, however, for that to be the
case. Mayer had sent him as a gift marked not return-
able.

With Gable still thrashing like a decked marlin, and
just as effectively, Cohn sent Capra casting for Claudette
Colbert, who was under contract to Paramount, but
about to start a four-week vacation. Colbert had made
her first film with Capra in 1927; it had been a disaster
she'd never forgotten. The atmosphere was so hostile when
he went to see her even her poodle attacked, biting him
soundly "in the tail." Nothing could keep her from her
vacation in Sun Valley, she shouted. Nothing. Except
$50,000 and a written commitment that the film would
be shot within her allotted four weeks.

She got herself a deal.

The picture rolled the last week in November, and,
owing to a remarkable spirit that infected both cast and
crew (who often worked through the nights), wrapped
on the eve of Christmas Eve. Capra insists that the rhythms
produced had nothing to do with anyone's suspecting the
film was "a masterpiece." He may be right, or he may
not have realized that some message was getting them
all subliminally.

After a few days of working out his anger at Mayer,
Clark turned into *Night's* clown. He frequently broke up
in a take where the humor hadn't been obvious until it
was played. One day, rehearsing a close-up with Colbert,
he put a hammer down the front of his pants and then

pulled her to him in a clinch not in the script. When she let out a scream that brought everyone running, he took out the hammer and laughed so long Capra had to call a second lunch break.

"Clark turned out to be the most wonderful egg," Capra says. "He just had a ball. What I believe is that he was playing himself, and maybe for the only time in his career. That clowning, boyish, roguish he-man *was* Gable. He was shy, but a lot of fun with people he knew. He was very sensitive about those God-damned ears, but he made jokes about them. After a shot, he'd ask, 'What'd they get—an ear?' He didn't look like anyone else. It was not only physical; he had mannerisms that were all his own: ways of standing, smoking—things like that—and a great flair for clothes. Whatever came natural to him, I let him do."

Certainly the Gable of *It Happened One Night* was the most relaxed Gable seen in any of his films to that date. The role draped over him the way his custom-made clothes did: with casual perfection.

What he wore in the film became important American fashion: a Norfolk jacket, a V-neck sweater, a snap-brim hat with the brim adjusted to his moods, a trenchcoat with the belt tied instead of buckled.* What he didn't wear was more important. In a motel sex-tease scene he gives Colbert a lesson on how men undress and strips down to his pants. He wore no undershirt because it would have been impossible for him to remove one with any grace, and it was essential for him to look naked enough to threaten Claudette's virtue. Audiences assumed Clark Gable wore no undershirt because real men didn't wear them. Within a year, the impact of this minor dramatic business was felt by underwear manufacturers, who complained in a group to the film industry that Gable's bare chest bankrupted a small but stunned portion of the garment industry.

Gable seemed larger than ever in the film, and that was Capra's doing. Filmgoers hadn't comprehended his

---

* Clark considered a trenchcoat his "lucky coat" and wore one in nearly every modern film in his career. Burberry made him one in 1939 for *Comrade X* which he used for twenty years. In MGM's public auction in 1969, the Burberry was put on the block, and a representative of the firm sent from London to buy it. The coat, however, was sold to an anonymous bidder for $1,250.

size before because other directors stood actors on boxes around Gable. Capra juxtaposed him with normal-sized men standing flat on the ground, and Gable dwarfed them.

But as Capra points out, there was nothing manipulative in his intentions. He didn't plan to make Gable a bigger man, or T-shirts obsolete, or a fad of pipe smoking, or arks of buses, or a hit tune of "The Man on the Flying Trapeze." He just wanted to keep his project rolling and finish "the bloody film." When he did so, the only congratulations offered were for meeting his deadline. Clark, certain he had had a good time making a flop, geared for his return to MGM. Life would go on as though *It Happened One Night* hadn't happened at all, except for one thing: Mr. Gable would divorce his agent.

Frank Capra was a client of Berg/Allenberg, and kept them abreast of his surprise at Gable's versatility. Capra believed Gable had a storehouse of talent that hadn't been tapped yet. When he had a rough cut of the film, he ran it for the agency. Allenberg turned to Berg and said, "I'd like to get him." Berg told Gable the agency wanted him. Allenberg told Minna Wallis Gable wanted out. Berg went to Ruth Collier and Minna and said, "We'll give you twenty-five thousand for Gable's contract."

That's Phil Berg's story.

Minna Wallis says, "Not true. *Not true at all.* I wish it had been. Money never entered into it. Clark and I talked it over thoroughly. Then I talked to Bert Allenberg, who was a darling man—used to golf with Clark—and we decided, that's what he wants, that's what he can have.

"Well, I was just a woman. This was big organization. I was upset; can't say I wasn't hurt. But Clark was the one to be considered. And if he had stayed with me, he would have been unhappy no matter what I did, and I probably couldn't have done the things Bert Allenberg did for him. Bert *worshipped* him, and he was crazy about Bert."

Phil Berg insists money was exchanged. "We didn't steal clients," he says, "we bought them. In fact, I was the one who *started* buying contracts."

Whether Clark was bought, stolen, or given away, he signed with Berg/Allenberg, but remained a friend of Minna's all his life. Rumors still persist that they were lovers, but proof of that is as impossible to produce as the check that passed from Berg to Wallis. "It was a relationship that is difficult to explain," Minna says. "I adored him, just adored him. He was sweet and wonderful to me always." She gestures around the living room of her Palm Springs home. "Look at the pictures he gave me. They're all signed, 'I love you.' He came to my house a lot because we were very dear and very close. Clark, George Brent, Errol Flynn, Jack Barrymore—they looked on me as a mother figure, I guess; I don't know.

"I remember one night he came here for a dinner party. We were playing cards or something and he said, 'Minnie, who's that handsome guy in that picture over there?' I said, 'That was you, twenty years ago.' He loved to tease me; he was my friend. This is typical: I was having a romance with George Brent. There was a problem or something—I don't remember—and Clark called. I was crying. He said, 'What the hell's the matter, Minnie?' It was a very hot day and he lived over in the valley. I lived in Beverly Hills, but before you could say *anything*, there he was, with a pair of trunks on, no top, in this roadster. And he said, 'Come on, tell me what it's all about.' "

He owed her a lot. It is to his credit that he seemed to know it.

25

They would show him who was boss, all right, all right. Four weeks in the slums was only half his punishment. The rest of it would happen in his own back lot. Bad Clark. *Bad.* They sent him a wire to report to MGM before the year ended. And told him to shave his mustache. It was like being in the Army.

He was assigned to play a dedicated, unsmiling intern in *Men in White*, and he threw himself into the role full tilt. Clark could take himself very seriously when anyone else did, and *Men in White* was *serious,* the way "Marcus Welby" is serious. Myrna Loy was his co-star; and that, at least, was a happy event. They had met before, and had, from the start, a special relationship that grew better with each of the seven films they shared. Miss Loy lights up, recalling their first meeting.

"Minna Wallis (he was her baby) called and asked if I wanted to go to a Mayfair party. I did, of course; they were charming parties. Everyone in the industry belonged to the Mayfair Club. It was started because there wasn't anywhere we could go to dance; it was impossible being exposed to the public. Just film people belonged and we met once a month for a dinner dance at a hotel. The press was there, too, of course, we never did anything without reporters around. Anyway, I went with Minna and Clark and Ria were there. He had *arrived,* you realize, and Minna was hysterically proud of him. I thought he was marvelous looking. Minna introduced us and I said, 'My ears stick out, too.' He laughed.

"He was a good dancer . . . 'Dancing in the Dark' we danced to. Isn't it funny that I remember?

"It seems incredible that we were never lovers. We never were; we were friends. He was very gentle with me. I was like a little sister. He could also get very annoyed with me. I was very unrealistic, he thought—always falling in love.

"I guess he wasn't my type."

He was Elizabeth Allan's type, and she his. A nubile English beauty, with a small part in *Men in White,* she was his souvenir of the film, or maybe the first notch in his belt for 1934. "Clark had a Babbitt mentality about sex in those days," says Anita Loos. "That old, early American male idea that you must take on any girl that comes your way."

It was more complex than that, but he was, indeed, quick with the requisite pass. Typically, Zita Johann recalls meeting Clark at a Hollywood party, the first time she'd seen him since *Machinal.* "He came very late, dressed informally. He wanted to talk about old times and we went to a room where we could be alone. You know how some men are; they think they have to make a pass—they're almost obligated to. He tried and I got out of it. It was nothing objectionable, but there just was no

attraction for me, or for him. He was really very detached.
His wife came in and sort of took over."

Ria did her best with a very difficult role: the little wife
who shouldn't be there. As soon as *Men in White* was
completed, MGM sent Clark on a cross-country promotion
tour. Though Ria went with him, there is no mention of
her existence in any of the dozens of newspaper features
the trip spawned.

In New York, they stayed at the Waldorf, pampered
and adored. It was the first time they had been back to
Manhattan together, and both tried to recapture the
magic the city had originally bestowed on them. They
shopped, ate out glamorously, and went nightly to the
theater. They had a good time, but there was a mighty
difference in their lives that probably was clearest to
them where they had memories together. There could be
no strolling hand-in-hand up Fifth Avenue; Clark had to
keep his hands free to sign autographs. There could be
no whispered criticisms of a play quietly shared; Clark
had to stand up for applause between acts. He didn't need
Ria to pick his clothes anymore; store managers stumbled
over themselves to see that he got only their best. Women
didn't just look at Ria with envy in the restaurants; they
came to the table and groped at her husband. Crowds
gathered in the streets to see him. Women of all ages stood
crying outside the Capitol Theater where he made personal appearances—crying because they'd seen him, crying because they hadn't.

Escorted by studio flacks, whisked about in limousines,
guarded by New York's finest, he was the most gracious
of idols: laughing, smiling, waving, kissing when kissed,
loving when loved. The message was getting to him: they
are cheering for *me*. They know *me*. They want *me*. Intellectually, he knew—with a perception that belied both
his age and his profession—that the crowd cheering him
today could trample him tomorrow. Emotionally, he was
reached deeply enough to wonder, Am I who I am?, and
to surrender to the wish: Yes, I am.

What interviews he gave, he gave in Howard Dietz's
office, flanked by MGM publicists. Reporters could see
him, but got little from him except inanities and plugs for
Men in White (never a word in any of the interviews
about *It Happened One Night*, scheduled to open mo-
mentarily at Radio City). Some of the quotes might have

been credited "coached by Josephine Dillon," whether they were studio handouts, or words Clark actually spoke, as claimed:

> I like to play any part that offers definite opportunity for characterization. I don't care how large or how small it is, if it is a part with a purpose, or a part that enables the player to get and hold audience attention while he is on the screen or stage. And I like roles that give a good entrance. I feel if you can get on there in a manner to get audience attention, the battle is half won.

Even in a brief press conference, the New York entertainment press got the full Gable message. Noted Regina Crewe in the New York *American*, February 11, 1934:

> . . . If he likes you he'll give out. If not, he's mum as a mollusc. If you click with him he's all grins and dimples and laughing blue eyes. If not he can scowl most effectively. For he can be tough. As tough as gentle. I'd rather have him for a friend than foe.
>
> The secret of his appeal is an open book once you've met him. For women he combines the boy quality with a wealth of forceful, virile manhood. . . . For men his magnetism is a matter of being all masculine. . . . Broad-shouldered, deep-chested, he's irreproachable in white tie and tails. But you know, too, that he's at home in boots and windbreaker. . . .

Across the country the reactions to him were the same: female hysteria both contrived and spontaneous; and press acceptance, peppered with surprise and reluctance. Gable evoked the Valentino syndrome—women sneaked into his hotel rooms and his bed, fans stole his cufflinks, watch, handkerchiefs, bathrobe—but he wasn't Valentino, the store dummy. The artifice of all the matinee idols who had preceded him was gone. Gable was the main attraction of the freak show, but he wasn't a freak. Gable, the man, was better than Gable, the fantasy.

He genuinely, desperately wanted to shut out the sounds he heard, and not be changed by them, but he was a man trying to stay afloat in a tidal wave. There was too much, just too much; too many willing women, too much fine wine, too many mornings after, and too much guilt. He wanted to be free of Ria and responsibility, free to test his wings and potency, but the tether she provided was the only lifeline he could see. Sometimes, going home to Ria seemed the only safe thing he could do. Mobs of frenzied fans were great when he was protected and they were controlled by a studio, but when he was beset unexpectedly, that was something else. A Los Angeles businessman named Marshall Schacker remembers, as a boy, going with Clark and Ria's son Al to the Venice Amusement Park: "Gable was mobbed in a way he usually wasn't—people reaching for him and screaming. I was so frightened I started to cry. Then I looked at Clark. He was trembling. We ran into the reptile house and waited —it seemed like hours—till the crowd went away." A grown man, a man's man, can't cry. But the impulse had to be there.

Clark still needed Ria, and she knew it. However, the tether had to grow longer and longer. "Mother was conscious of Clark's carousing, but tried to rise above it," says Jana. "She was that type of person. Even if she felt he was having an affair she was willing to overlook it." One of Ria's routine chores, now, was to issue a denial that she and Clark were splitting. Is the story ever any different for the wife of the people's choice?

With no fanfare whatsoever, *It Happened One Night* opened at Radio City, on February 23. It got mild reviews, ran for one week (NO SECOND BIG WEEK HOLDOVER), and moved into local theaters. Within a month it became the must-see film that critics re-reviewed, magazines overfeatured, and the public stood on line to see over and over and over. Why, one ponders in retrospect, had no one in Lotusland realized how starved the grieving world was for comedy? Why did no one know that in the cold, dark months *It Happened* was being shown, movie theaters were a refuge for families without fuel, men without jobs —people who had ten cents to spend for warmth and found a double feature longer-lasting than two cups of coffee? Anita Loos offers a simple answer: "Depression? Who knew there was a Depression? We didn't know anything that was going on, we were working too hard. At MGM we were together all day and half of the night. We had our cliques, yes, but everybody was so busy, you just didn't have time for anything except work and worry about work. It was like this—I'll never forget in 1940 . . . some of us were sitting around listening to the radio and they were talking about the fall of Paris. We had all been to Paris, and loved it, and some of us cried. Aldous Huxley came by and wanted to know what was going on. I said, 'We're sad about Paris.' He said, 'Why, what's the matter with Paris?'

"We survived on disinterest."

So as millions laughed and sang at the adventures of Colbert and Gable, Gable was at work as Blackie, the gambler, in what the *Hollywood Reporter* declared was "the type of role he does best: a do-gooder gangster." The film was *Manhattan Melodrama*; the producer, David Selznick. A youngster named Mickey Rooney debuted in the picture. Myrna Loy and William Powell co-starred, looking awfully good together to director W. S. ("Woody") Van Dyke. In his hands, and under Hunt Stromberg's supervision, they promptly became Mr. and Mrs. Charles in *The Thin Man*. Clark proceeded into *Chained*, a shipboard soap opera with Joan Crawford, who had proceeded, off screen, to the new man from three previous films, Franchot Tone. She became Mrs. Tone in October, 1935.

Romance—the legitimate kind—made its way, too, into the house in Brentwood. Father Gable was courting his brother's widow, Edna; and Jana had fallen in love with a young doctor in Houston named Tom Burke. Jana, independent even as an adolescent, needed nothing from her family. Will Gable, however, needed all the help he could get. Clark made arrangements for his father to be given $500 every month, and agreed to buy him a house so he could marry. Clark could afford the handouts—the studio had exercised an option that raised his salary to $3,000 a week. He resented them, nonetheless. It seemed now that for every gesture his father made, he paid. Will, for instance, soon after he married Edna, ordered a small marker for Addie's grave in Chestnut Corners. Clark knew the marker had been placed when he got a bill from Meadville, from John M. Grizzie Memorials.

By mid-summer, about the time Thalberg returned to find himself nearly powerless at MGM, the success of *It Happened One Night* finally got through to Mayer. An order went out to get some humor into the firmament, and Clark was dispatched to *Forsaking All Others*, with

noted comedienne Joan Crawford and Robert Montgomery.
Rosalind Russell, Charles Butterworth, Arthur Treacher,
and Billie Burke were also dispatched; the stock company
was expanding in every direction. It was the last Gable
film to be released in 1934, and one of the pair of overt
comedies Clark would make for MGM before the powers
decided to take him seriously again (*After Office Hours*,
with Constance Bennett, released in February, 1935, being the other).

Forsaking All Others opened Christmas week and delighted the critics. That good news, coupled with the
sustained excitement of *It Happened One Night*, plus an assignment to work next on *Call of the Wild*, a story he
loved, put Clark in an unusually generous mood for the
holiday season. Jana recalls, "He gave Mother a robe and
gave me a robe, not quite as fine as Mother's. He gave
me a pair of perfume bottles, quite lovely, and he gave
her a pair of lamps, quite lovely. Then he bought me a
ring, and he got her a finer ring. Now that's three gifts; I
think that was very lovely. Mother actually told him he
had bought too much. She never spent so much money
on me, you know."

It was a particularly memorable Christmas for Jana, not
because of the gifts, but because it was the last she ever
spent with her stepfather.

It was Clark's last Christmas with Ria.

26

The 1934 Academy Awards were scheduled for presentation on February 27, 1935, at a dinner at the Biltmore Hotel in Los Angeles. Nominees for awards in
fifteen categories were announced on February 23. *It
Happened One Night* was nominated in the five categories considered major: best actor, actress, director,
writer, and picture.

There were only three nominees for Best Actor, all of

them MGM contract players: Gable, William Powell (for *The Thin Man*), and Frank Morgan (for *Affairs of Cellini*). Claudette Colbert competed for Best Actress against Norma Shearer and Grace Moore in the official nominations; Bette Davis was entered into the competition as a write-in on many ballots.

It had been such a vintage year for the industry that twelve films were nominated for Best Picture. Unpretentious *It Happened* was up against such heavies as *Barretts of Wimpole Street, Cleopatra, House of Rothschild, One Night of Love, Gay Divorcee,* and *Viva Villa. Of Human Bondage* and *The Merry Widow,* not in the running for best picture, competed in other categories.

Clark, amazed that he was nominated, scoffed at the notion he had any chance to win. His role was not a serious one, and none of the seven previous Oscar-winning actors had been in a comedy. He wasn't even a sentimental favorite. One week before the nominations were announced he had returned from location shooting for *Call of the Wild*, where, for the first time, he had behaved unprofessionally—showing up late and unprepared—and gotten into open battles with director William Wellman. Rumors had spread from Mount Baker, Washington, where the company had been snowed in for weeks, that Clark was shacked up with Loretta Young, and that their romance, not the weather, was the cause of the expensive delays *Call of the Wild* was experiencing. Indeed, Clark had been guilty, at least, of excessive clowning around, which Miss Young, at the least, had found totally endearing. When she complained about his "string of cuss words" he whittled her a billy club out of balsa wood and suggested she clobber him with it every time he swore. One of the many "funny, sexy jokes" passed around was a doormat made of rubber bosoms stationed outside Gable's dressing room. Ria was upset by the stories which had filtered down the mountain, and the industry gossips thought it a bit much that the married Mr. Gable had become an item with Miss Young because Miss Young and the married Spencer Tracy had been one.

Under the circumstances, Clark suggested that wild horses could not drag him to the dinner, where he and Ria would be the main course. What Ria read into the circumstances was that the Gables had to show up—he in white tie and tails, she in a gown and orchid. Jana, in all innocence, pleaded with Clark to attend because she believed he was going to win. And somehow the two of them convinced him.

Claudette Colbert was so sure she wouldn't win that she booked herself on a train to New York the night of the presentations. It is a favorite Academy story that she was whisked off the train by a group of Columbia enthusiasts, appeared at the dinner in her beige travel suit, cried when she accepted her Oscar, then dashed back to the train, which was held in waiting for her.

One thousand people attended the dinner, another six thousand wedged into the Biltmore lobby, thousands more stood in the street outside the hotel. It was the kind of crowd that gathered to gawk at all major film events, but it was a night like no other to that time in Hollywood. In recent years, television audiences have witnessed the kind of joyous hysteria that mounts as one film wins award after award. This was the first such happening.

Master of ceremonies Irvin S. Cobb orchestrated the mood, opening sealed envelopes the contents of which were guaranteed secret for the first time by Price-Waterhouse. In time, he was shouting into the microphone "You guessed it. It's something that . . ." and the guests in the Biltmore were shouting back: "Happened One Night." Robert Riskin took Best Writer; Frank Capra, Best Director; Claudette Colbert, Best Actress; Clark Gable, Best Actor; and *It Happened One Night,* Best Picture. It would be thirty-five years before another film would capture as many top awards (*Patton,* of all things, in 1970), and no other co-starring actor and actress would win simultaneous Oscars until 1975.

Clark found the event threatening. As he was led from the podium, clutching the Oscar, he mumbled to no one except himself: "I'm still going to wear the same size hat . . . the same size hat."

One day, ten years later, a six-year-old boy named Richard Lang was playing with a toy car in the study of Clark's house in Encino. He found that a funny-looking gold statue on Clark's desk made a perfect target for his car, and played with the car and the statue all afternoon. Most of the time the car killed the statue, but sometimes it missed. When it was time to leave, Richard decided to ask if he could take the target home. He took the statue off the desk and carried it to his "Uncle" Clark.

"Hey," he said, tugging at Clark's sleeve, "you want this thing?"

Clark looked down at Richard, and blinked at the sight of his Oscar in the boy's hand. Then he smiled and said, "No, you can have it."

Richard's mother was in the room, visibly embarrassed. "Clark, don't be silly," she said. And to her son, "Put that back where you got it."

It was a charged moment, Richard looking from his mother to his friend and back again. Clark shook his head. "No, no, you keep it," he said to the boy. Then, to his mother, "Having it doesn't mean anything; earning it does."

Clark gloried in his award; the world gloried in him. It was one large step for common mankind, the knighting of Clark Gable. A large step, too, for fun and balls and sex appeal—and exiled actors.

He had made *Call of the Wild* on loan to Twentieth Century. For the remainder of his years at MGM, he would make only one other film on loan, and that to W. R. Hearst, to whom he had a long-standing commitment. In March, 1932, Hearst had wired Irving Thalberg from San Simeon: "If we are nearing date for next picture should we not be considering cast, especially leading man? Can we have Clark Gable again or is he permanently alienated or appropriated? W. R." Thalberg responded with an assurance that W. R. could have C. G., but by the time Clark was available, Hearst had gotten mad at Thalberg for casting Norma Shearer in two stories he wanted for his Marion, and moved Miss Davies, her bungalow, and Cosmopolitan Productions to Warner Brothers. Thus Clark made *Cain and Mabel* away from home in 1936.

If there was any doubt about his status at MGM before he won the Oscar, there was none ever after. Immediately following the presentations, Phil Berg began negotiations for a new contract for him, and Clark became one of the sixteen designated stars of his studio,* with full star treatment: special dressing room, his own hand-picked crew, and an elite seat in the commissary—at something called the Director's Table. This large table was on a screened-in porch attached to the main dining

---

* Actually, there were eighteen official stars in 1935, but Mayer counted the three Marx brothers as one star.

area, and housed, daily, up to thirty people: three or four directors, a coterie of writers and department heads, and a very select trio of actors: Clark Gable, Spencer Tracy and Robert Taylor, the latter two just risen in the firmament. It was the studio center of pun and games, envy and macho. No actress ever sat at the table, or participated in the legendary ceremony that ended every lunch there. A cage of dice was passed, with the check, to the lunching men. Each man spun the dice—there were three, so the numbers ranged from three to eighteen—and low man paid the check.

One day Herman Mankiewicz rolled a four, and passed the dice to Donald Ogden Stewart, ordering him to roll a three and save him money. Stewart rolled a ten and said, "Only God can make a three." Such witticisms were cherished at the table, but in time they wore thin on Gable, as did being stared at by other diners in the commissary. Since his appearance at the table was compulsory if he ate at the commissary, he often chose, over the years, to eat in his dressing room, or if there was time, in one of the pubs near the studio. Clark's way of dealing with people or situations he didn't like was to avoid them. Strickling remembers, "If someone offended him, he'd say, 'Keep him away from me, I don't want to see so and so.' Or he'd say, 'I'm not having lunch at the commissary because so and so is there; he upsets me. I'm going to drive out and lunch someplace else.' Any time he didn't talk, or shine himself up, you knew to stay away from him. Next day it might be a whole different story."

Another member of Strickling's publicity department, Kay Mulvey, termed these withdrawals of Clark's his "black moods." That is what he went into when he was told he would play Fletcher Christian in *Mutiny on the Bounty* as soon as *Call of the Wild* wrapped. *Mutiny* was a Thalberg project; he had bought the property despite objections from Mayer. Charles Laughton and Franchot Tone were already signed for the film when he chose Gable, and there is some suspicion that Thalberg wanted him not because he thought he was right for the part, but because since his return from Europe he had tried unsuccessfully to get him away from Selznick. Selznick, now, was planning to depart from MGM to go into independent production.

Clark objected to the role on all possible grounds. He

feared his voice would sound flat against the British accents of the other players, that he would be upstaged by Laughton and/or the *Bounty*, that he would look absurd in knickers, pigtail, and shaved face. His main concern, however, was that Christian was too much a dandy; that in playing him he would finally make real his father's obsession with the unmanliness of acting. (Indeed, Marlon Brando proved how sissified Christian could be in the 1962 remake of *Bounty*.) It took the combined pleading of Thalberg and Mannix to get him into the picture, and, of course, *Bounty* turned out to be one of the most important films of his career, and one he most enjoyed making. The picture, an arduous production shot in eighty-eight days, was a big money-maker for MGM, and won the 1936 Academy Award. Gable was nominated for Best Actor, as Christian, but lost to Paul Muni as Louis Pasteur.

It was during the unusually long preparation of *Bounty* that Jana began planning her marriage to Dr. Thomas Burke of Houston, Texas. Jana wanted Clark to give her away, and planned her wedding accordingly. She says, "I wanted to be married in Houston because I had most of my friends there, and I had to be married during Lent because that was the only time Clark could come. He had finished *Call of the Wild* and was between pictures, as I remember. I couldn't be married in the church of my faith, which was the Episcopal Church—in those days you couldn't be married during Lent—so I was married in the home of my friend who went away to school with me, Nellie Green. Clark had told Mother he just didn't know if he could get here or not, and Mother was terribly upset because the invitations were out and so on. Everyone was agog because Clark Gable was coming to give the bride away. Frankly, when my engagement was announced, some of my friends didn't even know that Clark was my stepfather. I worked for a little organization called the Assistance League, which is sort of like the Junior League, and they couldn't believe it when I told them. I laughingly said I'd have to put a red sash around the white dress so they could see the bride.

"You see, he told Mother he didn't know if he could come or not, and he told me that he would be here and I expected him. He very definitely said, 'Yes, Sister, I will be there.' There again, he seemed to love to devil Mother about things."

Clark attended the wedding, paid for Jana's trousseau, and gave her a diamond bracelet which Ria designed. Jana would see him only once more, in 1938, when her son, Tom, was two years old. "I was in Beverly Hills visiting Mother and Clark heard I was there, I guess through the grapevine, and he called me. He was working at MGM and he sent a car for me. He wanted to see me and he wanted to see my son. He was very sweet with Tom. I remember he asked me if Tommy, my husband, had wanted this child to be a boy, and I said 'Yes,' and he said, 'I've never understood why men want sons. If I ever had a child maybe then I could be convinced.' I thought that was so strange for him to say, I really did. He picked Tom up, and just seemed to be pleased with the whole visit. And that's the last time I saw him. Some people said that Clark and Mother got a divorce because he didn't want to be a grandfather. I think that's ridiculous, really. I think even Clark would have laughed at that."

If any one thing dealt a final blow to the Gable marriage it was Oscar, the ultimate success symbol. With such tangible proof that he had achieved, Clark no longer needed Ria to reassure him he would, or to fall back on if he didn't. Ria had officially become what Joseph Mankiewicz observed as a classic casualty, the Hollywood wife, a woman of no identity, and with no function. Mankiewicz asks, rhetorically, what a star's wife can be: "Partner, wailing wall, even whipping post? Forget it. What with producers, lawyers, agents, business managers, publicity men, secretaries—his professional life and income are so compartmentalized even he doesn't know what they are."

As though thinking specifically of Ria, but speaking generally, Mankiewicz sees this kind of wife as "completely helpless." "Her physical attractions are faded; at their best they were no match for those, the best in the world, that beguile her husband relentlessly. Her man doesn't leave of a morning, after all, for a corporate structure in which he merely fills a niche. He goes off to a fun fair where he's the brass ring on the merry-go-round. He no longer needs her. Not at all."

Clark and Ria separated and reconciled a few times in the early months of 1935. As likely to get sympathy as a stroke victim in a subway, she was stoic about the separations. She let him go without a murmur, believing she was merely lengthening his tether until he could get over the magnitude of what was happening to him. His house had been quieted; Father Gable and Jana were in homes of their own, and Al was at military school. Selznick was gone from MGM, thus removing Clark's irritant at the studio. Ria believed Clark just needed time, and eventually all would be well between them. She was wrong.

He made *China Seas* with Jean Harlow, Wallace Beery, and Rosalind Russell, exhibiting in the production a new bravado. He was now going in for derring-do, refusing to let stunt men replace him in dangerous shots. One scene director Tay Garnett remembers in particular required the Gable character to harness a steamroller that was crashing around the deck of a ship: "Grinning, Gable dismissed his stand-in and said, 'I'm doing this one myself.'" Garnett couldn't stop him. "When Gable decided to risk his neck," Garnett notes, "his neck got risked." The macho paid off. When the film was reviewed in the *New York Times*, Gable was singled out as "outstanding." The reviewer wrote, "It is a role which demands vigor, an infectious, devil-may-care philosophy and the stinging passion of distempered blood, and while Gable has displayed these qualities before, it is one of his most convincing portrayals."

When *China Seas* was finished, Clark had his lawyers start a separation agreement for him and Ria. He then left on an extended trip to South America, where, to his surprise, he found he was even more of an idol than he was at home. He stayed several weeks, dashing from city to city and country to country to keep from being harassed. If he stayed too long in any one hotel, his room would be stripped by souvenir hunters, his exits blocked by hysterical mobs. When he could bear the mauling no longer, he flew to New York for a rest. There columnists spotted him with Elizabeth Allan, and a socialite named Mary Taylor, among others. When he disembarked from a TWA plane in Los Angeles on November 18, 1935, he made light of the New York romance rumors, but confirmed his separation from Ria. Shortly thereafter, all the world knew he had moved into the Beverly Wilshire Hotel.

Ria bought a house in Beverly Hills, hired a couple to help run it, and feathered in for a long wait.

PART FOUR

KING

(1935-1942)

27

For the first time in fourteen years, Clark Gable was without a woman to answer to, and the freedom was breathtakingly becoming to him. His power to set off currents in a room just by entering it, once noticed by a select few, now was felt everywhere he went. Women could barely look at him without blushing. "I think every woman he ever met was in love with him," says Loretta Young. Certainly, most women felt an immediate attraction to him.

Joan Crawford believes that at the time Clark wanted to break from Ria, he finally realized his effect on women and relished it. She also believes his ability to charm heightened as a result of the roles he played. "He knew where he was the minute he looked at a woman. He knew what he would get back from that woman if he gave her the right look; he'd seen that reaction on the screen too often not to know. And he loved it if there was a new woman around and he could walk into a room and hear her sigh. He didn't even have to hear—he could see.

"Let me explain something about people raised in films. We learned a lot from acting. I learned to read by reading scripts. I learned how to react—learned strength and humor—from parts I played. I would rehearse lines I had in a picture and use them for myself, let them become a part of me.

"I think Clark took the humor and sex from the characters he played. We all did it, but not consciously, believe me. Hepburn is still part *African Queen*, part *Philadelphia Story*. Barbara Stanwyck, she's always been strong, but she's taken this strength from her pictures. She's drawn on every character; I know her well enough to say that.

"The trick is not to lose your identity. To draw on the characters when you need them: the charm, humor, strength, this and that. We didn't know it, but we grew through the years, playing characters."

"He made you feel twice the woman you thought you were," says Ursula Theiss, who knew Clark later, in the years she was married to Robert Taylor. It could be a line from a Gable film.

Howard Strickling describes Clark's initial approach to a woman:

"The first thing he always did, you know, he'd look her over. She'd know damn well that he was sizing her up head to foot. And he was looking at her eyes and he was looking at her lips, you know, and she'd know damn well that he was sizing her up while he was squinting at her, and she'd wonder what this guy was thinking about, you know. He'd ask her a lot of questions about herself or something about her dress. Or he'd remark about something, like where did this come from? or why do you wear your hair like that? and he'd have a few laughs with her. If he sensed she didn't respond the way he expected, he might clam up a bit. But mostly, they responded, you know."

Joan Blondell still sighs remembering him. "He *adored* women—not in a lechy way; he loved beauty: soft hair, beautiful deep eyes. His eyes would sparkle when he saw a beautiful woman. And if he liked you, he let you know it.

"He was boyish, mannish, a brute—all kinds of goodies. When he grinned you'd have to melt. If you didn't want him as a lover, you'd want to give him a bear hug. He affected all females, unless they were dead.

"I remember being at a big party—I don't recall whose; somebody doing the tent bit. I was leaning against a bar. Something made me turn and look across the room, and there was Clark, framed in dames, looking a little uncomfortable, I'll admit. He kind of winked at me, as though to share his amusement. He couldn't take it all seriously. A lot of women tried to run him ragged. Even visitors at the studio were brash with him, rubbing against him, handling him. He had to be pretty *damned* level-headed."

He was that most cavalier, most desirable of men: a married bachelor, game for anything. Studio pimps all over town offered him starlets, and he accepted them as his due. On his own, he went after bigger game. For many weeks after he first moved into the Beverly Wilshire, he tried to topple Mary Pickford, only recently divorced from Douglas Fairbanks (who was making the scene with a willowy blonde named Lady Sylvia Ashley). Miss Pickford was an interesting choice for the newly freed Mr. Gable. Once "America's Sweetheart," she was now reigning Empress of Hollywood, mistress of Pickfair, a true living legend. She had been worthy of the god Fairbanks; she was worthy of the god Gable. She was eight years his senior, rich, and a very strong lady. (In all his life, Gable never made a lasting attachment with a weak one—or, after Josephine Dillon, a poor one.)

Clark, however, used the wrong approach to Mary. He called her only when her staff was off, and only to invite himself to her house. Miss Pickford turned him down for a month of Thursdays, and would qualify for the short list of women who didn't sit and stay on Gable's command, except for one thing: she later regretted her decision and suspected she must have been out of her mind to reject him.

She does give lie to the statement Clark's male admirers so often make about him, however: that he wasn't a chaser. Certainly, he was more often pursued than the pursuer, but he chased when the spirit moved him, just like any other mortal man. The statement repeated even oftener—"Clark never married anybody; they married him"—is a mouthful of caramels, impossible to chew, much less to swallow. Clark married whom he chose, when he chose. He was even turned down by at least two women he wanted to marry. What can be said (albeit ungrammatically) is that nobody divorced him; he divorced them.

At the time of his separation from Ria, divorce was not an issue. Clark had no reason to get one, and Ria believed she would never need one because Clark would eventually return to her. Under the terms of his seven-year contract with MGM (signed July 29, 1935, but retroactive to December 13, 1934), Clark was to earn $4,000 a week for three years, $4,500 a week the next two years, and $5,000 a week for the last two years, for a minimum of forty weeks a year. Should he make more than three films in those weeks, he would be paid

an additional $25,000 per film.* His separation agreement
with Ria gave her half of his earnings. He could no
longer afford to be as extravagant as she had considered
him.

At no time in the negotiations of the MGM contract
was there any discussion of Clark's getting a percentage
of the profits of his films. For one thing, Phil Berg believed "in cash, not percentages," and for another, MGM
and Twentieth Century had a pact never to give percentages, and to blackball stars who demanded them.

There did not appear to be any discussion, either,
about Clark's refusing an MGM contract to freelance
at $100,000 per picture—the going rate for movie stars—
which, if he had made at least three films a year, would
have given him substantially more money. Phil Berg
didn't believe in his clients freelancing. "Seven-year
contracts locked them in, yes, but they got sponsorship,
good material, and a continuity in what they did."

What Clark seemed to want from his career was the
security of guaranteed work plus guaranteed leisure.
He was assured, by contract, of a minimum of six
consecutive weeks of "lay-off" a year, and he was much
more protective of that time than he was of his earnings.
After 1935, he never exceeded three pictures a year. Had
he been interested in money alone, he could have pushed
to work more. In the first five years of his life in talkies
he made a total of thirty films. In the next twenty-four
years he would make thirty-six. For the success-oriented
who aren't driven by demons, not having to work every day
is the surest sign of accomplishment.

Clark ended 1935 with the making of an undemanding
"woman's" picture, *Wife vs. Secretary*, with Jean Harlow
and Myrna Loy. It didn't matter what kind of picture he
made; the public simply worshipped him. Near the end
of the year he had gone to San Francisco to make an
appearance at a premiere as a favor to Columbia Pictures. Marco Wolff, whose Orpheum Theater Clark graced
on this occasion, recalls the night as being like no other
in his memory. Local newspapers ran the announcement
of Gable's coming in banner headlines. The night of
the premiere such masses of people oozed into the streets

---

* An abridgment of the twenty-one clauses of this twenty-six-page
contract appears in the appendix.

near the theater that cable cars couldn't run. Inside the theater there was no way to quiet the audience. "It was pandemonium," says Mr. Wolff. "The M.C. tried several times to introduce other guests; he couldn't. The audience kept chanting: 'Ga-ble, Ga-ble.' Finally he shouted 'And now . . .' And that's all he could say. The whole house stood up and roared. Gable walked on stage and the audience just kept shouting and applauding. I have never seen such an outburst. They stayed on their feet and Clark said a few words. Then he walked off, dazed."

He could have believed he was permanently enshrined —had he been some other man. But it was elemental to Clark Gable to distrust, to anticipate inconstancy. Proof of fame's infidelity was all around him in the form of abandoned actors. Just ten days into the year, in fact, John Gilbert died at age thirty-eight, an alcoholic unlamented by the public that had chanted for him almost as loudly as it was chanting for Gable. Clark knew the graves on which he walked. Knew them all too well.

There was a newness, though, about life for him as 1936 began, and a promise. Freedom and status secured, anything could happen. He was a twenty-two-year-old thirty-five-year-old. "Cocky" is the peculiarly applicable word. "You wouldn't have liked me then," he told Anita Colby when they dated in the forties. He caroused to the limit of his physical endurance.

With the world more than ever his oyster, he rebelled more openly than ever at his first film assignment of the year, an adventure-love story called *San Francisco*, with the studio's recent acquisition Jeanette MacDonald. The film was her baby, and she wanted Clark as its father, wanted him so badly she waited without pay for him to be available. It was precisely Miss MacDonald, America's new singing sweetheart, that Clark objected to. Clark hated to be sung at; feeling it was one thing if you could sing back and defend yourself; quite another if you just had to stand and smile beside some prima donna.

There were features of the project that attracted him, however. His role would be one familiar to him and his fans: "Blackie," the gambler with a heart of unmined gold. His sidekick would be Spencer Tracy, whose acting skill awed Mr. Gable. The director would be Woody Van Dykes' "man's man" and one hell of a director. And the special effects would be the earthquake destruction of San Francisco.

Nevertheless, Clark was rigid about not appearing in the film until, as the story goes, Eddie Mannix told him that Jeanette had gone without salary to get him as a co-star. Such was his reverence for money, legend has it, that he could not deny himself to someone who had gone without it for his sake.

Clark's ultimate acceptance of the role did not end Miss MacDonald's sacrifices. Clark so openly ignored her existence anywhere except on camera that she occasionally broke into tears over his indifference. She asked one of the publicists on the film to find out what she had done to anger him. Clark said Jeanette ate too much garlic.

Did he really? Did she really? Clark was known to have had aversions to at least a handful of women in his lifetime. Columnists Sheilah Graham and Dorothy Manners were two in particular, both of whom committed their sins in print. Greer Garson is the only actress other than Miss MacDonald whom Clark reportedly couldn't abide, and Johnny Mahin suggests that was because Clark felt Greer "put on airs." Maybe Miss MacDonald also put on airs. Or maybe she didn't work when she had her period. Mr. Mahin mentions that as something else Clark couldn't forgive in an actress.

What must always be kept in mind about Clark Gable is that he was an actor, and an actor's emotional reflexes are as developed as a dancer's muscles. An actor's turning cold needs no more explanation than a dancer's leap. However, it is quite possible that Clark ignored Jeanette MacDonald because he was so absorbed by Carole Lombard he didn't need to exercise his charm on the set. To put it another way, it could be that his chronically itching ego—an affliction all actors suffer—was finally getting sufficient scratching. For by the time *San Francisco* was under way, so was Hollywood's nomination for the romance of the decade.

Gable and Lombard, Lombard and Gable. Clark and Carole, Carole and Clark. Even the Windsors were only the Duke and his Duchess. They were never David and Wallis, Wallie and Dave. They were never the king and his queen, like Clark and Carole, Carole and Clark.

28

Carole Lombard was a self-made, self-proclaimed original who seemed, in the mid-thirties, to live by the motto "Ain't nobody not gonna know who I am." On her own, and later in league with publicist Russell Birdwell, she made more waves on the West Coast than the Pacific Ocean. Kiss-assy with the press, she was never one to louse up an active evening with anything that wouldn't make the papers. Her publicized flamboyance reached such a peak by the time she became Gable's girl, she had to stay awake nights thinking of ways to one-up herself. In the wacky party department, the practical joke department, the dirty word department, she simply had no peers. "She was flying all the time," says Jean Howard, former wife of the late Charles Feldman. "Fast and light," Miss Howard terms her. Strangely, she wasn't considered fast and loose. Before Gable, Lombard was openly "linked" to only three men: William Powell, whom she married in June, 1931, and divorced, without alimony, in August, 1933; singer Russ Columbo (1934); and writer Robert Riskin (1935). Biographers claim she had her share of affairs, and if she did, she had them discreetly. "She wasn't a sleep-around girl," says Buster Collier, who was one of her many male buddies. "Anyway, a lot of guys were scared of her."

Gable wasn't scared. He was sexually curious. "He always liked the dishy dame," says Joan Blondell. Carole was the dishiest of them all. In addition to becoming the All-American Fun Girl since he had made a picture with her in 1932, she had also become one of the highest paid actresses in the business, and nobody could figure out how, because, unlike Clark, she had never—with any of her forty-four films—been one of the top ten box office attractions.

A former pie-in-the-face Sennett cutie, her image in

talkies was diffuse. She was most successful in the few comedies she had made, particularly, *Twentieth Century*, with John Barrymore, in which she could be both slapstick and droll. Producers didn't ask for *a* Carole Lombard, because they didn't know what that was. Carole really hadn't solidified as either an actress or a film personality when she caught Clark's fancy. She was classically celebrated for her celebrity.

It happens in the life of every Don Juan: the realization that all females being equipped with the same parts, the only fun in sex is the game of sex. Not "will I make her?"—that too often goes without saying—but how long will it take to happen, and how will it happen? Gable, when he homed in on Carole, was so bored with making out like Gable he went to a whorehouse for his pleasure. He also took the untaxing route of waitresses, script girls, and other anonymous females, whom he didn't have to call the next day. In recent years, stories have circulated that he was impotent in normal circumstances. Howard Strickling put that aside with "hundreds of women would testify to his virility." *Hundreds,* he said. Certainly, many of them would be testifying about the years after Carole. But that would still leave an unusual number with whom he performed before her.

Carole Lombard flickered on the periphery of his vision when she was dating Russ Columbo. He had tried to date her "on the side," as was his fashion in his marriage to Ria, but Carole wasn't interested. Like some golden trout he had glimpsed and missed, she stayed in his mind. If the chance ever came, he'd have to try for her. He never really could resist a challenge.

Carole started life as Jane Alice Peters in Fort Wayne, Indiana, on October 6, 1908. (As any astrology buff knows, that made her a Libra, and therefore right for Aquarian Gable.) She was the third child and only daughter of Fred and Elizabeth Peters, who appeared to be a well-matched pair of attractive, substantial citizens. Fred and Elizabeth, however, had problems—all, it is said, related to an accident Fred had had before the children were born, which left him with a bad limp and severe headaches. Fred was able to tolerate his lameness, but Elizabeth (known as Bess, Bessie, or Petie) was unable to bear his reaction to the attacks of nearly paralyzing pain in his head. When Carole was six, Bessie took her and the boys, Fred Jr. and Stuart, to California for a vacation. They never went back to live in Fort Wayne, and Carole grew up knowing her father only as an occasional guest in her mother's Los Angeles home. When he died at age fifty-nine in 1935, she did not attend his funeral, saying that her doing so would turn the event into a carnival.

Bessie was Middle-America bred, but pure California in spirit. Even quicker than she adjusted to the climate, she adjusted her life to the guidelines of Bahai, numerology, and astrology, passing her belief in the latter two directly on to her daughter. It was through some weird numerological calculations that Jane Peters eventually became Carol Lombard and, later, Carole Lombard.

Bessie and her children were a tightly knit, interrelating group, of which Fred Jr. (nicknamed "Fritz") was the one serious member. Carole was doted on by them all. She was a child the family couldn't get out of their hair: a questioning, hyperactive companion to her mother; a funny, competitive pest to her brothers, who were her first choice as playmates. Bessie wanted Carole to be a tap-dancing, beribboned little girl. Carole wanted to be one of the boys.

Director Delmer Daves lived on the same Wilshire Boulevard block as the Peters family when he was sixteen. Carole was thirteen at the time. Fred was seventeen, Stuart, sixteen. Delmer and the boys were what he calls "front door friends." He remembers, "We sat on the steps and talked boy-talk. Carole was the kid sister and really beneath our attention. She teased me about it later. She'd say, 'You son-of-a-bitch, you never bothered to move your God-damned ass off those steps and let me go into the house.' Carole, at that time, was not an attractive girl; she was scrawny. I didn't pay any attention to her, really. She teased me about that, too, when we —as they say—grew up. Carole, with her four-letter words. She said, 'You fucking bastard, you'd never even looked at me.' "

Daves didn't look. Movie producer Allan Dwan did, and, in 1921, cast Jane Peters in a Fox silent called *A Perfect Crime*. It was not the beginning of a spiraling career, but it confirmed Jane's ambition to be a movie star.

Lombard chroniclers usually insist that Bess was not a

"stage mother." It must be noted, however, that Bess had once aspired to the stage herself, and she enrolled her daughter in a Los Angeles dramatic school as soon as she was of age. She also did nothing to discourage her daughter from quitting school to try for a film career at age fifteen. And at the beginning of what would have been her junior year in high school, Bess Peters's little girl signed her first studio contract with her mother's full approval.

The contract, with Fox Films, turned the teenaged Jane Peters into a Jazz Age starlet named Carol Lombard who competed in Charleston contests at the Cocoanut Grove, nipped bootlegged gin out of flasks, cavorted with the richest boys in town, and in all other ways behaved like a fictional flapper. She loved dancing, tennis, and the shock effect of profanity—and was expert in all three. An actress who knew her in those years remembers being in a crowd with Carole and some beaus at an afternoon party. "The boys were talking in the corner, and they were howling. I said to my date, 'What are they laughing at?' He said, 'Carole,' and I said, 'What did she do now?' and he said, 'I can't tell you.' Well, I coaxed him a little, and he gave in. He told me that one of the guys had taken her horseback riding and when she came back she said, 'I don't know why the hell everybody thinks this is fun; it's like a dry fuck.' "

The fun and games—and the studio contract—ended in a single moment for Carole, in the winter of her eighteenth year. She and a date were in an automobile accident which shattered the glass of his Bugatti. A shard sliced through the right side of her face, leaving a deep gash from her nostril to her ear. The wound required fourteen stitches, which she endured in a four-hour procedure without anesthesia to have the optimum chance of not being disfigured. Her whole future, after all, was in her face. The healing process of the wound and subsequent plastic surgery took nearly a year, during which Carole saw only close friends and family. In that year, Fox dropped her option, and when she went back to work it was for Mack Sennett, as a rather chubby $50-a-week bathing beauty. That the accident put her at a crossroad in her young life is clear in this note she sent to tennis champion Alice Marble in 1934 when Miss Marble was in a sanitarium.

You don't know me, but your tennis teacher is my teacher and she has told me all about you. It really makes very little difference who I am, but once I thought I had a great career in front of me, just like you thought you had. Then one day I was in a terrible automobile accident. For six months I lay on a hospital bed, just like you are today. Doctors told me I was through, but then I began to think I had nothing to lose by fighting, so I began to fight. Well—I proved the doctors wrong. I made my career come true, just as you can—if you fight.

Miss Marble* became one of Carole's closest friends and most ardent causes. Being Carole's close friend often meant more than a casual commitment. It could be a life-style. A sort of gang buddy to all the Sennett players, Carole chose as confidante a six-foot, 250-pound clown named Madalyn Fields, whom everyone called Fieldsie. Fieldsie was in every way as dominating as Carole (the son Fieldsie one day would have waggishly called her "Captain Bligh"), as emancipated, as fun-loving and as smart. She was not, however, as ambitious, and when her days at Sennett looked numbered, she gave up her career to foster Carole's, becoming her business manager, secretary, and advisor. After Carole divorced William Powell, the two women lived together in Carole's Hollywood Boulevard house, giving rise to a rumor they were lesbians.

Carole was rescued from the declining Sennett productions in 1928 by Joseph Kennedy, who gave her a starlet's contract at Pathé, where she made the transition to talkies, and no impression whatsoever. Her option was dropped, she freelanced a while, and then in 1930 she went to Paramount with a seven-year contract starting at $375 a week.

Paramount used all its shopworn tricks to promote her, but her fortunes did not change until she became the favorite client of agent Myron Selznick, who taught her how to in-fight; the favorite mannequin of designer Travis Benton, who made her a clothes horse; and the wife of

---

* Alice Marble won her championships before female tennis players had a commercial value. She supports herself today by working as an athletic director in a senior citizens housing development in California.

William Powell, who gave her class. At no time was she an overnight sensation. No miracles of public recognition served her as they did Gable. Hers was a grueling, rung-by-rung climb over and around the crops of over-bleached Kewpies proliferating in Hollywood in the early thirties.

It is said that Carole turned herself into the post-Powell screwball the world came to know and love to hype her vacillating career, and that is probably true. The task, however, was not distasteful to her. No one had a better time participating in her capers than she did. She thought it was genuinely funny to serve guests at a black-tie party out of bedpans; to load her house with hay and wear pigtails at a formal dinner; to invite guests to view the work of her decorator, William Haines, and then empty the house before they arrived; to take over the Venice Amusement Pier to entertain a few hundred of the elite of Hollywood plus some great carpenters, grips, and plumbers. Indeed, she did show up at a party in an ambulance-borne stretcher, did tie a few directors into strait-jackets, did trick Myron Selznick into signing over to her 10 percent of all his earnings, did buzz around Paramount on a motor scooter, and more and more and more. It takes a tremendous amount of energy to power this kind of personality, and Carole had more than required.

Devoted to her mother, who lived in Brentwood with Fred Jr., Carole opened her house to all Bessie's poker players and fellow travelers in the occult. On any given Sunday afternoon, Carole's guests included at least two mind readers, an astrologer, a numerologist, and a tennis coach who was a lesbian. When Carole began talking about marrying Russ Columbo, a monumentally vain man with an unsavory reputation and a questionable career, some of the locals began to wonder quite seriously where her head was. And until Columbo was shot in an alleged accident and Carole started dating the apparently normal Mr. Riskin of *It Happened One Night* fame, some of them figured her to self-destruct before she was thirty.

Beneath all the weirdness (or in addition to it), there was Carole, the compassionate busybody, who couldn't bear anything to be wrong in the life of a friend. There are simply dozens of stories about her handouts to the fallen,

her discovery of the unrisen, her ministrations to the sick,
and her machinations in behalf of the underpaid.

Perhaps nowhere did she butt in so relentlessly as she
did in the career of Alice Marble who called her, as did
her other friends, Missy Carole. "Our backgrounds
were similar," says Miss Marble. "Neither of us had a
father, and both of us had older brothers we competed
with like crazy. The only thing that troubled me about
her was that she had such a good-sized entourage of
people I didn't like. But she was such a kindly person."

Alice was a semi-invalid when Carole met her, and a
sad sight. Once a natural beauty, she weighed 175 pounds
when she was released from the sanitarium, and had a
bad case of acne. Carole, for whatever mystical reasons, didn't believe Alice had tuberculosis and sent her to
a doctor who concurred, told her to lose weight, and get
back to the tennis court. Carole supervised her diet and
Alice lost forty-five pounds, after which Carol sent her to
a dermatologist who cleared her skin, after which Carole
decided Alice didn't know enough about clothes. To
rectify that, Carole sent her to USC to take a course in
costume design, and also took her to "a little tailoring
shop" to help her pick fabrics. "She'd almost always
wind up footing the bills and what could you do? She
wanted me to be so good. Every time I tried to pay her
back she said, 'Oh, shit, forget about it.' She was always
embarrassed when people wanted to thank her. So whenever I won a championship, I'd give her a silver tray.
I must have given her twenty-five over the years, and
she treasured them."

When Alice got back into local tournaments, Carole
was present to cheer her on, to promote her to the
press, and to present the trophy if she won. (Carole's
tennis game was, according to Alice, "Very good. And
especially good when the cameras were on. God, what a
ham. What a *ham*.")

Not content to see Alice succeeding at a game which
paid only in glory, Carole then told her, "Now, honey,
you have an awfully nice natural voice, and your footwork
is great. Why don't we just set you up with some lessons
at Paramount?" So Alice had vocal lessons, drama lessons, fencing and dancing lessons. Carole was the first
to congratulate her when she debuted as a dinner club

chanteuse at LaMaze's on Sunset Strip, just as she was the first to call her after she won at Wimbledon.

When Clark reeled in Carole, he didn't know just how rare a fish he'd caught.

29

Clark got his opportunity to approach Carole at a party given early in 1936. There are at least three versions of what that party was—a Jock Whitney gag party, a Valentine party given by the Countess di Frasso, or the annual Mayfair Ball benefiting the Motion Picture Relief Fund. More than likely it was the last, where Clark appeared with an MGM employee named Eadie Adams, and Carole was escorted by her favorite walker, Cesar (Butch) Romero. Louella Parsons reported that Clark and Carole danced and looked very cozy at that ball, given January 23, which one can accept or reject at will, but in any case, by the end of February, Clark was driving a white jalopy festooned with red hearts, which he bragged had been given him by his girl, Carole Lombard.

The attraction was instant and probably overwhelming for them both. Neither of them was unaware of the little matter of audience impact, and both had to realize how stunning they looked together. Many a beautiful couple has been initially stimulated by the image of what a beautiful couple it is. Clark and Carole, with arms linked, fairly shimmered. Helen Gurley Brown remembers the spectacle of that pair at a premiere as being indescribably awesome. Mrs. Brown was only a little girl when she saw them with the beams of spotlights crossing behind their heads—a very poor girl whose mother had scrimped to save the dollar each needed to sit in the stands erected for the public at premieres—but she remembers Gable and Lombard as being the most glamorous vision of her life, which has had more than its share of glamorous visions since. Carole and Clark could

WANTED
ITEMS DONATED TO THE STOREHOUSE
117 So. Brdy.

Auction will be August 13th

We need anything but clothes.
Will pick up.

Call evenings . . .
886-2216
886-7825
886-3260
882-1403

3. | **AUTO & TRUCKS**

WEEKEND
SPECIAL

CAR CORNER

1973
truck
speed
with
with
Sturg

'74 G
22,000

'68
Go

and

com-
ister

PETER
Kranzburg, S.
886-9333

© 1977 United Feature Syndicate, Inc.

have spent months just basking in the perfection of their joint reflection.

She found him different from what she expected: a shy man, a worrier—a man with a lifetime occupation of recovering from a traumatic youth. Clark found her more than he had expected. She was bottled soda shaken too hard and released—yes. But she was a sensitive, giving person who anticipated his every mood, every need; she was there before he could cry out. In no time at all, he was calling her "Ma" and she was calling him "Pa" or "Pappy." What strange terms of endearment for such a beautiful couple.

Noel Busch wrote for *Life* an on-the-spot description of Carole at the height of her romance with Clark:

> . . . She gets up too early, plays tennis too hard, wastes time and feeling on trifles and drinks Coca-Colas the way Samuel Johnson used to drink tea. She is a scribbler on telephone pads, inhibited nail-nibbler, toe-puller, pillow-grabber, head-and-elbow scratcher, and chain cigarette smoker. When Carole Lombard talks, her conversation, often brilliant, is punctuated by screeches, laughs, growls, gesticulations and the expletives of a sailor's parrot.

Clark must have felt he had a bobcat by the tail, or that a bobcat had him by the tail. All evidence indicates that he started out the pursuer and ended up the pursued (chasing Carole till she caught him, as it were), but there's no knowing what he would have done had she withdrawn her attention from him, because she was quick to move if there was trouble between them. There was, for instance, the matter of the gift she sent him the morning after a quarrel the night before. She bribed a Beverly Wilshire Hotel attendant to take a pair of doves to his room while he slept. He woke up with them fluttering over his head, had them caged and returned to her for safe-keeping. Ever after she sent him doves—live or fake—whenever there was need of a peace offering between them.

By the spring of 1936, the movie colony was aware that Gable and Lombard were a serious matter, at least on Carole's part. Mrs. William Wyler (Margaret Tallichet), who was a protégé of Carole's at that time,

articulates what was the community consensus: "It was
obvious to me right away that Carole was madly in
love with him. Just from the way she spoke about him,
I never saw them together. I can only say that I felt she
was enormously in love, and that she was going to see
that this situation was handled properly on every level.
As I look back on it now, I just think that she had such
enormous energy, you see—that was one of her main
qualities. When she would zero in on something, that
was it, and she wanted this relationship, so therefore
I am sure that on every level she was going to make it
come about. She was the driving force, perhaps because
she just had more energy than he did. Maybe it was
glandular, or I don't know what. Also, of course, she
wasn't stupid. She was bright, very bright."

They didn't have a great deal of time to spend together in the first year of their affair, because both were
going from picture to picture. Early in the year, Carole
was finishing the gaily romantic *Princess Comes Across*
and starting work with her ex-husband on *My Man God-
frey,* a Depression comedy that, in retrospect, is one of
the most vicious attacks on the rich ever produced in
Hollywood. Clark was into *San Francisco,* aching from
the combined effects of his loathing for Jeanette Mac-
Donald and his admiration for Spencer Tracy. So convincing was the image of Gable and Tracy as Quixote
and Panza (or Pinocchio and Jiminy Cricket) that it's
difficult to believe they made only three films together.
They were a rarity in film history: a pair of top male
stars, one of whom willingly played the eunuch. No
such thing exists today in the pairing of Redford-Newman,
or Newman-McQueen, or Caine-Connery, or Beatty-
Nicholson, etc., etc. Tracy, indeed, did tire of the role,
otherwise the combination might have gone on to become
Astaire and Rogers.

Clark and Spence worked silkily together, but they
caused each other a lot of grief. Strickling says, "Spencer
Tracy would have given his right arm to have been the guy
Clark Gable was—to be loved and respected and worshipped. Clark would have given his right arm to have
been recognized as the actor's actor, you know—what
Spencer Tracy was. But Clark Gable was Clark Gable.
This was one of the tragedies of his life; he couldn't
play character parts."

Most people at the studio thought the men were very close because they did so much kidding around. Tracy would hit Gable in a brawl and Gable would crumble hard to make Spence think he'd really injured him. Tracy would milk his big scenes so long Gable would shout, "Christ, die already, will you, Tracy?" Together they would visit a set where Loretta Young was working and tease her unmercifully. Miss Young thought they cared for each other like brothers; so did Joan Crawford. Howard Strickling, who knew better, terms them "friendly enemies." What they were, really, was rivals on Mt. Olympus, jostling each other on the box office attraction lists, challenging each other jokingly so neither had to be the first to draw a weapon. Anita Colby remembers that when she was dating Clark, Tracy taunted her about dating "such an old man." "I'm going to tell him what you said," Anita told Spence. "Go ahead," Spence replied. So she did, and Clark shot off a wire to Tracy: "I'll show mine if you show yours—birth certificate, that is."

It remained for Carole to keep Clark buoyed during *San Francisco*, a job she undertook with her usual enthusiasm. Whenever he was free, and she was, they went gadflying: the races, the Trocadero, tennis matches, boxing matches, skeet shooting, parties. They usually went alone because there were few friends that both liked, or that liked both of them. Fieldsie was skeptical about Clark; she thought he was a baby, and totally dependent for his existence on a strong woman. Had he been anything else, Carole probably wouldn't have been so in love with him, so Fieldsie's criticism was meaningless.

The more sophisticated (or pseudo-sophisticated) of Carole's friends found Clark dull. Mrs. Basil Rathbone, one of the elite hostesses of the village, thought "Clark and Carole were *divine* together, but Clark was a bit rough. He wasn't my type; I never went for rugged he-men." She didn't invite them to her parties but they crashed one of the formal ones, in fishing clothes. Carole's idea, of course; nobody snubbed *her* and got away with it.

Clark didn't like Carole's sycophants—some specifically, and the idea of them in general. Most of Clark's man's-man friends admired Carole for her ease in becoming one of the boys, but an occasional one found her language unbearable. Johnny Mahin, for instance, says, "There was so much more to her than the swearing;

that's what made me mad. She could be a gracious, charming woman. But I hate to be around girls who say shit and fuck. I hate it. I was always uncomfortable. I'd get up and leave. Carole always embarrassed me. Everything was fuck and shit, fuck and shit. Clark loved it. He'd laugh; never try to stop her. She'd never swear if there was somebody visiting on a set; she was very careful. It was only around what she felt was a pal, or the crew and the grips."

Even people who were amused by Carole's language found it bewildering. Says Margaret Wyler, "She was an absolutely eye-opening person to me because she was this curious mixture. She was beautiful, obviously—exceedingly beautiful—and *very* feminine and *very* glamorous, and used language like I had never heard. I had never heard anyone, male or female, talk like that.

"I used to puzzle about it because I found it so *unusual*. I was young and not terribly perceptive, but even then I understood that it had to have begun as a sort of defense mechanism. I really felt that, strongly. She would tell stories about crazy parties where, as a very young girl, she had been tossed into the wildest of surroundings. I felt then, and I feel now, that that was the defense she built for herself so as not to be as vulnerable as she probably was. This was something she'd picked up and grown within herself.

"I don't recall her talking that way when she was with her mother or brothers, or not as much, though it had become, to a certain extent, second nature to her. But you didn't feel it was something she was born with. It was a tool she had adopted.

One of the couples Clark and Carole enjoyed was Kay Francis and Delmer Daves, who, Mr. Daves says, lived together from 1935 through 1937. It was Delmer's impression that Clark was living in Carole's house, which he may have been, but his official residence was the hotel. "We were all chums," he says. "Kay was a free spirit like Carole, and Clark loved women who could make him laugh. Carole would invite Kay and me up to dinner. We sat in a big room which was, aside from the bedroom and kitchen, the only room in the house. We were fed the drinks and that kind of stuff. We'd tell naughty stories and get a little drunk—not really drunk, just high. Then Carole would say—and this was inventive and very

1936—'Is everybody hungry?' We'd never move from our chairs. The butler would come out and put a table with folding legs right beside you and serve the soup, and we'd go on talking and never move. Then the next course, and we'd be having a drink in between, and then dessert, and we'd never leave our chairs. We'd arrive, have drinks, eat, the tables were removed, and then we'd have our brandy and tell funny stories we'd heard on our travels."

What Mr. Daves seems to be crediting to Carole is the invention of TV tables, but the point is that Carole never did things the conventional way, which Clark admired about her even more than her friends did. He could never anticipate her. She was such a marvel to him he couldn't stop telling "Carole" stories. Long after she was gone, he told Howard Hawks about the first time he took her duck hunting. As Hawks remembers, Clark said: "We had dinner and some drinks and played poker and the guys just loved her—you know how she could talk; swear as good as anybody. We got up early in the morning to go out to the duck blind. It was foggy and you could hear the ducks and the geese honking up above the fog. We just sat there and she said, 'What'll we do?' I told her we just waited. She said, 'I can think of something better to do.' And we made love twice in the duck blind, which wasn't an easy thing to do."

The lovers simply couldn't be together as much as both wanted. Carole tried to synchronize her work schedule with his, but it wasn't possible without one of them going on suspension. Perhaps both should have. Clark had some free time due him after *San Francisco*, but Carole was scheduled into *Swing High, Swing Low*, with Fred Mac-Murray, a badly reviewed comedy. When Carole finished that, Clark was making *Cain and Mabel*, an extravagant vehicle for Marion Davies, the only good thing in which was a spectacular carousel W.R. later took to San Simeon to delight guests at a party. Carole was then loose, but Clark was dispatched on a promotion tour that nearly got him killed in New York where frenzied fans tried to over-turn his limousine, attempting to shake him out of it. After that incident, he wouldn't allow his accompanying publicist, Kay Mulvey, to ride in the same car with him.

Also, in June, Clark launched his career in radio—and the idea of a star-studded "Lux Radio Theater"—

appearing on the air with Marlene Dietrich in *Morocco*, for a fee of $5,000. He was such a hit he was then asked to launch "Camel Caravan" for $6,500 and all the cigarettes he could consume. He appeared with Madeleine Carroll, voicing *Men in White*.

Time magazine reported, in August, 1936:

> Easy-going and informal, Clark Gable is credited with breaking the Hollywood taboo against permitting audiences at broadcasts. . . . By the terms of his Metro-Goldwyn-Mayer contract, Actor Gable may make four annual commercial radio appearances. This year's two remaining broadcasts have already been engaged by Camel. This week, Actor Gable was thoughtfullly thumbing the scripts of *The Last Mile, What Price Glory?, Little Old New York, Journey's End* and *One Sunday Afternoon*. . . .

Actor Gable was a busy man, so busy he didn't have time to read the new book everyone was talking about, particularly in Hollywood, where David Selznick had bought the movie rights for $50,000. It was a first novel by a petite Southern lady named Margaret Mitchell. Its title was *Gone With the Wind*. Everyone said it was a woman's book, and anyway, how could he possibly read such a huge tome when he had to make a half-assed comedy with Joan Crawford (*Love on the Run*), keep taking bows for *San Francisco*—the biggest-grossing film MGM had ever had—and see his girl, who was a veritable dervish. Furthermore, his girl had moved into a Bel Air house where people couldn't see him seeing her quite so easily, and the trek from Beverly Hills was getting annoying. There was only one thing to do: rent a house near Carole's, and so he did, one owned by Rex Ingram, Howard Strickling's old boss. At some point he also went on a hunting trip and brought back a baby cougar for Carole. There was nothing wrong with Clark's energy, either.

There were so many of them in that small world they peopled who lived as though each moment were their last. Did they have some mass puritanical guilt about having so much for doing so little? What punishment did they all anticipate, and for what? Why was it that each time the bell tolled, the reaction was that it tolled for them all?

On September 14, 1936, Irving Thalberg died of pneumonia at age thirty-seven. In a recent book about him, former MGM story editor Samuel Marx recalled:

The studio closed Wednesday, when services were held at the B'nai B'rith Temple in Los Angeles. It had the grandeur of a great MGM premiere: crowds on the sidewalk watching for celebrities, Whitey Hendry's policemen keeping order, Howard Strickling's alert, sober-faced staff scanning each arrival, recognizing the notables, separating them from the nobodies, directing the select into the auditorium.

Clark Gable was an usher at the funeral.
The road to Forest Lawn was always paved with glory.

30

In the year 1937, Clark reached a degree of popularity it is difficult to imagine in this decade of anti-heroism. Public affection was given him in an unconditional way it has been given few but war or sports heroes in this country. Surviving film clips of his public appearances have the irresistible emotional tug of a ticker-tape parade. The crowds were euphoric with love; their idol stalwart, humble—worthy. The corny mid-thirties household phrase, "Who do you think you are, Clark Gable?" tells a lot about what the public thought Clark Gable was; in essence, a man beyond criticism.

His importance to MGM doesn't begin to be indicated by the salary the company paid him. He had become, as Clarence Bull puts it, "the big rock in the studio foundation." In the months before Thalberg's death, the producer was planning to leave MGM to form his

own company. As part of the impending agreement on his
departure, he was permitted to take with him a half-dozen
or so of the major stars—anyone except Gable. If he took
Garbo, he would have to share her with the company,
but anyone else would mean nothing to the survival of
MGM—except Gable. There was a tacit understanding
among all employees that Gable was to be protected and
comforted at all costs. Eddie Mannix and Howard Strickling were to be heeded without question because Gable
trusted them. Fieldsie's son, Richard Lang, now a television
director, says, "The secret of Clark's surviving his own
fame was that he was protected by the people around
him. If a building was falling, for whatever reason, they
would throw themselves over him. If I were to make a
film about a man like Gable, it would be the story of a
man who gets a car cheaper than anyone else. At first
this seems like luck, then it seems divinely ordained."

The studio's hovering was supposed to be so subtle
Clark wouldn't know he was being coddled. He had the
same illusion of freedom as a head of state taking a
walk through Central Park with a secret serviceman
behind every tree.

Mayer wanted a regular report on the progress of the
Gable-Lombard affair. He also wanted to be kept informed
on the temperature of Ria Langham. In addition to his
usual concern for the welfare of wronged wives, and
morally pure image of his stars, he had a mighty scheme
he was sure would one day hinge on the financial condition of Clark Gable. If there was ever a clue that
Clark and Carole wanted to get married, and that Clark
would therefore need a divorce, and therefore money—
he had to be the first to know. What Mayer wanted was
to get into Selznick's projected production of *Gone With
the Wind*. The people's choice for Rhett Butler was
Clark Gable, and only Clark Gable. To get Gable, Selznick
would have to borrow him. When he came for the loan,
L.B. could write his own conditions.

The more letters that poured into the studio (and to
Selznick) casting Clark as Rhett, the louder Clark insisted
he wouldn't make the film. He felt there was no way
he could play the part that wouldn't fall short of public
expectations. Carole did nothing to change his feelings.
She wanted to play Scarlett O'Hara, and she feared that
she would have no chance if Clark were cast as Rhett,

because Selznick wouldn't risk damaging his picture with pressure from inevitable groups of the morally outraged. Mayer needed a sword to hold over Gable's head. The threat of suspension would be that sword only if Clark were desperate for money. So the romance was being watched for reasons neither Clark nor Carole could suspect.

Ria was also unaware of the highly placed intrigue. She still didn't believe Clark was in love with Carole, and as long as they didn't do anything outrageous—which they didn't—she could still hold her head above the affair. Her path crossed that of the lovers occasionally; all survived the encounters. Ria told friends and family often over the years, "Clark never did anything to embarrass me." Ria had an impregnable dignity, and people that mattered respected her for it.

Clark started work in the new year on what, in present jargon, was an ego trip. It was time, all thought after the two mediocre pictures he had last made, that he had a property worthy of a great star, time for him to break from the predictable and show what a serious actor he could be. Unfortunately, with Thalberg gone, the taste level for "serious" properties at MGM had dropped several notches. Clark, when taking himself seriously, had no judgment at all.

What was acquired for him was a Broadway hit called *Parnell,* about the Irish Nationalist whose chance to lead his country to home rule was ruined by his involvement with a married woman. To play a historical figure in those days was as prestigious as a fan magazine writer publishing in *Saturday Review.* Clark was flattered by the project and even agreed to work with a "heavy" director (John Stahl) with whom he neither hunted nor boozed. When he learned that Joan Crawford had refused to take the role of his lady-love, he stopped speaking to her and remained icy toward her for five years.

Myrna Loy, who took the part Crawford rejected, thought *Parnell* was a lovely story and a lovely movie. She might be the only person alive who thought so. Early in the production, cast and crew had listened to a rebroadcast of the Duke of Windsor's abdication speech. Miss Loy suspects the event colored Gable's performance. The mood on the picture was consistently melodramatic. "I learned about another side of him at that time," she recalls. "He was a man who loved poetry and fine literature, read it, and knew it. He would read poetry to me sometimes during breaks, but he didn't want anyone to know it."

The poet in Clark surfaced rarely and usually surprised anyone confronting it, all his life. Wayne Griffin recalls being at a party with him in the fifties where the after-dinner game was a guessing one. "The person who was 'it' asked a question and then left the room. One person would write an answer, then the person who was 'it' had to guess who it was. One of the questions was 'What do you cherish most in your memories?' The answer was, 'The smell of heather after a rain.' Everybody sat there saying, 'Who the hell wrote that? Who's the poet in the crowd?' Well, it was Gable. Nobody could believe it."

His conflict between closet-poet and he-man made Clark a rigid, embarrassing Parnell. The film was a disaster. Disaster, in terms of the Gable of the thirties, didn't mean people stayed away from his picture; it meant that they went to the film, hated seeing their idol tarnished, and wrote angry letters to the studio. Clark's fans never again suffered such an insult. He might make bad pictures, but in them he was always indisputably Gable. His fans would see him die in only one more film: *Run Silent, Run Deep,* released in 1958. And the great percentage of the films he would make after *Parnell* would be directed by his kind of men: Vic Fleming, Jack Conway, Clarence Brown, Bill Wellman, John Ford, Raoul Walsh, etc.

No one at MGM "blamed" Gable for *Parnell.* In fact, on March 26, he received a bonus of $25,000 with a note from "E. J. Mannix." The note said the money was "in appreciation of the cooperation and excellent services rendered by you. . . ." Can the owners of a gushing oil well get mad at it for spitting a single pebble?

In January, Clark had placed his handprints and foot-prints in wet cement in front of Grauman's Chinese The-atre, one of the stranger publicity rites stars endured to insure their immortality. Jean Garceau reported in her book, "The crowd of fans that day was estimated as the largest ever on hand for the ceremony. This record stood for twenty-four years. . . ."

On his thirty-sixth birthday came another tribute to his stature, a party at the studio at which MGM's cute new child star, Judy Garland—a young lady brought in to knock Shirley Temple off the charts—sang to him a song with a verse composed just for the occasion. ("You Made Me Love You" was the song.)

Her rendition made L.B. cry. (Indeed, it was moving to Gable, too.) Mayer was so touched, however, that he had Judy sing it to a photograph of Clark in *Broadway Melodies of 1938*, and sing it to Clark himself at every major gathering of his barony. In 1949 Clark finally told Judy what he thought of the gesture: "Goddamn brat," he said. "You've ruined every one of my birthdays. They bring you out from behind the wallpaper to sing that song, and it's a pain in the ass."

Yet another tribute to Clark's status occurred in April, with the public trial of an Englishwoman named Violet Norton, under indictment by the U.S. Post Office Department for mail fraud. Ms. Norton had been writing extortion letters trying to get Clark Gable to support a fifteen-year-old girl she claimed was his child. Every star worth his salt was involved in a paternity suit, but this was a convolution nobody had yet thought of. In fact, so much was learned about the wholesome career of Clark Gable in the three days of trial, a few people wondered if it was the MGM publicity department that had invented it.

The case was open and shut from the start. Violet claimed Clark had sired the child in England, and it was quickly established that Clark had not been issued a passport to leave the United States before 1930. The trial, it seems, could have ended there, but it didn't. The public got to meet an array of characters in Gable's life (witnesses for the prosecution): his father, some of his Oregon employers, and Franz Dorfler, whom no one had known how to locate until Bert Allenberg looked in his kitchen and found her working there. Miss Dorfler confirms, with gentle pride, that she had had a very bad time in the first years of the Depression, and had indeed taken work as a domestic. After the trial, however, she was given an MGM contract and stayed on the company payroll for ten years.

Another person employed by MGM as a result of the trial was a Los Angeles *Examiner* reporter named Otto Winkler. The official story on his hiring was that Clark was so impressed with Winkler's coverage of the trial he asked Howard Strickling to add him to the publicity department. However it happened, Winkler was hired as Clark's personal public relations man, and eventually was trusted by him perhaps to a greater degree than even Strickling was.

So faithful was Otto to his job that Clark expected to see him every single day he worked, and got moody if Otto didn't show. So loyal was Otto that within five years after the Violet Norton fiasco, he would be dead, the direct result of having failed for the first time to carry out to the letter a mission of trust for Clark Gable.

Violet Norton was deported, her sad cockney testimony stored, for all time, in the morgues of California newspapers. "This ere Clark Gyble's an arrant fraud," she had said. "'E's Frank Billings, that's oo 'e is, I can tell by the whye 'e mykes love to that Joan Crawford—just the syme as 'e did t'me."

Millions of women understood her flight of fancy.

31

Even though *Parnell* had been planned as the film that would change Gable's image, the studio had another typical Gable vehicle being polished for him, *Saratoga,* in which he would play "Duke," a bookie with a heart of gold dust. Jack Conway was assigned to direct, and Anita Loos to tailor the script for Clark. For a while there was no leading lady scheduled, and columnists, as far back as the fall of 1936, announced that Lombard would be loaned by Paramount for the part.

Carole wanted very badly to make a film with Clark, but she had complicated contractual obligations, and went, instead, into Selznick's *Nothing Sacred,* her only Technicolor film. Jean Harlow entered *Saratoga,* tying together the two productions with an incredible daisy chain. "Baby" was quite publicly the paramour of Carole's exhusband, Bill Powell, who had become a great pal of Carole's. "Baby" was Gable's pal, and therefore Carole's pal. A few months earlier, Powell and Harlow had made *Libeled Lady* with Spencer Tracy, who became such a pal they had chosen him, at a production party, as one of the first to know they would marry. Harlow, however, first had to finish *Personal Property,* a comedy with Robert Taylor, for which MGM had tried, unsuccessfully, to borrow Carole Lombard. *Personal Property* was supposed to do for Taylor what *It Happened One Night* had done for Gable, who was helping Taylor finesse a man's-man image by the hunting-fishing route he had taken himself. Taylor's affair with Barbara Stanwyck was second in news value only to that of Clark and Carole's; the fact that they had made a very successful film together gave Carole hope that she and Clark would be able to do the same.

Somehow, movies were made anyway.

Harlow didn't look well as *Saratoga* rolled. She was bloated and her complexion was chalky. She was edgy, too, even with her publicist, Kay Mulvey, to whom she was very attached, and she complained frequently of being tired. On a Saturday, late in May, with the picture perhaps 90 percent finished, she collapsed on the set. As Walter Pidgeon remembers:

"I was doing a scene with her just before lunch. It was all lit and she and I stepped into the lights to shoot it, when she suddenly doubled up in my arms and said, 'I have a terrible pain.' I called to Jack Conway, 'Baby's got a pain.' He told her to go have lunch in her dressing room and rest. I never saw her again. A week or ten days later we were working on the back lot. I was sitting with Conway when he was called to a phone about ten or fifteen feet away. He came back and said, 'Oh my God, Baby's gone.' "

Studio releases said Harlow had died of uremic poisoning. To this day, however, the circumstances of her death are as disputed as those of Marilyn Monroe's. The most persistent story is that Harlow had had an acute gall bladder attack but that her mother, a Christian Scientist, had not permitted her to be taken to a hospital. Friends, including Gable, supposedly were refused admittance to the house where Harlow lay writhing, until Mayer ordered them to defy her mother and remove her. She died in the Good Samaritan Hospital shortly after entering it. Because the studio had not released anything on her illness or shut down the set while she malingered, the news of her death came as a complete shock to the press and public. Both assumed there had been deliberate secrecy and, therefore, something to hide. Certainly, the air of mystery was compounded by stories like this one, from Clarence Bull, about her final sitting for him, for *Saratoga's* poster art:

"The last portrait taken, Jean looked at me. I looked at her. We both had tears in our eyes without knowing why. Slowly she came up to me and put her arms around my neck and whispered:

" 'Clarence, I'll never be here again.'

" 'Nonsense, Jean, we have fashions to do in a few days.'

" 'I don't mean that. I mean it's goodbye to—to everything.' "

Once again, Clark Gable found himself an usher at a chapel in Forest Lawn. And this time, a pallbearer as well —shouldering the coffin of a twenty-six-year-old woman who had lived ten lifetimes, and none at all.

He went with Carole to the funeral, witnessed with her the hysteria of the crowds along the roads, inhaled with her the fragrance of thousands of dollars' worth of flowers (including what appeared to be a mammoth Valentine from L. B. Mayer: a huge heart made of red roses, split by a golden arrow), and listened with her to Jeanette Mac-Donald singing "Indian Love Song," to Nelson Eddy singing "Ah, Sweet Mystery of Life."

The people who loved Jean Harlow, whatever she was, and Gable was one of them, were deeply, honestly shaken by her death. Their grief was made more bitter by the news that this towering star had left a total estate— cash, furs, jewelry, everything—of about $25,000. The flowers at her funeral had cost nearly as much.

There was the matter, then, of wrapping *Saratoga* and delivering it to a public eager to see Jean in her farewell appearance. Mayer issued a few press releases about re-shooting the entire picture with another actress, a gesture later known as running it up the flagpole to see if anyone salutes. The news was met by a great outcry of protest from exhibitors, so a young lady named Mary Dees was cast as Harlow's ghost, the script hastily rewritten to show the Harlow character only from the back, and the shooting resumed.

Among the blond hopefuls who tested for the part was a sixteen-year-old beauty named Virginia Grey. Perhaps because he was in a particularly vulnerable mood, or per-haps because he found a certain kind of female irresistible, Clark couldn't forget the girl Jean Garceau refers to as "little Virginia." He first got her bit parts in two of his films. He later gave her a featured part in his life. "Gable and Virginia Grey were together longer than anybody else in history," Richard Lang says. Howard Strickling says, "Clark and Virginia had a great relationship. If he was lonesome, you know—I mean Virginia was always there. I mean, if he was in a mood, Virginia was there, you know." Friends still wonder why they never married. Miss Grey has never married at all.

Jean Harlow's funeral was on June 9, 1937. *Saratoga* was released on July 23, the same year. It was, of course, a box-office smash. Spotting Mary Dees was such a great trivia game it clung to a generation straight through *The Late Show* and *The Late, Late Show*. There still are people around who can tell you which scenes with Harlow were not really with Harlow.

Harlow was gone, but Gable was Gable, better than ever, and just in time to pull himself from the mire of *Parnell*, which had opened the week of Harlow's death. All of Clark's good friends had a wonderful time teasing him about his terrible flop, particularly Carole. She had *Parnell* stickers printed and, according to Jean Garceau, for years "stuck them in everything imaginable. . . . Clark's books, his clothes, the food, and other unexpected places." Carole had to have had an extraordinary sense of timing, as well as a psychic sense of the strength of her man, for she clearly felt safe attacking him on dangerous ground. Not only did she rib him about his single failure as an actor, but also about his false teeth, his big ears, his ego, his stinginess, and his virility. A witness to the relationship could well have considered her a first-class ball-breaker, but none ever did. Could anyone picture Jackie pasting "Bay of Pigs" stickers all over the White House? It's unthinkable. Yet Carole excelled at just such jokes, and Clark reportedly adored her for it.

There was, however, a distinct change in their lives together after Harlow's death; probably because of it. Clark, with more free time than he'd ever had, withdrew from Hollywood's gay life—Carole's ambience—into the activities that gave him peace. If Carole wanted to be with him, she had to do what he chose to do: hunt, fish, and take to the hills on horseback. She also had to trade her hangers-on for people who would share Clark's outdoor activities. That she did all this with her incomparable verve added to her legend and secured her in Clark's affection as nothing else could have.

It was contrast that made Carole appear so unusual in the role of sportsman's companion. Clothes-horse-glamorgirls just didn't do things the way Carole did in the land of glitter. They didn't get up at four A.M. to make breakfast for a bunch of guys, didn't mount a horse before sunrise, didn't risk breaking a nail or getting a sunburn. Contrast made Gable a studio hero in the same kind of way; he didn't behave like other stars. He made no queer demands, showed no temperament, talked to common people. Clark and Carole seemed so special because they weren't bizarre where being bizarre was the norm.

Carole worked as hard as she played in 1937, worked harder than she ever would again. Her income that year was $465,000, earned on three films and three radio shows. Taxes and expenses ate all but about $50,000 of the figure, but that horror story almost paid for itself in square inches of newsprint. Russell Birdwell, now her press agent by way of her association with David Selznick, issued a release about Carole being delighted to pay taxes for the privileges of living in America, and the story was so widely circulated President Roosevelt wrote her a personal note of thanks. Fieldsie, who did Carole's tax returns (and Clark's as well), got a letter from the IRS saying the return had been checked and would not be audited. It was a matter of pride to Fieldsie to demand such a letter on every return she filed.

Nothing Carole did, however, could gain for her the public acceptance Clark had without apparent effort. Carole campaigned for stardom—calling Louella Parsons once a week, giving endless interviews. Clark had no campaign. Carole believed the public could be won; Clark didn't believe in the public at all. Carole thought a star was as good as his latest trick; Clark, as good as his latest picture. Carole earned more; Clark was better loved. Perhaps it was this balance that kept Clark and Carole from competing in the way that was so historically destructive to Hollywood romances.

In the last week of November, two Carole Lombard films were released simultaneously in neighborhood theaters. At the same time, the twenty million readers of fifty-five Chicago *Tribune*–New York *News* syndicated papers were asked to vote, on published ballots, for the king and queen of Hollywood. In the week that followed the newspapers tried to create as much suspense as possible over the result of the popularity poll. There was, indeed, curiosity over who the female would be. Clark Gable, however, was the obvious choice for the male, and he took first place a length ahead of second choice, Robert Taylor. Myrna Loy was elected queen (followed by Loretta Young). Carole was not even a runner-up.

On the rainy evening of December 8, Clark and Myrna were presented with velvet and tin crowns before a live audience in the El Capitan Theatre in Hollywood, and a network radio audience on NBC. Photographs of the event show him at his handsomest in a herringbone tweed suit with leather buttons and workable buttonholes, contrasting vest, white shirt, polka-dot tie. He was trim, clean, and he towered over Miss Loy and Ed Sullivan, who presented the crowns. "No queen ever stood beside such a good-looking king," Miss Loy said on the air. Nothing could have been more obvious to the 1,500 people in the theater. Clark, crowned first, had no chance to return the compliment. He recited, with warmth, the brief lines Otto Winkler had written for him: "I've played newspaper reporters and Klondike miners and lots of other roles, but this is the first time I've ever been a king. I want to thank all those readers who made me one."

Clark called Myrna "Queenie" after that evening. People never seemed to be called by their rightful names in the movie business anyway. In addition to nicknames already mentioned, for instance, Tracy was "The Iron Duke"; Bill Powell, "William the Fourth"; and Victor Fleming, "The Mad Monk." None was to his nickname, however, what Gable was to his. For months Clark had been called "King" by toilers at the studio who interpreted his shyness (aloofness? reserve?) as regality. To them, too, his size was also his karma. A man who could be recognized a hundred feet away—from the back—filled doorways, looked down on the heads of moguls, and seemed twice the size of men his own height was a king among men. And so, most people at some time called him the King, and even when it was said as the purest of jokes, it never sounded totally funny.

Strangely, Carole did not choose the occasion of Clark's coronation to pull any of her usual stunts. Bill Powell sent Myrna Loy a large box of sour grapes. Carole

let Clark find his own way to put "the king bullshit" in
perspective. Playing Parnell, Clark had tripped over his
ego; she couldn't let him forget that. But his being the
King was a role other people saw him in, and it reflected
on her, as his choice of a suitable woman. There was glory
in being the King's mistress, but there would be more in
being the King's wife. Carole wanted to marry Clark, have
children, work less. There were clues that she was going
to get what she wanted, but that it was going to cost more
than either she or Clark had expected: Carole began to
sell whatever furnishings and jewelry she owned of real
value. And L. B. Mayer began discussing his terms
through his emissary, Eddie Mannix, for the loan of
Clark Gable to *Gone With the Wind.*

32

What was it Ria wanted that was dictating the course of
so many lives? At first, it was just Clark. She wanted him
back, and so did her son, Al. Says Jana, "After Clark left
Mother, Al tried to have some sort of relationship with
him, but Clark didn't seem to want it and it hurt my
brother very much." Ria was hurt for her son, and hurt
for herself when it became obvious Clark loved Carole in
a way he had never loved her.

She reconciled herself to the fact that she couldn't have
Clark. What she asked as compensation was a share of the
money MGM had been putting in trust for him since December, 1934. Says Jana, "Mother was told by her lawyers
that she was entitled to part of that trust and that's what
the whole rigamarole was all about. Mother was told by
her lawyers that she had helped him and this should be
hers. I don't remember any other details; I was married
and living in Houston and had my own life. But I remember Mother telling me her lawyers said she certainly was
entitled to that money, and that she was going to get it."

Ria couldn't have demanded anything more complicated

to get. Most assuredly, Clark didn't want to give her that storehouse of cash, which was all that stood between him and insolvency. Carole couldn't stand Clark's penny-pinching. What she couldn't comprehend was that he lived on nearly every cent he earned—or, rather, every cent he had left after payments to Ria and his father. He was an incurably tight man locked in a hopelessly tight situation.

Furthermore, MGM didn't want to surrender money that Clark couldn't touch until he had satisfactorily fulfilled all his contractual obligations. "No studio trust fund was ever set up in altruism," says Phil Berg. All that nice, forced savings MGM had been stashing for Clark was really the studio's only hold on him.

In his first move toward divorce, the King was in check.

After his first move to procure Gable, David Selznick was in shock. In the deal offered, Gable could be Rhett only if MGM got half of *Gone With the Wind*. Selznick would pay MGM Clark's salary, now up to $4,500 a week, plus 3 percent for the company coffers. Then Selznick would accept $1,250,000—estimated to be half of the cost of making the film—in return for which MGM would get half the film's profits. Additionally, MGM's parent company, Loew's Inc., would distribute the film in return for 15 percent of the gross.

Louis Mayer had a personal income in 1937 of $1,300,000, largely from his percentage of the profits of MGM films. He was, with that income, the highest-salaried man in the United States. (Average income in that Depression year was about $1,500.) No one wanted to see him one cent richer, particularly David Selznick. What the bartering Mayer was doing was destroying his son-in-law's innards. There was another ulcer-making aspect to the deal: United Artists had distribution rights to all Selznick's pictures until 1939. If Loew's was to distribute *Gone With the Wind*, the film couldn't even get under way for more than a year.

Selznick was not without alternatives, as Gable was. David could return to MGM as a vice-president and producer of the property he owned. Or he could get a deal elsewhere, as, for instance, at Warner Brothers, which offered Errol Flynn and made much milder demands. Or he could try to get Gary Cooper, from Sam Goldwyn, to play Rhett. Or he could cast Ronald Colman as Rhett, or Warner Baxter or some unknown—and have half the world happy to club him to death with a first edition of the book. He even thought wistfully of an actor no longer on earth. "We have buried the man who should have been Rhett Butler," he told John Gilbert's widow.

In the first months of 1938, Selznick capitulated to Mayer, and Clark was signed into captivity. News of the deal would not be released until late summer because of Selznick's contract with United Artists.

Clark had a full year to fume over the use made of his body, and to get nervous about playing Rhett Butler. "There are going to be six million eyes on me," he told a friend, "all daring me to fail." How he hated to have to live up to other people's expectations of him.

Fortunately, he had the immediate distraction of work on a film that was just his style: *Test Pilot*, with Myrna Loy, Spencer Tracy, Lionel Barrymore, and, in a minor role, Virginia Grey. Vic Fleming was directing and the Air Corps was cooperating, with use of its base, March Field near Riverside, and its new bomber, called a B-17. Clark would be working mostly at the base, which meant he could be away from studio nonsense and in the company of men he admired. One man he met, Al Menasco, was to become a lifetime friend. Menasco was an engineer, had been a test pilot in World War I, was a friend of Jimmy Doolittle, and knew all there was to know about motors. Clark got to know him through his stunt-flying stand-in, Ray Moore, who was staying at Menasco's house for the duration of the filming. Menasco was helping to get the planes needed for the picture's numerous aerial scenes. Unit director of the flight scenes was a flier named Paul Mantz; he became the third of Clark's 3-M buddies during the film. It was Menasco, Moore, and Mantz—and Gable, off, whenever possible, on a new adventure.

One of the adventures, according to Myrna Loy, caused the temporary disappearance of Tracy from the picture. "Vic and Clark and Al were going to Catalina one afternoon; Paul was going to fly them over in a B-17, maybe let Clark take the controls for a while. They asked Spence to go, but he wouldn't and they figured he was afraid. Spence was so angry with them I asked him why he didn't go with them. At first he just said he didn't want to. Later he told me he wouldn't go because he was on the wagon. He said, 'I couldn't go with those bastards; they're going to get drunk.'

"After dinner they all came back very full of themselves. Spence walked right past them, without talking, and the next morning, didn't show up for work. I told Clark what had happened and he was terribly chagrined. He wouldn't have gone, ever, if he'd known why Spence wouldn't go. After that, we tried to track down Spence, but he got away. He went on a twenty-four-hour drinking spree."

When they stopped playing cock o' the walk, Gable and Tracy did some genuinely fine acting together. Clark marveled at the way Tracy was able to steal a scene without saying a line, without a hammy gesture. He said of him, for publication, "The guy's good and there's nobody in this business who can touch him, so you're a fool to try." The guy's being good made Gable better than he'd ever been in the kind of tough-tender scenes he was always uncomfortable doing. "I watched him grow in *Test Pilot*," Miss Loy says. "There was some very poetic stuff in the film, and he was afraid he couldn't do it." He did it all so well the flow of flying-buddy affection went back and forth between him and Tracy on the screen like melted mercury.

While Clark was giving his best to *Test Pilot*, Carole was at Warner Brothers trying to pump adrenaline into a corpse of a picture called *Fools for Scandal*. This was her turn to trip over her ego. She had contracted, without her agent, to do the picture, succumbing to Jack Warner's promise to treat her like visiting royalty—no, like resident royalty; like Bette Davis, queen of Warner Brothers. The film was badly scripted and badly directed, and when it opened on April 16, even *Photoplay*'s reviewer recoiled in disbelief. The kindest of the critics suggested Carole had played in one too many screwball comedies; others suggested she go somewhere and cool off. The hostility in the reactions to the film knocked the wind out of her.

Test Pilot opened April 22, and was lovingly received by everyone.

Carole didn't like playing seesaw. She informed Myron Selznick she would accept no more comedy roles, and no more roles at all if they kept her from Clark's side. She had other important matters to tend to as well. Fieldsie was going to marry director Walter Lang; Carole had to get herself ready for the happy day of the wedding, and the dreaded day she would be without Fieldsie's gift for making order. Friends needed her special brand of care:

Bill Powell was sick, emotionally shattered by the loss of Baby, physically shattered by cancer surgery. Writer Donald Ogden Stewart—for whom only God could make a three—had been in a serious accident and had no place to go to recuperate because he was separated from his wife. Carole offered him a room in her house, and all the attention she could spare.

As silence becomes noticeable when it follows a prolonged period of noise, Carole's withdrawal from her normal pursuits became noticeable to her friends. Most of them attributed the change in her—the normalizing of her —to her desire to please Clark. Surely, he was the center of her existence, but Clark liked Carole to be wacky and unpredictable. More than likely, Carole's fear that she'd gone too far with the public had as much to do with her cooling it as Clark did. There was still a Mardi Gras in progress honoring the search for the perfect Scarlett O'Hara, and still hope in Carole that it would be she.

It is hard to imagine, in present contexts, how involved the public was in the casting of this fictional heroine. There was actually a New York *Times* editorial supporting Norma Shearer for the role after thousands of her fans had written her asking her not to take it. Norma had had a slim chance of getting the part, anyway—another MGM star to plague Selznick?—but she made a public statement of withdrawal from the campaign to pacify her followers. A list of the women being considered, tested, or promoted for Scarlett was a list of living actresses under the age of forty: Bette Davis, Paulette Goddard, Miriam Hopkins, Joan Crawford, Katharine Hepburn, Jean Arthur, Loretta Young, Joan Bennett, Margaret Sullavan, Claudette Colbert. Among the unknowns plumbed were a New York model one day to be known as Susan Hayward and an RKO contract player named Lucille Ball. Not to mention the legions of Southern belles who were suddenly vacationing in Los Angeles, stage-whispering "Fiddle de dee, y'awl," in the lobby of the Beverly Wilshire. Selznick used more than 150,000 feet of film screen-testing for Scarlett.

Paulette Goddard was rejected because the public thought she was too naughty; no one believed she had really married Charlie Chaplin, with whom she was living. Norma Shearer bowed out because the public thought she was too nice; Miss Shearer had been too convincing as

Thalberg's Good Wife and fabled widow. What kind of image would Carole have to create to become Scarlett, sitting as she was, under David Selznick's nose?

She enlarged her menagerie of household pets: dogs, cats, doves, and people—and plunked herself next to Clark, wherever he was. When, in early summer, he started another Myrna Loy co-starrer called *Too Hot to Handle,* fan magazines carried pictures of her cozied next to Clark on the set; he in his canvas director's chair, she in director Jack Conway's. Clark hadn't liked it when Josephine watched him work, or when Ria did. There is no reason to believe he was any happier with the presence of Carole just out of range of the big lights.

Carole's constant attention to the comfort of her man, however, won her three fans who were indispensable to the progress of her romance: Eddie Mannix, Howard Strickling, and Otto Winkler. In agreement that Carole was the best thing that ever happened to Clark, the three of them ran interference between the affair and the Mayer, who was always on the side of the wronged wife (while it served his purpose), and always against anything that might impair the morals of the human race, e.g., a publicized affair between two consenting adults, one or both of whom was an MGM star. Once Clark was committed to *Gone With the Wind* insiders knew Ria was going to get her settlement eventually. But Howard et al. could keep L. B. off the lovers' backs while the mills of the gods were grinding.

What Howard says of Carole today may be colored by hindsight, but it is said with deep feeling: "Carole was one of the smartest women I knew. She knew what she wanted and knew how to handle it. When she made up her mind she wanted Clark Gable and nobody else, she wanted him one thousand percent. She didn't want to take him and mold him like all the other gals had done (they made a great mistake, you know). She wanted to be his wife. She was a boudoir girl, but for him she just ran outdoors. She did everything with him he'd wanted to do all his life. They played. The only playmate he'd ever had in his life was Carole. I say he was still a little boy from Cadiz, Ohio, when Carole got him. You know, they say you can't take the country out of the boy . . . and Clark was a hick kid at heart. He became very sophisticated later on. Carole did everything she could for Clark."

No one pretends the lovers were without conflict. "People who laugh as hard as they did, fight hard" is the sort of thing friends say, or, as Joan Blondell puts it, "They weren't cows, you know, they were juicy people." Carole didn't trust Clark at all with aggressive women, and she resented his past affairs. She knew she would always have to keep a wary eye on him, but accepted that, and felt up to it. She felt he needed her and she had never before loved a man who needed her. Her first husband was a fussy, self-sufficient man who, she told Alice Marble, "acted even when he was in his pajamas." Columbo was a mamma's boy who put Carole on a pedestal and lavished her with gifts and attention. "His love for me was the kind that rarely comes to any woman," she said after his funeral. Riskin was an intellectual who, she suspected, wanted her to be something she wasn't. Clark took her as she was, but, she suspected, could also leave her that way. To keep him, she had to insinuate herself so thoroughly into his life he couldn't function without her. Pa . . . Pappy . . . The Big Lug . . . Moose . . . any way she called him, Gable was a full-time job.

33

On August 25, the casting of Rhett Butler was officially announced and a photo released of Clark, David Selznick, and L. B. Mayer, leaning into a piece of paper which, noted the caption, was a contract. Clark was wearing the sickest smile a camera ever recorded.

There was time for him to make one more picture before *Gone With the Wind* would consume him for twenty weeks; it was Robert Sherwood's *Idiot's Delight*, directed by Clarence Brown, co-starring Norma Shearer. The Hollywood press assumed Norma had gotten Clark as a bonus for having so gallantly delivered Scarlett back to the people. She may have, but Clark had seen *Idiot's Delight* two years before—on Broadway, when Lunt and Fontanne were shining in it—expressly because MGM wanted the property for him.

Clark worried, typically, about being able to "fill Alfred Lunt's shoes." He needn't have. Sherwood tailored the screenplay so perfectly for him no one could imagine anyone else was ever "Harry," the hoofer. His characterization of that lovable phony was, and remains, a Gable gem. In a "Puttin' on the Ritz" tap routine, which Carole rehearsed with him—he, full of anxiety, she laughing uncontrollably—his comic talent nearly soars. Gable's appeal pivoted on the way he laughed at himself, on screen and off. On screen it was with a certain smile; off screen, with a memorable quip. "Hold onto the trapeze with your teeth," Clarence Brown directed him. "What do I hold onto my teeth with?" asked Clark.

Carole worked herself into a jealous froth over Clark at the start of the picture, behaving, for the first time, like his pet shrew. She suspected Miss Shearer of having designs on her man and rushed to their set whenever she could. She also demanded a replacement for one of the dancers cast as a member of "Harry's" dancing troupe, because she had seen the girl make a pass at Clark at a party. "Get that whore out of here," she reportedly shouted to Clarence Brown, who complied, not for Clark, but because Carole was under the protection of Eddie Mannix. Oddly, she did not ask for a replacement for Virginia Grey, who was also in the dancing troupe.

Perhaps embarrassed by her own behavior, Carole resorted once again to the kind of gag gifts that always served her so well. Among other goodies, she sent Clark a huge tutu and huge ballet shoes, and arranged for a huge silly bouquet of flowers to be handed him on the last take of the hoofing scene. When the picture was finished, she sent gifts to the entire crew in Clark's name, but fooled no one. It was common knowledge that Clark didn't believe in that common practice. Clark gave so few idle gifts that when he did give one it became an event. The late Larry Barbier, who was in charge of MGM's still department, told the tale of how he became the owner of the famous Valentine car Carole had given Clark. Clark spent over $1,000 having the car painted black and souped up enough to go one hundred miles an hour. Then he tired of it, and Barbier asked if he could buy it for his teenaged son. As Barbier often told it:

"Clark said, 'Hell, no. Do you think I want him to wrap himself around some telephone pole and kill himself?' I didn't argue. You learned not to argue with Clark. He was stubborn as they came. But a few weeks later, after I promoted him a new station wagon with special gear for hunting, he drove me to the nearest Department of Motor Vehicles. Then he asked me for a buck. He said he was going to sign his old black car over to me, but damn if he was going to pay the buck transfer fee, too. That was just like him.

"When I told the boys on the set about the car, they said I must have had him hypnotized."

It is an interesting statement on their personalities and relationship: Carole gave so many gifts that few had real meaning. Clark gave so few that each was memorable. Carole was a giver, Clark a taker. But her giving stopped, and his accepting stopped, when either felt used.

Being a lady of leisure didn't become Carole, and, while Ria remained an obstacle to her marrying Clark, did more harm than good to their relationship. Therefore, when Clark signed for *Idiot's Delight*, Carole committed herself to a David Selznick film that promised to put her career on an improved course. It was a drama of young marrieds called *Made for Each Other*, and her co-star was a young actor named James Stewart. Her working while Clark worked put them back in the rhythm that seemed best for them. He, in particular, seemed to take more pleasure in their time together when they had to steal it.

Clark was under tremendous pressure as 1937 drew to a close. His role in *Idiot's Delight*, which looked so easy for him, was demanding, nonetheless. "Harry" would have been less demanding if Rhett Butler had not been shadowing him wherever he went. Over and over and over Clark read *Gone With the Wind*, trying to understand the character of the man he would have to be for five long months. He would have liked to have had a script to study, but then, so would Selznick, who had chewed up a battalion of writers, including F. Scott Fitzgerald, and was still seeking the ultimate creator. Selznick had no script, he had no Scarlett. He had a pocketful of Benzedrine to fight fatigue (he was known to go three days at a clip without sleep), and the conviction he was going to produce the greatest movie ever made. That he was beginning to convince everyone else in Hollywood added considerably to Clark's tension.

Carole concentrated on proving herself a capable dramatic actress, and on clearing the path to becoming Mrs. Gable. Before she had started *Made for Each Other,* she had hired Jean Garceau, a happily married, efficient member of Myron Selznick's staff, to replace Fieldsie as her secretary-business manager. As soon as she finished the picture, she assigned Jean to a major expedition: hunting, with her, for the perfect house to settle in with Clark. She had told Jean, the day after she hired her, that she and Clark would marry as soon as he was divorced. Mrs. Garceau, a lady with a remarkable sense of propriety, did not ask when that would be. Ria, in New York to escape, for a while, the endless gossip about the lovers, told Adela Rogers St. Johns: "I've always told Clark he could have a divorce any day he asked me for it. And he can. Today or tomorrow. But he's a businessman as well as a movie star. He knows one must be businesslike about these things. It's only fair. I gave him a good many years of my life, and taught him a great deal."

In mid-December, Clark made a strategic error in dealing with Ria. Responding to studio hysteria over a *Photoplay* article listing Gable and Lombard as one of several pairs of "Hollywood's Unmarried Husbands and Wives," Clark permitted the publicity department to release an announcement from him that he was going to ask Ria for a divorce. It was one too many public insults for Ria, who had assumed that when the inevitable happened, she would do the announcing, and the divorcing. The self-serving callousness of Clark's unexpected move sparked a quick and angry message to him from her lawyers that she would contest. Columnists then informed anxious fans that the Gable divorce had "hit a snag."

Carole had had enough of snags and procrastinations, and this latest hitch could not have come at a worse time. She and Clark had just bought a house in the San Fernando Valley that both had long admired—with $50,000 of her money. She had just gone with Clark and Jean Garceau to look again at the property, and hear Clark say, "I've always wanted a place like this. It will be the first home I've had since I was a boy that I can really call my own. Ma, I think we're going to be very happy here."

Something had to be done to salvage the mess, and

Carole went to friends with her frustration. Russell Birdwell suggested a new lawyer be brought into the case, and
recommended a prominent one named W. I. Gilbert, whom
Clark consulted and retained. Within days, newspapers
carried the following statement from Mr. Gable:

> I regret bitterly that a short time ago a story was
> printed to the effect that I would seek a divorce from
> Mrs. Gable. Mrs. Gable and I had a fine life together
> until the time came that we both realized we could no
> longer make a go of it. After years of separation it is
> only natural that Mrs. Gable should institute proceed-
> ings that will assure her freedom.

This apology went nearly unnoticed in the light of the
more startling news from the Western front that an English
actress named Vivien Leigh was signed for the role of
Scarlett O'Hara. But Ria saw Clark's mouthful of humble
pie, and, her pride soothed, planned to go to Nevada
when the holiday season was over. From the single available clue—in a contract between Clark and MGM
negotiated after *Gone With the Wind* was concluded—it
appears Ria probably did not get her settlement immediately. The new contract revoked and terminated the trust
estate in 1940, giving all the money to Clark. The New
York *Times* reported Ria got a settlement of $286,000
payable in three years. There is no indication of whether
that represented all or part of the trust.

In *Idiot's Delight,* Clark buys Norma Shearer a seventy-
five-cent trinket and tells her, "That's the most expensive
present I ever bought a dame." The line broke Carole up
every time she heard it.

The house Carole and Clark chose to buy had been the
weekend retreat of the colorful one-eyed director Raoul
Walsh, who, in his memoirs, said that Clark had asked him
to sell it to him, regularly, for three years before it was on
the market. The house in Encino was a small, two-story,
California interpretation of a Connecticut farmhouse, built
in 1926 by an MGM designer named Malcolm Brown.
The exterior was white-washed brick, the interior done
with lots of wood paneling, random-planked floors, and
fireplaces. Since the Valley was always at least ten degrees
hotter than any other area around L.A., the house had no
central heating. It also had a kitchen just adequate for a

weekend cook, and limited facilities for live-in help. Compared to the luxury-laden mansions of Bel Air and Beverly Hills, the kindest thing that could be said about it was that it was cozy. Carole and Clark knew the house needed considerable work to become the enchanted cottage they envisioned.

The great beauty of the place was the acreage that sloped down away from the house, and then up the low hills around it. Southern Californians call the layout a ranch; an Easterner would call it an estate. There were twenty acres in all, with a semi-tropical lushness one might expect to find in the northern West Indies. All sorts of fruit trees flourished on the land: orange, grapefruit, lemon, fig, peach, plum, apricot. There were also giant copper-colored eucalyptus, and huge lacy locusts. Around the paddock and nine-stall stable were fields of alfalfa and oats.

Encino, in the thirties, bore no resemblance to the congested suburb it is today. Traffic did not move, bumper to bumper, through the canyons at rush hour. There was no rush hour. The hills and valleys behind Bel Air sprawled vast and open. Coyotes howled in them. Rattlesnakes sunned on their rocks. Nights were so still in the Valley you could hear the Pacific hitting the shore twenty-five miles away.

Clark and Carole chose a very modest place away from the very madding crowd. And, of course, their choice surprised the group in Hollywood that never could comprehend their tastes. "Such a simple house (not even a swimming pool, my dear), and so *far* from everyone." It wasn't as though they had to go all the way out there to find land. Vic Fleming had a lovely twenty-acre ranch in Bel Air. And Howard Hawks had 360 acres, right near Vic, where he was going to build one day.

Clark and Carole. Carole and Clark. Their legend grew and grew.

34

The fictional Rhett Butler was described as a man who towered over other men: tall, broad-shouldered, narrow-waisted; powerful but graceful in motion. He had black hair, a black mustache, a cynical smile, an arrogant air, and a way of looking at women that made them feel naked. Surely it is no wonder that readers of *Gone With the Wind* saw Clark Gable as the incarnation of Margaret Mitchell's ingenuous erotic fantasy. Rhett was a distillation of every "Duke" and "Ace" and "Blackie" Gable ever played. But to the end of his days, Clark's answer to anyone who said so was a rigid, "When the book was being written I was a four-dollar-a-day laborer in Oklahoma and not in anybody's mind for anything." The bulk of *Gone With the Wind* was written in the late twenties when Clark was under Josephine's tutelage, but the point is, he simply didn't see himself as Captain Butler. "I don't want the part for money, chalk, or marbles," he had told Selznick. The fact that he had it anyway didn't mean he would bend to it; Clark went into the production nose-deep in defenses.

Early in December, when director George Cukor asked his players to start their "Southern" lessons, Gable took his first rebellious stand. Memo, to George Cukor from David O. Selznick, December 8, 1938: "For your information, I am informed by MGM that Clark Gable refuses under any circumstances to have any kind of a Southern accent."

One of the things decided at their next meeting was that the production by-law was, whatever Gable wants, Gable gets. The one thing Ann Rutherford, who played one of Scarlett's sisters, remembers most clearly today about the making of *Gone With the Wind* is, "Nobody pushed Clark Gable around. Just nobody pushed him around. I don't think anyone would have looked at his looming presence and crossed swords with him."

The production of the film had gone through three years of tension before the first foot of it was shot. It would never know any other mood.

Joe Mankiewicz wonders to this day why Gable and Leigh didn't fall in love during the five months they spent creating sexual tension between Rhett and Scarlett. The answer goes beyond Clark's involvement with Carole, and Vivien Leigh's with Laurence Olivier, to the power struggles continuously raging on the set. Ann Rutherford terms the relationship between the two stars "amicable." Clarence Bull, last of the Hollywood romantics, recalled, in his memoirs, the first time the two met (to pose for the film's first publicity stills):

We had been waiting for over an hour for Vivien Leigh. . . . The shots were in costume. Clark was pacing back and forth. . . .

"I couldn't make love to that dame now if she were the most beautiful woman in the world!"

And then, a rustle of silk, the sweet smell of lilacs and there *was* the most beautiful woman in the world, standing behind him, touching his shoulder, whispering like a summer breeze. . . .

"I quite agree, Mr. Gable. If I were a man I'd tell that Vivien Leigh to go right back to merry old England and . . ."

Gable turned and looked. Leigh looked back. The look in their eyes had flash bulbs in it. Slowly Rhett Butler took Scarlett O'Hara by the arm and walked onto the Southern staircase, talking and smiling as though they'd known each other all their lives.

The distrust between Clark and David Selznick reached nearly paranoid proportions. Knowing how far the producer had had to crawl to get him for the film, Gable was sure he would try to get revenge on him. Knowing how desperately Gable had not wanted to do "Rhett," Selznick was half mad trying to anticipate Gable's revenge on the whole picture. Clark officially went on payroll on January 23, 1939. The day before, Ria had announced to the press that she was leaving for Las Vegas to start divorce proceedings. Selznick was sure that one thing Gable would do to the production was leave it to marry Carole and take a long honeymoon. Selznick was so self-absorbed he underestimated the celebrated Gable professionalism. Gable was too self-absorbed to realize that nothing mattered as much to Selznick as making *Gone With the Wind* the greatest film in history.

Once the picture was really under way, Selznick behaved like a mother whose handicapped child just entered its first gym class. No one could be trusted with it. He couldn't bear being away from the set, and he hovered over Cukor in a way considered unethical, immoral, and unforgivable by directors and actors alike.

Shooting moved so slowly that after two weeks of production the picture was seven days behind schedule. One step forward, two backward. In those two weeks, Cukor directed only one scene with Gable, but Clark was on the set each day of the six-day work week, playing gin rummy and eating onion sandwiches. "Selznick would rather have you around and not need you, than need you and not have you around," Ann Rutherford says. The picture was not being shot in sequence, but in isolated scenes for which a shooting script had been okayed by Selznick. There was no complete script. Most of the initial scenes centered on Scarlett. Vivien Leigh, therefore, got most of Cukor's attention. Clark's relationship with the directors was, in Cukor's word, "Polite."

On February 12, George Cukor was relieved of his duties as director, and production suspended. A few days later, man's man Victor Fleming was named director and Gable was named rat's rat of a localized civil war.

Everyone knew Clark had fretted about Cukor for a year because he was considered a woman's director. Vivien Leigh and Olivia De Havilland (as Melanie), who adored Cukor, burst into tears when they heard he was fired. Selznick tried to take the heat off Clark by assuming full responsibility for the firing. Cukor blamed Selznick's shattered nerves but didn't really know what had happened. He told Gavin Lambert in 1970: "Perhaps Gable mistakenly thought that because I was supposed to be a 'woman's director' I would throw the story to Vivien—but if that's so, it was very naïve of him and not the reaction of a very good or professional actor." Years before, he had told another reporter, "It is nonsense to say that I was giving too much attention to Vivien and Olivia. It is the text that dictates where the emphasis should go, and the director does not do it. Clark Gable did not have a great deal of confidence in himself as an actor, although he was a great screen personality; and maybe he thought that I did not understand that."

Jean Garceau says, "Clark just wasn't getting along with Cukor at all. He felt that Fleming would put guts into the picture. He worked on them till they did get Fleming. He was spunky about things at the studio."

Says Strickling, "Gable personally complained about George Cukor."

Fleming had not been sitting around waiting for Selznick's call; he was directing the final sequences of *Wizard of Oz,* a production lulu in itself. Gable had to work at persuading his friend to take on *Gone With the Wind;* Fleming didn't want it. Gavin Lambert reports in *The Making of Gone With the Wind* that when Fleming saw the footage that had already been shot he said to Selznick, "David, your fucking script is no fucking good." Lambert also reports production manager Raymond Klune remembering Fleming "as a dour man, notably foul-mouthed and anti-Semitic." Klune told Lambert that Fleming often asked him how he could keep on working "for all these Jews." Clark, in his buddy's company, seemed equally anti-Semitic, which shocked his other friends. They had never considered him a prejudiced man, and attributed what Jean Garceau calls "his unfortunate remarks" to his general dyspepsia.

On March 1, when shooting resumed on the picture, Fleming's job was to control a nursery school full of high-strung brats, and answer to a crazed headmaster. Among other irritants, Vivien Leigh showed up every day with a marked copy of the book in her hand; Olivia De Havilland and Miss Leigh went to George Cukor on Sundays for tutoring; and Leslie Howard (Ashley Wilkes) hated his role, thought the film a bore, and said so repeatedly. It was inevitable that Fleming—tough, cold, and unshakable as he was—would eventually have the biggest tantrum of them all. After a few months he feigned a nervous breakdown, stayed away from the set for two weeks, and when he returned, split the remaining directorial duties with *Gone With the Wind* director number three, Sam Wood.

There was no question that Clark needed Fleming to survive the holocaust. Though he had all of his MGM cohorts supporting him on peripheral matters—his physical comfort, his billing, the use made of him for publicity, etc.

—none of them could stop Selznick from making almost daily changes in the script, could make Clark comfortable with the seven Technicolor cameras that enclosed him (this was his first color film), or help Clark get through scenes he felt were beyond his scope as an actor. The worst of the latter was one shared with Melanie in which he was required to cry. He could not, would not do it. He wanted the scene rewritten, or his back turned to the cameras, or, he claimed, he would walk out and never act again. Fleming was able to coerce him, gently, into shooting the scene two ways: with tears and without, promising to use only the best of the footage. He was also able to assure him that crying was not always unmanly, and in this case, would make Clark seem a bigger man than ever to his fans. No man had ever given Clark permission to cry before. The scene was a breakthrough for him both professionally and emotionally.

Carole had a theory that Clark's interest in acting was an expression of a Walter Mitty in him no one else seemed to sense. If this was so, it compounds the reason he didn't want Rhett to cry. Clark's heroes didn't weep. Clark Kent might; Superman wouldn't. Carole told Adela Rogers St. Johns:

"Clark's got so much imagination and so much more vitality and love of life than anybody else. He wants to live more, faster, harder, crowd in more experiences. He doesn't want to settle for one life, one job. So, he gets to be boss of a rubber plantation full of man-eating tigers. He can be a con-man, a pilot, a gambler saving lives in the San Francisco earthquake, a doctor, a hard-boiled reporter. He can go to Alaska in the Gold Rush, lead a mutiny, be a minister, killer, prize-fighter, politician. He can sail the China Seas and fight the Civil War—all that's just Gable having his idea of life, of fun."

Selznick supported Clark whenever he thought Clark's complaints had bearing on the ultimate perfection of the film. There was, for instance, the matter of Clark's ill-fitting wardrobe, which started bothering the star weeks before shooting began, and enraged him for weeks after. The costumes for *Gone With the Wind* were a collective work of art worth more than $150,000, and a matter of infinite importance for Selznick. Miss Rutherford recalls, "He had an Italian bootmaker making incredible shoes for us—beige and black, all handstitched. Our petticoats were trimmed with Alençon lace. I'm just talking about things that didn't *show*. I told Mr. Selznick I didn't understand why he was spending so much money when none of it would show, and he said, '*You'll* know you're wearing it.' "

Clark wanted the same kind of attention to his own wardrobe and just couldn't get it. He assumed, then, it was part of Selznick's revenge, to make him look ridiculous. Finally, on April 3, went a memo to a Mr. Lambert that was signed "DOS" but had strong overtones of Gable:

> I spoke today to Walter Plunkett about Gable's costumes. I think there is no excuse for their fitting him so badly, especially around the collar. . . . I think it is very disappointing indeed to have the elegant Rhett Butler wandering around with clothes that look as though he had bought them at the Hart, Schaffner, and Marx of that period and walked right out of the store with them. . . . The trick about collars on any man with a large neck . . . is to make the collars slightly large so that they don't press against the neck and make it look as though it is bulging. Look at Gable's own collars in private life and see how well he looks in them, and then compare them with our collars. As a matter of fact, look at how well he looks in his own clothes, generally, and compare the fit and the tailoring and the general attractiveness with what I regard as the awful costuming job we are doing with him.

It was too late in the malignant relationship for such gestures on Selznick's part to have any meaning for Clark. Nor did he ever try to hide his feelings. "Clark is a very nice fellow," Selznick wrote in a memo to his East Coast story editor, "but a very suspicious one, and very quickly and not infrequently gets the notion in his head that people are taking advantage of him." He wrote in a long letter to Carole Lombard, "All through the picture he was frank in expressing his suspicions that I intended to do him in. . . ."

On March 5, before Fleming had directed even a week's shooting, Ria was granted a divorce from Clark, on grounds of desertion. Selznick took a deep breath and waited for the other shoe to drop.

35

If Carole was upset at not playing Scarlett, she surely
didn't show it once the film began. Carole always had so
much to *do*. There were not only the events of her own life
to tend to, there were the things that kept happening to her
friends. For instance, "Doagie" Devine (wife of Andy)
was due to have a baby sometime in January (1939).
Doagie was a real buddy; she shared a trailer with Carole
at the duck club in Bakersfield when the guys went up for
the hunting season. Carole and her friend Sally Cobb gave
Doagie a baby shower at the Brown Derby which was
marvelous and hilarious—but Carole went a step further.
She had the *delivery* catered by the Brown Derby. As Mrs.
Devine recalls:

"When our boy was born—our second boy, Dennis—
Carole and Clark came and sat in the fathers' room at
Cedars of Lebanon Hospital. They sat with Andy and
waited. It was her idea to order food. See, there was no
one in Delivery that night except me. I went in at seven in
the evening for induced labor, because I was late. They
said it might take a while, which it did. Clark and Carole
got there—I guess it was about ten o'clock. Everybody
was thirsty and hungry. Especially thirsty. They thought,
well, it's going to be a long siege, better have some nourish-
ment. So they sneaked the stuff and Benny, the Brown
Derby waiter, up the back elevator. Cold cuts, drinks, and
the waiter. I kept running across the hall. I'd get a little
labor pain and go back."

Doagie had a baby, and Fieldsie had a baby, and Carole
was pregnant with ideas for a house that needed remodeling and decorating. She knew exactly what she wanted it
to look like—warm, textured, lived-in, authentically New
England. Though she had a decorator, she scouted antique
shops with Jean Garceau for the things that would make
the house personal. Decorating was the fun job, the rest
was a series of headaches. Mrs. Garceau wrote, in her
book:

The place was like a lodestone. Every spare moment Clark or Carole had, we raced out to check the progress of the remodeling and the construction of the caretaker's cottage. The three of us spent many hours sitting on the floor before a huge fire in the dining room, deep in plans and specifications . . . while workmen swarmed around us.

When it became obvious that the ranch couldn't possibly be ready for occupancy before the summer and that it was going to cost two fortunes to make it livable, Carole started looking for a film assignment. Married or not married, Clark would be tied to *Gone With the Wind* for months. Nothing she could get involved in could take as long as what he was already doing. RKO had a property that appealed to her: a story about a tormented man whose conniving wife won't give him a divorce to marry the one girl in the world who can make him happy. She signed to make that rather timely drama—*In Name Only*— with Cary Grant as her co-star, and signed for three other RKO films as well. The deal she made was a rare one: $150,000 per film, plus a small percentage of the profits. No major studio would have considered such a contract.

Even after Clark and Ria were officially divorced, Clark didn't know what to tell Carole about marriage plans, except that as soon as he could get away, they would be wed. A bigger problem was figuring a way to marry without causing a street riot.

Late in March, Clark found out he wouldn't be working the last days of the month and that, coincidentally, a fulldress premiere of *Alexander Graham Bell* would draw the elite of Hollywood and most of the local press to San Francisco. It was the perfect time for the world's favorite lovers to escape unnoticed. Clark called Otto and asked him to come to Carole's house with Howard, who recalls the moment. "Clark said, 'Well, we've decided. We're going to do it. What do you think?' Carole said, 'I've got to call Bird and we'll all get together.' Well, Otto and I said, 'No Bird. As far as we're concerned, we don't trust him. We'll handle it or else. What'll it be? If you're marrying Clark then Birdwell will handle it. If Clark's marrying you, then we'll handle it.'

"She said, 'You dirty so and so's. You're both in love

with my old man. What the hell chance have I got or has
Birdwell got—so you handle it.' "

Otto had married his wife, Jill, just the week before at a
quiet ceremony in Kingman, Arizona, 357 miles away. He
felt it was a safe place to take Clark and Carole, and that
they could drive the round trip in the allotted time. They
left for Kingman with Otto at four-thirty on the morning of
March 29, were married in the home of a Protestant minister, and were back in Carole's house before twenty-four
hours had elapsed. On their way home, Otto phoned
Howard to tell him it was okay to release the big news, and
Howard set up a press conference for the next day in Carole's house. He also called the Brown Derby to cater it.

Carole called her mother, and then tried unsuccessfully
to phone Louella Parsons, whom she had promised would
be the first to know of the marriage. Not being able to
reach "Lolly," she wired her, but the news had already
broken and Louella was so put out nothing Carole could
say could undo the insult. Later, when Louella went to
Europe, Carole had her bathroom refurbished as a small
gesture of apology. When it was finished, she and Clark
and Fieldsie went to Louella's house and put notes and
streamers all over the ornately decorated room. Carole
capped it all with a promise that Lolly would be the first
to know when Carole became pregnant, which the Gables
hoped would be very soon.

Clark and Carole seemed both radiantly happy and
newlywed shy at their press conference. He wore a navy
suit, white shirt, and silk tie. She was dressed simply—the
way he liked her best and the way she looked most beautiful—in a man-tailored, gray-flannel suit. Except for the
flaring white handkerchief in Clark's pocket and the slim
gold chain on Carole's left ankle, their style would be as
elegantly fashionable today as it was in 1939.

The press conference was noteworthy only because it
was an unusually subdued one for Carole. Clark was as
diffident as he always was, but Carole was equally diffident, and that was a marked change for her. To the most
innocuous questions, Clark replied, "We'd rather not answer that," and Carole giggled nervously. The reporters
never did learn whether the Gables wanted children,
whether their careers would mix, or what, precisely, Carole could cook. The most intimate information they got was

that the Gables hoped to visit the New York World's Fair when it opened. Carole Gable was a different person from the Carole Lombard who had talked candidly to reporters about everything from eye shadow to sex, and once announced at a press conference that Clark wasn't circumcised. It looked as though Miss Madcap had gone straight. Maybe even square.

The next day, Clark was back to work on GWTW. The Gables moved to Encino in July and Clark almost immediately began to show off his picture-postcard house to his friends. He was prouder of the home than of anything else in his life, and gave Carole full credit for producing it. To Hollywood, the house was a monument to Clark's modest self-image; simply the most unpretentious setting imaginable for such an imposing royal figure.

The house was entered through a small, wood-paneled vestibule, to the left of which was a stairway, and to the right, the living room. It might be expected that a man of Clark's height would choose rooms with high, vaulted ceilings. There were no such rooms in the house. The living room ceiling, wood-paneled, but painted white, as were the pine-paneled walls and woodwork, was no more than eight feet high. The dining room ceiling was beamed, and appeared even lower. What made the rooms seem big enough to accommodate so large a man was the uncluttered way Carole had had them decorated, and the light colors she used.

The living room was carpeted wall-to-wall in sunny yellow wool. The two largest pieces of furniture—a pair of skirted Lawson sofas—were also yellow. A pair of large green club chairs and a pair of oversized wing chairs in red linen were the remaining upholstered pieces. All the tables in the room were authentic colonial pine pieces, and small scaled. Sunlight flooded the room, despite awnings outside, through four large windows made of antique American glass. The entire window wall had draperies of white, green, and red flowered linen. On the opposite wall was an antique cabinet housing a collection of pitchers. The tables held large ashtrays, few *objets*. Fireplace accessories for the high-manteled fireplace were polished brass. Near the fireplace was a spindle-backed slipper chair, the cushion of which was covered in the drapery fabric. Carole liked to keep huge bouquets of informally arranged fresh flowers in large vases on the wood pieces against the walls, small arrangements on the low tables. There were no magazine or newspaper racks because Clark wouldn't permit reading matter to accumulate.

Behind the living room was Clark's gun room, one wall of which—thirty feet long—housed his ever-expanding armory. There were lounge chairs and built-in couches in the room, making it the perfect place for gentlemen to have cigars and brandy.

The dining room was the masterpiece of the house. It was entered through sliding doors from the living room, but had a very different ambience: cool and dark, rather than warm and sunny. A vast room with a tavern feeling, it had a large, open bar on one wall, a white-washed brick fireplace on another. The walls were of natural pine, the highly polished floors of dark oak. There was an oval-shaped braided rug under the rectangular dining table, a smaller braided rug under a round wooden game table. All the chairs were captain's chairs, uncushioned. In built-in hutch-style cabinets, Carole displayed a collection of rare pink Staffordshire, the only pink showing in the entire house, or on her; Clark hated pink. An unusual service-bar attached to the fireplace held a huge sterling lazy Susan. There were china teapots tucked into niches in the horizontal beams, antique horse prints on the walls, and a chandelier made of old oil lamps over the dining table.

When the dining room was used, even for just the two of them, the table, which could seat ten, was always set very formally, without either cloth or placemats to hide the patina of the wood. Carole's china was Spode, her crystal, Waterford, and her flatware antique, pistol-handled sterling. Informal meals were served on a large screened-in patio decorated with Early American furniture painted and upholstered in yellow.

The vast kitchen was as gleaming and modern as the best appliances of 1939 could make it, and contained a room-sized walk-in refrigerator. Other downstairs rooms were a powder room, a maid's room, and a bedroom-suite that had been turned into a yellow toile office for Jean Garceau, fully equipped with intercom, file cabinets, telephones, etc.

The entire upstairs was composed of two adjoining bedroom suites: a brown and beige one for Clark on the side of the house with the eaves; a white and blue one for Carole on the other side. Clark's double bed had a

headboard of brown tufted leather. Carole's double bed
was a mahogany four-poster, fully flounced. Both suites
were carpeted in an off-white wool; Carole's also had
white fur throw rugs and a concert harp. Bookcases were
built into the wall behind Clark's bed, as was a small bar,
so neither "Ma" nor "Pa" would have to go downstairs to
fetch his nightcap. His study contained an antique pine
desk, a prop from *Gone With the Wind* which Clark accepted from David Selznick when the film was completed.
His elaborate beige marble bathroom had no tub in it—
only a shower.

Carole's white marble bathroom and adjoining mirrored
dressing room were the only "Hollywood" rooms in the
house, and went all the way: white fur on the floors, crystal chandeliers on the ceilings, silver sconces on the walls.
Both His and Her dressing rooms had the lavish and spectacular built-in wardrobe accommodations due two such
lavish and spectacular wardrobes.

There was no guest room.

In the first months in the new house, Carole went
through some unsettling, quite typical, help problems.
What the Gables needed as a house staff, both decided,
were a cook, a maid, and a butler-valet. Carole had had in
Bel Air a fine cook named Jessie and a trustworthy maid
named Juanita. Neither, however, was willing to move to
the primitive Valley, and the parade of women who replaced them kept the house in constant turmoil. In time,
both ladies changed their minds and rejoined their mistress, who then hired as valet a big, handsome fellow
named Rufus Martin. The three house servants, all of
them black, became a vital part of the family. The caretaker, who lived in a separate cottage with his wife, had
less intimate contact with the Gables and was replaced
after a year or so.

Martin, who could wear Clark's clothes and duplicate
his voice on the phone, was a very low-key man who rarely
spoke an unbidden word. Observers felt the relationship
between Martin and his boss was totally impersonal—
unlike that between Clark and his studio man-Friday, Lew
Smith—but Martin stayed with the star for twenty years,
quietly shining his shoes and seeing to his well-being. An
artful coddler, he put him to bed when he was drunk, made
sure he ate his breakfast when he had an early call to work,
and went to the studio with him to see his clothes were in

order when he started a new film. "He was a very unusual man," Strickling says. He was a man of extreme loyalty. Not once in his lifetime did Martin utter a word to anyone about his boss.

Jessie was a mammoth woman whose Southern cooking was famous all over the Valley, as was the elegant way she prepared the down-home meals Clark loved: steak, roast beef, stewed chicken and dumplings, spareribs and baked beans, devil's food cake, and homemade ice cream. Lunch, when the two stars were home together, was a simple affair, served on trays on the patio between one and two P.M. Dinner was never served before nine, because Clark liked to have a few drinks, catch up with the day's business, read the mail, return phone calls, study a script (with Carole cueing him), and unwind, all before eating. When her boss was making a picture, Jessie was under orders from Mrs. Gable to cut down on the cake, potatoes, and cornbread, and she did so without Clark's noticing he was on a diet.

"Everything centered around Clark, his likes and dislikes," Jean Garceau observed. Indeed, everyone noticed there was only one star in the Gable household. Says Mrs. Garceau, "I used to have to pinch myself, to say, my gosh, I am working for Clark Gable. Look at him, he's right here. It doesn't seem possible."

Strickling saw the Gable household in mythical proportions, a manifestation of Carole's all-encompassing love. "She built this house for him out in the valley and everything in it was oversized. The ceiling was *that* high and the dining room table was *twice the size* of an ordinary dining room table. The chairs—the legs on them were tremendous. Everything in the house was. His chair was four times the size of the ordinary chair. The highball glasses were twice the size of any ordinary highball glasses. The dish she served the mashed potatoes in was twice the size of an ordinary dish."

Benny Massi, the Brown Derby waiter who went with the food Carole frequently ordered either for parties or for dinner on the Sundays Jessie was off, says that the only instruction Carole ever gave him concerned Clark. She would say, "I don't give a damn what you do, but I want you to take care of my pappy; give him anything he wants."

Carole made it understood that, to satisfy Mr. Gable, the house was to be kept so clean it could pass white-glove inspection any hour of the day or night. Jokingly she once told Alice Marble she had bought a magnifying glass to check for dirt under the furniture.

The house, *gemütlicht* though it was, did not de-glamorize Carole. Though she romped around the ranch all day in khakis and pigtails, by sunset she was all velvet or silk, with her hair coiffed, her nails polished, and her pedicured feet tucked into satin and maribou mules. She was, after all, still a half million dollars' worth of movie star.

If, as the thirties drew to a close, there was a man anywhere who had everything, it was the master of the house at 4525 Petit Avenue, Encino. And he knew it. "Joe Lucky," he called himself.

Joe Lucky was the same guy who told Jean Garceau, "I never got anything I didn't work for."

36

"To be with Clark and Carole was like spending the day in the sun," Andy Devine says. Such was the pleasure of their company to the people who had it. The Gables were out of the mainstream of Hollywood social life, but they had a small circle of friends who gladly would have amputated limbs for them, had they been asked. "He was a pretty private guy," says Andy. "When he came home there was a certain group he liked to be with. People with whom, as he said, 'he could take his shoes off.' " Some were "Carole's side," others, Clark's. There were Fieldsie and Walter Lang; the Menascos—he had opened a Ford agency in Culver City; Nan and Harry Fleischmann, he of the Bakersfield duck club; Buster Collier,* who knew Carole

---

* William Buster Collier Jr. started in Hollywood as a child star in silent films. Later he was a Warner Brothers producer, and then an

from her Sennett days, and his wife, Stevie; Tuffy Goff ("Abner" of "Lum and Abner") and his wife, Liz. The last couple were ranch people, like the Gables, as were the Devines, who raised sheep and goats ("and had some hogs") on their five acres in Van Nuys. Newlyweds Howard and Gail Strickling raised chickens on their ranch near Clark's. The Stricklings didn't socialize with the gang, they were just there, nearby, in case.

Added to the clique were members of the family: Bessie, Freddy, and Stuart, who were around for holidays and parties; and Father Gable, who came by with Edna to supervise jobs like mending split-rail fences.

Clark and Carole, who earned $600,000 annually, lived in the little compound on the prairie, with horses (His, a show horse she gave him; Hers, a polo pony he gave her) and dogs (His, a pointer; Hers, a dachshund; Theirs, a boxer) and a stray cat. There were feathered friends, too: offspring of the first pair of doves Carole had sent Clark; and the rooster and Rhode Island Reds the Devines had given the Gables as a housewarming gift "right in the living room at the party."

A war had begun in Europe, but it wasn't going to spoil the fun. Walter Lang was convinced there was going to be a revolution in their own backyard, but that wasn't supposed to spoil the fun either. Clark shared Lang's conviction that one wrong step in the wrong direction and it would be all over, one way or the other. Old-timers were around, asking for money, and a constant reminder of what could happen. "They had money stashed all over the place," Richard Lang says. "They were very unsure about what was going on, but they were all strong people. It was understood that if you had a personal problem, you worked it out; if the problem was cosmic, you ignored it. They played their way through adversity, with leather cases of games and booze. If somebody was in the hospital, the gang would arrive with Monopoly."

Carole supplied the style.

"One time," says Andy Devine, "we were all going to

---

agent working with Charles Feldman. While with Warner Brothers in England, he received one of the most famous cables ever dispatched from filmland. It read: MERRY XMAS HAPPY NEW YEAR TO YOU, STEVIE AND BABY—STOP—WE ARE NOT TAKING UP YOUR OPTION—STOP—. The cable was dated December 25, 1937, and signed "Warner."

the County Fair out at Pomona, and we were going to have a picnic. But Carole sent her butler ahead with a station wagon full of food. He was there, all set up, with red table-cloths. We had a million laughs."

A guest at a party at Fred MacMurray's remembers Carole "in the most gorgeous white gown I'd ever seen. Fred had a beautiful pool—a fish pond. There were maybe thirty people sitting around it—it was summer and very hot. Carole jumped into the fish pond. Boom—like that. Clark laughed and laughed, saying, 'Isn't she wonderful? Isn't she darling? Isn't she marvelous?' Carole went in the house and came back wearing a pair of Fred's pajamas."

Buster Collier remembers getting a call one afternoon from Carole, to come right over; the yellows were running off San Diego. "We drove to the ranch, had dinner, and a few drinks. They made *some* drinks, let me tell you. About midnight we started driving to San Diego. We got there about five in the morning, boarded a boat, and all of us passed out. Just passed out."

The gang usually did wait for a call to assemble. Right from the start it was clear you didn't intrude on Clark and Carole; you didn't drop in on them. "They were a sexy couple," says one of the group. "They were all over each other. And Sundays were for making babies."

The honeymoon was interrupted early in October, twelve weeks after Clark completed *Gone With the Wind*, with an order for him to return to work. (Assignment: *Strange Cargo* with Joan Crawford.) Carole was due to return to reality later in the month, to star in a hospital drama for RKO called *Vigil in the Night*. Three days before she was to start work, she was in Cedars of Lebanon hospital with a disease highly contagious in Hollywood: appendicitis. She reportedly had an appendectomy and was home in a few days, at work within three weeks. Maybe it was. Maybe she did. Surely some of the reported appendectomies in filmland involved somebody's appendix being removed, but some friends claim Carole had a miscarriage. Maybe she did.

Both their films were heavy dramas, and quieted the stars down a bit. Clark's role as an escaped convict in *Cargo* was the meanest he'd played in years. Carole's dedicated nurse in *Vigil* was the most serious character she created in her entire career. Clark also was not over his anger at Crawford for abandoning him on *Parnell*. There was, further, renewed drama occurring in the *Gone With the Wind* department. First, there was a battle between MGM and Selznick about Gable's billing. By contract with Selznick, Clark's name was supposed to appear above the title of the film. Eventually MGM capitulated to Selznick's wish to have his own name above the title. Then plans for the December 15 Atlanta premiere got under way, and confusion reigned west, east, and south. Too many people were in on the act: MGM's publicity departments on both coasts, Selznick and staff on West Coast; a contingent of politicians and club women in Georgia. All of them pressured for their own ideas about how extensive the festivities should be in Atlanta, who should participate, and when. The big questions were whether Clark would agree to go to Atlanta at all, and if he did, how much could be asked of him. Next biggest issue was whether there should be bands, parades, luncheons (how many), dinners (how many), and dinner dances (how many). There was no question about a formal premiere being held, but there was a major crisis over the distribution of tickets. The Grand Theatre had 2,000 seats. There were 40,000 requests for them. Tickets were $10 apiece, profits to benefit the Atlanta Community Chest. Scalpers were selling them for $200 each.

Howard Dietz threw all of MGM into hysterics when he got caught between Atlanta's mayor and Georgia's governor in the ticket hassle. To make peace with the politicians, he offered the governor a free banquet for seven Southern governors he'd invited to the film, and told the mayor Clark Gable would escort his daughter to the ball after the premiere. There just wasn't anyone who would mention this to Clark, and the memos crying "Foul" and "Help" inundated Strickling's office.

The number of memos, letters, phone calls, and telegrams exchanged over every picayune detail of *L'Affaire Premiere* must have sent communications stocks soaring. Howard Dietz got one telegram from Selznick that was four feet long, and said, in part, "I WANT YOU TO BE VERY CAREFUL OF THE PAPER YOU SELECT FOR THE PROGRAM. SOMETIMES THEIR CRACKLING MAKES IT DIFFICULT TO HEAR THE DIALOGUE." When Dietz then wired Selznick not to worry about the programs, he added: "HAVE MADE TIEUP

WITH GONE WITH THE WIND PEANUT BRITTLE COMPANY
ASSURING EACH PATRON OF THE PICTURE A BOX OF PEANUT
BRITTLE AS HE ENTERS THE THEATRE."

When trouble was stamped out in one place, it flared in
another. Very late in November, someone in Atlanta requested that Clark show up a day earlier than scheduled.
Clark, by that time, was angry at MGM for "using" him,
and as punishment, withdrew Carole from the trip. (He
later okayed her going.) His champion turned out to be
David Selznick, who included these statements in a long
memo to Kay Brown:

> You must bear in mind that Gable has been op-
> posed to this whole trip from the outset. He is still
> squawking about the ball, claiming that going to the
> opening is bad enough, but that selling thousands of
> tickets because of a personal appearance by him at a
> ball is a little thick. . . . I feel that whatever he does
> for us is in the nature of a great favor, and that we
> should regard it as such. . . . He is the biggest star in
> the world, and any time he wants to show his face for
> three minutes, he can get a fortune for it. . . .

At the eleventh hour, when the minute-by-minute
schedule finally had everyone's approval, Clark learned
that Victor Fleming wasn't going to Atlanta because he
had been insulted, he thought, by Selznick, and so Clark
refused to go. Strickling's version of that brouhaha is as
follows:

"What happened was, Vic Fleming had never been to a
premiere in his life. He'd never made any personal appearances. He was the shyest, most bashful guy in that
way. But his wife had always wanted to go to a premiere.
So finally she and Carole framed up something to get Vic
to Atlanta and they bought special luggage for him. They
were all set, and they were all going together, and then
came the program for the premiere, and they had slipped
Vic's credits. He got hurt and refused to go to the premiere.
So we got into the act, and finally Carole and Clark said
they would go, if we would take them along.

"So Olivia De Havilland and David and Irene Selznick,
and Birdwell, all went by train. I promoted C. R. Smith of
American Airlines, who was just getting started then, to

get a plane, a DC-3, for Carole and Clark and Otto, and
we flew."

Before contingent number two departed, Otto sent a
night letter to Walter Winchell exclusively informing him
that Carole would be going to the premiere with Clark—
their first honeymoon trip. Strickling says:

"We always encouraged Gables and Taylors never to be
sneaking in alley ways. To go in the front way. 'If the
press wants to meet you, go ahead and meet them'—because they had built this image that they were He-guys
and He-guys don't go sneaking around back alleys.

"We left for Atlanta about midnight, and our first stop
was Tucson, Arizona. We got there about six o'clock, just
daylight, and Clark had a little hangover. There were
about five thousand people around the plane. He said,
'Jesus, I want something hot like ham and eggs. I'm going
to a restaurant.' Nobody would go with him. So he goes to
the door. He says, 'Hey, folks, you know how I feel? I've
just been up all night. Will you let me get some ham and
eggs at that place over there?' They said, 'Sure,' and they
made way for him. He walked in the restaurant and talked
to all the waitresses, had his ham and eggs, bought some
stuff for Carole and all, walked back to the plane and said
goodbye.

"When we got to Atlanta it was like a feud, you know.
C. R. Smith, he fell for Carole like all the guys did. He was
big, like Gable. A great big guy. The parade in Atlanta
was supposed to start at one o'clock. When we reached the
airport, Smith said, 'You want to come down now or fly
around a little?' I said, 'Let's fly around a little bit. Keep
the parade waiting.' He got a big kick out of it.

"In Atlanta they had all kinds of arrangements made to
sneak in here and sneak in there. Clark said, 'Listen, I
came here. They begged me to come. The people want to
see me. I don't want to go ducking in back doors.' He
stayed right out in the open, all the time. He was the first
one to come down the ramp of the plane."

On the weekend of the premiere, which the governor
declared a state holiday, the population of Atlanta went
from 300,000 to one million, and everyone wanted to see
the movie stars. All through the weekend, people lined the
streets, leaned off rooftops and out of windows, sat in trees.
Ann Rutherford says, "Even before the picture started,
everybody had a sense they were in on something that

could be a milestone. But we couldn't have imagined what would happen in Atlanta. There was *nothing* like Atlanta. Everything worked. There was dancing in the streets. All the buildings were turned into Tara. Bands kept playing. People kept shouting and laughing and cheering. Everywhere you went you were in a parade."

To appease the crowds screaming for Gable the night of the premiere, Clark agreed to say a few public words. He walked to the microphone at the entrance to the theater, gently unlinked Carole's satin-clad arm from his, and said, "Ladies and gentlemen. Tonight I am here just as a spectator. I want to see *Gone With the Wind* the same as you do. This is Margaret Mitchell's night and the people of Atlanta's night. Allow me, please, to see *Gone With the Wind* as a spectator."

He did not see the entire film that night. Says Strickling, "Inside the theater he met Margaret Mitchell for the first time. All the reporters were there and they asked her, 'Did you think of Clark Gable when you were writing the book?' She said, 'I'll never tell anyone except Mr. Gable.' They looked around for someplace to be alone, and she said, 'Let's go in here,' and she took him in the ladies' room."

They stayed there until the intermission of the three-hour and forty-five-minute film. No one who is alive today knows what they said to each other.

Despite, or because of, the rave reviews *Gone With the Wind* and its cast received, Clark was nervous about attending the Hollywood premiere, where his friends, family, and peers would be out in force. Clark got tickets for Jean Garceau and her husband, and a car pass for them so they could arrive among the stars' limousines. He wanted to do the same for his father, but Bill didn't see any reason for all the fuss. He agreed to attend the opening, but he wouldn't wear black tie and he wouldn't do anything that would bring attention to himself.

Clark and Carole, assiduously avoiding David Selznick and his group, went to the premiere with Marion Davies and Raoul Walsh. Carole wore a dazzling gold lamé gown and cape designed by Irene. Earlier in the day, her hairdresser had been at the ranch getting her groomed. She glittered from head to toe, and was mobbed, with Clark, by fans and photographers. As they went to their seats, a drunk tried to pick a fight with them, and Clark's nerves went. He didn't want to sit through the picture, and the belligerent man gave him an excuse to hide for the evening. With Carole, Marion, Raoul, and a bottle or two of Chivas Regal, he sat out the film in the manager's office. Carole's game, for the four hours, was answering the phone with, "Sorry, no reservations; sold out for a year."

The Gables did not attend the New York premiere, but did go to the 1939 Academy Awards presentation at which Gone With the Wind received ten awards, the highest number given one picture to that date. Clark had been nominated for Best Actor, and knew, from an early break in an evening newspaper, that he lost to Robert Donat in Goodbye, Mr. Chips. He publicly endured the ordeal of being overlooked for an Oscar he deserved, to cheer for Vic Fleming, who did not attend the affair but was named Best Director.

It would be several years before Clark would see Gone With the Wind in its entirety—Anita Colby believes she was the first person to sit through it with him, at a private screening in the mid-forties—and twenty years before Clark would admit to anyone that he thought he had done well in the picture. Says Jean Garceau, "I think he was proud, in his heart. He never said so to me. What he did admit being proud of was Carole, in Atlanta. When they came home from that trip, she went upstairs to dress, and he came and sat down in my office and started to talk. I never heard him so articulate as he was about that experience. He was so proud of her. He said, 'People were just agog at Mama—she was so beautiful. They were all at her feet.' "

What Clark had at his feet was MGM. On January 25, 1940, more than two years before the expiration of his 1935 contract, he signed a new contract that acceded to his stardom in every way. Twice the length of his previous contract and incorporating its standard clauses, the new contract awarded him the money in his trust estate and guaranteed him the new salary of $7,500 a week, for a minimum of forty weeks a year. It also guaranteed him an eight-hour workday between the hours of nine A.M. and six P.M., and an annual eight-week rest period between September 1 and December 1. For the first three years he would not be required to make more than three pictures a year and would have two weeks' rest between pictures; for the next four years, two pictures a year, four weeks' rest

between them. The new contract revoked the studio's right
to lend Gable or assign his contract; its right to require him
to make personal appearances. In direct deference to his
stardom, he was guaranteed first-class lodgings and transportation on locations ("If you are to travel by train we
agree to furnish you a drawing room . . ."), and a star or
co-star credit on the screen and in all advertising and publicity for any of his films, with his name to precede the
name of any co-star. And, unlike any of his previous contracts, this one granted him the option to terminate his
employment after five years.

The only hitch in the contract was Clause 26, making
Clark "available at all times in Los Angeles or any other
place we may designate." This meant that Strickling, Mannix, or Hendrickson of the legal department had to know
where Clark Gable was 365 days a year. It also accounts
for Jean Garceau's panic when Clark was out of reach of
a telephone or Western Union. For instance, late in January, Clark and Carole and the Fleischmanns drove to the
La Grulla duck club near Ensenada, Mexico. When, after
a few days, they didn't get any duck, they drove farther
south, to Hattie Hamilton's Club, to try for geese. Phone
service in both places was terrible, but Clark tried to let
someone in each club know where he was at all times.
They spent a few days wild-goose chasing, then headed
back to Ensenada and into a downpour which turned the
roads to pure mud. They stayed overnight in sleeping bags
in the station wagon, and then went on to La Grulla, arriving twenty-four hours later than expected. In those
twenty-four hours, during which Jean tried vainly to reach
both clubs, stories that the Gables were missing broke in
Los Angeles papers, and Howard Strickling ordered Otto
Winkler on a Livingstone expedition to Mexico. When the
press learned the Gables weren't missing after all, Otto
was accused of having created a publicity stunt, which was
totally uncharacteristic of him. Had the press accused
Birdwell it would at least have had a plausible case.

In the months following the openings of Gone With the
Wind, Clark and Carole stayed home and played farmer.
Clark's dream became making the ranch pay its way. He
joined the Citrus Association, which sent laborers in to
pick fruit, and worked with the caretaker planting, prun-
ing, and spraying the groves. He also decided to enlarge
his collection of chickens to six hundred, and sell eggs; and

to raise a couple of steer for beef for the ranch. The egg box Carole designed had a crest—a chicken wearing a crown—and a label, "The King's Eggs." It was of no inspiration to the chickens, however. They laid so whimsically the King couldn't deliver on a regular schedule, and so wound up using most of the eggs himself. He fared no better with the other ventures. Over the years, the fruit trees were assaulted by nature, either with bugs, frost, or drought—and never grew either in sufficient quantity or quality to sell. When the steer were slaughtered and the beef served in the dining room, no one could eat it because the calves had become a part of the family. What the Gables wound up with were mountains of bills, and the sights, smells, and sounds of a working ranch. It was good enough, and it kept Clark from thinking about the public that waited outside his walls to consume him.

His aversion to making public appearances became stronger and stronger. Alice Marble remembers asking him to introduce the finals of a tennis match in 1940. "He said, 'Walk across the court?' I said. 'Well, Honey, there's a card and you read, this match will be between . . .' He said, "I couldn't do it. I would be shaking so badly, I couldn't do it to save my life.' "

He would not permit photographs to be taken of the interior of the house, and he tried his best to keep the exact whereabouts of the ranch unknown. Nevertheless, hundreds of fan letters reached the house every week, and so did an occasional fan. Jean Garceau, who handled all mail, inspected the fan letters before she turned them over to the studio for answering. She says, "There were some letters from the same people over and over again and I had to keep what I called a MAD WOMAN file for those that might prove dangerous. These letters were mostly salacious, and written by mentally disturbed women who were almost always perfectly normal to see or to meet. It became very troublesome if they tried not only to write but to come to the ranch and try to get at him, which just drove him up the wall. This was a touchy situation because you had to try to get rid of them, and if they refused to go we could not lay a hand on them because they might say we hurt them and then there'd be a legal mess. So if it became really bad I would have to call the studio police to come out. By the time they got there the crashers were long gone into the bushes."

Keeping the location of the ranch a secret from the public turned out to be impossible. The occasional "mad woman" who trespassed became encampments of teenagers, cars full of tourists, and then sightseeing buses which drove to the front door and stopped to let the passengers stare while the driver lectured. Once the house made its way onto maps of the stars' homes, Clark had to fence the property and install an electric gate at the foot of the driveway. By the time they celebrated their first anniversary (at the track in Santa Anita), Clark and Carole were talking about looking for a home that would be farther away and harder to find. This search couldn't take place, however, until both finished their next films. Clark had started *Boom Town*, a film which proclaimed it was about "Men born of the lasting miracle that is America," late in March; and Carole was to begin her third RKO picture, *They Knew What They Wanted*, late in April.

Carole's going back to work was considered a therapeutic move by her friends. Had she been pregnant, she would have stopped working, but she wasn't, despite a year of Sundays, and she was depressed about it. Her career wasn't going the way she had hoped, either; *Vigil in the Night*, which brought her excellent reviews, failed completely at the box office, making her profit-sharing experiment a failure as well. Clearly, there were matters that the Gables, with all their combined power, couldn't control.

37

Boom Town was a rolling-off-a-log job for Clark. A story about a pair of wildcatters (Gable as "Big John," Tracy as "Square John") and their women (nice girl, Claudette Colbert; bad girl, Hedy Lamarr), it was partly filmed at oil fields near Los Angeles, which Clark found fascinating because they were such an improvement on the ones he remembered from his youth. Jack Conway directed, Johnny Mahin wrote the screenplay. Together they fashioned a film that was ideal for Gable, so much so, that Tracy sulked all through the production. Clark was home with a cold for four days in mid-April, went back to work, and was accidentally socked in the mouth by Tracy's stand-in. The blow cut and bruised his lip, damaged his dentures, and put him out of commission for a week.

While *Boom Town* was being shot, the studio readied another vehicle for Gable and Lamarr, a *Ninotchka* spin-off called *Comrade X*, to start in August. Mayer thought the pair produced sparks, and figured another Gable film would establish Hedy as a top star. They were not Rhett and Scarlett, however. Lamarr was not fiery enough for Gable, on screen or off, and her feeling that he was a nice man with no sex appeal showed on screen and off. As a co-starring team they were funny, which was fine for the farcical *Comrade X*, but L.B. was not about to turn gorgeous Hedy into a comedienne. Carole had nothing to fear from her, in any way at all.

In June, Paris fell to the Germans, but life seemed to proceed as usual for the folks who gamboled in and around Hollywood. The war was beginning to hurt the movie industry—the embattled countries of Europe were neither importing films nor exporting currency—and its moguls began to anticipate a crippling depression. The mood in the playground was, more than ever, to make every minute count. Shutters weren't being slammed against the threatening storm; the storm, if it would come, would be greeted with one huge hurricane party.

In July, Carole threw one of her annual tented outdoor affairs for the Gable clique. The Brown Derby catered, dispatching both Benny, the waiter, and Bob, the head chef. There were checked tablecloths, flowers, and candles in wine bottles on the tables, a hot dog stand with all the gear under the tent, and a buffet table groaning under stew, steaks, turkeys, and all the fixings. There was a dance floor, and a bandstand complete with band instruments, but no band. Carole's gimmick for the night was that the guests had to be the band, but only one of them could play an instrument: Fred MacMurray—and he brought his own saxophone. Clark diddled with the drums and a flute, Buster Collier played the bass fiddle, and everybody else hummed. "It was freeze-ass cold in the tent," recalls

Stevie Collier. Photographs of the party show a lot of pretty ladies truckin' on down in fox jackets.

The Gables threw parties only for close friends. Occasionally, Carole had a formal dinner for film biggies, and she and Clark attended a few as well. Hollywood, at this time, gave the impression, via the press, that it was a wildly social place; it was not. People who needed to be seen went out. Others did not. The Gables' life was not so different from the lives of other active couples in the business. It was, after all, a factory town, and people got up early to go to work. Social life centered on dinner parties at home. Carole and Clark went to fewer of these than some couples did, both because they lived out of range, and because Clark's career was secure enough to allow them to say "No" when he chose to. They were not, however, reclusive. They went to premieres and other important film functions; they went to the track, tennis tournaments, and ball games. And when they traveled it was almost always with friends.

Before Clark started *Comrade X,* he and Carole went to Arizona with the Menascos to shop for a ranch. Though they didn't find what they wanted, they loved the Arizona mountain country and planned to return for another shopping trip. "When we find our place, Jeanie," Carole told Mrs. Garceau, "you and your old man are going to come up and live with us. We'll be just one family and have a lot of fun."

They had many plans, but work always stalled them. When Clark finished *Comrade X* in October, Carole was into her last RKO film, and back to being everybody's favorite screwball. The picture was a domestic comedy called *Mr. and Mrs. Smith,* for which Carole chose Alfred Hitchcock as director and Robert Montgomery as co-star. Resorting to old reliable gags to publicize the picture, she gave a birthday party on the set for her hairdresser and served cold-cream-filled ice-cream cones; directed Hitchcock in his trademark walk-on scene, making him do take after take after take. Naturally, both events were covered by photographers. The latter got a spread in *Life.*

Duck season was well under way while Carole was still working, and Clark was restless at the ranch, eager to start for Ensenada. Carole suggested he go without her, and wait in the blinds for her to join him, but he wouldn't do that. For the first time, Jean Garceau began to notice that when Clark was at the ranch while Carole worked, "he was lost without her." They were able to leave in their faithful station wagon in November, with the Fleischmanns. The Colliers and Bergs joined them in La Grulla.

They roughed it, the way a king's hunting party should rough it. Carole had a new mink-lined poplin jacket. Clark had a new camera and made movies every time somebody opened his eyes. Unfortunately, he didn't know the camera's quirks, and shot the first 5,000 feet of film with the shutter closed. When few ducks appeared in their sights, they decided to go to Laguna Hanson, in the mountains, and called Clark's *Test Pilot* buddy, Paul Mantz, to fly them there. He appeared at the controls of his Sikorsky S-38 Twin Engine Amphibian, flew them and their gear to the isolated lake, and then waited, to fly them out again. The only place to stay on the lake was a cabin occupied by Mexicans, whom they paid to leave. "Nothing in the cabin had worked for a thousand years," Stevie Collier remembers fondly. The ladies in the group struggled with the coal stove, and since no one wanted the thousand-year-old beds, they all slept in sleeping bags on the floor. Using the outdoor bathroom facilities, Carole got poison ivy and was attacked by yellow jackets. Undaunted, she waited until she got home to go to bed and cry.

Only one thing really disturbed the Gables' determination to lead the best of all possible lives, and that was their unfulfilled, desperate wish to have children. "They were forever checking sperm," reports one of their friends. "They tried every position known to humans," reports another. "They would have done it hanging out a window if somebody said you got pregnant that way."

They were involved in a game called "Who's infertile?" which no one ever wins. (The game ends when either player is destroyed.) Doagie Devine says Carole was the infertile one. Fieldsie swore to the day of her recent death that Clark was. It would have been so bad for his image if it were known, she said, that Carole took the rap for him. Clark and Carole, for a time, didn't know who was, but Carole most assuredly blamed herself initially. In a crested carton she distributed "The King's Eggs"; why couldn't she produce "The King's Child"? As much as she wanted a baby for Clark, she wanted one for herself. She wanted to take care of a child, give to one, love one.

On December 27, 1940, the New York *Times* reported that Clark Gable had entered Johns Hopkins in Baltimore to check out an injury he'd gotten from a horse in 1933. In her 1960 book, Jean Garceau reported Clark went to Johns Hopkins to check out "a shoulder he'd injured while filming *San Francisco* in 1936." Friends say Clark and Carole went to the hospital for a fertility work-up, and more than likely, they did.

Over the years, writers have often cited Carole as the source of stories about Clark's impotence, or other inadequacies as a lover, most frequently quoting her as saying, "I love Pa, but he's a lousy lay." It is inconceivable that, if she did say it, anyone would have taken her seriously. She was a notorious tease; little of what she said off the top of her head was taken as gospel—except this silly statement. Other famous lovers have needled each other publicly about their performance in bed (Taylor and Burton, to name one pair) as a clear and obvious joke. What better gag could Carole toss off than the suggestion "Gable isn't Gable after all"? Chances are, however, that if Gable weren't Gable at *anything,* Carole—a self-appointed guardian of her husband's image—would be the last person in the world to say so. She knew Clark's needs better than anyone else in his life, went far beyond the normal in catering to them. Is it possible that, knowing how fragile was his sense of masculinity, she would disparage it to people she barely knew? In candid photographs of the two of them, she is at his feet, on his lap, flopped over him like a rag doll—always touching, touching, touching him. Indeed, in some of the photos she looks like a mother who can't keep her hands off a child of whom she is excessively proud, but she leaves no doubt she is a smitten woman. It seems a waste to bring up the matter at all, except to shoot it down. Until someone offers home movies of Clark and Carole in the act, the curiosity about what these glorious movie stars did in bed will simply have to be suffered.

The talk, which persists to this day, about Clark's infidelities to Carole began after their trip to Baltimore, and was strong enough to muddy the legendary love story. One of his alleged affairs, with a starlet he met during *Gone With the Wind,* reportedly lost the young lady her MGM contract. "He was a promiscuous man," Howard Dietz says unconditionally. Another man who knew the

Gables says, "He was running around a lot. But that's not to say he didn't love Carole. That's only really wrong in the wife's eyes. The other guys say, 'Atta Boy!' I think Carole knew about most of the women and would let him have it about most of them. She screamed at him every six, eight weeks, and he was a good boy for a while." One of Carole's friends says, "Clark was a typical Aquarian. You could walk in his room and find him in bed with some broad and he'd look you right in the eye and say, 'What's wrong?' Sure he was screwing around; he didn't see any reason not to."

There was unmistakable tension in the Gable household as the second year of their marriage drew to a close. As far as anyone knew for certain, it was caused primarily by a hiatus in Carole's career. There was also the continuing matter of their inability to secure privacy, and the matter of the war in Europe edging closer to home.

Before they had returned from their Baltimore trip, Clark and Carole had a VIP tour of Washington, D.C. President Roosevelt learned they were in the capital and invited them to join a few other guests who would sit in the Oval Room while he gave his year's-end Fireside Chat on network radio. They were fittingly honored by the invitation, and sensibly distressed by the nature of the speech. Roosevelt made clear his conviction that Germany intended ". . . to enslave the whole of Europe" and then ". . . dominate the rest of the world." He urged the country to support Great Britain, and increase its defense efforts, and hinted at the necessity to institute rationing of certain foods and luxury items. After his speech, he invited the Gables to stay and talk, which they did, for about half an hour.

Clark and Carole took the visit very seriously. When they got home they began what Jean Garceau called "laying in food supplies, for the ranch-to-be, storing them in one of the waterproof barns." These food supplies, ostensibly for a home they hoped to own one day, bore remarkable resemblance to those being hoarded by many people who suspected imminent shortages: hundred-pound sacks of sugar, cases of canned goods, bottles of oil and molasses. Carole also bought ten galvanized metal garbage cans, four-feet high, and had them filled with beans. Mrs. Garceau asked Carole, "Why on earth did you buy so many beans?" and Carole replied, "Pa likes his baked beans. We must never run short!"

On January 31, 1941, Clark received the following night letter at home from Eddie Mannix: CONGRATULATIONS AND WISH YOU A HAPPY BIRTHDAY. ALSO THANKS FOR THE DUCKS AND GEESE. AM EATING DUCKS TONIGHT AND GEESE SUNDAY AND WILL BE THINKING OF YOU. IF YOU GET A CHANCE TO COME IN HAVE A HELL OF A STORY FOR YOU. BEST REGARDS.

The hell of a story was *They Met in Bombay,* a badly conceived film in which Clark was to play a jewel thief with a heart of gems, co-starring with Rosalind Russell. He started work on it in March. Though neither he nor Miss Russell was happy with the script, they had a comfortable relationship and enjoyed working together. She has often talked about the ease of doing a love scene with him, which, she says, came from his remarkable grace. She claims he had a way of standing which made his screen kiss seem totally natural. "He was a very graceful person with his body, and there wasn't all this enormous clinching and awkwardness. His rhythm and timing were much like a ballet dancer's." (Delmer Daves, somewhat more critical of Clark's clinch scenes, actually timed the rhythm of them when he directed him in 1952, and discovered a kind of conga beat: one, two, three, kiss.)

Miss Russell was more solicitous of Mrs. Gable than most of Clark's leading ladies. She had a maid who hand-stitched leather gloves, and sent Clark home with dozens of pairs of them for Carole, who appreciated all the levels of her thoughtfulness.

The Gables' second wedding anniversary occurred during the making of *Bombay,* and Carole arranged a surprise party for the occasion, catered by the Brown Derby, right on a set. Earlier, she had thrown a fortieth birthday party for Clark at the ranch, which the Brown Derby catered, and Benny the waiter remembers as a happy event presided over by a doting wife.

Carole spent most of her time presiding over one thing or another because she had no work. Her RKO contract was not extended, and her association with David Selznick was in limbo, despite her film commitment to him, because of Clark's hatred of the man. She read dozens of scripts, and saw many of them go into production with her professional rivals. As the months went by, she blamed

Myron Selznick for her inactivity, accusing him of not
getting material to her fast enough, and not selling her to
the studios. She asked him to release her from her contract with him, which extended through 1943. He refused.
She turned the matter over to W. I. Gilbert, who first tried
to settle with Myron, and then submitted the matter to
court for arbitration. There was no precedent for the case,
and it lingered over several weeks. When it was decided,
the industry proclaimed it a victory for Carole, though certainly it was a mixed one. Carole got her release, but she
had to pay Myron $27,500 estimated commission on
future work; and she had to pay all the court costs. She
signed with a new agent, Nat Wolff, who was an occasional
hunting companion of Clark's. Their joint efforts eventually
got her assigned to two films, one a comedy with Jack
Benny for fall production called *To Be or Not to Be*, the
other called *They All Kissed the Bride*.

While she still had time on her hands, she helped the
Garceaus build and decorate a Cape Cod cottage, which
Clark so admired he ordered a similar one built for his
father. Both houses were within five miles of the ranch,
and Carole dashed from one to the other, fussing over
matters of taste, delighted to be of service.

She also did a little fussing around MGM. She wanted
the studio to send her 16mm prints of *Free Soul*, *Susan
Lenox*, *Dancing Lady*, *Mutiny on the Bounty*, *San Francisco*, and *Boom Town*. Her initial request wound up in
the hands of the legal department, whose Mr. Hendrickson wrote her a letter saying it was against company policy
to comply with her request. When a copy of his letter circulated to the other executives, there was much rustling
around, and then a note from Hendrickson appended to
the carbon, which was recirculated. The note said: "Miss
Lombard spoke to Mr. Mannix on Saturday evening at a
party at which time Mr. Mannix indicated that he would
endeavor to get the films for Miss Lombard. Otto will
call her and tell her that he was advised today that the
above letter had been mailed to her and that I had no
knowledge of her discussion with Mr. Mannix last Saturday evening."

Without further ado the films were delivered, and instructions sent from Mr. Mannix, to whom it concerned,
that the cost of the films would be charged to overhead.

Clark took only a short rest period after *Bombay* because he anticipated the picture would be badly reviewed and wanted to do another immediately. He chose to play a heartless frontier gambler in *Honky Tonk,* a film the studio considered unworthy of him, and asked Jack Conway to direct it. The good girl, and therefore his girl, was to be played by newcomer Lana Turner; the bad girl, and therefore his ex-girl, by Claire Trevor. From the moment the film began there was an explosion of rumors about Clark and Lana, and Carole responded to them wildly, threatening to make a scene of her own at the studio, threatening to kick both Turner and Gable in the ass, etc. She visited the set a few times, and then was requested by studio executives to stay home. Miss Turner recalled for a *Ladies' Home Journal* article:

> We rehearsed our first love scene—ours was a wonderful chemical rapport which came over on film —and suddenly I turned around and froze. There was beloved Carole Lombard, Mrs. Gable! She seldom came on the set but I guess she wanted to see who the new kid was. Well, it's one thing to work with a King but quite another to have his Lady there. I retreated to my dressing room and when director Jack Conway came to say we were ready to shoot, I wailed, 'I can't!' Whether Jack told Clark, I don't know. I just know that while I sat in my dressing room suffering, beautiful Carole disappeared.

In the same article Miss Turner declared of her relationship with Clark: "Ours was a closeness without intimacy. There was a dear loving for him but never an affair. No way."

Honky Tonk was shot so quickly that when it was previewed rumors of an affair on the set were still warm on the lips of Lolly and Hedda. In a rare move, the Gables attended the first preview, and held hands throughout it. The feline sex appeal of the young Lana Turner (she was really the first sex kitten, Bardot notwithstanding) and the tomcat sex appeal of vintage Clark Gable became something close to erotic on the screen, and the team was declared box office dynamite. To Carole's dismay, MGM executives left the preview determined to team Gable and Turner again, as soon as he caught some fish, or shot some birds, or whatever that was he did when he wasn't working.

Clark and Carole went to the Rogue River with the Fleischmanns, but were so put upon by locals who knew which cabin Clark used they had to leave. Without the Fleischmanns, they rented a cabin cruiser on Lake Mead and spent three days alone, which they probably needed. By this time, whenever they were away, either Jimmy Fidler or Walter Winchell inevitably announced the Gables had split.

For the opening of duck season, the Gables and the Fleischmanns took off for South Dakota, but were grounded by bad weather, and wound up in Kansas City. Excessively fussed over by the owner of the hotel where they were trapped, Clark had a tantrum and called the airline, ordering it to get him and his party out of Kansas instantly. The airline warmed up its largest transcontinental plane and flew the four to Omaha, whence they were driven to Watertown, South Dakota. They stayed only one day because again the natives besieged them. When they learned they couldn't fly out because of bad weather, Clark bought a Ford (he always carried two to three thousand dollars in cash) and they drove home, straight into a formation of reporters seeking a confirmation of their separation.

They decided, that night, that when Carole finished her picture, they would put the ranch on the market and move somewhere—anywhere they would be left alone. Carole, however, would never have a chance to take care of selling the ranch. She would live on it for the rest of her life, and Clark would live on it for the rest of his.

38

Behind the scenes, 1942 began like this:

Wire to Howard Strickling from W. G. Bishop (date obscured):

> RE YOUR LETTER JANUARY 5 ON MASSEY HARRIS
> CATALOGUE AND CALENDAR, THEY WILL DELIVER
> FROM NEAREST DEALER TO THE GABLE RANCH ONE OF
> THEIR LARGE TRACTORS FULLY EQUIPPED PLUS A CER-
> TAIN SUM TO HIS FAVORITE CHARITY AS PER CORRE-
> SPONDENCE SENT TO YOU UNDER DATE OF JANUARY 2.
> UNDERSTAND COMPANY WILLING TO STEP UP CHARITY
> CONTRIBUTIONS CONSIDERABLY IF CAROLE LOMBARD
> ALSO AVAILABLE FOR PICTURE. AGENCY WILL PREPARE
> SKETCHES AND HAVE REPRESENTATIVE AVAILABLE
> WHEN PHOTO OF GABLE WITH TRACTOR IS TAKEN.
> PLEASE ADVISE SOONEST.

Wire to Bill Bishop from Howard Strickling (date obscured):

> CLARK GABLE DEFINITELY INTERESTED IN MASSEY
> HARRIS TRACTOR AND PROPOSITION WHEREBY HE WILL
> RECEIVE TRACTOR PLUS CERTAIN SUM TO CHARITY
> PROVIDED PROPOSITION SATISFACTORY. BELIEVE CAN
> ALSO ARRANGE FOR MRS. GABLE. TO DATE WE HAVE
> NEVER RECEIVED CATALOGUE SO DON'T KNOW WHAT
> MASSEY TRACTOR IS. IF YOU WILL HAVE THEIR REP-
> RESENTATIVE CONTACT US MONDAY AS TO TYPE TRAC-
> TOR WILL GIVE DEFINITE DECISION THEN.

Wire to Bill Bishop from Howard Strickling dated January 16:

> CLARK GABLE OKAY ON MASSEY HARRIS TRACTOR.

WOULD LIKE THE MODEL #81 WITH PLOW CULTIVA-
TOR AND OTHER EQUIPMENT. AS HE IS NOW WORKING
WILL TAKE THE PICTURE ANY SUNDAY WITH MRS.
GABLE PROVIDED SKETCHES ARE SATISFACTORY.

On January 16, 1942, at 7:20 P.M. (PST), Mrs. Gable
was killed, along with her mother, Otto Winkler, and nine-
teen others, when the TWA twin-engine DC-3 in which
she was a passenger crashed into a vertical rock cliff near
the top of Potosi Mountain, thirteen minutes after leaving
Las Vegas, Nevada.

On January 16, 1942, Carole Lombard Gable was dead
at age thirty-three. Dead because the war blacked out
beacons that might have kept the pilot on course. Dead
because of patriotism that took her from home to sell.
War Bonds. Dead because of nervous energy that made
her board a plane in the middle of the night instead of
waiting for a morning train.

Dead.

She would never be in the photographs of the tractor.

Or on the ranch again, or in the duck blinds, or on her
motor scooter, or under the dryer, or in her mirrored dressing room, or on a set, or at Clark's side, at his feet, in his
arms.

"Why Ma?" Clark asked over and over in his anguish.
How could anyone answer, when everyone felt such pain?

The attack on Pearl Harbor and Roosevelt's declaration
of war the following day affected the Gables the way it did
everyone else in America. They were angry and frightened, somewhat disbelieving, eager to do their part. Clark,
much more conservative, politically, than Carole, had been
an isolationist, a matter of no relevance at all once the
war began. Meeting Roosevelt had made him a temporary
Democrat, and also gave him the impetus to write the
White House volunteering his services, and Carole's, to the
war effort. The President answered him, urging the two
stars to stay at what they were doing because films were
necessary for morale.

The war seemed closer to people on the West Coast
because they were vulnerable to direct attack. In Los Angeles, as well as in other major cities, there were immediate air raid drills, black-outs, brown-outs, and other
civilian efforts at mobilization. People of the film industry,

bred to drama, pitched in with perhaps a bit more flare than necessary, but with a spirit that has become legend in the domestic history of the war. Robert Montgomery and James Stewart enlisted before the war began, setting a precedent followed in short order by their peers. Carole wanted Clark to apply for a commission and get into the Army. He wasn't sure what a man of his age could offer, but agreed to investigate. Meanwhile, he was asked to head the actors' division of the Hollywood Victory Committee, and threw himself earnestly into the job.

Carole finished *To Be or Not to Be* in mid-December, and let Jean Garceau know their usual wild Christmas shopping spree was postponed for the duration. With few exceptions, their friends would get cards telling them of contributions made in their names to the Red Cross. The Garceaus, considered part of the family, received, on Christmas Eve, an Early American bedroom set. (The Gables had given them a dining room set as a house-warming gift.) Clark, who usually gave Carole diamond and/or ruby jewelry for Christmas (one year he also gave her a Cadillac convertible), this year gave her diamond and ruby earrings. Carole usually gave Clark sporting equipment, but succumbed to sentiment and bought him a solid gold cigarette case, engraved: "To Pa. I love you. Ma."

Parties were down to a minimum on the social circuit, but Ernst Lubitsch, who directed *To Be or Not to Be,* was so pleased with the painless way the film had proceeded he gave an extravagant bash to celebrate its completion. Clark and Carole attended with all the luminaries a favorite director could muster. Carole was particularly happy to go because she felt the picture was one of the best she'd ever made.

Clark had to report for work on *Somewhere I'll Find You,* the Lana Turner picture, around the fourteenth of January. Carole urged him to inquire about a commission before the film began, knowing he would be tied up for months, once it did.

In New York, Howard Dietz had been "drafted" by Secretary of the Treasury Henry Morgenthau, to promote the sale of War Bonds. In this capacity, Dietz organized a program that would send movie stars on War Bond tours, and to launch it in Indiana, he chose the most famous Hoosier available—Carole Lombard. His request

for her participation went to Clark, not because he was
her husband, but because of his position on the Victory
Committee. Carole was thrilled with the "invitation."
Clark sent Dietz his okay, and Dietz set January 15 as the
big day. Carole was to leave for Indianapolis by train on
January 12, selling bonds at stops en route. Dietz's implicit
instructions to all participants in the program was that
nobody was to travel by plane. He wanted minimum risk
of accidents or delays. Carole's round-trip Pullman accommodations were fully booked for her from the moment
she agreed to go.

Carole wanted Clark to go with her, but he couldn't because of his film commitment. As his surrogate, he chose
Otto Winkler, who swelled with pride, being asked. "He
trusts me to take care of his old lady," he told Strickling,
and then bought a gray, pinstriped suit—the kind, Strickling noticed, "that Clark wore a lot." Carole wanted her
mother to go, also, and Fieldsie. Neither was an odd
choice; they were the women closest to her.

Irene whipped together a few black ensembles for
Carole, who also packed the memorable gown she wore to
the ball in Atlanta: a strapless black velvet creation with
an overskirt drawn to the side with a huge rose. For Bessie, Carole made a whirlwind shopping tour of her favorite
shops, and then stopped for lunch, with her mother, at the
Brown Derby. There she saw Benny Massi, who remembers her wearing "a long mink coat, from the top to the
bottom," which was probably a sable coat she had in her
wardrobe. She told him, "I'm going on a tour to sell War
Bonds and I want you to take care of my Pappy if he
comes here. I'll see you when I come back; we'll have a
nice party."

Fieldsie was ill the day the group departed and couldn't
make the trip. Clark was away, reportedly in Washington
looking into his future military career. Carole gave Jean
Garceau a handful of notes to give him, one each day,
while she was gone. That she already had in mind to fly
home is clear; there were just five notes, rather than the
seven or eight that would have been in order had she
planned to take the train. Howard Dietz called her to urge
her once again to take the trains scheduled, and then
called Otto to caution him to see that Carole obeyed the
order. Carole didn't tell them—she told a reporter in Salt

Lake City—that she planned to be at the first preview of *To Be or Not to Be* on the eighteenth.

She left on the morning of January 12, in a sober mood, asking Jean, as she had asked Benny, to take care of her old man.

When Clark got home, on the thirteenth, he found, in his bed, a buxom blond dummy bearing a note, "So you won't be lonely." The joke was to remind him to keep his hands off Lana Turner and other such attractive creatures while she was gone.

Young Robert Sterling, on leave from the Air National Guard, was cast as Clark's brother in *Somewhere I'll Find You*. He recalls that when they started work, on the four-teenth, Clark's stand-in, Lew Smith, came to his dressing room ("Next door to Clark's but somewhat lesser in gran-deur") and said, "Pappy would like you to come for coffee." When he went, Clark told him about the dummy Carole had made, and asked him to help make one to put in Carole's bed. On Clark's dressing table, Sterling noticed, was a tall crystal vase holding a single rose. Clark said, "Carole sent it. That somabitch thinks of everything." A string of fake doves she had given him the year before were draped over the top of his mirror. "She was just a groovy lady," Sterling says. "He adored her.

"We worked three days, creating a male dummy in free moments. And on the third day, about five o'clock, when my ass was dragging, Clark stopped at my dressing room and said, 'Come on, Junior, help me with this.' " Sterling helped him to his car with the dummy which was, he says, "amusingly vulgar." (It had a large, erect penis.) As he got the monster into his car, Clark said, "Don't hurry to work tomorrow; I'm going to be late." He winked and drove away.

Jill Winkler was invited to the welcome-home dinner, as were Carole's brothers and Freddie's wife, Virginia. The house was filled with flowers, the table set and gleam-ing. Clark was so moved by the way the place looked, he called Jean to thank her.

Carole, Bessie, and Otto were due at the airport in Bur-bank around seven. They had left Indianapolis at four A.M. The flight was seventeen hours, and they gained time coming home. Otto had called his wife from one of their stops to tell her he had tried to get Carole to wait and take the train, but just couldn't contain her. He'd even flipped a coin with her, he said—and lost.

Neither Jean nor Clark had spoken to Carole since the fourteenth, but she wired each of them on her way home. She asked Jean to have her hairdresser and manicurist at the house in the morning, and told Clark, "Hey, Pappy, you'd better get into this man's army."

Her tour had been incredibly successful. In Indianapolis alone, she sold over $2 million worth of bonds. She had signed thousands of autographs, shaken thousands of hands. When she led the singing of "The Star-Spangled Banner" in the Cadle Tabernacle, backed by three military bands, she broke, for the first time, and cried. After a powerful farewell victory salute, she listened to the loving cheers of her fellow patriots, prouder of herself than she had ever been.

She was too emotionally high to sleep and too tired to sit. A *Life* reporter suggested to her that she get some rest, and then take the Saturday train. She told him by the time she would be on the train, she could be asleep in her own bed, and that she couldn't stand "choo-choo's."

If only and if only—if—and if—and if.

The plane was delayed all along its route, and Clark was kept informed of the new arrival times by Larry Barbier, who had gone to Burbank to meet Carole. The news that the plane was down near Las Vegas was first received by Barbier, who contacted Howard Strickling at a garage where he was overseeing work on his car. Howard told Larry to charter a plane, called Clark, and left to meet him at the airport. Ralph Wheelright drove Clark, Jill Winkler, and Stuart to the airport. Freddie and his wife started for Las Vegas by car; Eddie Mannix took a scheduled flight. The Garceaus went to the Gable ranch, where they were joined by the Bergs and the Goffs. All of them feared the worst.

Howard Strickling says of the plane trip, "As I've said, Clark was the biggest man I ever knew, in every way. I mean, in his size, too—he always seemed so big to me. In the plane that night, I thought he was going to squash me. He was so tense, you know, because he sensed what had happened. You knew you shouldn't talk to him. You knew not to say 'It's going to be all right' or 'I'm sorry.' "

Search parties were just leaving for the site of the crash when Clark arrived in Las Vegas. He learned that several witnesses had seen the plane flying off course, and others had seen a fire on the mountain where the crash was assumed to have occurred. It was obvious that the search would take most of the night, for there were no roads up the snow-covered mountain; only narrow trails. The first search party was a small one composed mostly of Army personnel. The second included stretcher-bearing mules, medical personnel and supplies, and deputy sheriffs to guard the wreckage. Clark asked to go with the second group, but was persuaded by his friends to stay behind. Eddie Mannix and Ralph Wheelright made the tortured climb in his place, and carried with them for decades the sight and smell of the carnage that was found. Many years after the tragedy, Mannix told another MGM executive that Carole's burned body had been decapitated. Though it would be fervently hoped that Clark was spared this grisly detail, Mannix said it had been told him.

The inhuman ordeal in Las Vegas dragged out for three days, during which Clark's friends were more awed than ever by his stoic composure. Al Menasco, Buster Collier, and Phil Berg were among the close friends who flew to Las Vegas once the news was officially released. Buster says, "Clark put on the greatest act of his life, trying to keep everyone else from crumbling." He saw to the comfort of returning members of the search parties, took long walks with Collier, a ride with Al Menasco to a spot where he could see the crash site, and waited, in near silence, for the bodies of his wife, his mother-in-law, and his trusted friend to be brought down from the mountain. He asked Ralph Wheelright if he thought Carole had known . . . Wheelright said no. He asked Al Menasco what he thought had happened, and Menasco told him. He himself told the group waiting at the ranch, "Ma's gone," when he knew for certain that was so. He was on the train that bore the bodies to Los Angeles, and at Forest Lawn immediately afterward to make funeral arrangements.

He purchased three modest crypts: one for Bessie, one for Carole, and next to Carole's, one for himself.

Because Carole had died in the service of her country, the Army wanted to give her a military funeral. The Hollywood Victory Committee wanted to erect a monument in her honor. Clark refused both offers. Carole's will, dated August 8, 1939, specified:

I request that no person other than my immediate family and the persons who shall prepare my remains for interment be permitted to view my remains after death has been pronounced. I further request a private funeral and that I be clothed in white and placed in a modestly priced crypt in Forest Lawn Memorial Park, Glendale, California.

Clark stayed with Al Menasco and did not return to the ranch until after the simple funeral for Carole and Bessie on January 22. That night, Jean gave him the last note Carole had written, and Clark broke apart. Except on a tense day on the set of *Gone With the Wind,* no one had ever seen Clark Gable cry before. When Otto was buried the next day, Clark was Jill's comfort and strength.

He was a changed man. A man who had been to some dark and terrible place, and returned. Lazarus. People were afraid to go near him, though he showed a softness and a compassion he had never shown before. He was gaunt and hypertense—so much so his doctor warned him not to drink. But that wasn't what people noticed about him. He smelled of death. Of metaphysical death.

Ma was dead. Mother was dead. That's what happened, that's why life was so strange: Ma was *dead.*

A part of Clark was dead, too, and only Howard Strickling spotted what it was. "The boyishness he had, you know. The little boy was gone."

Carole Lombard died and the little boy she loved died with her.

The question was, what kind of man survived her?

PART FIVE

HERO

(1942-1952)

39

The picture that emerges of Clark in the aftermath of the tragedy is that of a sad and aimless wanderer, "inconsolable and unapproachable."

He could not work, of course, and production of *Somewhere I'll Find You* was suspended. The initial task of his day was just getting out of bed to face his grief and the painful feelings that complicated it: the rage, bewilderment, and guilt. The gnawing, clawing guilt. He was alive; she was dead. He was alive; Otto was dead. He was alive; Bessie was dead. Howard Dietz wrote Clark about his own feelings of guilt at having sent Carole on the tour, and Clark was able to send him a gentle letter of absolution. Otto just wasn't aggressive enough to keep Carole off the plane, he wrote, and the tragedy was too strong to dwell on the whys and wherefores. It was one thing to write this to a friend, another to accept it himself. Images of how Carole might have died tortured him, and no amount of information on the crash could take away his fear that she had known, that she had suffered. Over all was the unreality of anyone as ferociously alive as Carole being vulnerable to death.

He could not bear to participate in the details of running the ranch. Says Jean Garceau, "When Carole was there, they did a lot of playing around outside together and Clark loved to run the tractor and play at gentleman farming. I just carried out their orders. After she was gone, the job of supervision fell to me. There were the citrus trees, which had to be irrigated, pruned, sprayed and cultivated. We had rose gardens, paddocks, six acres that had to be planted to rye grass. There were the stables, a huge barn (with only one cow), the dove cotes." There was also the household to run, which meant keeping the servants in line, supervising the buying, planning the meals, shopping. "I tried to run the home just as Carole had run it, as that was what pleased Clark," she says. Her standing order was that nothing of the life-style of the house was to change; Mr. Gable was to dine with flowers and lighted candles on the table, china, crystal, and silver set as usual, even to the finger bowls.

He ate alone. One day, when Adela Rogers St. Johns stopped in to see how Clark was doing, she asked him why he didn't invite some friends to dinner. He replied, as though it answered everything, "Ma always did that."

He tried to run away. Strickling says, "He'd get into the car and drive up to Oregon, all by himself. He'd drive out in the Valley, just drive and drive, to all kinds of places, sometimes not knowing where he was going." Automobiles couldn't take him fast enough, so he bought a massive motorcycle and began tearing through the canyons on it. The motorcycle helped; it required his full concentration. He could also ride with someone without having to talk, and he chose Al Menasco as his cycling companion.

He made himself walk the ranch, slowly, painfully. He walked along the split-rail fences circling the property. He wandered to the stables, stopping to pet the horses, but not able to mount one. He went out to the garage and stared at the station wagon. He walked among the orchards, and through the alfalfa fields. Touchingly, everywhere he walked he was followed by Carole's dachshund, Commissioner, who, before his mistress's death, wouldn't go near him.

The meanderings were so private a communication, the help in the house turned away from the sight. When one would ask, "Where's Mr. Gable?" another would just point to a window, indicating somewhere outside. There were many days, Strickling says, Clark talked to no one.

When he did talk, it was always about Ma—how she looked, the funny things she did, the plans she had had. Mostly he talked to Jean, Al Menasco, Harry Fleischmann, the Langs, and Howard Strickling. With few exceptions he avoided the people he had known through Carole. Says Andy Devine, "It was just that any time he'd run into you, it would make him think of Carole. He would talk about her—and only about her. After a while, we didn't see him at all."

One of the relationships Carole had sponsored ended abruptly and bitterly: the one with her brothers. There are many unpleasant stories about why Clark and the brothers stopped speaking, but none can be verified. The logical assumption is that one of the causes was Carole's will, which left everything to Clark and contained this clause: "I have . . . intentionally and with full knowledge omitted to provide for heirs living at the time of my decease." As often happens in estate distribution, many people were angry at being overlooked. None, perhaps, had as much reason as the two men who had lost both their sister and their mother, and reportedly they did blame Clark, particularly for Bessie's taking the trip. It did not help their feelings any that a story was circulating about Clark and Carole having had "the fight of their lives" before she left, over Clark's lingering affair with an MGM starlet.

The estate amounted to more than a half-million dollars, not including the ranch, which had been purchased in Clark's name. About $21,000 was in furs and jewelry. Carole left behind capes of ermine, beaver, and fox; coats of sable, and Persian lamb; jackets of fox, lynx, and caracul; wraps of marten and sable; and a sable muff. The jewelry left was not so extensive, because she had taken the ruby and diamond pieces Clark had given her to Indianapolis. (Only a small, mutilated portion of one of them was recovered from the crash, and Clark wore it around his neck in a specially designed gold locket.) Among the other assets were three hunting guns: a 20-gauge Remington, a 410-gauge Winchester, and 12-gauge Browning; 230 chickens; and an interest in five film properties. Carole, indeed, had been the sum of her parts.

Nothing of the estate could be touched until the will was probated, so Clark was spared, until he was better fit for it, the distribution of her personal belongings. Eventually he sold her car and disposed of her wardrobe, giving much of it to Jean Garceau. He gave her hand-tooled saddle to the wife of their riding instructor, and to Adela Rogers St. Johns, two books Carole had been reading before she left on the tour: *The Cloud of Unknowing* and *Cosmic Consciousness*. Anything that was part of the decor of the house remained in the house, precisely where Carole had placed it. Carole's bedroom suite was kept clean, closed, and intact, except for the concert harp, which seems simply to have disappeared, but may have been sold.

A part of Clark's flight from the haunted ranch was his decision, once again, to sell it. He sent Jean Garceau house hunting in Bel Air and Beverly Hills, and she did so earnestly, though without believing that Clark would really move. Her belief was reinforced by the fact that nothing she took him to see quite pleased him, but she continued the charade as long as it was required.

Clark's house hunting gave rise to column items that he was going to quit films and enlist, and those rumors prompted two telegrams.

Wire to Clark Gable, from Captain Sy Bartlett, Washington, D.C., January 23, 1942:

HAVE JUST HAD FAVORABLE DISCUSSION ABOUT YOU WITH CHIEF OF ARMY AIR FORCES GENERAL ARNOLD. I BELIEVE THERE IS A GREAT JOB FOR YOU TO DO WITH THE AIR CORPS. IF YOU'VE TAKEN ANY OTHER STEPS WOULD SUGGEST YOU DO NOTHING UNTIL I ARRIVE. MY GREATEST CONCERN IS THAT WE DO NOT, REPEAT NOT, CONFLICT WITH STUDIO PLANS. REGARDS.

Wire to Clark Gable from H. H. Arnold, Lieutenant General Chief of the Army Air Forces, January 23, 1942:

CAPTAIN SY BARTLETT, WHOM YOU KNOW, HAS JUST BEEN TRANSFERRED TO THE ARMY AIR FORCES. HE INFORMS ME THAT YOU WISH TO JOIN THE AIR FORCES. IF WE DO NOT, REPEAT NOT, CONFLICT WITH YOUR STUDIOS FUTURE PLANS FOR YOU, I BELIEVE IN MY CAPACITY AS CHIEF OF THE ARMY AIR FORCES, THAT WE HAVE SPECIFIC AND HIGHLY IMPORTANT ASSIGNMENT FOR YOU. CAPTAIN BARTLETT WILL BE IN CALIFORNIA WITHIN A FORTNIGHT AND WILL DISCUSS MY PLANS WITH YOU.

The wires were sent to MGM, where they were immediately sidetracked.

Wire to Captain Sy Bartlett from Howard Strickling, January 23, 1942:

WIRE TO GABLE RECEIVED BUT NOT GIVING IT TO HIM AS DO NOT THINK IT ADVISABLE TO DISCUSS WITH HIM AT PRESENT TIME. SUGGEST YOU TELEPHONE ME SATURDAY AT STATE 41702. REGARDS.

The studio did not want to lose Gable to the service,

ever, and conspired to keep him a civilian as best it could. Even before he reported back to work, his favorite writers and directors were asked to locate properties for him. As soon as he agreed to complete *Somewhere I'll Find You,* Strickling wired Dietz to release the news there was ". . . another picture planned for Gable called *Shadow of the Wing,* a thrilling story of the Army Air Corps to be directed by Victor Fleming. Sam Zimbalist to be producer." When production resumed, he wired him to announce again, "After filming present film, Gable starts *Shadow of the Wing,* story of soldier of fortune who joins Air Force."

Clark began working again on February 23, responding to no pressure except his own. Director Wesley Ruggles (who had also directed Clark's only film with Carole) cautioned cast and crew "not to baby him." No one did. When anyone tried, Clark turned to stone. One matter that disturbed him was that the studio kept him on payroll during the weeks he hadn't worked, despite his request to the contrary. Many memos were stuffed into the studio legal files about the issue, until this final report was filed by Mr. Hendrickson on March 3:

At Mr. Mannix's request, I went to Stage 22 to talk to Gable relative to his wishes in connection with salary during the period he was absent from the studio, January 17 to February 22 inclusive. I advised Gable that on January 27, 28, or 29, we received certain word from Phil Berg and from his secretary to the effect that he desired to be taken off salary as of January 16 . . . and to be resumed on salary the day he reported to the studio on Monday, February 23, as he did not wish to be paid during a period in which he was not rendering services. I advised him that we had continued to draw his checks throughout this period of time at the specific instructions of Mr. Mannix. He nevertheless reiterated that he did not wish to accept any pay during his absence.

Once the matter was settled, Clark wanted no more dallying. On March 4, Hendrickson informed the payroll department: "It is most urgent that Gable's check for the three-day period ending February 25, 1942, be mailed to him today."

The set of *Somewhere I'll Find You* was closed and

guarded by studio police. Unlike the good old days, when Clark had left his dressing room open to all callers—and often sat outside it so the crew would feel free to approach him—he now made it clear he wanted to be alone. He ate in his dressing room with the door shut. When occasionally he sat outside to get some sun, he had the police insure his privacy. Working gave him some distraction from mourning Carole, but brought him face to face with the depth of his dependency on Otto Winkler. He couldn't stop expecting him to poke his face in the dressing room, couldn't stop the impulse to call the publicity department, and say, "Where the hell is Winkler? Well, tell him to get his ass over here." Strickling wanted to appoint a replacement for him. Clark said not now, and not ever.

The change in Clark at work went beyond his withdrawal, to something which showed on the screen; his sense of humor was gone. It takes no special perception to spot it in the film when it is run today. The engaging undercurrent of fun, irrepressible in the Gable persona, had become an undercurrent of anger. In many scenes he seems to be flinching from the camera, afraid of what it will catch if he looks it in the eye. Physically, he is the same super-virile figure who wears his coat collar turned up and lifts his lady as though she weighs less than a poodle puppy. But he is grouchy, dour, different. Parts of the film which deal with the tragedies of the war in Bataan, with death and the threat of death, must have been excruciating for him to handle.

His discipline got him through his scenes, but the worst part of the day was the end of it, when he had to go home. The hours he used to spend with Carole before dinner were always bubbling ones, almost manic with her ceaseless chatter. Now there was no reason to curtail the cocktail hours, and all the reasons in the world to continue it through his lonely dinner and into the night. Jean Garceau stayed at the house for dinner the first week of shooting, but he couldn't let her continue to do that. Instead, he looked for an excuse not to go home, and found one.

One day in March, Joan Crawford, to whom he had not been civil in years, sent him a note at the studio saying, as she recalls, "If you'd like to stop by and have a quiet dinner, I'll be home rather late tonight and all this week." It was not Joan's first gesture of empathy after Carole's death. She had volunteered, the day she heard the news of the crash, to take Carole's scheduled role in *They All Kissed the Bride,* and donate her salary of $125,000 to the Red Cross. Her agent made the deal. When he took his usual 10 percent, she fired him.

Clark accepted her invitation to dinner the day he got it, and every other day until his film was finished. "He needed someone to talk to, and I just listened until three in the morning. He knew I would never repeat anything he said. He was a moody man who needed a pair of broad shoulders to lean on. One night, I said, 'Clark, you have got to stop this drinking, you've got to.' He started to cry, and said, 'I know I must.' "

He didn't stop drinking, but when the shooting finished, he did make an attempt to fight his grief. He went to Arizona with Al Menasco, and to the Rogue River with Robert Sterling, who remembers some of the details. "We'd take a case of champagne and a case of Scotch, and split the bills. We had a guide named 'Pop'—a big, heavy man who talked all the time. I remember we'd been out awhile and hadn't had a strike. Pop changed our hooks, and we started pulling in the trout—nine inches long. When we got five or six apiece we pulled in on a bank so beautiful you couldn't believe it. Pop told Clark, 'You clean the fish' and told me, 'You build the fire.' We had a drink, ate fried fish, took a nap, then fished some more. We did pretty much the same sort of thing every day. Clark was easy to be with, but not easy to know.

"I remember being impressed with what great taste he had. He had groovy luggage and leather packing cases, cashmere sweaters, and whipcord slacks. He'd let himself go in his fishing clothes, but they were the best, and so was his gear. He had tremendous style, no matter what he did, or what mood he was in. There was a riffle on the river they named for him: 'Gable's Riffle.' "

Despite Strickling's releases, Clark had no intention of making *Shadow of the Wing,* or any other film, for that matter. Not being in uniform in 1942 was tough for any man, and for a man like Clark, nearly impossible. Vic Fleming wanted Clark to make the Eddie Rickenbacker story. Clark thought it was time he stopped playing and got into a real uniform. But he brooded and inquired and hesitated because he feared he would be turned down. What he did not know was that late in May his draft board sent Eddie Mannix notice that Clark Gable's classification was about to be considered, and that Mannix was busy trying to get him deferred. Among other things, he had the legal department preparing an affidavit which would contain proof that Clark was essential to the war effort as a movie star. Hendrickson wired Dietz the news, asking for help:

> . . . We would like to point out as accurately as possible the number of people who view pictures in which Gable appears. We would also like to substantiate as nearly as possible any figure which we designate. We are under the impression that various polls such as the Gallup Poll, etc., are conducted. . . .

Ralph Wheelright memoed Hendrickson:

> For your information, Clark Gable's been in the first ten of national box office favorites for the past ten years in the poll conducted by Quigley Publications through the votes of some 10,000 motion picture exhibitors. Although he has never been first, he has always been in the first ten and usually in the first three.

Rumors persisted that Clark had accepted a commission as a major in the Air Corps. He had not. He had, however, made up his mind to enlist as soon as he could get his life in order. He wanted the ranch to be maintained, though on a tightened scale. He released two servants with the understanding they would return when he did; Rufus Martin got a job in a defense plant; Jessie, another position as a cook. He had all except fifteen of the chickens sold, the food Carole stored sent to hospitals, the cars jacked up, and the horses set out to graze in the hay field with a couple of others belonging to friends, so there would be no need for mowing.

On August 11, Eddie Mannix wired Clark:

> HELLO POP. WAR DEPARTMENT NOTIFIED ME ABOUT YOUR ENLISTMENT. NOW DON'T GET OUT OF TOWN UNTIL I SAY HELLO TO YOU. REGARDS.

The same day, Clark drove to Jill Winkler's house on his motorcycle to take her an engraved gold I.D. bracelet as a farewell gift. He told her: "I'm going in and I don't expect to come back, and I don't really give a hoot whether I do or not."

The next morning, Ralph Wheelright took him to a recruiting office in Los Angeles and watched while an enlistment officer recited, "You, Clark Gable, a citizen of the United States, do hereby volunteer to enlist this twelfth day of August, 1942, as a soldier in the Army of the United States of America for the duration of the war plus six months . . ." and Clark replied, "I do."

Later that day, Howard Strickling wired his daily news items to Howard Dietz:

CLARK GABLE WAS SWORN INTO THE AIR CORPS AS A PRIVATE TODAY AND LEAVES TODAY FOR MIAMI WHERE HE WILL GO INTO OFFICERS TRAINING SCHOOL. [*Sic*] ANN SOUTHERN AND MELVYN DOUGLAS TO STAR IN THREE HEARTS FOR JULIA TO BE DIRECTED BY EDWARD BUSELL. . . .

The next day Strickling wired Colonel Arthur Innis of the War Department:

EVERYTHING WORKED OUT VERY SATISFACTORILY ON GABLE INDUCTION AND CLARK APPRECIATED ARRANGEMENTS YOU MADE. MAILING CLIPPINGS FROM LOCAL PAPERS WHICH THOUGHT MIGHT BE OF INTEREST TO YOU. REGARDS.

He was serial number 191-257-41, but that didn't make him GI Joe.

40

Private Gable applied for admission to Officers Candidate School, became Corporal Gable, and was assigned to Miami Beach for the thirteen weeks of training that would make him a second lieutenant—if he survived the ordeal. It sounds great—Miami Beach, what a deal. It wasn't. The

Army had annexed the Beach, stripping the hotels and turning them into vertical barracks, and the whole area into a giant, restricted base. It was a few degrees more comfortable than most military camps, but it was at least twenty degrees hotter. The late summer of 1942, in fact, was one of the hottest in Miami's history with temperatures rising well over one hundred nearly every day.

Getting there had been a nightmare for Clark, who had really hoped, for once in his movie-star life, to make a public move without being a public spectacle. No word had been released on his destination, but somehow it got around. On August 15, when he reached New Orleans, such crowds surrounded him that he missed his train connection and arrived in Miami Beach a day late.

It was a great way to start. "Oh yeah," the guys at the school said to each other. "Here comes the King." Adding to their skepticism was the fact that Clark was inducted with an MGM cameraman named Andrew McIntyre, who never left his side. When Clark told Jean Garceau he had been charged with seeing the two of them reached Miami Beach on time, he said, "I enlist as a private and find myself in charge of a two-man contingent." An Army officer told reporter Bill Davidson, "Gable is the only private in the history of the Army who had his own orderly."

He had a lot to prove to the sweating cadets, but it didn't hit him at first. All he knew when he got to Miami Beach, and into his three-bunk room, was that the sight and sound of the marching men in the street chilled him right to the marrow. It was almost sensual, the cadence of "SOUND OFF, ONE-TWO; SOUND OFF, THREE-FOUR; SOUND OFF, one-two, three-four." Here was a world he'd never made, and wanted with every fiber. Jesus, if only they'd let him be just a guy among guys. A soldier among soldiers chanting "Left, left, I had a good job and I left, left. I left my wife and forty-eight kids and I left, left."

On his first day in the camp, a gentleman from the Air Force asked if he'd mind if they photographed him shaving off his mustache, and the Associated Press wired the picture of Clark, shaving and grinning, to newspapers all over the country. "I'll probably be cooler anyway," said Clark, as his razor removed the famous hairs. There were no photos of him after his hair was crew cut, out of deference to his ears.

Raymond Green, a Philadelphia radio executive, was at OCS with Gable. He recalls that when word spread that the star was in Miami, few of the cadets believed it because (a) they couldn't believe someone with his pull would go to OCS rather than to OTS (Officers Training School) with a direct commission and (b) he was too old. (At forty-one, he was at least twenty years older than many of the men at the base, but within his own class, where the youngest men were thirty-three, he was of average age.) They figured he was a new boondoggle, and though they were curious about him, decided to ignore him and let him play his game, or, more to the point, act his role. "Hey, you know who's here? Clark Gable," a GI would say. Another would reply, "Why, are they making a movie?"

In a very short time, Green says, "We began to realize he was the real McCoy. But still you'd say to yourself, 'Only an actor can act the way he does.' He was the All-American hero, the energetic superman gonna do it the hard way; a flag waver of the first order. We were all, all those things, but he was Clark Gable. The day he walked in he had more military bearing than most of the men had when they left, partly because of his natural posture, and partly because he was an actor, I'm sure."

Clark realized very quickly that he was being watched and tested. He put himself under tremendous pressure. Not only did he want to succeed and show the young squirts a thing or two, he also wanted to be liked. It bothered him worse than ever that women lined the streets of Miami hoping to get a glimpse of him marching to and from mess. What he didn't know was that he had become unrecognizable. In his khakis and overseas cap, without his mustache, running at half-time in a sea of men, he had at last what he had wanted for years: anonymity. "Gable didn't look particularly good in his khakis," recalls writer A. E. Hotchner, who was a class ahead of him at OCS. "He looked wilted. My memory of him was how much he perspired. He was always soaking wet." In the first weeks, even his cook wouldn't have recognized him; he had a boil on his nose covered with a large bandage that was as good as a mask.

The thirteen-week crash program designed to convert the soft flesh of civilians into the tough hide of officers was a notoriously grueling one. "Ninety-day wonder" was a left-handed epithet for someone who was force-fed in three months what West Point cadets learned in four years. "The object of the course was to crack you," says Hotchner. "You were kept in a state of nervous and physical exhaustion. If you fainted once, you got a black mark; twice, you were washed out."

Clark's first letters home (mostly to Joan, who passed them around to his friends) were filled with his shock at the rigors of his eighteen-hour-a-day, seven-day-a-week schedule. Like the rest of the cadets at the base, he was permitted no outside contact for the duration of his stay. Married officers had "wife privilege" one night a week; everyone else bit the bullet. "I'm being a very good boy," Clark wrote Jean, "too damn good. That's got to end when this is over." He wrote his letters the way he studied: in the dark, sitting on a toilet after "lights out."

Seven or eight hours of the day were spent in classrooms, where, says Mr. Green, "they were pumping information into us." At the beginning of a class, the men were handed mimeographed sheets containing the information given them in their lectures. "Gable would sit through class looking like he was half-asleep, and you'd wonder whether he was listening at all. Then he would get top grades in his exams. One day I asked him how he did it. He said, 'It's easy; I memorize everything on the sheet and give it back to them.' It was just like studying a script to him. Maybe he didn't retain anything, but so what?"

In his peculiar civilian job, Clark probably had better training for the tough grind of OCS than most of the rookies, few of whom had ever worked a six-day week, a fourteen-hour day. The years he had made a movie a month served him well in the Air Corps. He wished he'd had something in his life that had prepared him as well to scrub floors.

Something very fine emerged in Clark Gable in Miami, something which had begun to show immediately after Carole's death. His preoccupation with his own needs and interest only in people who satisfied them became a genuine concern for others—on a vast scale, all the fine young men at the base; on a personal scale, his friends at home. He wanted involvement in other lives, he wanted to be sent gingerbread and cookies, he wanted the home fires kept burning. His letters to Jean were impressively articulate and grammatical, but most of all, they were humane.

They began with "Honey" and a round-up of business matters he'd attended to ("I've signed the checks and they're enclosed," etc.). Then, sounding like a college senior, he wrote about how tough classes were, how hard he was working. "The courses are getting as stiff as a groom on his wedding night," he wrote, but when he used the word "hell" it was written "H——." He sent love to Al, Howard, and Fieldsie. He urged Jean to make sure, if her husband went into service, he got a commission. He worried about Jill Winkler properly handling her legacy from Otto. He wanted Jean to see that she didn't spend it all, that she realize "the importance of having a little when things may not be so easy."

Raymond Green says, "I think those of us who knew Clark Gable as a soldier saw the real man more than anyone else perhaps in his whole lifetime. He was not a movie star to us." Hotchner's prevailing feeling about Clark was that he was a man of great honesty. "The last time I talked to him," Hotch says, "he had doubts he would make it. He had progressively wilted, and he looked just awful. He was thin, and looked exhausted, really worn out. He was having trouble on the hikes and marches. I said to him, 'Don't worry, they're *not* going to flunk you out.' He said, 'Maybe they have to, just to show this is so tough and impartial they can flunk Clark Gable.' I said, 'Well, that's a point.' He was down, but everybody was. Nobody was singing in the shower."

"I sometimes wondered if he had a death wish," says Mr. Green. "We talked about what we wanted to do after we got commissioned. We were both in the entertainment field, and were eligible for special services. He didn't want that. He wanted to fight, wanted a daring job in the middle of everything. He never talked at all about what he would do when the war was over; he had a cut-off point in his mind.

"I walked beach guard with him a few nights. At that time, there was a threat of Nazi subs coming in and dropping spies. The beach had to be protected, and one or two nights a week you pulled beach guard. I was in charge of eight guards patrolling a one-mile strip; each guard walked an eighth of it. When I made my rounds, I would stop and talk to the men for a while. One night, Clark talked to me about Carole and what a tragic death she had had. I don't remember what he said specifically, but

I remember how sad he seemed on that beautiful beach, with the sky close the way it is over water, and the moon full—all alone, thinking about his wife.

"Another night I walked with him, there was a thunderstorm, and a lifeguard stanchion right near us was hit by lightning and exploded. I told him I was going in to get him relieved from guard duty. He wouldn't let me. I said, 'You're carrying a rifle, you could get killed.' He said, 'So?' He had no fear of death and he didn't seem to care. If he died, he died."

On October 27, 1942, Corporal Gable was discharged to accept his commission. The following day he became Second Lieutenant Gable, serial number 056-5390. General Arnold gave the commencement address to the 2,600 graduates assembled on a sun-baked golf course; and Lieutenant Gable spoke for the men, at their request. He said: "I've worked with you, scrubbed with you, marched with you, worried with you over whether this day would ever come. The important thing, the proud thing I've learned about us is that we are men. . . . Soon we will wear the uniforms of officers. How we look in them is not very important. How we *wear* them is a lot more important. . . . The job is to stay on the beam until in victory we get the command 'Fall out.' "

Clark then learned what Hap Arnold had in mind for him. He was to form a film unit and make a propaganda movie about aerial gunners, the reason being that there were so many casualties among gunners the Air Force was having trouble getting them. He was assigned, with Andy McIntyre, to Gunnery School at Tyndall Field in Florida, where, on November 8, Clark was made a first lieutenant. Their aerial gunner and photography training would continue at Fort Wright, in Spokane, through January, 1943.

Clark's first move as an officer was to let his mustache grow in, his second was to ask Jean Garceau to order some custom-made uniforms for him, and send him, *please*, his English shoes.

In December, he was given a short furlough and flew home, arriving on the nineteenth. He had not seen the ranch since August, and had to leave it before Christmas, so he held the celebrating down to a minimum. He saw his father, Howard, Al, and a few other friends, and attended a dinner party at Jill Winkler's, which was also attended by Virginia Grey. Jean Garceau wrote, "It had been several years since Clark had seen her and she had grown into a beautiful woman. This was the beginning of their wonderful friendship, which lasted many years."

His close friends at the studio gave him a farewell party his last night home. For the event, Benny Thau tried to get him a date with an exquisite new MGM contract player named Kay Williams. Miss Williams, who thirteen years later would be the fifth Mrs. Gable, refused Benny's "request," and Eddie Mannix's, who also called her. Mr. Thau, who still can't believe he talked to a woman who refused a date with Clark Gable, says Miss Williams couldn't attend the dinner because she was being watched by a man the newspapers called "a mysterious South American known only as Macoco." Miss Williams had married "Macoco" (Martin de Alzaga Unzue, a nightclub owner) the previous month. She divorced him the following August.

Clark ended his brief foray back into his own world with these parting words to Jean Garceau: "You know I have everything anyone could want, except one thing. And all I really need and want is Ma."

He spent the holidays with the men at war, and on January 7, 1943, received his aerial gunner wings. Newsreels taken of that event—of Clark stepping out of file, getting his wings pinned on, saluting, and returning to his ranks—show a proud man with a face fairly bursting with pleasure —a different man from the one sworn in in August with his eyes full of tears.

He was mobbed all along his route to Spokane. When he settled there, the Army issued a press release saying: "Lieutenant Gable will appreciate it if the public will not interfere with his training. He wishes to be treated like every other member of the Service."

41

On January 28, Lieutenant Gable (with Andy McIntyre) was assigned to the 508th squadron of the 351st Heavy Bombardment Group, 1st Air Division, Eighth Air Force —which was being readied for action in Europe. His base was in Pueblo, Colorado, his commanding officer, Colonel William Hatcher. "Hatcher's Chickens" they called the 351st. Their historian, recording in the Group log the arrival of Gable and McIntyre, wrote: "Lt. Gable was charged with the duty of making a training film showing the day-to-day activities of a typical heavy bombardment group in training and in action; the 351st had the honor of being the star of the film." That was all.

Clark chose as his writer Johnny Mahin, who was in Combat Intelligence, "stuck in a training course some place in New Mexico—awful." Though they were neighbors in Encino, as well as friends at work, for the first months there was a strain in their relationship. Mahin was teaching aircraft identification when Clark called him, and scouting for a more inspiring job. "I had my dreams, too," he says. "I had hopes of breaking the German code or something. When Clark asked me to go overseas with him, I told him I would, if I couldn't get a better job. I said, 'I'll come and tell you if I get a better offer somewhere, but I'll do my best to see what we can do with what we're allowed to do.' Later, when the Colonel gave us carte blanche—like permission to install hammers in the bomb bay and give cameras to co-pilots, gunners and tail-gunners, plus our own two cameramen—I forgot I ever said that."

Clark didn't forget. He was hurt by his friend's conditional acceptance. Says Mahin, "When we got to England, suddenly I found the Colonel and Clark going off to London, or Clark going to parties, and John wasn't along. I said, 'Wait a minute, Bub. You and I are equals in this thing now. Come on, I don't want any of this stardom; I want to be in on the fun, too. We're working equals and we're going to be playing equals.' He said, 'Well, John, do you remember what you said'—he'd been carrying this all along—'that if you got a better job you would leave me?' I told him I'd forgotten all about it and was just as happy as could be. He said, 'Come on, let's go get drunk.' " John was forgiven when his constancy was assured.

Hatcher personally flew Clark in a B-17 to New Mexico to get Mahin. Says John, "It was the first time I'd seen him since Carole's death and he was far more serious than I knew him to be. Quieter. He looked a little stunned. He didn't know whether he was going to be any good at what he was committed to. I had that feeling. An actor worrying about his role, really. He had a role to play, damn it. He was America's hero going out to help, to be with the kids, none of whom believed he was going to do anything at all. They thought it was just a hippodrome thing, and they never thought he was going to expose himself to any kind of danger. They said it was a lot of bullshit. It nearly killed him that the kids shunned him. All the brass was crazy about him, naturally, because they wanted their pictures taken. The correspondents would come around in a group and of course the Colonel would be in everything. The boys resented that."

They resented, too, that while they were training to go to Europe to get shot at, he was flying around the country picking his production crew—which called itself "The Little Hollywood Group"—and tooling in and out of Los Angeles to get equipment, taking officers with him to the ranch, on the way.

Clark's inability to comprehend how much his privileged position antagonized "the kids" came from the core of the essential lie of his existence. He didn't understand that feeling as though you are a common, ordinary guy doesn't automatically make you one. He worked so hard at denying he was any kind of king, sometimes he didn't know when he behaved like one. He equated honesty with homogeneity, and the fact that the two are not equal bounced him around like a yo-yo on an elastic string. When he was accepted even though he was Clark Gable, it was because he was a nice king who didn't have to be nice. He couldn't—or didn't want to—see that.

He didn't know what to do to win "the kids" of

his Group, for whom he would do anything, but what he could do best was press the royal buttons. For instance, while he was still based in Colorado he exchanged wires with various MGM executives about an insignia he wanted made up for the Group. An excerpt from his wire to Strickling reads:

INSIGNIAS SHOULD HAVE SOME HUMOR IN THEM, AT THE SAME TIME, COLORFUL: BIRDS CARRYING BOMBS OR ANYTHING THE ART DEPARTMENT CAN DREAM UP. WOULD LIKE TO HAVE FIVE OR SIX DESIGNS TO PICK FROM. THIS IS A SWELL GANG HERE AND THEY WILL APPRECIATE ANYTHING WE DO. . . . LOVE TO ALL. CLARK.

The whole of the studio's art department was put to work on the project under the personal supervision of its brilliant leader, Cedric Gibbons. A wire back to Clark said Gibbons would like to know "the dimensions of the areas of fuselage to be covered by the insignia and if possible the type of plane the group uses." When Clark supplied that information, the drawings appeared like magic.

Ever the reluctant monarch, he used his power when it would bring the results he wanted, but the power embarrassed him. Mahin tells of a time in England when they had a three-day pass to go to London to get some film developed. Hotel space was very difficult to get. Clark, by then, was a captain, an automatic promotion he got before he went overseas in April. "We were playing bridge in the Colonel's room," John recalls. "I said, 'You'd better make some reservations, Clark.' He said, 'You make them.' I said, 'No, you'd better make them, Papa, because, you know—just mention the name.' Very shyly, he called the Savoy. He says, 'I'd like to reserve two rooms for Saturday night . . . Two rooms . . . You haven't any? . . . Well, look again, I'll just wait a moment . . . My name? . . . Gable: G-A-B-L-E . . . No, not *Mr.* Gable, *Captain* Gable; Captain Clark Gable . . . Just got two, huh? . . . Great.' He hated to say it. "Not Mr. Gable, Captain Gable. Captain Clark Gable.' You had to see the expression on his face. We were sitting there dying, screaming with laughter."

The 351st Group, operating B-17s, was assigned in late April, 1942, to a base in Polebrook about eighty miles north of London. Clark flew there with Mahin and Colonel

Hatcher, still considered a glory hound by the men of the Group. It didn't help that when their gear was taken off the plane, among it were crates of oranges, chocolate bars, and other items known to be in short supply in England.

Clark weighed about 195 pounds, and was qualified to fly at 30,000 feet. In a short time, his weight went up to 230, a result, Mahin says, of the kind of food he was eating. "He didn't eat in the Combat Officers mess, where they got the good food. He could have eaten there, but he didn't want to. The non-combat officers got brussels sprouts and potatoes, spam and beans. God awful. We all put on pots." In Clark's case, the pot was potentially dangerous, because he was a non-combat officer, and his weight wasn't watched. No one expected him to fly missions, but he did, and on one of them, cruising at 30,000 feet (on oxygen), he got a slight case of the bends.

As part of his effort not to be singled out, he refused the Army's offer of special housing. He stayed in the officers' quarters, in an eight-by-fifteen room next to Mahin's. They were together constantly, and John got to know him as intimately as any man ever had. One of the things that first registered on Mahin was Clark's cleanliness fetish. He says, "I don't think I ever saw him undressed until we were out in the war. He came in my room, the first time, just in his shorts, and I saw that he shaved his chest and under his arms. I guess it sort of shocked me because I remember saying, 'By God, you shave.' He said, 'Yeah. I can't stand hair. You smell with it. It makes you sweat more.' And he would never take baths. At the base there were just bathtubs—and Englishmen, you know, just don't bathe much anyway. He'd say, 'How can you sit in that tub, with all that dirty water coming off of you?' He went to Petersborough, the nearest town, and bought all the plumbing and everything, and rigged up a shower for himself."

He had no scars on his body, Mahin says. If his memory is correct, it puts to rest the stories of Clark's appendectomy.

He had his uniforms made by a Bond Street tailor who braided silver wings on them "like the English." Clark found that much neater than pinning on metal wings.

He couldn't stand laziness, John says, or waste. "He was a very frugal man. Once I walked into his quarters and he was mending his leather belt himself and doing a very good job on it, taking some strong cord, and sewing it through with a leather needle he'd found somewhere, I guess over in the workshop.

"He loved animals. Loved cats, stray cats."

He rarely talked about Carole, but he frequently fingered "the thing he wore around his neck that had a very odd shape, kind of like a kidney. It had some jewelry of Carole's in it; I never asked him what. One day he was touching it unconsciously, and I said, 'That's something to do with *her*, isn't it?' And he said, 'Yeah, it's all they found of her, John. All I have left of her.'"

One of the things which most surprised Mahin was his own reaction to the man. He says, "I always felt like he needed protection, somehow. He called me 'Father John' —that was his nickname for me. Why John should protect Clark Gable—it's just silly. He could make mince meat of me physically, and he had all the armor of assurance and everything.

"I don't know, he was wary—like an old stud dog approaching some new bitch that might turn around and bite him any minute. And he was so innocent sometimes; he made me feel like an old man. One night, we were just sitting around quietly and he said to me, 'John, do you believe in all that hooey?' I didn't know what he was thinking, so I didn't know what he was talking about. I said, 'What hooey?' He said, 'Oh—Jesus, God, and all that shit.' And I said, 'Well, I was raised in a religious family and always went to church, but I don't now. I don't believe Christ was anything more than a great philosopher, but there must be *something* more powerful than us, otherwise it doesn't seem to make any sense.' Then he said, 'You know what I think? I think the only religion is a good man in love with a good woman.' I said, 'Well, that's kind of powerful, isn't it? It's something I guess we're all seeking, and something that makes the world go around, so I guess that's as good as anything.' He was as serious as he could be.

"We were quiet again, and then I said to him, 'I know you're scared.' He said, 'Yes. It's murder up there. They're falling like moths. Like dying moths.'"

When they first got to England, John found it sad that the men weren't accepting Clark, and tried to help. Hatcher allowed the star to make the Group's first mission, on May 14; an attack on an airdrome at Vcourtrai,

Belgium. John says, "I was in the tower when he and the Colonel went up, and I said to the guys, 'I hear Gable's up there.' They said that was a lot of bullshit; Gable wasn't going on any missions. Even when he came back, they said it was a milk run, and so what? It wasn't, really, 'cause he was damn-near killed. A twenty millimeter came through the plane, knocked the heel off his boot, and went out just a couple inches over his head. After his second mission, though, which was a tough one, the kids adored him. They couldn't stay away from him. And he was proud that he did it."

Once the kids adored Gable, the feeling about him was unanimous. Everybody wanted him around—enlisted men wanted him on their softball teams, officers wanted him at their parties and parades for dignitaries, the press wanted pictures and quotes (coming back from a mission on which he manned the nosegun he said, ". . . I could see the German pilot's features. The guy won't be around long if he keeps doing that. I don't know how we missed him. I didn't hit a damned thing myself"), British royalty wanted him to grace their mansions. Lady Dewar frequently invited him to dinner with John, whom she called his *aide-de-camp;* Lord Gramson took him to his country place for a weekend and made an anglophile out of him.

Even Hitler wanted him. Goering offered any flier who could bring him in a promotion, a leave, and a reward equaling $5,000. Mahin says that Clark, knowing Hitler wanted to "put him in a cage like a gorilla," refused to carry an escape kit with phony identification on his missions. Clark had said he would never bail out if his plane was hit. "How could I hide this face?" he asked. "If the plane goes, I'll just go with the son of a bitch."

That women wanted him goes without saying. Whenever he was accessible to the public, he was mobbed. Mahin recalls a trip they made to Blackpool. "We were taking pictures of kids up in R and R [rest and recreation] and we were photographing on the street. There were crowds watching, and the Bobbies were trying to keep them away because it was impossible to work. One woman broke through the crowd, a woman of about fifty, I guess, and jumped on him, piggyback. Her skirt was up and her shanks were hanging out, and he looked so silly, the crowd started to laugh. He shouted, 'Father John, get this son of a bitch off me, get her off.' He was almost crying. I was hauling her, and a constable was hauling her, and she kept yelling, 'I FOUND YA! I FOUND YA!' It looked so awful, I felt so sorry for him."

Other times when it was Clark who was pursuing, John felt bewilderment rather than sympathy. He says, "Clark never talked about his conquests, which I liked (it seems the best ones don't), but he was a sucker for anything. I don't know. Strange-looking women. I imagine he was a pretty vital guy sexually. I mean, he had to have that stimulation, it didn't really matter with whom. There was one woman—really ugly, with a big horse face . . . I said to him, 'Why in God's name, her?' And he said, 'Well, she's there.' Nobody would have believed he was sleeping with this woman, except the two of us who knew it. The kids wouldn't have believed it.

"I don't mean he didn't like good-looking women; he did. He looked plenty—he didn't leer, but he looked. He just seemed to think he got into less trouble with the ugly ones." Perhaps he was being respectful to Carole's ghost, for whom "the ugly ones" would be no competition.

The collective impressions of Captain Gable in England are of a man on the run. Somewhere he had acquired a British motorcycle, which he rode around the base. An enlisted man of the 351st remembers that the guys used to love to see him zooming around. They played games with him, blocking his path, then scrambling when he pretended he was going to run them down.

He regularly visited anyone he knew who was even remotely near by. In London, he ate dinner at the home of old flame Elizabeth Allan, who was married and had children; he called on Adele Astaire, the wife of Lord Charles Cavendish. David Niven recalled that Clark was a frequent visitor at his cottage near Windsor Castle. Clark, he wrote, used the cottage, and the company of Niven, his wife Primmie, and infant son, as "his refuge from military life."

He was also a passionate tourist, enchanted with the English countryside, where he could sometimes wander without being recognized. Mahin recalls his going into cottages and asking how the thatching was put on the roof, how the beams were attached. Mahin, who was also a tourist at heart, went sight-seeing with him, poking with him into churches, castle ruins, and old graveyards.

Gable was more than a peripatetic civilian in Army

clothing, however. He was a duty-bound man, performing to the letter every job assigned him. His involvement at the base didn't begin and end with the Little Hollywood Group. He was an operations officer on call like any other, as tense as any other when word came to stand by for stand-up missions, as anxiety-ridden as any other when Fortresses returned dropping the double red flares that meant there were wounded aboard. He knew every man who left on the missions, and missed every one who didn't return. Sometimes he volunteered to write the saddest of all letters to the widows and families of "kids" to whom he had become particularly attached, feeling he knew enough about grief to say the right thing.

In the perverse way that familiarity with death can give balance to life, his involvements at the base eased his personal melancholy. What he began to understand was that he had not been singled out by the gods for special punishment. It was not his hubris which brought about Carole's death, or anything he was, or had said or done. To men who still thought they were going to live forever, Clark's exposing himself to German shells when he didn't have to seemed a death wish, but it was really an affirmation of his existence. Clark was not seeking his own death, he was coming to terms with mortality. Which is not to say he was without fear or despair. In a way, he didn't want to go home; he was attracted to the Air Force, but he wished to be assimilated by it, not to use it as a means to his end.

He was sufficiently tormented to drink himself unconscious, given the chance. He was close enough to the brink to lose control if pushed. One day he went to a hospital to see one of the turret gunners he knew who had been pulled out of a shattered plane, mortally wounded. The surgeon in charge, a colonel, took him to the bed where the boy was suspended, wrapped like a mummy, with only his face showing. The doctor said the gunner was loaded with morphine and wouldn't know Clark was there. "He has maybe a few hours left," the doctor said. He then described his injuries, pointing to them: three ribs gone, lung gone, spine severed, etc., etc. While he was talking, Clark saw tears welling out of the boy's closed eyes and rolling down his face. He grabbed the doctor's arm and pushed him into the hall outside the room. "What are you doing? Get your hands off me," the doctor shouted.

Clark, his face red and hands shaking, seized him by the collar and shoved him against the wall. "If you ever do anything like that again, I'll kill you," he snarled. Then he let him go, turned his back, and stormed out of the hospital.

Mahin, who witnessed the attack, said, "Jesus, Clark, that guy was your superior officer. I know he was wrong, but you can't let go like that; you'll get yourself run right out of here." Clark didn't answer.

As the months went by, somewhere in the ranks above him it was decided that Gable was taking himself too seriously, and becoming a hand grenade with a loose pin. Frank Capra gives the most specific evidence of this. In London on his own film assignment for the Army (he was a lieutenant colonel), he met one of Clark's commanding officers and asked how Clark was doing. The general gave him an earful. "How's he doing?" he shouted. "He's scaring the hell out of us. The damn fool insists on going on bombing missions and he wants to be a gunner, yet. No officer mans a gun; the guy's crazy. You know what it would do to us if he gets himself shot? I'm pulling every string there is to get him out of here. He gives me the willies. He's trying to get himself killed, that's how he's doing."

Late in October, when he had shot 50,000 feet of film, Clark and his Little Group were sent home. Clark's orders were to report, with John, to General Arnold in Washington. Before he left, he was awarded an Air Medal "for superior performance of duty." He also wore an American Campaign Medal, and a Europe-Africa-Middle-Eastern Campaign Medal with one bronze service star. He made it clear to anyone who asked that they were not hero's medals, which was not only humility, but also truth. Nevertheless, he left behind him a heroic impression. "He was a human with heart," says one former sergeant of the 351st. "I'll never forget the day Bob Hope and his troupe came over to entertain us. There were thousands of us sitting out on a field, Gable tucked in somewhere with the guys. Hope stood up at the mike, trying his damnedest to get Clark on the stage. He couldn't even get him to stand up. Hope kept saying, 'Where is he? I know there's a celebrity out there. Where is he?' The guys laughed and some of them shouted, 'Here,' and started to applaud and whistle. Clark smiled and gave half a wave, then put his head down. The applause and whistling went on, gee, it must have been ten minutes. Everybody thought he was great."

42

He didn't feel like a hero, any more than he ever felt like a king, but he had no more control over being treated like one than being treated like the other. He had assumed he would go quietly to Washington, get his orders, and leave. Instead, when he arrived at the Pentagon, the corridors were lined with cheering employees, and one hundred reporters awaited him at a press conference arranged by the War Department. Mahin, knowing how Clark felt about public speaking, offered to scribble some notes for him to follow. Clark said he wouldn't need them. He took a deep breath and faced the crowd. "I was absolutely amazed at the way he rose to the occasion," says Mahin. "He was simply magnificent. Charming and gracious, and modest." The gist of his simple remarks was that the boys he met were doing a great job, their morale was high, and that war was very different from movies. His dignity and modesty made him more of a hero than ever.

His meeting with General Arnold presented another kind of shock. Arnold welcomed him back, and welcomed Mahin, who reported in with him. He then said, "Well, Clark, what was it I sent you to Europe for? I've forgotten." Clark said, "To make a film. There was a gunner problem, sir." Arnold said, "Oh. We've licked that."

Clark looked at Mahin and went white. Mahin said, "Well, we've got all that footage, so we'll have to think of something else to do with it, General." To Clark he said, "We've got enough film, don't worry." The General said, "Go on out and do anything you want, any way you want to."

Clark was officially assigned to report in January to the Air Force photography studio at Fort Roach in Culver

City. Since he was under no restrictions, however, he chose to work at MGM, where he could pick his own editor and move on familiar ground. His first visit to the studio in November somewhat resembled Marc Antony's return from Egypt.

The thing no one could spoil for him was that he was home, and the ranch had flourished under Jean Garceau's faultless care. There was fresh orange juice—all he could drink, and his thirst for it was unquenchable. There was fresh cream from his pampered cow. Father Gable had planted a Victory Garden that yielded fine fresh berries and vegetables. The chickens did their bit, and supplied fresh eggs. Any question in his mind about selling his house vanished in the warmth of the Valley, and Clark seemed, to the people nearest him, to be restored to his old self, the signs of maturity in his face, the gray in his hair, the youthful energy in his movements combining to make him handsomer than ever. Assuming he would be sent to the Pacific when his films were completed, he doubly cherished his days at the ranch. Once again he was out on his tractor, whitewashing the fence, tampering with his motorcycle, riding his horses, and worrying a ball around with his dogs. Carole's little dachshund had died while Clark was away, but Virginia Grey, who was now living nearby, bought him another, named Rover. God was not in His heaven, and all was not right with the world, but there was peace and order in one quiet corner for Clark Gable, who knew enough to make every minute count.

On November 28, Harry Fleischmann died of a heart attack. Clark was not yet home a month and he was driving to Bakersfield to the funeral of one of the finest men he knew, driving to his favorite duck club to comfort a precious friend who was suddenly a widow. By then, however, he had become a man who lived with his back to a wall.

Early in December, Clark signed a new contract with MGM which changed only a few clauses of the 1940 contract that had been suspended when he went into service. It was a two-picture-a-year deal, guaranteeing him $7,500 for forty weeks, payment to commence when he left the Army. The contract engaged him as "Actor, Executive, Producer, Associate Producer, or Director" and ended his day at five o'clock instead of six. He agreed, in the document, to appear "in television productions if they become a substantial part of our business," which he hoped they wouldn't. Clark, from the start, saw television as a threat to the medium that had made him rich, and steadfastly refused to perform on it the rest of his life. He made only two television appearances, both in the late fifties. One, when he presented an Academy Award; the other on a bit of film promoting one of his movies on the *Ed Sullivan Show*.

The December 8, 1943, contract was originally drawn for seven years. It was changed to twelve years by a letter to Loew's from the Commissioner of Internal Revenue, sent in response to a query from MGM about Gable's participation in the company retirement plan. The letter stated in part:

> Mr. Gable's existing contract would expire when he was approximately fifty years of age, and under normal circumstances his career as a star in moving pictures would be about over. If he could be assured of employment for ten or twelve years in the future, he would be minimizing to a substantial extent the normal risks in the motion picture industry.

Three years later, the contract was revised to include a clause which stated that if ever Howard Strickling was not employed by MGM, all Clark's personal publicity would be subject to his own supervision, and nothing issued without his approval. It was a flat statement; Gable trusted no one at MGM except Howard. Many years earlier, Clark had told Andy Devine he was looking forward to the day he could walk down Washington Boulevard, take out his dentures, and throw them through L. B. Mayer's window. Such was his feeling about the company that coddled him, and his career in general.

On schedule, in January, 1944, he started the tedious job of making sense of the miles of footage he brought from England. MGM gave him one of their finest film editors, Blanche Sewell (for whom Clark would stand deathwatch a few years later), and all available facilities. Johnny Mahin worked on a narration for Clark, Eddie Mannix hung around to make sure the boys got everything they needed and wanted. The studio was intensely proud of Captain Gable; the extent of its deification of him would eventually do him more harm than good.

The year began for Clark with a wrenching ordeal. A new War Bond campaign was being started locally, and to open it, Clark was asked to speak at the launching of the Liberty ship *Carole Lombard*. The crowd assembled for the christening numbered over fifteen thousand. Mayer presided over the ceremony; Irene Dunne was to christen the ship. Clark spoke with fists clenched at his sides, and openly wept when the champagne bottle was sent across the hull of the ship sliding into the sea. Except for the photographs of Clark sneaked at Carole's funeral, no sadder pictures of him were ever published than those the press snapped at this event.

He was a man with a great storehouse of courage, and he wished for something other than his angst to challenge it. Clark Gable needed a dragon, a windmill, a war. Instead, he had a souped-up motorcycle and a standing golf game at the Bel Air Country Club. He didn't hit golf balls, he tried to decimate them. One day Adolphe Menjou shouted at him in frustration, "For God's sake, Clark, this is a matter of mind and judgment, not muscle and force!" The one hole-in-one he ever hit (a 215-yard drive) he hit with such fury he bent the shaft of his iron.

Clark saw a lot of the Langs at this time, and began dating Kay Williams when he wasn't with Virginia Grey. One of Clark's friends says that, according to Kay, the relationship was welded on their first date when Clark said to her, "Why don't you go upstairs and get undressed?" and she answered, "Why don't you go shit in your hat?" The twenty-five-year-old, twice-married Miss Williams was clearly his kind of dishy dame. He took her to star-studded parties, to Air Force dances, and to nightclubs. He liked being seen with her.

Without what he considered a hero's assignment for the Air Force, Clark began to feel foolish in his uniform. Vulnerable to anything done in the name of patriotism, he became involved in an organization called the Motion Picture Alliance for the Preservation of American Ideals, against Fascism and Communism. Formed in February by Hollywood's political right, the MPA, by spring, was causing deep furrows in many brows in the industry. Considered divisive by its foes, and threatening by minority groups, the Alliance vowed it would "refuse to permit the effort of Communist, Fascist and other totalitarian-minded groups to pervert this powerful medium into an instrument for the dissemination of un-American ideas and beliefs."

In April, Captain Gable appeared at an MPA meeting

where James McGuinness, chairman of the formulating committee, said, "The alliance has been the victim of a smear campaign and had been accused of being anti-Semitic." The Los Angeles *Times* reported that McGuinness "denied that the organization was anti-Semitic and pointed out that the most active opponents of Communism in the United States were members of the Jewish race." Hollywood's most famous "Conservatives" lent their names (and some of them, a great amount of time and effort) to the Alliance: John Wayne, Walt Disney, Hedda Hopper, Robert Taylor, Ward Bond, Victor Fleming, Adolphe Menjou. Johnny Mahin, who was also a member, says that Clark was involved only because so many of the members were his friends. Gable allowed himself to be used, others say, but didn't go to meetings and was never active in the "pinko-hunts" the MPA is remembered for. Nevertheless, as late as 1953, the name Clark Gable still appeared on the list of members of the executive committee.

In May, Clark was made a major, but still had no new orders from the Air Force. When D-Day came and he still had no orders, he asked to be discharged from the service. On June 12, he was "relieved from active duty as a Major, on his own request." His return to civilian life was heavily celebrated in Hollywood, which, in the bleak war years, leaped on any excuse for a party. The Langs invited fifty people to a breakfast-at-midnight bash for him, among them, the Mannixes, Stricklings, Flemings, Goffs, MacMurrays, Ann Sothern, Bob Sterling, Virginia Bruce, and Kay Williams. There was a three-piece band at the party and everyone sang, Clark rendering "Cowboy Joe" and "That's Friendship."

The studio gave him a stag party one night, and mammoth dinner party the next, to which, as a favor to a friend, he escorted actress Jan Clayton. Miss Clayton gives the night she dated Clark Gable its due place in her memories, recalling that Clark had a terrible hangover from the stag party, wore prewar civvies (to her disappointment because "he looked gorgeous in his uniform"), and had borrowed his caretaker's Ford. She was living in a tract house he couldn't find, so he arrived late, by which time every woman in the tract was watching from behind a Venetian blind. At the party, Miss Clayton says, Clark was charming and affable to her, but "Susan Hayward walked in, and his attention was gone. Susan had an intense way of looking at men that was universally misinterpreted. It wasn't sex; she was terribly myopic. She was trying to *find* them." Miss Hayward didn't respond to what Hedda Hopper called "Clark's knack of taking one look at a girl and flattering her to swooning point." When Miss Clayton told her after the party that Clark had stared at her all night, she said, "He *did?* Why didn't somebody tell me?"

"Anyway," says Miss Clayton, "he took me home and kissed me good night, and I kissed him back because at least eighteen women had ordered, 'Kiss him for me.' It was a lovely evening that changed neither his life nor my own."

Clark continued working on his films—five in all—which were scheduled for use in recruiting and training programs. In September he delivered them to Washington, and then went to New York for a rip-roaring vacation. There he ran into lovely Dolly O'Brien, ex-wife of, among others, a sportsman he knew named Jay O'Brien. From their first encounter at the Stork Club, Clark and Dolly were a steady item around town.

Willowy Laura ("Dolly") Hylan Heminway Fleischmann O'Brien was a beautiful blond, blue-eyed, Palm Beach belle, known for her offbeat wit and elegant lifestyle. A regular in society columns, she was most famous for having divorced yeast millionaire Julius Fleischmann with a settlement of $5 million, shortly before he fell from a polo pony and died, and left an estate of $66 million. A very independent lady six years Gable's senior, she found him attractive, but a bit older than she liked her men. Dolly didn't believe in compromising on any level. When she traveled by train, her luggage contained bottled water and silk sheets, as well as one of the great wardrobes ever to ride the rails. When she said she liked young men, she meant she liked being surrounded by young men. It was fortunate for the lady that she had the money to support her tastes, but she would have been a dazzler even without it.

Clark left Dolly reluctantly—and only temporarily. In December he spent two weeks at her Palm Beach villa. He was, in his fashion, quite smitten, and called her regularly when he got home.

Throughout the fall he went, like a lemming, to Bakersfield, paying his own kind of tribute to his lost friend

Harry. When Nan Fleischmann decided to sell the club, he was so upset friends suggested he ease his distress by buying it himself. That would have meant parting with cash, however, and that he wouldn't do. "Money doesn't mean anything to me," he told Wayne Griffin. "Anything more than the air I breathe." He continued to hunt at the club, even though it had changed hands, until 1947, when a strange incident involving him with game wardens made him angry enough to end his membership.

According to Frank Capra, who was on the scene, "About seventeen or eighteen guys, including Clark, went to Bakersfield for opening day of the season. Clark couldn't get up with us at 4:00 A.M. because he was stewed or something. The ducks were plentiful that morning, and some of the guys overshot. When they brought the ducks in, they put the extra ones on his strap—maybe twelve or thirteen, and the limit was ten. I think they thought that was funny. Well, Clark got up later, went out and shot a few ducks, and here he comes, bleary-eyed, with the wardens waiting for him. They said, 'Mr. Gable, you've shot a double limit.' He said, 'How is that?' They said, 'You went over the limit this morning; here's your strap.' He didn't hesitate a minute. He said, 'If they're on my strap, they're my ducks.' Frank Morgan couldn't stand it; he said some of them were his. So the wardens grabbed Morgan, too, and took both of them to the local hoosegow. They had to pay a five-hundred-dollar fine, and suffer all the embarrassment of the damn thing getting in the papers. Clark was no game-hog. He didn't hunt to kill. He went hunting because he liked to talk dirty, drink, and make passes at waitresses."

Indeed, reporters treated the event like the big news it wasn't. It was grimly announced on radio, and newspapers ran headlines (some bannered) reading, "Clark Gable cited on Game Law Charge." Strickling and friends pleaded with Clark to call a press conference and tell his story. He wouldn't. "It's not that important," he said. What was important to him was that the men who'd done the deed hadn't come forward to say so. That was worse sportsmanship than cuckolding a Mason. Camaraderie being a religion with him, he never hunted at Bakersfield again.

Clark spent many hours with Nan Fleischmann after she sold the club and moved to Pacific Palisades. Strictly as a friend, he dropped by to cheer her, using constructively some of the lengthening hours he had on his hands. Dropping in on friends was a new pastime for him. He had never sought company so openly before. "Gregarious" was not a word that had ever applied to him. It applied now. In Palm Beach, with Dolly O'Brien, he became something more, and that was "social." The interest in and response to new people and places were good for him; the idleness causing all this was not. He drank too much. His friends worried about his drinking, but never risked doing anything except joke with him about it. Howard Hawks, for instance, had a rule about Clark's dropping in for a drink at his spread on Morago Drive. If Clark was driving the caretaker's old Ford, he could have his Scotch. If he was driving a high-powered car, he couldn't. "We laughed about it," Hawks says. "You could hear him tooting his horn all the way up the driveway if he was in the old car."

Clark's heroic consumption of alcohol ceased to be a laughing matter when he wrapped himself around a tree in the middle of a night in March, too drunk to find the Wilshire Boulevard cut-off from a traffic circle. Fortunately for his image, the tree he ran into was on the lawn of agent Harry Friedman, who knew the business well enough to call Howard Strickling rather than the police or an ambulance. It was four or five in the morning, as Howard recalls, and Friedman said to him, "Howard, geez, your friend is bleeding; what shall I do?" Howard told him he was too far to come quickly, so he would send Ralph Wheelright and Whitey Hendry. "In the meantime," he said, "tell Clark to talk to no one. And have them get the car out of there as fast as they can."

Howard explains, "It wouldn't have been particularly good to have some photographers go out and make a picture of Clark Gable lying on the lawn covered with blood, and his car all cracked up, because they all would say, 'Who was with him?' you know. They always said, 'There was some woman with him and you hid her.'"

Wheelright called a doctor, who called a surgeon; the Stricklings arrived in time to take Clark to Cedars of Lebanon Hospital. There he got ten stitches in his head and shoulder, and was placed under observation. Howard had to take away his clothes to make him stay in the hospital, but within three days he talked Jean Garceau into bringing him a suit, and his doctor into releasing him.

Once he was hospitalized, there was no way to keep the press from closing in. The story the reporters were told was that Clark had swerved into the tree to avoid hitting a drunken driver, who did not stop at the accident. The press printed it, but no one believed it. Those who were told what MGM claimed was the true story behind the newspaper story didn't believe that either. Rumors persist that the *true* true story was so damaging that MGM issued a fake true story to fog it. "Who was with him?" people still ask. "What were they hiding?"

The new outgoing, humanitarian Gable did not spend his time idly in the hospital. He struck up a friendship with the beautiful young actress Susan Peters (wife of Richard Quine), who had been shot in a hunting accident, and paralyzed. Miss Peters was writing magazine articles as therapy. Clark gave her an exclusive interview for publication, the first and only one he gave after being discharged from the Air Force.

It was the kind of thing Carole would have done.

43

The change in MGM between the summer of 1942, when Clark finished his last film, and the winter of 1944, when he was looking for his next, was so vast a decade could have slipped through those two and a half years. For one thing, more stars than there are in heaven shifted. Among the women, Garbo, Shearer, Crawford, MacDonald, and Loy were gone—either freelancing or out of the sky altogether. Replacing them in the heights were Greer Garson, Katharine Hepburn, and an assortment of female specialty acts: warblers Judy Garland and Kathryn Grayson; *wunderkinder* Margaret O'Brien and Elizabeth Taylor; submarine Esther Williams; sugar-substitute June Allyson; and a collie named Lassie who was really a male. Hard-core pin-up girls were not Mayer's style; the only one at MGM was Lana Turner.

Many of the male stars were in service, their places taken by Mickey Rooney, who did not go into the Army until 1944; Gene Kelly, who went in the Navy in '45 and was out in '46; and Van Johnson—darling of ankleted young ladies known as bobby-soxers—who was 4F because of a head injury he got in an automobile accident.

There were also changes at the executive level. Mayer had become such a passionate follower of horse racing that he bought a breeding farm, where he was trying to raise his own winners. This stable of four-legged stars who didn't talk back took so much of his time he was barely seen at the studio. His executive power was divided among Eddie Mannix and two other executives. One of his most important producers, Hunt Stromberg, was retired because of illness; another, Bernie Hyman, died of a heart attack. They were replaced by Pandro Berman of RKO, and Joe Pasternak of Universal, neither of whom was particularly challenged by the times, because, once again, the public was so hungry for entertainment it would have been possible to draw a crowd to a *musical version* of the telephone book. (The wartime passion for movies peaked in 1946, when 80 million Americans weekly attended a film. Today, 22 million is considered good.)

In this strange new world, no one seemed to know what to do with Clark Gable. The creative powers were all assigned to look for a property for him, but they didn't know what to look for. MGM, heavily into the production of musicals and family whimsies, was out of the rhythm of Gable vehicles. Furthermore, they didn't see Gable as Gable anymore, they saw him as some kind of saint. When they did come up with a property they thought right for him, they had to contend with his own interpretation of his film image. Adela Rogers St. Johns was hired specifically to find him a story, and even she couldn't find something that pleased both the front office and the star. When she expressed her frustration to Clark, he told her what he thought the public wanted from him: "They see me broke, in trouble, scared of things that go bump in the night but coming out fighting. . . . They see life with a high price tag on it, but they get an idea that no price is too high if it's *life*. . . . I am not going to make any motion pictures that don't keep right on telling them that about a man. Let's get that understood. The things a man has to have are hope and confidence in himself against odds, and sometimes he needs somebody, his pal or his mother or his wife or God, to give him that confidence. He's got to have some inner standards worth fighting for or there won't be any way to bring him into conflict. And he must be ready to choose death before dishonor without making too much song and dance about it."

The result of all this awe of the Gable image was that in the next three years Clark would make only three films, *Adventure, The Hucksters,* and *Homecoming,* none of which was worthy of the prewar actor. Only *Adventure,* the first of them, was popular with his fans, and that was because Gable was back and Garson had him. America had missed *him,* and loved *her.*

He began *Adventure* in May, soon after V-E Day, at the tail end of the gloom that had settled on him when he was discharged. Still adjusting to civilian life and finding it hollow, still drinking too much, he started the picture ill equipped for it. Like many of his fellow screen stars, he found acting pointless and demeaning after being at war. Howard Strickling, noting that Gable's ambition was gone when he resumed work in 1945, blamed its death on Carole's. If this was a reason, it was probably one of several, including his Air Force service, and the fact that he felt he had reached a pinnacle as Rhett Butler and had nowhere to go except down. Chances are, if Clark had felt he could do anything else that would produce as much income, he would have ended his acting career in 1942.

The only security he had ever had about acting seemed to come from the momentum built up doing one picture after another. That momentum long gone, he suffered real stage fright when *Adventure* began. Joan Blondell, the giddy blonde of the film, recalls that Clark perspired a great deal when he was working, and that his head shook when there was any tension on the set. Vic Fleming, the film's director, was able to take few close-ups because of the shaking, and had to adjust the script accordingly. (David Niven has said that the shaking came from Gable's taking Dexedrine to fight the weight his drinking was putting on him.)

From time to time, Clark came out of the doldrums and was able to laugh and kid around with the crew and cast—all except his co-star, Miss Garson, whom he disliked unequivocably. "He didn't talk about his service at all," says Miss Blondell. "He didn't want to." One evening he brought her to the ranch for dinner and showed her around the house. She says, "He had Carole's room just the way she left it, but said someday he would change it. Her silver bottles were all shined and in place in her bathroom, and there was even some strange douche thing still there. He had bought every picture Carole ever made, and looked at them, often. He spent a lot of lonely hours at that house." She did not find him radically changed; she had always considered him a deep man, and thought him merely deeper. "He was still fun and juicy and damned consistent about who he was," she says. "I never considered Clark a typical movie actor. That's a bad profession for men. They become picky and fussy and do a lot of talking to mirrors. Clark wasn't like that, ever."

He liked the undemanding company of the make-up girl on the film, Dotty Pondell, and often went to her house at the end of the workday. Sometimes he took "Joanie" (his name for Miss Blondell) with him. "He'd go get some steaks," she recalls, "make them himself, and eat with us in the kitchen wearing a towel apron."

Adventure was released in December. Today Gable's friends recall it being badly reviewed, but in fact, the picture was well received by many critics, including *Time* magazine's, who said, ". . . the steady gleam of the picture is the inimitable, jugeared, perdurable Clark Gable, back from the wars and still going strong." Recollections of the reception of the film may be clouded by memories of Clark's aversion to Howard Dietz's "Gable's Back and Garson's Got Him" ad campaign. Clark hated being called "Gable," hated being got by Garson, hated the repetition of the slogan. He wound up hating the picture more than he hated *Parnell*, but it was a sign of the return of his good nature that friends could tease him about it and make him laugh.

When the picture was completed, Clark took a trip to the Rogue River, and returned again at loose ends. Wayne Griffin, who had joined the radio department of Berg-Allenberg, tried to get him to do some radio shows. "It's a quick seventy-five hundred bucks, Clark," he said. Clark answered, "If you were invited to go down to the butcher shop on Saturday and earn fifty bucks by handing stuff out over the counter, would you be interested?" Wayne said, "I'm not going to answer that because I know what you're leading up to. You don't want to do it, but you should."

Griffin was able to talk him into doing a play, *Take Her Down* (for "Cavalcade of America"), about a heroic submarine commander, on the basis of his duty to the war effort. Kay Williams accompanied him to the broadcast. After the war ended in August, there was no way to talk Clark into doing another radio show. *Take Her Down* was his last.

Clark's ever-increasing gregariousness now propelled him into something called the Morago Spit and Polish Club, a middle-aged motorcycle gang that convened every Sunday in Howard Hawks' Morago Drive driveway. It was a group, says Mr. Hawks, that "didn't care too damn much about the usual social life that centered around how big you were." Regulars were Ward Bond, Vic Fleming, Andy Devine, Keenan Wynn, Bill Wellman, Al Menasco, a couple of stunt riders, Hawks, and Clark. It expanded and contracted; sometimes there were as many as twenty cyclists revving up on the Hawks ranch at ten-thirty Sunday mornings. Mrs. Hawks, the beautiful model called "Slim" (later Mrs. Leland Hayward, and still later, Lady Nancy Keith), complained bitterly about the racket they all made before they took off over the hills, but she had Spit and Polish Club shirts made for them, and had lunch ready for them all, never knowing when they would come back, but knowing they would be starved when they did.

The gang was competitive, but not about speed or tricks. The competition was over who had the best, shiniest machine. Most of the men had Harleys; Clark rode a Square 4 Aerial, whatever that was. Fleming was the only wild one of the bunch. Clark was a careful, easy rider, who, in his later years, got the ultimate compliment when James Dean said of him, "He's a real hot shoe. When you ride, you wear a steel sole that fits over the bottom of your boot. When you round a corner, you put that foot on the ground. If you can really ride, you're called a hot shoe. Gable rides like crazy."

The Sunday rides usually ended at the Devines' ranch. Says Andy, "We had this long 'Liar's Bench' made for our house. All the riders would sit and drink beer and tell lies about what they'd been doing on their motorcycles. Then the guys would go outside and shine their bikes—spit and polish, you know." In fact, they spent more time polishing their machines than riding them. Occasionally they would pack them in station wagons, drive hundreds of miles to an open area, buzz around for fifteen minutes, eat a picnic meal, and drive home. It was a curious thing for grown men to spend so much time at.

Soon after the release of *Adventure,* MGM bought Frederic Wakeman's hit novel *The Hucksters* for Gable's next project and Clark responded to it like an angry blowfish. The novel was an attack on the advertising business that had burgeoned into "Madison Avenue" in the wartime economic boom. Its hero was a bit of a rotter, its heroine adulterous. The thought that MGM would consider it suitable for Captain Marvel affronted him. So the studio ordered the book castrated, and Clark cooled his heels. Eventually, writer Luther Davis produced a palatable screenplay that was largely a satire on soap commercials. He made the hero a scoundrel with a heart of suds who winds up emptying a pitcher of water over the head of his ludicrous, power-mad boss; and the heroine a genteel English widow. Clark's friend Jack Conway was assigned to direct, and the film went well. Deborah Kerr played the English lady (her first American film role), and Ava Gardner a sexy lady. Clark had tested with both women and fully approved them. MGM felt that was the wisest course, considering his behavior with Greer Garson. Miss Gardner particularly amused him; she was his kind of no bullshit buddy. When she had first come to Hollywood, she had announced her ambition was to marry its king. He was married to Lombard, however, so she married Mickey Rooney, number one at the box office, instead. By the time she did meet Clark, she was Mrs. Artie Shaw, and when next they would work together, Mrs. Frank Sinatra. She never seemed to run into him when she was between husbands.

In any case, had she done so, she would have had to get on line. From the day Clark left Polebrook for Los Angeles he became the number one catch of the hemisphere. "Women flocked around him like moths around a candle —duchesses, show girls, movie stars, socialites—name them, he could have had them," said sage old Hedda Hopper. Clark responded like an ice cream freak seeing his first Howard Johnson's soda fountain.

Women, women, women, women. For at least five years, that was the story of his life.

44

Hollywood in the immediate postwar years was the most glamorous spot on earth. When the rubble of the war could be cleared from the paths to the famous watering holes of the super-rich, it would pale as a playground, but for a moment in the history of hedonism, there was no place like it. Hollywood's appeal in the twenties was that it was crazier than the crazy times. In the thirties it was rich and fur-clad alone in a starving world. In the postwar years, money wasn't a universal problem; drabness was, tackiness was, deprivation was. Hollywood seemed to suffer none of it. There were parties every hour of the day and night, night-clubs like Ciro's and the Mocambo to dance in, restaurants like Chasen's and Romanoff's to eat and be seen in. There were men to play with—men who had always been choice, but were now doubly appealing because of their roles in the war—either real or on screen.

Where there are desirable men, there are gorgeous women; Hollywood was bursting with them: robot-looking creatures, pompadoured, heavily made up, girdled so tightly they were unpinchable, uplifted by bras that gave them pistol-pointed breasts even in the strapless numbers that were the fashion. Very different from the passively near-naked Hollywood ladies of the thirties, the postwar breed had the wartime sex appeal of Sherman tanks. The "look" was Rita Hayworth, Betty Grable, Carole Landis, Ann Sheridan, Veronica Lake. Subtlety was dead.

Thus when a beautiful studio executive named Anita Colby learned Clark Gable was at a party at the home of her boss, David Selznick,* did she feel free to say

---

* Clark made up with Selznick soon after he returned from England, telling him he had made a resolution to do so on a mission from which he hadn't expected to return. He said he had thought to himself, "What did that guy ever do to me except force me to be in the most important film I ever made? If I get out of here alive, I'm going to

to a Selznick starlet named Jennifer Jones, "Let's go. He's divine. I want to meet him." The fact that they weren't invited didn't faze Anita, nor did the fact that the party was dressy, and she was wearing an angora sweater over a cotton dress. (Jennifer was a nervous wreck, but she had reason to be; she was Selznick's girl and hoped no one knew that.)

Anita was not concerned, either, that Clark was "very involved" with her friend Kay Williams, whom he had brought to the party. Anita tugged on the sleeve of her friend Joe Cotten and whispered, "I want to meet Gable. Do you know him well enough to introduce me?" Cotten nodded and took her to Clark and his date. "Hi, Kay," said Anita. "Hi," said Kay, turning quickly to talk to someone else. Anita shook Clark's hand, noticed it was "cold as a dead man's," and was whisked away by Harry Crocker to dance.

Anita Colby was a prize among Hollywood women. In addition to being a renowned beauty (as a Conover model she had been on as many as twelve magazine covers in one month), and being a rare female power in the business (earning $100,000 a year as a consultant for Selznick Productions), she was the girl who said "No" to everyone. A forerunner of the Doris Day film virgin, she was thirty and had never been wed—or laid, as far as anyone knew. Her wholesome blond good looks— she was called "The Face" as a model—her gaiety, her sexual cool, and her brain were Anita's stock-in-trade. Men adored her.

People danced belly-to-belly in the flirty forties. Men "cut in" on other men when they wanted to dance with their partners. Clark cut in on Harry Crocker. "Where's Kay?" asked Anita. "Don't know," said Clark. Since no one would cut in on the king, they danced uninterrupted. "I was married to a lady who had frizzy hair like yours," said Clark. "An Irish biddy with a terrible temper." When the music stopped, Clark asked Anita where she lived, and she told him. She then said, "I've covered you with angora feathers."

He said, "No, you haven't."

She said, "You look cute."

---

apologize." For a time after he got home, he made a point of liking everyone.

He said, "I do?"

She said, "Yes, cute as a chicken."

He said, "You're a nut."

And Anita was home free.

Now there were in Clark's life: Virginia, the girl next door; Kay, the girl Wayne Griffin thought Clark was in love with; Dolly, whom Clark thought Clark was in love with; Anita, the new one; Carol, the fish catcher; and Betty, the golfer.

Carol?

Carol Gibson. "Rainbow's" daughter—of the We Ask U Inn on the Rogue River. "On his last trip to Oregon," Jean Garceau reported, "Clark almost lost his heart to Carol, now a tall, willowy brunette." Clark told Anita he never liked brunettes because they looked dirty to him. Carol was one of the exceptions. He had gone with her and some friends to the mouth of the Rogue for salmon, caught a batch, had them canned, labeled, and shipped home. Young Carol he labeled "My girl on the Rogue," and left in Oregon. But he couldn't think of fishing without thinking of her in her waders.

Betty?

Betty Chisholm, dignified, rawboned blond widow (and Jones sausage heiress) Clark met on a trip to Phoenix. Noted Jean Garceau, "Her home was on the Arizona Biltmore estates and Clark frequently went to see her, staying at the Arizona Biltmore so they could ride and golf together, for Betty played an excellent game."

Clark's game was juggling his collection, not too difficult to do with the ones in strategic out-of-state locations, but somewhat complicated with the three in Los Angeles. There were no hasty weekend trips made to court the out-of-towners because after Clark disembarked from his last Flying Fortress, he wouldn't go near an airplane. When he did start to fly again, in 1952, he had an "airplane clause" added to his MGM contract that said he would fly only in planes having two or more motors and with "duly qualified and licensed pilots." He also had to know "the make of the airplanes" in which he might be required to fly. His fear of flying was no joking matter.

The collection kept growing, with only one dropout, Kay Williams. Before one of Clark's trips to New York about a year after he and Kay became an item, they said goodbye and thought, at the time, they meant it. Kay became the fifth wife of infamous millionaire Adolph Spreckels.*

Slim Hawks eventually filled the gap left by Kay. When she and the director were divorced, Slim accompanied Clark on a few hunting and fishing trips and communicated with the rest of the harem about who was the current favorite. "He wants to get you over the hill and into the feathers," she told Anita, who was determined he would do no such thing. Slim didn't like social occasions with Clark because she couldn't stand the way people carried on about him, in public or at parties. She preferred being with Leland Hayward, who was a terribly attractive man whom no one outside the industry recognized.

Anita, on the other hand, found Clark's celebrity exciting. "I loved walking into a room with him," she says. "He was a dream and a darling, and the loneliest, most insecure man in the world. If we'd go to a party, he'd shake like a leaf. I went to an Air Force dinner with him once. He was the honored guest and had to make a speech. Here was this man who was the biggest showoff in the world under the lights—shaking so much I thought he was going to drop dead. He said to me, 'Look at you; anybody'd think you owned the place.' "

Anita's relationship with Clark, as far as she was concerned, was strictly buddy-buddy. "I loved him, but I wasn't in love with him," she says. "I would no more have thought of going to bed with him than with the man in the moon." Many times when they were together,

---

* The late Adolph Spreckels, heir to a sugar fortune, was arrested on his first honeymoon for possessing marijuana, and accused of wife-beating in his first divorce. His second divorce settlement was made when his eighteen-year-old wife of three months threatened to expose a diary that he kept which was "hotter than Boccaccio's Decameron." During his third divorce suit (from his cousin, Geraldine Spreckels) he was accused of flying into wild rages and physically abusing his wife. His fourth wife charged him with being a Nazi sympathizer who knocked her down and beat her. Soon after his fifth marriage (to Kay) a dancer sued him for beating her, maiming her "in sadistic frenzies," and trying to set her afire. His sixth wife divorced him after one month of marriage, testifying in court that he had dislocated both her arms and both wrists and then fractured her arm. He was regularly in court for drunkenness until, in 1961, he died of a brain hemorrhage brought on by an unexplained head injury.

one or another of Anita's family would be with them—
her mother, sister, or a cousin or all three. Clark got
the message; whenever he asked Anita to travel with
him, he always assured her there were chaperones. Once
he called her from Pebble Beach and said, "I'm here
with Primmie and David [Niven] and the whole gang.
Come on up, I'll meet you at the airport." On another
occasion he called her from Arizona (a curious overlap;
that was Chisholm territory) and asked her to come with
her cousin, a doctor. "Give her a weekend away from
the bedpans," Clark said. The two women joined him and
took him to church for Sunday morning mass. His celebrity nearly crippled him that weekend. He had water
on the knee and had trouble kneeling. "He was too stubborn to lean on me, so I told him to leave," says Anita.
"He said he couldn't because people in the church had
noticed him. When we got out, he had to go to bed for
a week."

Anita felt Clark trusted her enough to pour out his
heart to her. She doesn't know whether he did the same
with the others. He told her he was in love with Dolly,
had asked her to marry him, had been turned down, and
was very hurt by her refusal. The weekend in Pebble
Beach began with his saying, "Guess what: Dolly's getting married tomorrow. I hear he's got something that's
as long as here to Fifth Avenue." He did not grant Anita
the privilege of being as raw. Once, she recalls, she said
"damn" in front of him and he got very angry. "I never
heard you say that before, and don't do it again," he said.
She gasped, "How can you say that when you were married to Lombard?" He said, "That was a different thing. It
was like music from her. It's not natural with you,
and not like you."

Anita was like Carole only in the gifts she sent. There
was, for instance, the mammoth horseshoe covered with
flowers and bars of flea soap she sent for good luck when
he started *The Hucksters,* and the dinghy for his new
swimming pool, the craft she named "King III" so the
salesclerk wouldn't think he didn't have any other boats.
The dinghy was the end of a long story. Clark put the pool
in after the war as a gesture of amenity to his friends
and their children. He had never wanted a pool, but was
entertaining so much he thought it would be nice for
his guests. Workmen took three months to complete the

job, during which Clark stayed in one of the worst rages his friends had ever witnessed. It had been a house rule, starting with Carole, to have workmen around only when Clark was away because he couldn't abide the mess they made. This was the first time he was exposed to the dirt of excavation and the rest, and he was furious about the delays that kept the ranch in turmoil. He told Anita he had seen and felt enough dirt when he was young to last him all his life. He told her about how he had slept in dirty beds still warm from the filthy bodies just out of them, about the foul talk of men in an oil field, about how he had to wear wet jeans that chafed him because he only had one pair and when he washed it there was no time for it to dry.

So when the pool ordeal was over, Anita sent a boat, which she and her sister rowed around the new luxury until Clark discovered it left marks on the pool sides and gave it to his father.

At some point, Clark's girls were snapped to attention by the addition to their ranks of Standard Oil heiress Millicent Rogers, the most colorful of all Clark's female connections. Thrice-married Mary Millicent Huddleston Rogers Salm VonHoogstraeton Peralda-Ramos Balcom was a lady to be reckoned with. A dark-haired, pale-eyed, willful clothes horse whose wild collection of costumes (designed by such giants as Schiaparelli, Mainbocher, and Charles James) recently landed in an exhibition at the Metropolitan Museum, Millicent was likely to show up anywhere, and wearing a parachute if that was her mood. Millicent got the ideas for her outfits from museum archives. Some days she was an authentic reproduction of an Indian squaw, some days a Tyrolean peasant, some days a *caballero*, some days Marie Antoinette. She was in her mid-forties when she met Clark, and, according to society columnists, living quietly. In Hollywood to see him, however, she took a fancy to a small monkey belonging to the designer Adrian, bought one for herself, and wore it on her shoulder. Once she met Clark, probably in Southampton on one of his New York trips (she had a home there and one in the Tyrol), she stalked him relentlessly, even to courting Jean Garceau, who struck terror into the hearts of the Los Angeles girls. She took Jean to lunch, and sent her some of the 24-carat jewelry she carved as a hobby—a collection of which she also sent Clark the Christmas she was pursuing him. She was madly in love with him, and it was this obvious much-reported fact, the other girls decided, that did her in after only a year in Clark's favor. When their romance ended, she sent him (and Hedda Hopper) this eerie fare-well letter:

My darling Clark,

I want to thank you, my dear, for taking care of me last year, for the happiness and pleasure of the days and hours spent with you; for the kind, sweet things you have said to me and done for me in so many ways, none of which I shall forget.

You are a perfectionist, as am I; therefore I hope you will not altogether forget me, that some part and moments of me will remain in you and come back to you now and then, bringing pleasure with them and a feeling of warmth. For myself, you will always be a measure by which I shall judge what a true man should be. As I never found such a one before you, so I believe I shall never find such a man again. Suffice that I have known him and that he lives.

You gave me happiness when I was with you, a happiness because of you that I only thought might exist, but which until then I never felt. Be certain that I shall remember it. The love I have for you is like a rock. It was great last year. Now it is a foundation upon which a life is being built.

I followed you last night as you took your young friend home. I am glad you kissed and that I saw you do it, because now I know that you have some-one close to you and that you will have enough warmth beside you. Above all things on this earth, I want happiness for you.

I am sorry that I failed you. I hope that I have made you laugh a little now and then; that even my long skinniness has at times given you pleasure; that when you held me, I gave you all that a man can want. That was my desire, that I should be al-ways as you wished me to be. Love is like birth; an agony of bringing forth. Had you so wished it, my pleasure would have been to give you my life to shape and mold to yours, not as a common gift of

words but as a choice to follow you. As I shall do
now, alone.

You told me once that you would never hurt me.
That has been true, even last night. I have failed
because of my inadequacy of complete faith, en-
gendered by my own desires, by my own selfishness,
my own ability to be patient and wait like a lady.
I have always found life so short, so terrifyingly
uncertain.

God bless you, most darling Darling. Be gentle
with yourself. Allow yourself happiness. There is no
paying life in advance for what it will do to you.
It asks of one's unarmored heart, and one must
give it. There is no other way. When you find happiness, take it. Don't question too much.

Goodbye, my Clark. I love you as I always shall.

Millicent did not marry again. She bought a house in
Taos, New Mexico, and lived there almost reclusively.
When she died in 1952, a Taos house owned by a friend
was made into a museum in her honor. Her estate was
divided among her three sons, but ten thousand dollars of it was left to a friend to be used for a party on
the first anniversary of her death.

That was Millicent.

Dolly divorced her fourth husband and was back in
Clark's collection before anyone knew how to spell her
latest name. Dolly was crazy about Clark, her friends
say, and would have married him had she been able
to remove him from Hollywood.

It has to appear from this list of, say, active involvements, that Clark did nothing after the war except
womanize. Indeed, his career in these years was in-
cidental to him. After *Adventure* and *The Hucksters*
he made *Homecoming* and *Command Decision*, in both
of which his roles were pompous and forgettable. "I'll
do everything they say until my contract runs out," he
told friends. However, his relationships with his women
didn't appear to be much more important to him. One
could guess from the report of the cook who found him
happy when she took his breakfast to his room, and from
Jean Garceau who often found him despondent during
the day, that he woke up, looked around, panicked, and
reached for something to distract him. He'd play golf,

see friends, and maybe call someone for a date as a convenience, or an afterthought. He traveled a great deal, also as a distraction, but he'd leave excitedly on a trip, get where he was going, and find himself lonely again. If there was no comfortable woman around, he'd pick up the phone and send for one, the way he called home for his saddle when he located some good riding horses, or for particular suits when he unpacked and missed them.

For a while after Millicent faded out, Carol Gibson was the girl most often conjured when Clark went to the phone. Before he started *Command Decision,* he went to Oregon for steelhead, and while there organized a party, with Carol, to boat downriver and camp in farmhouses on the way. When he finished *Decision,* he went to New York on a promotion trip with Howard Strickling, then suggested they go to San Francisco for Easter and have Gail Strickling and Carol Gibson join them. He had promised Carol he would show her San Francisco one day, he said, and she was a fantastic girl. He loved the way she fished with the gang, a flask of bourbon in her hip pocket to swill when she got cold. He called her Junior.

Gail remembers Carol arriving in San Francisco with a little suitcase in which she had a pair of Levi's and a black suit. Clark had with him his custom-made suits and a derby he wore every Easter. The years he joined the Stricklings' Easter egg hunt at their ranch, he wore the derby with a safari suit. In San Francisco, for an egg hunt around the group's hotel suites, he wore it with his gabardines. He said it was something he had always wanted as a kid and had bought on his first trip to New York. He had had derbies as a teenager, but not the big-city kind.

He escorted Carol to every corner of San Francisco and had a ball. After the Easter egg hunt, he wanted to take a ride on a cable car. The women didn't want to join him because the weather was terrible, but he went anyway, still in his derby, and dragged Howard along. The people who got on the car with them wouldn't get off until Gable did. He had planned to disembark at Fisherman's Wharf, but it was pouring, so he got off, went around the other side, and got on again, the entire crowd on the car following right behind. They sang all the way back, waved to everyone on the street, and kissed Gable goodbye when he left.

Soon after this gay trip, he proposed to Anita Colby.

Anita was stunned. She had no idea he was that fond of her. She knew he respected her and admired the way she handled herself socially. He had had her hostess a few parties for him, and he took her to the choicest of the parties he attended. He was attentive when she was sick, and jealous when she spent time with other men. But he had never given her a gift, or been anything but a pal. Clark loved to laugh, and Anita loved to make him laugh. That was all, she thought.

Then one day she decided she'd had enough of being a Hollywood nanny, and made plans to go back to New York. Clark went to her house to say goodbye. "We were sitting by the fireplace looking at each other," she recalls, "and he started this strange conversation. He said he had been baptized a Catholic, and would go to a priest about joining the Church and annulling his marriages. He said we could have a fine life together, have children, live any way I wanted. He told me later that my eyes got like saucers, and he thought I would say yes. What I was thinking was, 'How do you say no to Clark Gable?' I told him I wasn't ready for marriage, and wanted to go home. I also told him he drank too much—he drank Scotch in vases by that time—and he said, 'That's because I'm lonely.'

"Poor darling. He was so ready for marriage. I said to him, 'Please don't get married right now; you're so anxious, you might make a mistake.' He assured me he wouldn't, and said he would see me soon in New York. After I left, he wrote me, 'The sun has gone from California.' We did see each other, but the subject of marriage never came up again."

Clark went forward with Virginia, Carol, Betty, Slim, Dolly, and Joan.

Joan?

Joan Crawford. Followed by Joan.

Joan Harrison.

And parties and hunting and fishing and traveling. None of which could make life stand still.

45

Soon after the beautiful trip to Pebble Beach he had made with the Nivens, their friends, and his, twenty-five-year-old Primmie Niven was dead. Her death was as sudden and as inexplicable as Carole's had been, and perhaps even more unbearable because the cause was so silly. There was a party around the pool at Tyrone Power's. After a barbecue dinner, the guests, including Clark, went inside to play games. The gang always played games: charades, snooker, rummy, magician, marbles—name it. This night they played in the dark a hide-and-seek game. Primmie opened what she thought was a closet door and plummeted into the basement of the house, hitting her head on the cement floor. Twenty-four hours later the concussion killed her.

Within a year, Father Gable's wife Edna had a serious heart attack while Clark had as house guests a famous polo player and his wife. Soon after they left, as Clark was setting up his first vacation trip to Europe, Edna died. There had been too many funerals. Clark did not attend this one.

He left for New York to spend a few days there before sailing (July 12, 1948) on the *Queen Mary*. Anita and Slim saw him off, Dolly met him when he arrived in France, as did the Stricklings. He relaxed in Deauville for a while, playing baccarat at the casino, golf with the Duke of Windsor at his hotel, and King with Dolly at Elsa Maxwell's royal gatherings. He went to Paris and discovered cuisine, hired an open car and valet and motored to Switzerland, drunk—on pleasure. He had been in Europe three weeks. As he entered his first Swiss hotel, he got word from Howard Strickling that his father had died of a heart attack on August 4. He boarded the next luxury liner for New York. This funeral would not take place without him, but it would have to wait. His father was already dead, and wouldn't know that Clark would not get on a plane to hurry to his side. Clark did his mourning aboard ship, rarely leaving his room.

Soon after burying his father, Clark sold the house he had built him at a price far below the market value, a move that exasperated Jean Garceau who was already frustrated by Clark's rigidity about money. Friends urged Clark to buy land in the Valley; it was booming with the postwar housing shortage, and as sound an investment as anyone could imagine. He wouldn't do it. Jean talked him into going into the stock market, but he would invest only $25,000, a pittance to him. His money was to go into savings accounts, he insisted. Since savings accounts were insured only for $10,000, he had cash in banks all over town.

When the subject of money was broached to him, he usually changed it to talk of his shaky career. Particularly did he discuss this with Wayne Griffin, who had become an independent producer. Wayne wanted Clark to incorporate, as so many stars were doing, but Clark said that sounded too complicated, and refused. His mind was on the cataclysmic changes at MGM, and he didn't want a lot of detail work to distract it. In 1948, MGM's net profits sank to slightly more than $4 million, lowest since 1933, worst year of the Depression. When production costs were figured, it was learned that the company was running $6.5 million in the red. Things were so bad Mayer auctioned his race horses and began to appear daily in his office. That being insufficient to shore up the sinking company, he looked for a Thalberg or Selznick to put the place afloat. He chose forty-three-year-old Dore Schary, an Easterner enamored of "message" movies. Clark was of the group in Hollywood who believed message delivering was strictly for Western Union. He was also a member of the Motion Picture Alliance, whose guiding spirit, MGM's James McGuinness, considered the liberal Schary pink—perhaps even red. McGuinness spit all over Schary's ideas, until, after eight months of tension, he left MGM with two other top executives. Outsiders thought these departures averted MGM's pending civil war, but insiders knew the studio was still divided into pro-Schary and anti-Schary camps. Men like Mannix and Strickling were Mayer people. Their job, as they saw it, was to keep the peace at any price, to keep Mayer secure. Gable was not pro anything, and he didn't trust Schary as much as he had trusted Selznick.

Schary clearly proved himself untrustworthy when, as his first thought for Gable, he got an old studio property called *Quo Vadis* off the shelf, and promised to turn it into a major epic. Gable sent word through his agent that he did not wish to appear on the screen for three hours with his knees hanging out. Not wanting to be completely negative, however, Mr. Gable mentioned that he would be happy to perform in any film that resembled *Fountainhead, Foxes of Harrow, A Lion Is in the Streets,* and *Miracle of the Bells*. In fact, Mr. Gable wondered why none of those properties had been acquired for him, but, of course, that was before Mr. Schary's time.

He tried rankling Schary with a game he played very badly: hold-up. Wayne Griffin owned a script for a comedy Clark liked well enough to buy into. Griffin went to Schary, offering the comedy, Clark as its star, and himself as producer. Schary liked the package. He offered $137,000 for the script, and a producer's salary for Griffin. Clark would work on his regular salary, by contract. Wayne went to Clark with the news, and found him playing with Rover.

"Look what this little bastard does, will you?" he said. Clark threw the ball, Rover retrieved it, but instead of returning it, set it down near a couch, and looked up at his master. "He's ready for me to find the ball now," Clark said, and went looking for it. "He thinks I don't know where it is," he said, chuckling. He "found" the ball, threw it, the dog retrieved it, and so on, for half an hour.

Wayne, saying he was sorry to interrupt, told him about Schary's offer. Clark said, "Not enough money. Go see him again." Wayne suggested they ask $200,000 for the script. Clark said, "Five hundred thousand." Wayne said, "Are you kidding? He'll never go for that." Clark said, "Try." Schary nearly went into a coma before he turned down the project. Griffin bought back Clark's interest in the script, which is still for sale, should anyone be interested.

Clark's first film for Schary was *Any Number Can Play*, in which he was Charley King, a gambler with a heart condition who is "a nut for human dignity." The only notable thing about the picture happened during the making of it; Alexis Smith's pivot tooth got stuck in Clark's mustache, causing cast and crew to break into uncontrollable giggles. At least somebody else's teeth were funny for a change.

Clark struck up a friendship with Errol Flynn during the filming. Flynn was on loan to Metro, and they ate lunch together often at a nearby saloon that showed 16mm films of old prizefights. He told Wayne Griffin that Flynn was "a colorful bastard, tough as nails." He also said Flynn was killing himself with cigarettes "like I'm killing myself." Griffin suggested it wouldn't hurt if Clark modified not only his smoking, but also his drinking. "You're going to undo your liver and everything else," said Wayne. Clark replied, "You paddle your canoe and I'll paddle mine," his standard answer to any of Griffin's suggestions about his vices.

Jean Garceau recalls that she saw very little of Clark around this time. When he was free, he went to Oregon to shoot ducks with Carol, or to Phoenix to play golf with Betty. When at home, he courted Joan Harrison, an English dazzler who worked for Alfred Hitchcock, shared some parties with Joan Crawford, and called on Virginia. He had to fend off Paulette Goddard (whose surprise remark about him to Anita Loos was that he was a great gourmet); she was a bit too eager for his present mood. And he made a pal of Ida Lupino, whom he knew through David Niven.

The Lupino household was always filled with her family and friends, so much so that Ida had a bulletin board in the kitchen where itinerants posted their whereabouts. Clark would call her unpredictably and ask if he could come by and sit awhile, and sit he did, with her, or her little English aunt, or anyone else who was around. He talked about Carole a lot, Miss Lupino says, and about his sadness at not having any children. One night, after work, he took her to a party at David Niven's. He was tired, but they were having such a good time they stayed very late. When he took her home, he went in the house for a nightcap. Ida went to the kitchen to make some eggs, and when she returned to the living room, he was asleep on a couch. She put some gladioli in his hands. "In about a half-hour his eyes opened and he looked at the flowers and screamed," she recalls. "He thought things like that were very funny."

Courtesy of Buster and Stevie Collier

Clark and Carole

Bettmann Archive

The most familiar face in the world became the most familiar voice; Clark popularized radio dramas for the unheard-of fee (in the late thirties) of $5,000 per show.

Courtesy of Jean Garceau

A proof from the last photo-sitting Carole did before departing on a fatal war-bond selling trip. A piece of one of the pair of diamond and ruby clips she wears, gifts from Clark, was found among the ruins of the plane in which she was killed. Clark wore it in a locket around his neck.

UPI

Ma was dead. Clark left Nevada, where she died, with two close friends: Eddie Mannix of MGM (left) and Al Menasco.

CAROLE HAD ASKED HIM TO ENLIST AND HE DID . . .

Wide World Photos

August 12, 1942, he was sworn in as a private in the Air Corps. He was forty-one, OCS was tough, Miami Beach was hot but Gable was Gable.

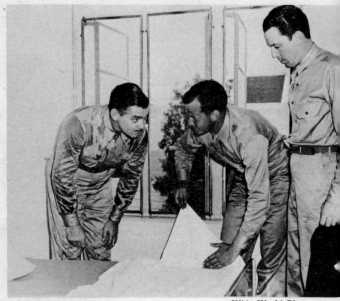

Wide World Photos

Promoted to captain, the star's wartime role was to make a recruiting film for which he recruited his own crew, called "The Hollywood Group" by the guys at the Polebrook, England, air field.

Wide World Photos

Bettmann Archive

Wide World Photos

Among Gable's crew, to the right: Captain John Lee Mahin, Lieutenant Andrew McIntyre, Lieutenant Howard Voss, and Sergeant Robert Boles.

The men at the field started out thinking Gable was a hippodrome thing, but ultimately considered him fearless and "regular."

Museum of Modern Art/Film Stills Archive

Worse than flying bombing missions over Germany was the task of attending the christening of the Liberty ship *Carole Lombard*. Beside Clark, who had been promoted to major, was Fieldsie Lang, Carole's best friend. Irene Dunn broke the bottle; L. B. Mayer tried to smile.

Bettmann Archive

Home went the hero, to MGM and a meeting with the other heroes, Lieutenant Commander Robert Montgomery, Lieutenant (Jg) Robert Taylor, and MGM executive Eddie Mannix.

UPI

Motorcycles were Clark's first post-war passion. He had commandeered one in England and tore around the base there as he later did around the studio. With him is a studio mechanic; Gable was often with mechanics.

Courtesy of Minna Wallis

Wide World Photos

UPI

THESE WERE A FEW OF HIS FAVORITE FRIENDS . . .
First agent Minna Wallis (above opposite)
Steel heiress Millicent Rogers (below opposite)
"Slim Hawks" (above)

Wide World Photos

Model Suzanne Dadolle

Actress Elizabeth Allan

UPI

Betty Chisholm

Courtesy of Anita Colby

Anita Colby

UPI

Actress Virginia Grey

Bettmann Archive

Socialite Dolly O'Brien

Museum of Modern Art/Film Stills Archive

Joan Crawford

UPI

Mogambo co-star Grace Kelly

Wide World Photos

. . . in Solvang, California, in the presence of her nephew, Timothy Bleck (left, dark suit) and sister, Mrs. Basil Bleck (on Clark's right).

Wide World Photos

They honeymooned in Honolulu . . .

Wide World Photos

returned home on the *Lurline* . . .

UPI

settled on the Encino ranch . . .

UPI

socialized with the Z. Wayne Griffins . . . and were estranged
within eighteen months.

He rediscovered Kay Spreckels, whom he had dated in the forties, married her, and became Father Gable to her chil-

UPI

dren Joan and Adolph. Content at last, he let his age show
where it would.

UPI

Arriving in New York with Kay in 1957.

Wide World Photos
Rehearsing for the 1958 Academy Awards Dinner.

Copyright © 1961 Seven Arts Productions, Inc.
Released through United Artists

Clark made Arthur Miller's *The Misfits* as the highest-paid star in film history: with Arthur Miller (above), with Montgomery Clift (below). He died in November 1960, shortly after the film's completion.

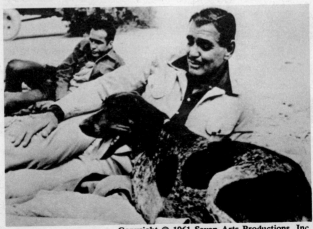

Copyright © 1961 Seven Arts Productions, Inc.
Released through United Artists

Kay gave birth in March 1961 to John Clark, who now attends school in Switzerland. Kay and John Clark at a 1970 premiere of a Disney film.

Copyright © 1961 Seven Arts Productions, Inc.
Released through United Artists

One thing about Clark's movements at this time that none of his friends—even Jean Garceau—knew, was that he kept a suite at the Bel Air Hotel. According to lawyer Greg Bautzer, who lived at the Bel Air for ten years, Clark kept the suite as a hideaway for about a year. The suite had its own driveway off a side street so Clark could come and go without using the hotel entrance. The hotel switchboard and desk provided further protection, and there were few visitors to the suite, either male or female. The front of his rooms opened on the hotel swimming pool, which he used after midnight when it was usually uninhabited. One night he dove into the pool not realizing there was a woman in it—a young girl, actually; an eighteen-year-old New York model under contract to one of the studios. He was terribly embarrassed to find her there because he had no clothes on. The next two nights he joined the young lady for a swim, normally clad. After that, she didn't see him again.

"He was a great swimmer and loved to swim," says Bautzer, who swam with him. Jean Garceau claims Clark hated swimming and rarely went in his own pool.

Bautzer says Clark got to the hotel late because he was working (though that can't be the reason because he quit at five), ate dinner late in his room, and sometimes had an after-dinner brandy with him, either in Clark's room or his own. Bautzer was "stuck on" Joan Crawford about this time, he says, but was quickly taken out of the picture by Gable. He "fired and fell back," flattered even to be a runner-up when competing with the King. His most vivid memory of the man was being in his suite when they heard a squeaking noise outside. "A puppy had fallen into the pool and was swimming frantically because it couldn't find a way to get out of the water. Without a moment's hesitation, Clark, fully dressed, dove in the water and pulled out the dog. He then called a bellman and told him to find the owner and return the poor creature."

Once a few too many people discovered Gable's presence at the hotel, it no longer served a purpose, and he left.

He bought himself a rare Jaguar XK-120, and took it on the desert to see if it really would go over 125 miles an hour. Maybe it gave him the seclusion he had wanted from the hotel. Maybe it was another companion like

Virginia and Betty and Carol and the Joans. Maybe he used it to drive his demons—a change of pace from their driving him.

He began to talk about retiring, a way, perhaps, of getting reassurance about his career and his vitality. Most people ignored the subject as too ridiculous to discuss, so Griffin was his patsy for this game, if that's what it was. He told him, "You can't retire, Gabe; you'd be bored like hell just sitting around counting your money." Clark said, "Well, you know, it's been a great life. If it's over—I have no quarrel."

"You talk like you're ninety years old," Griffin said.

Clark said, "I feel that way."

He and Griffin finally worked together on Clark's second film for Schary. The film, *Key to the City*, with Loretta Young and Frank Morgan, was produced by Griffin from another script he owned. Before filming began, Clark was visited by Duke Wayne, who came to warn him there was a Communist in the crew Schary had lined up. Clark called Griffin and asked how they happened to be using the man in question. Griffin said, "Gabe, I checked his politics. The kid was listed on a lot of things, but not involved. I think he was used, and I don't think it's anything to worry about, but I'll talk to Schary about it, and if there's anything wrong, I'll ask him to get off the picture." Duke then got on the phone and said, "Kiddo, think about it hard because you don't want to do something to Clark, or get him mixed up in something." Schary told Griffin the man had been checked out and found pure when he was hired. Griffin and Gable accepted that.

Even with his friend as producer, Clark stubbornly clung to his five o'clock quitting time. He admitted to Miss Young that he felt like a dog walking out when everyone else was still working, but he had made an issue out of getting the clause in his contract and was honor-bound to it. Clark's leaving early slowed down production, which was suspended briefly when Loretta, who was Mrs. Tom Lewis, had a miscarriage. When the film wrapped, Miss Young and her husband gave a Thank God It's Over party which Clark and Wayne attended in high spirits. Midway into the party they learned that Frank Morgan was dead. They left at once to see if they could be of help to his widow. Clark was a pallbearer at the funeral.

Right after New Year's, Vic Fleming died at age sixty-five.

Clark's moods were so mercurial now, and so talked about, that Virginia Grey felt it necessary to make a rare comment about him to a reporter who hounded her. She said, "He's lonely. Everybody tries to tell him what to do, how to run his life, what pictures to make. His nature makes him listen to everybody, and weigh things carefully. The result is that he's been stung and stung bad a few times, so he tries to withdraw."

Many years later, Clark told reporter Joe Hyams, who commented on the star's remarkable ability to deal with whatever came along: "I don't know whether I'm able to *cope* with problems, but I am able to face them."

To Clark Gable, "facing" a problem meant doing something about it. He had been lonely too long.

PART SIX

GENT

(1952-1960)

46

One morning the week before Christmas, 1949, Clark called Jean Garceau as she was leaving for work. "Are you sitting down?" he asked her. She assured him she was. "Jeanie," he said, "I'm going to be married." Jean blinked at the phone receiver, swallowed hard, and said, "Well, fine. But to whom?"

He said, "To Syl."

She said, *"Who?"*

Like a chorus of owls, Howard and Johnny and Wayne and L.B. and Lolly and Hedda and Dolly and Anita and Carol and all the folks giving odds that the fourth Mrs. Gable would be Grey, Harrison, or Chisholm, echoed the word: *"Who?"*

By the time they knew who, Clark and Syl were married—and divorced. Lady Sylvia Ashley—as the thrice-married Sylvia Hawkes called herself—didn't have a fighting chance in that marriage. A woman in her early seventies today, and in poor health, she still wonders what Hollywood had against her, and why anything written about her has inevitably been cruel. "I never wanted any publicity," she says. Still refusing to discuss having been Mrs. Gable ("It was a bad time in my life and I don't want to talk about it"), she believes, "I am a private person. I always have been."

In truth, she lost her privacy in 1934, when her first husband (for seven years) sued her for divorce in London, naming Douglas Fairbanks Sr. as co-respondent. It was a wow of a case which the whole world watched delightedly, the best tabloid entertainment available. Imagine the appeal of a Depression drama with this cast: Lord Anthony Ashley, heir to the Ninth Duke of Shaftesbury; his wife, Sylvia, a beautiful fair-skinned former show girl—lowborn but haughty; beloved movie star, Douglas Fairbanks; and his adored movie star wife,

Mary Pickford. When this gorgeous assortment of royalty on two sides of an ocean hung out their dirty laundry, they left it out for three years. That's how long it took for Lord Ashley to get his divorce, for Mary Pickford to choose to get hers, for Fairbanks to marry Sylvia, and for Mary to select Buddy Rogers as her next husband. Two years later, Sylvia Fairbanks was a widow, and once again known as Lady Sylvia Ashley to the Hollywood colony who, knowing nothing of her relationship with Fairbanks, decided she had been the downfall of the greatest star it had ever known. Furthermore, she got a lot of his money and took it to England instead of spending it in Bel Air.

In 1944, Sylvia married Edward John, Lord Stanley of Alderly, who started divorce proceedings against her a year later. There were suits and countersuits between them, dragging out for four years the divorce clearly in order for them both. In 1948, when Lord Stanley shed Sylvia, she shed his name, and headed for Los Angeles as Lady Sylvia Ashley. Her sister, Vera Bleck, brother-in-law Basil Bleck, and their two teenaged children lived in a house in Santa Monica, which Fairbanks had left Sylvia. They were a devoted group, and Sylvia stayed with them until, as Mrs. Gable, she moved to Encino.

She met Clark at a party and then confided to an English actor friend that she *must* see him again. He gave a party to which he invited them both, and they dated occasionally afterward. She was a stunning, effervescent lady, and a likely candidate for one of the compartments in Clark's love life. No one, however, took them seriously as a couple. They were not even an item. Onlookers judged Sylvia to be too delicate and too grand for Clark's taste; a meringue among the toll house cookies he preferred. They underestimated the woman who had legally attracted two lords and a mighty movie star. They also underestimated how exciting it might be to Clark to acquire such a one. "I've had every kind of woman," he told Elsa Maxwell after he married Sylvia. "Now I have a siren."

Another member of the English settlement in Hollywood observed, at a party at agent Charlie Feldman's, that "she was all over Clark like a tent. We knew *something* was happening," says the lady. "Sylvia was kissing him madly in the hall." That was Saturday, December 17.

Late the next day, Clark called Howard Strickling, told him he was at the home of Lady Sylvia Ashley, and wanted to marry her before another day passed. Howard said he'd come right over. Mr. Strickling would never admit such a thing, but one can imagine he took a large slug of gin and muttered a few choice words before he left for Malibu Beach, where there was a family champagne party in progress. Howard asked Clark if he was certain he wanted to go through with the marriage. Sylvia said he surely did, and Howard said, "I wasn't talking to you." That set the tone of her relationship with Howard.

Nevertheless, Howard arranged the wedding. He got close friends in Solvang to provide their house and secure a minister, and Sylvia and Clark were married on Tuesday, December 20, 1949. Present at the wedding were the Solvang homeowners, the Stricklings, two members of Howard's staff, an MGM photographer, all the Blecks, and Jean Garceau. It was a simple affair, with Sylvia in a high-necked, tailored, navy-blue wool dress, and Clark in a navy-blue suit and white shirt. Everyone was, to say the least, nervous. The press, immediately notified by Howard, took off like hyenas for the Gable ranch, and stayed there, clamoring at the gate, until the newlyweds sailed for Honolulu on a bona fide honeymoon—Clark's first. The Stricklings flew to Honolulu to make sure Oahu was ready for the Gables and greeted them when they docked. Dolly O'Brien sent a cable reading "Happy leis, happy days," which Clark found funny, but Sylvia found so insulting she stopped speaking to Dolly.

California papers banner-headlined the marriage story. Louella wrote, in the inimitable style that overtook her when she was breathless: "I doubt if any characters in history, and that includes Cleopatra and Antony, Helen of Troy and all the rest, equal the career of these two." A few readers wondered what she meant by that.

One of the few people who seemed happy about the event was Minna Wallis, who had returned to Clark's life as a good friend and hostess after Carole died. She says, "When they married, I thought, 'This is going to be great.' He loved to fish, he loved to shoot, and Sylvia did all those things in England. Howard Strickling, though, was very upset. He thought she was wrong for him."

Wayne Griffin was also a Sylvia supporter. "She was a real good egg kind of person," says Wayne. "A simple, uncomplicated woman. I don't know what broke them down because they laughed and joked and were kind to each other. I thought they were really an interesting, well-adjusted couple." As for the rest of Clark's friends, among themselves they called Sylvia "her ladyship," and they didn't mean it respectfully. Johnny Mahin recalls a dinner party for Clark and Sylvia when they returned from their honeymoon. "Hal Rosson gave it at Chasen's. There were about fifteen of us and Clark was a little drunk. *She* sat there like she was watching a bunch of animals in a zoo. She'd say to him, 'Well, now, who's that one and who's he and who's she?' as though we couldn't hear or didn't understand. We all kept up a rapid conversation. It was a big, round table, and it was awfully embarrassing. She had to leave early, too. She was a real one." Johnny didn't see Clark again until he and Sylvia were divorced. Then he said, "Good God, what made you marry her?" and Clark replied, "I was drunk."

The Langs, whom Clark had seen very regularly—at the parties they gave every six weeks or so, and at holidays —also bowed out in the Sylvia year. Their son believes they probably wouldn't have approved of anyone Clark married after Carole. And that really was the basis of the antagonism of most of his friends. They thought they wanted him to be married, but they didn't really want him to be married to anyone who wasn't Lombard. It should have been their problem, but by glance and comment, they transferred it to him. They responded to his marrying "an outsider" like executives respond when a new company president is brought in by a headhunter.

The friends claim it didn't take Clark more than three weeks to realize he'd made a mistake. That is a wishful exaggeration. The decline of the marriage was rapid, but not that rapid. Clark returned from his honeymoon looking better than he had in years: trim, tanned, bright-eyed, and happy. He turned the running of the house over to Sylvia, and seemed to enjoy the rim of sophistication it took on like a margarita goblet dipped in salt. That the salt cost money didn't seem to bother him, nor did the frenzied activity of getting things in order.

Sylvia's mode of living demanded more space than the house provided. She wanted a guest house, a sitting room for herself, and one for the staff, now increased by the appearance of her personal maid, and altered by the hir-

ing of a cook to replace Jessie. A two-bedroom guest house
and the help's sitting room were added to the house. Sylvia
found Jean Garceau's office the perfect spot for her own
sitting room—she dabbled in needlepoint and water-
colors—but absorbing it meant adding an office on the
Garceau house. All of this took place without a single
display of "mood" on Clark's part. The astounding thing,
considering the stories of the shrine made of Carole's room,
was that he did not complain, either, when Sylvia redeco-
rated it with her own English antiques, and had the walls
painted *pink*.

Sylvia had had Jean Garceau send to England for her
antique furniture right after the honeymoon—quite im-
periously, observers claim. The truckloads of furniture
crates stayed in the driveway until Sylvia could open and
ponder them, then most of the antiques were stored in
the stable. Sylvia intended to change the bulk of the
decorating in the house which was so Lombard it made
her uneasy, but she sensed she should be somewhat gradual
about it. In time she recovered the living room furniture
and added her antiques to the room. She did not like the
sentimental dining room, but did not suggest it be redone.
Instead, she told Clark she would like to build an additional dining room to house her beautiful furniture. A
friend of Sylvia's claims that when she announced this
Clark said, "Sure, Ducky Doodle, whatever you say," and
then got a look in his eyes that would have forewarned a
lesser lady than Sylvia. The same friend says Clark always called Sylvia "Ducky Doodle"—a tooth-grinder of
a name if ever there was one. Sylvia called Clark "Bird."
There was no Ma or Pa at Mayfair in the Valley.

Just as soon as the guest house was finished, Sylvia
invited a pair of titled English friends to stay in it. "To
have his lordship and ladyship visit so soon after the
honeymoon—that was stupid," says Minna Wallis. Others
considered everything Sylvia did dumb because it was
different from what they thought Clark wanted. The most
offensive sight to Gable's chums was Clark carrying Sylvia's tiny terrier, Minnie (as in Mouse, the wags claimed).
Hearing that Clark had bought Minnie a diamond collar
when he, Sylvia, and the dog were shopping one day made
a few of the men's men gag.

But it didn't bother Clark or he surely wouldn't have
done it. Gable was the man nobody pushed around—not

for long, anyway. It is interesting to note that as soon as the lord and lady left the guest house, Clark asked Jean to move her office into it. He said, "I need you here on the spot and so does Syl," and back she came. The office Clark had built on her home became a sitting room.

He thus cut down on the list of overnight guests, but he made no move to divest his home of the ever-presence of Sylvia's family, to whom she was very devoted. Her nephew, Timothy Bleck, was her favorite, and she spoiled him every chance she got.

Sylvia had the British touch with gardens, and had four formal rose gardens put on the grounds. She loved to tend them, and Clark loved to see them blooming. Jean Garceau delighted in them so much Sylvia had one planted at the Garceau house as well. (The exchanges between the Garceau house and the Gable house also involved a cabana Clark wanted built by the pool, "like the one Jeanie has.")

The menus at the Gable house changed from down-home to English and continental. The guest list changed the same way. Syl's social group included the Ronald Colemans, the Robert Douglasses, Charles Boyer, Louis Jourdan, the Winnie Gardiners (Sonja Henie), the Ray Millands, Cole Porter, Gloria Swanson, Joan Fontaine, Merle Oberon, the Nivens (David's new wife was Swedish model Hjordis Tersmedes), Brian Aherne, Sir Charles Mendl, and the Charles Feldmans.* All of these friends entertained Sylvia and her new husband, and she was quick to reciprocate. She liked to entertain and was as fond of the Brown Derby as Carole had been. Benny Massi says he was at the house at least once a week, and often twice. On Sundays Sylvia indulged what Benny terms "a bad habit." She invited all her English friends to come to the house and served champagne and "cold hors d'oeuvres in a Lazy Sue."

She had exquisite jewels and clothes, and Clark, in the first months, enjoyed shopping with her at Adrian's for the latter. He liked seeing her on the ranch in her tweedy

---

* Not exactly foreign, the Feldmans qualified under exotic: handsome Charlie, a much-loved agent, was called "the Jewish Clark Gable" by his friends. His wife, Jean Howard, was the only woman over whom L. B. Mayer was known to have lost his head. When Jean married Charlie, L. B. blackballed all his clients and attempted to get other moguls to do the same.

English country clothes. Like many Americans, Clark considered anything English classy, and even a little intimidating. It wasn't until he felt he was being colonized that his anglophilia began to dim.

Sylvia had a major time-consuming problem, and that was money. She was a rich lady, with diversified investments, but little cash. From Fairbanks alone, she had inherited a half-interest in the million-dollar Rancho Zorro in San Diego; the $50,000 beach house the Blecks used; an additional $15,000 worth of beach property; and films she sold for another $50,000. She also had close to a half-million dollars' worth of jewelry, and $37,000 worth of securities. Clark asked Jean to handle Sylvia's business affairs as well as his own, and it was like merging two conglomerates. Mrs. Garceau wrote in her book: "Her various legal and business affairs were so complicated that she was in constant correspondence with a battery of English barristers, and the muddle was compounded by the fact that her funds were frozen in England." Clark had not married an heiress to turn her into a philanthropy. He was accustomed to wives who paid bills, and Sylvia was not to set a new precedent. He made it clear that either she would have to go to England and defrost some cash, or stop spending.

For at least five months after his honeymoon, Clark continued to look spectacular. He didn't like anyone suggesting anything else. When Sheilah Graham saw him at a party and then wrote in her column, "Clark Gable threw back his head and exposed a neckline on which a thin ridge of fat was beginning to collect," he got furious. He was about to make a film that delighted him, and he felt he was in the peak of condition.

The picture, *To Please a Lady*, is the first of his postwar films in which he is his legend. Though it was not well reviewed, it was as good as any of the Myrna Loy or Rosalind Russell films he had made. In the film he plays a tough on the outside, tender on the inside racing driver taunted by a spoiled, snobbish columnist (Barbara Stanwyck). Miss Stanwyck is even more his speed than the racing cars. "You better listen to what I'm saying or I'll knock that smile off your face," he growls at her. "Knock it off," she says, meaning the smile. He does. Gable was really back, and Stanwyck really had him.

For the first time in eight years, he was happy making

a picture, and that shows, too. The production was loaded with his friends; Clarence Brown directed, Hal Rosson did the photography, Adolphe Menjou had a supporting role, and Clark found bit parts for his sidekick, Lew Smith, and old roommate Hal K. Dawson. The racing footage was shot at Indianapolis during the excitement of the Memorial Day races, which of course was thrilling to everyone involved. Sylvia was in Indianapolis to share the fun and make Clark comfortable. (She brought her nephew as well.) Al Menasco and his son showed up the day of the big race. Clark remembered, making this film, what it was he had enjoyed about acting. He told the studio to ready another property; he wanted to go to work again while his restored ambition was still with him. The choice was *Across the Wide Missouri*, a pioneer story, with Bill Wellman directing.

Sylvia left for England right from Indianapolis, taking Timothy with her. Clark declined to go because he didn't want to get involved in her financial complications. She returned in three weeks, still without cash. Unable to shake loose her money, she took instead $90,000 worth of jewelry. Sheilah Graham released this morsel in her column, unaware that Sylvia hadn't declared the jewels. The Feds swiftly moved in on the Gables, and Clark declared Sheilah Graham unfit for human consumption.

The late summer turned sour for Sylvia. Her nephew, Timothy, whom she left in Europe, became a nuisance for Clark, and she couldn't bear being caught between them. A wire from MGM's New York office to management on the coast read: "GABLE'S NEPHEW NOW IN PARIS REQUESTS ADDITIONAL PAYMENT HIS HOTEL BILL ABOUT $100. THIS IN ADDITION TO MONIES ADVANCED IN ROME. PLEASE AUTHORIZE." The request was okayed, but Clark and Sylvia quarreled about her indulgence of Timothy.

On location for *Missouri*, Sylvia got into much deeper trouble. Clark left first, in late July, for the rugged Colorado location. He drove, carrying Minnie and an extraordinary amount of luggage. In addition to the various items of her usual wardrobe, she packed her paint sets, needlepoint, and some new Western outfits Jean had helped her buy. Soon after she settled with Clark in their cabin at the ranch the unit was using, she attempted to make things cozy. As many people connected with the picture recall, she put "frilly curtains" on the windows, and had the place landscaped with trees, grass turf, and an instant garden. Clearly, she had good intentions. However, the rough-and-ready ensemble, placed at a respectful distance from the King by Wellman, who had not worked with him for years and wanted him properly treated, thought Sylvia was ridiculous. Alan Napier, a British actor in the cast, was the most sympathetic to Sylvia, understanding she was far out of her element. "She was a curiously attractive, even beautiful woman who was still playing the role of a Flapper in England—hair-do, everything. For whatever reason she was doing this, I admit she brought it off. She looked wonderfully young. She did try to fit in, I must say, but she didn't really know how."

Being as much in love with animals as most British, Sylvia couldn't see that Clark was embarrassed when she brought Minnie to eat with them at the tables cast and crew were sharing. She had delicate skin and couldn't take much sun; her staying covered or in the shade also prompted a lot of snickering. Clark fished whenever he had free time. Sylvia tried to fish with him, but had no skill at the sport. Minna Wallis had considered Sylvia sporty—but fishing Colorado creeks was very different from hunting quail on the continent. Wayne Griffin went to visit Clark, and he fished with him.

Sylvia was relieved when the horrid trip was over and she could return to the comfortable life of the ranch. What she didn't know was she had lost Clark, and wouldn't get him back. That their life took on shades of you-go-your-way-I'll-go-mine didn't threaten her; many people she knew lived that way. The Sunday "Lazy Sue's" resumed, but now Clark was frequently absent from them. He took off for Wayne's ranch to ride and practice roping, or just rode one of his own horses around his own ranch while Sylvia and her friends sipped champagne by the pool. Recalls Benny the waiter, "One day he was outside with a horse and he called me. He says, 'Benny, give me a beer. The hell, I'm so sick and tired of those English actors.' I knew they were not getting along very much."

Another day, Benny overheard Sylvia and Clark talking about their expenses. "She says to him, 'We got too much help; one of them has to go.' He says, 'None of my help goes.' And the next Sunday when I went over there, *her* help was gone."

Sylvia blithely continued gardening, painting, and

needlepointing, while Clark missed duck season, trout season, and salmon season. She walked around the golf course with him occasionally, but wilted on the hot days. Where she shone was at social events like the opening of the opera season in San Francisco she and Clark attended with the Griffins. There she could appear in velvet, jewels, and mink, her fair skin making her a stand-out among the outdoorsy California women. She and Clark looked regal together at such an event; the fact that he might fall asleep halfway through it only amused her. She reluctantly went with him to Al Menasco's new ranch in the Napa Valley for Thanksgiving, then perked up when they left for Nassau to spend Christmas in the villa of one of her friends.

They stopped in New York on the way home, and Clark went to Brooks Brothers for fittings on some suits—something he did at least once a year. John Garrity, a salesman in Brooks' custom department, always waited on him. "After the war," says Mr. Garrity, "Mr. Gable liked natural shoulders, trimmer, straighter-cut trousers. He came to us to look like a well-turned-out gentleman." This trip, "with Lady Ashley" as Mr. Garrity calls the then Mrs. Gable, was the first on which he'd ever come to the store with a companion. "He always seemed good-natured, except for that time. I remember they were in the fitting room with the little English tailor, Robert George. Mr. Gable was having a jacket fitted. Lady Ashley tried to tell him to have the shoulders widened. He asked her to leave the room. She did. You could tell he was angry. He had very good taste in clothes and knew just what he wanted."

Though people at all levels of the Gables' lives saw Clark doing a slow burn, they also saw him enjoying himself. He had a particularly good time at the ranch when there were children visiting. He liked neighborhood kids to use the pool, so long as they didn't do anything foolish, and he sat with them and joked with them. He liked visiting friends to bring their children with them as well. One of Sylvia's friends, Bob Douglas, whom Clark had met in London, had a five-year-old daughter named Lucinda, whom both Clark and Sylvia loved enough to invite to the ranch overnight. Lucinda called Clark "Auntie Clark," which always made him laugh.

The trouble with the Gable home with Sylvia in charge was that Clark was no longer the star of it. All of his wives had made Clark the focal point of their existence. Josephine and Ria groomed him; Carole mothered him. Sylvia simply afforded him whatever she was. She made him, for the first time in his life, feel like the stepchild which, as a child, he really was. The situation was so charged for him he couldn't face it head-on until it had become unbearable. Instead of telling Sylvia he couldn't stand having her family around all the time, or her pack of English immigrants, or her lack of interest in his hobbies—he withdrew.

Probably his most outrageous display of childish temper occurred on the night of his fiftieth birthday, a disastrous evening that illustrated the depth of the trouble between him and Sylvia. The first birthday party she had given him had been a formal dinner attended by her favorite European luminaries. She had grown wiser in a year, however, and decided his fiftieth should be celebrated by his friends eating and drinking his favorite things. She invited his: the Menascos, the Stricklings, and the Griffins, and hers: the Adrians and Merle Oberon. Then she said to Jean Garceau, "What does he really, really love to eat? It's his birthday, and I want the food he loves most."

Jean said, "Chicken and dumplings."

Sylvia said, "That's it, then. That's what we'll have."

Jean blanches today at the thought. "Well, of course, it was the last thing on earth that should be served at this gorgeous dinner party. You know, finger bowls and everything, and then chicken 'n' dumplings. It should have been pressed duck."

The chicken probably would have gone over as terribly chic and fun, except for one thing. The new cook made it the day before the party, left it out in the kitchen, and it spoiled. It didn't spoil subtly, so the group would die of ptomaine never knowing what hit them. It spoiled out loud, smelling so evil Martin hardly could bear carrying it to the dining room. When it was put on the dinner plates, it was so overpowering that after the first shock, there was nothing to do except make jokes. Everyone started laughing and telling ruined-dinner stories and pretending to faint, etc., when Clark suddenly pushed his chair from the table and stomped out of the room. He went to his bathroom, locked the door, and didn't come out for several hours. It was not the first time he'd done this ("If he didn't like something he would huff, go upstairs and sit on the john all evening," says Jean)—but it was probably the worst.

It was Clark's way of informing Sylvia the marriage was over, which he did say two months later. About to start another film, he had no intention of taking Sylvia with him. He walked into the house one evening in April, located his wife in her bathtub sipping champagne, said, "Sylvia, I want a divorce," and walked out.

Sylvia went to Wayne for help and Clark got furious that she would do such a thing. "She was desperate," Wayne says. "She loved him and wanted to save her marriage." She went to Minna Wallis, and Minna said, "You know you brought this disaster on yourself. The worst thing you did was try to change that ranch, because the ranch is his whole life to him. I told you, 'Leave it alone. This is his place. This is the way he wants it.'"

Sylvia didn't understand anything that was happening. Stunned, she left immediately for Nassau, and once there, called several friends to ask if they would talk to Clark for her. Jean Feldman obliged, asking him to come for a drink. He didn't mention the separation and when Jean brought it up, she says, "He turned off right away." Jean's analysis of the problem was that Clark didn't dislike Sylvia; he found something very foreign about life with her and didn't know how to handle it.

Anita Colby was in Hollywood at that time, and Sylvia asked her for help as well. She and Clark met for dinner and Anita broached the subject. "What happened to you and Sylvia?" she asked. Clark said, "Well, her family was there all the time." Anita, a family girl herself, said, "So what? That's to be admired." Clark then said, "I don't know what went wrong. I really cared for her."

Sylvia hoped that when she returned from Nassau she'd wake up and the nightmare would be over. Instead, she went to the ranch and found herself locked out of it. She filed for divorce in Santa Monica on May 31, and left the next day for Honolulu with the George Vanderbilts, on their yacht.

47

Clark showed no sign of remorse over his latest marital failure. In fact, he seemed to explode with relief. One night, rehearsing a brawl scene for his new film, *Lone Star*, he, Broderick Crawford (the film's heavy), Griffin (who was producing this one), and director Vincent Sherman tore apart a private dining room at Chasen's. Soon after, as a joke, Clark had a friend in special effects wire Griffin's new Cadillac sedan so it would go "Boom" when started. The technician went haywire, and the charge did considerable damage to the car, to say nothing of what it did to Wayne's blood pressure. When Clark got off the ground, where he had fallen in a laughing fit, he apologized and paid for repairs to the car and Wayne's clothes.

Having cauterized his belligerence, Clark then settled down to work with Ava Gardner, his co-star in *Lone Star*, a mediocre flag-waver of a western in which he and Ava seemed to be wearing hand-me-downs from *Gone With the Wind* and had lines like, (Clark) "You're a *lot* of woman. . . . You're a strange woman . . . but still a *lot* of woman." (Ava) "You know, you're a strange man . . . but quite a lot of man."

The effects of Clark's drinking showed on his face, badly enough for memos to be exchanged in the publicity department saying, "Gable doesn't look like Gable anymore," and questioning how much retouching should be done on the artwork. It is strange how much better he looks in both films he made when Sylvia was around than he does in this one. In any case, Clark always requested, from the start of his career, that his photographs not be retouched. "I want them to leave the character lines," he said. "Otherwise I look like twenty million other guys."

For the moment, however, Gable's face was not MGM's most pressing problem. The power struggle between Mayer and Schary was. Theirs was an extremely complicated corporate battle, the crux of which was Schary's success with several films Mayer had not wanted to make. The two men were in conflict over most potential properties, but Schary, having proved himself right on the right occasions, was able to go over Mayer's head and get approval. Their fights became more and more open, and more and more abusive. Mayer, unable to get corporate support, resigned on June 22, 1951—the resignation to take effect on August 31. There was shock in the industry, but little sadness anywhere except in the offices of such Mayer stalwarts as Mannix, Thau, and Strickling. Mayer was severed with close to $3 million of MGM's cash, 75 percent of which he was able to keep because of a special clause put in the federal tax law.* Schary was made head of the studio. A three-man executive committee, composed of Mannix, Thau, and L. K. Sidney, was appointed to serve directly under him. In the clinch, Mayer's people turned out to be MGM people after all. The old guard was consistent in its dislike of Schary, but united in the effort to maintain the glory of the lion of the industry. When, after two years, that effort failed, the picture drastically changed. Schary's office would become known as "Hollywood's Panmunjom," before, in 1955, it ceased being Schary's office.

The fall of Mayer proved conclusively to Clark that there was no height from which a man could not be tumbled. And his own career was losing height rapidly. He knew the old guard would support him, no matter what, but wondered how long the old guard would last. His MGM contract had nearly three years to go, but there was a statute on the books that would allow him to dissolve it sooner, if he chose. His divorce with Sylvia somewhere in limbo, it was not time to talk of retiring, and anyway, he didn't want to make any move that would jeopardize his studio retirement plan. So the clear and present problem was getting hold of properties that would do more for him than the likes of *Missouri* and *Lone Star*. Jean Garceau thought Clark should change agents, and that suggestion struck him as being sound. Phil Berg had retired from Berg-Allenberg, leaving Bert Allenberg in full charge of the client list. Clark liked Allenberg, but took Berg's early

---

* Louis B. Mayer died of leukemia in 1957 at the age of seventy-two, leaving an estate in excess of $7.5 million.

retirement as a personal affront. Of all the agency's clients, Berg says, Clark was the only one who stopped speaking to him when he left. Griffin arranged a meeting with Clark and George Chasin of MCA, a powerful agency bent on breaking the studio's hold on major stars. After a single lunch with the impressively dignified Chasin, Clark bought himself out of Allenberg's clutches, and signed with MCA.

Chasin's first move was to begin negotiations for amendments to Clark's existing contract. MGM began to amass a file on Gable that would provide evidence in case there would be legal proceedings with the star. In the file were memos reviewing cost and income of Gable's postwar films, and gossip-column items about his marriage and problems at the studio.

When Sylvia returned from Honolulu, Clark asked her to remove her belongings from the ranch. After a few weeks, she still made no appearance, and Clark feared the worst. Propelled by visions of being stripped to his last nickel, he left for the Nevada side of Lake Tahoe. He took up residence at the Glenbrook Lodge, changed his license plates, and established a Nevada bank account. For the next five months he would return only once to California (by law, his attempt to establish a Nevada residency would be aborted if he spent more than twenty-three hours outside the state before six weeks passed). On that one brief trip to Los Angeles, accompanied by the Griffins, he and Howard Strickling made the rounds of his banks. He withdrew all his money, stashed it in a suitcase, and returned to Nevada. After six weeks, when his residency was established, he sued Sylvia for a Nevada divorce. The Glenbrook Lodge closed for the winter, and Clark, wanting to make sure his residency was taken seriously, moved to a ranch in Carson City.

He was not on Elba. He rode, played golf, asked the Griffins to bring some of his guns so he could go hunting. The Garceaus also visited him, at his request, so Russell, a real estate agent, could advise him on Nevada property he was considering. It was his long rest period, so he was not stealing time from the studio. Nor was he pining for female companionship. At the ranch, he took a fancy to a lovely young brunette named Natalie Thompson, daughter of a Beverly Hills socialite. Natalie, who was also serving residency time, became Clark's girl in Carson City. When he was able to leave Nevada (but not return to

California, where Sylvia was suing him), he had the Garceaus buy him a Cadillac convertible and drive it to Phoenix, where he and Betty Chisholm met and entertained them before they flew home and Clark drove back to Natalie.

Clark was also visited in Nevada by MGM producer Arthur Hornblow Jr., who was scheduled to produce his next film, *Sometimes I Love You*. Hornblow appeared in the early weeks, when Clark was at Tahoe, to consult with the star about the film's script, director, and cameraman, as Clark's contract specified. According to a five-page notarized report filed by Hornblow, Clark agreed to do the film and get Ava Gardner ("our pretty girl-friend across the lake") to co-star. Later, when he saw the final script, Clark refused to do the picture, said he never committed himself to it, and called Hornblow a liar. Schary threatened to suspend him, and sent him a "cause of action" summons. Clark turned the mess over to Chasin, who was in the midst of trying to get Clark in on a new deal whereby he could work eighteen months in Europe and not pay taxes on any of his income. Everyone in Hollywood was lining up to board the same ark. The exodus that would ensue would move Sunset Boulevard to the Thames, and intersect the corner of Hollywood and Vine with the Rue de la Paix.

Clark found these loose-ended legal hassles as bad as putting in a pool. He actually felt relieved when Sylvia's lawyers got an injunction against his Nevada divorce, and his lawyers told him he'd best abide by it. He returned to his own ranch shortly after Christmas, and went on a binge of enjoying the feel of it in his hands and under his feet. He was out planting and plowing every day. He romped with his dogs, fed his doves, and restored his sense of identity. Natalie Thompson arrived, "to visit her mother," and was soon seen all around town on Clark's arm. Clark's friends worried about this one looking "so ga-ga over him" because this one was "so *young*." Natalie was soon gone, however, wounded by Cupid, but ambulatory.

Clark spent his fifty-first birthday alone with a coconut cake created by Jean Garceau and a friend.

Sylvia was due in California after her annual holiday trip to Nassau. Unfortunately, she hurt her back in a fall and was hospitalized in New York. Their settlement was imminent, all papers drawn and ready for signatures. Clark

asked Wayne Griffin to see Sylvia on his behalf. Says
Wayne, "He knew I liked her and that we all trusted each
other, and he thought it kinder to settle the thing through
a friend rather than attorneys." After his lonely birthday,
however, he decided to go along. On February 2, he left
with the Griffins on the Superchief. Griffin was active in
the campaign to get Eisenhower to run in '52, and talked
Clark into appearing at a bring-Ike-back-from-Europe
rally in Madison Square Garden. The day of the rally, he
took Clark to the hospital to see Sylvia, and nearly lost
him. "They got to laughing, joking, and talking," Wayne
reports. "They were like two youngsters. When the subject of the settlement came up it was clear Sylvia was not
going to make any trouble. What she wanted from him
was very small compared to what she could have asked.
If she had been avaricious, she could have hounded him
out of his eyeballs.

"They had the time of their lives on that hospital visit.
I had to leave, but I couldn't break Clark away. I called
about an hour later and he was still there. I was sure
there would be a reconciliation. He got back to the hotel
just in time to change and grab a sandwich, and he was
in a great mood."

His part in the rally was to talk to Eisenhower via
transatlantic telephone, their conversation to be broadcast
live. Clark rejected a long speech that had been written
for him and spoke extemporaneously instead. He told the
General the people were with him, and that should he de-
cide to run, he would be the next President. Newspapers
noted, in the coverage of the rally, that no one could tell
the difference between the voices of the two men.

When Clark returned to California he was in constant
conferences with Chasin about his contract for work
abroad. There were all sorts of nit-picky matters involved,
and Clark was in a balky mood. Two things kept the
negotiations going: Sylvia's upcoming settlement, and
Clark's interest in a script he had seen for a remake of
Red Dust, which Johnny Mahin had made even better,
Clark thought, than his original. The story was now called
Mogambo, and was set in Africa, the Gable character having become a white hunter. (King Solomon's Mines,
MGM's latest hit, was the influence.) The romances were
much stronger and not quite so comic as in the original.
The former Harlow part was less raunchy and more mov-

ing; the Astor role was now a woman not toyed with, but loved. Clark wanted to do the film so badly he agreed to star first in a picture he had once turned down. MGM thought, mistakenly, they had him where they wanted him, and tried to get him to waive the tax indemnity clause in his old contract. Chasin let them know that under no circumstances would Clark agree to the waiver, and said that if that was not acceptable, there was no point in discussing the rest of the contract. MGM agreed "to remain liable under the tax indemnity clause. In return, Gable must agree to leave England at his own expense every Saturday and Sunday . . . during the production of the two pictures in England prior to April 5, 1953, unless given express permission to remain."

Another swap was made, with MGM agreeing to drop the cause of action on *Sometimes I Love You* if Clark would do a third picture—the third picture to have a separate contract. MGM agreed to hold *Mogambo* for Gable, unless he postponed its production beyond the date of the seven-year statute that could be applied to his eight-year contract. Clark asked for a letter from the retirement plan committee confirming that none of his new contractual arrangements would interfere with or jeopardize his continued membership in the plan. Mannix stepped in and told Clark not to leave the country until he had such a letter. He received it.

All of these agreements were reached the same week Sylvia was granted a provisional divorce. She was awarded 10 percent of Clark's earnings for one year; 7 percent for the next four—a total of about $150,000. The divorce would become final a year later, and Sylvia would marry Prince Dimitri Djordjadze.

Clark sailed for Paris on the *Liberté* on May 6, 1952, with his guns and golf clubs. He was not scheduled to return until November 14, 1953. *This* was exile. But with all expenses paid, five days a week, and nearly a half-million dollars to pocket when it ended, it could be endured.

48

Clark's first vacation in Europe had been cut short by his father's death. He had a month, now, before starting *Never Let Me Go*. He was in Paris and it was spring. His life was defined and had purpose. He lost no time finding a lovely Parisienne to share the leisure he would soon earn. Her name was Suzanne Dadolle. She was twenty-seven, a successful *haute couture* model and a sculptured blonde who looked more like Lombard than any of the other women in his collection. They shared a romantic month, and Suzanne became his girl in Paris.

In London he settled into a suite at the Dorchester, and then went shopping for a new companion. He chose a Jaguar. Not an ordinary Jaguar, but a custom-built one that he believed could outrace anything on the continent. He'd learned all about racing cars in Indianapolis, and he knew that the trouble with conventional Jags was that they overheated, so he designed one with louvers the full length of the hood, and was so proud of it he almost came apart. It was the only machine of its kind in the world. He instructed Jean to sell his old Jaguar, which couldn't compare, and also told her to sell his motorcycle. Then he fidgeted like an expectant mother until he could get his gorgeous creation into an open space and let her rip.

He had great misgivings about *Never Let Me Go*, a pretentious anti-Communist drama, but was enchanted with his delicate, doll-like leading lady, Gene Tierney. He had hand-picked Delmer Daves to direct, borrowing him from Darryl Zanuck, and apologized constantly for asking him to work on such "a crummy story." When he asked Del to do the picture, he told him he was deeply in debt because he had had to pay mutual death taxes on Carole's estate. "He explained some of it to me, but I didn't pry," says Mr. Daves. "There were legal complications because everything they owned was mixed up together at the time she died. He said he was left almost penniless. He said he needed the eighteen months in Europe to get back on his feet again."

It was the first time Clark and Daves worked together and they got along like the old friends they were. "I never had a conflict with him of any kind," says Daves. "He was more like my son in the relationship; more son than friend. He needed a great deal of reassurance about his work. He would constantly refer to his stage background. It was—I don't know—his security blanket. He was always saying, 'Del, I'm really an actor,' and I would say, 'I know you are, Clark, you don't have to keep telling me.' Then he'd say again, 'You saw me in *The Last Mile*, you know I'm an actor.' He wasn't, truly, he was a personality—an immense personality. I couldn't make him bend in a scene; he was not flexible. I'd try to get him to put a little more shading into a scene, I'd say, 'Clark, you know you're coming out—bang—with this,' and I'd show him what he should do instead. He'd say, 'How's this, Boss?' or he'd call me 'Governor,' like the British. 'How's that, Governor?'—with a naughty grin on his face. I'd say, 'That's closer, Clark.'

"There was a kind of shy, wistful—I don't know how in the hell to express this quality about him, but I saw it time and again. Up on the screen he was a buffalo type who would bust through doors, but innately he was a gentleman—kind, thoughtful, and tender. Curious quality about Clark. Inside he was a gentle man in every sense of the word. He was courteous. Very courteous. He was a smiling man. All I think of about Clark was the twinkle in his eye. We would laugh every day about something.

"He could communicate beautifully. We shot some scenes in Cornwall where they didn't know who Clark was. But he would sit down and ask some fellow how he built his boat, whether he started with the keel or a total design. Cornishmen talk up hill and down hill, so Clark would talk up hill and down hill. He was adaptable to anyone. I'm sure when Clark did his racing picture, everybody on the circuit thought he should be racing, and in Cornwall, they thought he should be a fisherman.

"He hated to be alone. At Cornwall I put him in his own cottage at Mullion Cove. After his first night in it I said, 'Did you sleep well? It was quiet, wasn't it?' He said, 'It was too goddamn quiet; scared the hell out of me.

All I could hear was the sea gulls. I'm not good at being alone.' So he took my room at an inn, and I took his cottage.

"Then there was this childlike quality. For instance, he kept talking about his racing car, and wanted me to see it. Stars weren't allowed to drive themselves to locations, so I didn't even think about it. When we were in Cornwall he kept telling me the car would arrive any day. Well, one day I'm directing him in a scene, and suddenly Clark says, 'Jesus Christ, here it comes.' And up the hill comes this Jaguar he designed. His toy was delivered. I said, 'Obviously this is the end of our shooting for the time being.' He said, 'Would you—could you—remember your lines with this beautiful monster standing here?' I turned to the crew and said, 'Lunch. Everybody eat.' (We could cheat this way.) And I got in that car and for the next hour Clark and I took every curve in Cornwall —*Vroooom, vroooom*. He was a kid. That was the real joy of Clark, that he was a child, and a man. And slightly cornball."

The beautiful Miss Tierney (who is married now to Texan Howard Lee and calls herself Gene Lee) found Clark "an old-fashioned gentleman" who respected women, was rather serious and sweet. She says, "Working on a film, you expect to be taken to dinner by your leading man. Well, we had our 'date' in Cornwall. We went to a pub for dinner. I was depressed and not feeling well, and told him so. He talked about Carole. I also told him how hard it was on my feet to play at being a ballerina; I was a Russian one in the film. One weekend when he went to Paris, he came back with a gift for me: a tube of salve for my feet. He said they told him in Paris it was the best medicine in the world. It was so cute. A sweet gesture from a gentleman."

In Paris, Suzanne Dadolle was showing off a different kind of gift from Clark: a topaz ring some of her friends thought was a portable bridge table. She wore it on Bastille Day, when she and Clark danced in the streets of Paris, drank wine, and sang out loud in cafés, and at dawn went with *tout Paris* to Les Halles for onion soup.

The women he couldn't visit visited him. Joan Harrison showed up in London when Clark returned there from Cornwall. Betty Chisholm arrived for a brief stay a few weeks later. But it was Suzanne, who was in the right place on Saturdays and Sundays, whom he favored. When the seemingly endless production of *Never Let Me Go* concluded in late September, he took Suzanne and his Jaguar and started for Rome, where he fervently hoped he could rid his bones of the chill of Cornwall and London. He got as far as the Villa d'Este on Lake Como, took a look at the resort's famous golf course, called London for his golf clubs, and parked his car.

Clark remained at the Villa d'Este for three weeks. When he got to Rome in late October, he was greeted by frantic wires from *Mogambo*'s producer, Sam Zimbalist. The Mau Mau situation was getting very worrisome, he said, and it was urgent the picture get under way as soon as possible. The time had come for Clark to face a matter he had tried to forget when he left Hollywood, and that was the fact that he had to take a plane to Africa. As much as he wanted to make *Mogambo,* he had almost turned it down because there wouldn't be time for him to go to Africa by boat. *Mogambo* had prompted the "airplane clause" in his contract. If it had not been for that film, he would have had a clause about never having to fly to a location. He did have some curiosity about the new British Comets, the first commercial jets, and did board one in Rome on November 2.

Somewhere over a remote spot in Africa, the plane flew into a hailstorm and had to make a forced landing. The pilot located an open plain, and set the plane down on it. Small planes were sent in very quickly to pick up passengers and crew. Clark wrote Wayne Griffin that the hailstones had been as big as his fist, and that the plane looked like battered silver, done in very elite patterns. "I guess that if the hail didn't get me, my time will come when it will come," he wrote. "I guess I can fly in anything from now on."

He landed in Nairobi on November 2, and left a few days later with *Mogambo* director John Ford for an animal preserve at Mount Kenya, sixty miles away. They flew. For the entire first week of shooting the *Mogambo* cast flew to the preserve every day and returned every night to Nairobi.

The film began in a high-spirited mood that lasted the duration of the group's stay in Africa. Ava Gardner, playing the old Harlow role, arrived with her husband, Frank Sinatra, and secretary, Eileen Thomas. Her first day in

Africa was her wedding anniversary, and jet-lag or no jet-lag, there was a party in their hotel suite. Frank gave Ava a mink coat, which Ava looked at and tossed aside. "I would never let a woman treat me like that," Clark said to a friend.

Grace Kelly, whose twenty-fourth birthday occurred at the end of one week's work, was given a surprise party by Clark and the MGM unit publicist Morgan Hudgins.

Clark had MGM ship him his guns from London, and wired Jean for his favorite hunting clothes, a movie camera, and a steady supply of American cigarettes. The primitive appeal of East Africa got to him the moment they landed in the game preserve. He had found a place exotic enough and hot enough to make him totally happy; he didn't care if he never left. The threat of a Mau Mau attack added to the Walter Mittyness of the whole adventure. He was living a film as he never had before. There was no line between reality and unreality; real people carried pistols to protect themselves against real danger. Real animals lurked in real bush. Ava was probably never so much herself as she was playing the stranded show girl, "Honey Bear." No one ever seemed as vulnerable as wispy Grace Kelly. And Clark could accept himself as a white hunter, as he could well imagine that in another life he was a test pilot or a racing driver. He did, however, wire Jean to send him two of his old Stetsons, which he wore instead of safari hats on his hunting expeditions.

The safari formed to take the group to Tanganyika for a month's shooting was the largest Africa had ever seen. No expense was spared by either MGM or the British government in insuring the company's safety and comfort. An airfield was hacked out of the jungle to keep planes shuttling between Nairobi and the Tanganyika camp. The camp itself was established on the banks of the Kagera River. There were 149 whites in the camp, the British government announced, and 300 blacks. In addition to the tents that housed them, there were a hospital tent, a recreation tent, a projection-room tent, and a dance floor.

In addition to Clark, the fantasy white hunter, there were ten of the real thing. The eleven of them hunted game, which the Africans used as their food supply. Strangely, Clark was not interested in hunting the big game that could be seen all around the camp. One day, when all the real white hunters were elsewhere, the Afri-

cans spotted a crocodile on an island in the river. They got
very animated because they prized the creatures both for
food and their hides. They wanted to get this one, which
was sunning indifferently, and had no way to kill it. Enter
Clark, with trusty rifle. One shot—one—right between
the eyes. The crocodile, 150 yards away, lay dead. From
that day on, Clark's name in the camp was "Bwana," except to Grace Kelly, who called him "Ba," which is Swahili
for "father." They were very impressed with one another,
the King, and the Philadelphia Main Line beauty who
would one day be a princess. Grace went on hunting
trips in the bush with Clark. Clark read her poetry beside
the wide Kagera. They swam together in jungle lakes
and watched the rhinos go by.

Clark's only problem in the jungle was a lion named
John Ford, a fierce leader who dictated more than he directed. Ford, too, had trouble working around the palsied
trembling of Clark's head and hands that had shown up
since the war, but unlike the directors Clark was used to,
was abrupt about it. His entire working manner was abrupt.
One day Clark asked for an additional take on a scene
with Ava, and Ford cut him dead "in front of everybody,"
reports a witness to the scene. Clark walked off the set
and didn't speak to Ford again until the production moved
to England and Sam Zimbalist stepped in as peacemaker.
"Look, Clark," Zimbalist said. "Ford's a tyrant. He's
been used to John Wayne. When you get in there you just
say, 'Yes, Coach,' and everything will be okay." Clark
wound up an admirer of John Ford, but from a distance.

From Tanganyika the company went to Uganda. Clark,
Grace, Ava, Frank, and Morgan Hudgins took a weekend
trip from there to a beach resort on the Indian Ocean.
They flew in a bi-plane Clark later told friends was held
together with chicken wire. The company spread out all
over Uganda, from the desert to the high country. The
footage being flown back to Hollywood caused tremendous
excitement in the studio. Cheering cables were regularly
dispatched to the itinerant actors.

When the African location scenes were finished there
was still sound-stage work to be done, and the group
moved to London, where the pace was much slower than it
had been on location. (English crews take a lot of tea
breaks. Also sausage-roll breaks and pastry breaks.) Clark
got cranky about the English winter. He moved from the

Dorchester to the Connaught, which he found cozier, but nothing would ever make him enjoy the bleak weather. Even in July, he had kept the fireplace going constantly in his suite at the Dorchester. He drank more in London than he had in Africa, saying it was the only way to prevent frostbite.

London was brimming with people he knew from Hollywood; all of them huddled together while they waited out their tax breaks. Clark met them weekly at Tay Garnett's flat, where Garnett and his wife did their best to provide American fare for the homesick exiles. Ava was part of the group, as was Robert Taylor, the Alan Ladds, John Huston, and Lana Turner. Garnett's most memorable night with the group was one when Ava, dressed in a $3,000 ball gown, cooked fried chicken, and Clark "sat on the floor throughout most of the evening, crooning to a fifth of cognac." Mr. Garnett marveled over the fact that Clark "arose after a hearty dinner, leaving an empty Courvoisier bottle, and walked to his car as if he'd been drinking Uncola." (The "car" was the sexy Jaguar which Clark had stored in Rome while he was in Africa, and then had shipped to him in London.)

George Chasin was also in London, but on a special mission. He had in hand the script for a third overseas production which MGM wanted for Clark. He brought word that MGM did not wish, at that time, to negotiate a new long-term contract, but would consider a two-year extension of the old one, which was rapidly expiring. Clark agreed to make the film, which would be shot in Holland, but wanted a vacation before discussing the complex matter of future contracts. He was not only performing in *Mogambo*, but also helping to edit it. Every time he walked out of his hotel, he waded into a gale, and was dispirited. Though he had served only a year of his sentence, he was homesick. The Menascos were due in Europe to take a trip with him, and he wanted to wait until that was completed before trying to think.

Late in April, *Mogambo* ended; Grace Kelly left England; and Clark and the Menascos motored slowly to Rome. Suzanne Dadolle joined them the weekends they spent in France; the Griffins met them in Florence, where Clark was recognized and mobbed. "Doesn't this ever get to be a pain in the ass?" Wayne asked him, as a crowd of autograph hunters surrounded them. Clark said, "Well, it does. But I never forget what it was like to be poor, so I'm grateful that people pay attention to me."

When his California friends left for home, he continued touring, and then parked in Paris. Stateside gossip columnists began to run regular items about his imminent marriage to Suzanne Dadolle. Reporters staked out the Hotel Raphael, where he was staying. At the peak of the curiosity about Clark and his model, he left Paris for London. The Dadolle affair was over.

Clark moved into the Connaught again, and started story conferences and wardrobe fittings for the film to be made in Holland. It was called *Betrayed*, and Lana Turner was the co-star. His contract for the film was separate from any other, and for one picture only. MGM had flatly rejected a Chasin-Gable demand for an increased salary plus percentage of profits on future films. Clark would not renew under the old terms. *Betrayed* would be his last film for MGM.

49

Clark returned to California in mid-December, 1953, a richer, but embittered man. He had, in a sense, left MGM voluntarily, but no matter how the split was viewed, the studio had turned its back on him. The end of the relationship was not really of his choosing. He could not help feeling he had been used and discarded. Says Strickling, "He was disgusted, upset, and angry, and he wanted no part of MGM ever again. What really stuck in his craw was the fact that he got no percentage on *Gone With the Wind*. The thing is, he didn't ask for a percentage because he was anxious to pay off Ria so he could marry Carole. That's all he cared about. That's all she cared about. He got that. And then after Carole passed away he had this great bitterness because they wouldn't give him a percentage."

They wouldn't give him a print of the film, either.

Clark had a copy of every movie he made after 1930, but the studio wanted $3,200 for *Gone With the Wind*, and he wouldn't pay it. *Gone With the Wind*, by 1953, had grossed nearly $100 million, and was still going strong. Clark frequently mused with friends over the $10 million he would have made had he had 10 percent; or even the $1 million one percent would have yielded. His total lifetime pension from his share of the company retirement plan would be $400,000 if he took it in a lump; $31,000 a year if he took it when his contract expired; or $49,000 annually if he waited ten years to begin collecting. The money seemed paltry in the light of what might have been. He did not hold MGM exclusively responsible for the *Gone With the Wind* contract; he also blamed his former agent, Phil Berg. He felt Berg should have taken better care of his interests, and suspected him of being in collusion with the studio. His hurt went much deeper than resentment over one film, to the place in him that had no tolerance for disloyalty.

He had some ends to tie on *Betrayed* at the studio after the holidays. He informed Howard Strickling that he wished to come and go unnoticed, and that there was to be no fanfare of any sort to mark his last days on the lot.

While he had been in Europe, Jean Garceau, following his instructions, removed all traces of Sylvia from the ranch. The house was restored to its original fashion. Betty Chisholm was in it to greet him on his return, and he left with her to spend the holidays with some friends of hers who had a ranch in Texas. He shot duck, quail, turkey, and then went home to finish his work, professionally, but remotely.

His last day at the studio involved portrait sittings for Clarence Sinclair Bull—just as his first day had, twenty-three years before. He arrived for the sittings on time at ten in the morning, finished them, cleaned out the few remaining items in his dressing room (a framed *Parnell* poster among them), said his goodbyes, got in his Jaguar, and drove off the lot. He went for lunch, as he had done so often, at his favorite dive, where he stayed three hours talking to Clarence Bull and drinking a pitcher of memories.

Columnist Dorothy Manners published a caustic item about Clark's being fired and leaving the studio without a party or farewell, and got this wire from Howard Strickling:

Your item this morning about Clark Gable struck Leo in a very sensitive spot. Clark Gable, as you know, is one of the most popular and best-liked personalities to ever work at MGM. This goes from the bottom up and top down. Everyone regretted seeing him leave. This was unanimous. As you know, Clark left because he wanted to. MGM made every effort to have him stay. On the last day of shooting on *Betrayed*, Clark worked in the morning and there was one long parade of friends and well-wishers from every department from executives to back lot. Everyone wished him well and all expressed hope he would return. I am certain Clark could be elected mayor of MGM if ever an election were held. Just wanted you to have this information to keep the record straight. MGM appreciates and loves Clark Gable and you, too.

Many people cried when they saw his Jaguar pass through the back gate. They cried because they loved Clark Gable, and cried because he took with him the remnants of the passion and glory that marked Louis B. Mayer's MGM. The end of a cinematic era was at hand, and the one ahead held little promise.

Clark issued, through George Chasin, the following statement to the press:

I am discontinuing my long-term association with Loew's, Inc. after being with the company for more than twenty years, in order to avail myself of the opportunity of entering the freelance field. I want to express my great appreciation to the many friends and associates at Loew's, Inc., whose help I have had and with whom I have had the pleasure of working.

I wish also to pay tribute to my friends and associates who are no longer alive whose help and guidance over the years meant so much to me.

Ironically, this happened at a time when Clark was back at a peak of popularity he had not known in a dozen years. *Mogambo* had been released shortly before his return from Europe, and was a runaway success. White hunters seemed to have become the last men on earth to Americans of the chlorophyll age, and Gable as a white hunter the last sexy man on earth. Gardner and Kelly were the ultimate challenge to the Gable potency, and clearly, in the film, neither had ever had it better. The public interest in Gable was loud and clear. It took no time at all for Eddie Mannix to approach Clark with an independent production deal, and much less for Gable to reject it.

Chasin was getting offers for Gable's services from every film-maker in town. Clark was getting advice from everyone he knew about the course of his career. The suggestion that he become a director made him laugh. The idea of becoming a producer made him shiver. He really wanted to do what he had always done, but get paid more for it. He told Chasin he'd like to make ten films and then retire. He also told him he didn't expect to live to be sixty.

Leaving MCA to sow his future the way MGM had always done, he took off for Phoenix to ride and play golf with Betty. At home he sought the company of Grace Kelly, visiting the Bel-Air Hotel, according to an employee, "fairly regularly when she was staying here." He took her to the Academy Awards presentation; she was nominated for her supporting role in *Mogambo*, but lost to Donna Reed in *From Here to Eternity*. He received from her a tiny Mexican burro named "Ba." He planned to make her his co-star in his first freelance film, whatever it turned out to be. Friends of both believed they cared enough about each other to discuss marrying. Miss Kelly told reporters after the relationship ended, "Perhaps it would have been different, if it weren't for the difference in our ages."

Clark stayed in constant touch with Howard Strickling, calling him often to find out the latest gossip at the studio. And he loafed, adding bits of his life as Bwana to his life as abdicated king. He bought a jeep and had it upholstered in a souvenir zebra skin; he dressed in full safari uniform when Jean needed a hit man and called him to assassinate a rattlesnake in her backyard. The Stricklings and Joan Harrison found him sunning in safari shorts when they picked him up in Tucson to go deep-sea fishing in Mexico.

Everyone found him in a rigid mood about film properties. He didn't know exactly what he wanted, but he knew what he didn't want. Howard Hawks says, "When he got away from Metro, he got the idea he wanted to be a hero and that was lousy. He asked me to make a picture with him and I said, 'not while you're feeling this way.'" He had been feeling whatever way that was for a long time. MGM story editor Samuel Marx had gone to him in Nevada with a script Schary wanted to buy. Schary sent the editor to see the star, saying, *"You've got to get Clark; he won't do anything for me."* The story was about two Nevada gamblers in love with the same woman. Schary wanted Gable, Flynn, and Lana Turner for the film. Clark turned it down. He said, "I'm not going to do this picture. The girl can't make up her mind which one of us she wants. I don't make pictures where the girl is undecided."

He was in no hurry, and he wanted to make sure that the studios bidding for him weren't just planning to use him to impress their stockholders. He finally made a deal with Darryl Zanuck at 20th Century-Fox for two films, each to provide him 10 percent of its gross, with $400,000 guaranteed and up front. The first, *Soldier of Fortune* (a Gable kind of title if there ever was one), would be started in Hong Kong in the fall of '54; the second, a western with Jane Russell called *The Tall Men*, would be shot in Mexico under the direction of his old friend Raoul Walsh. Clark immediately asked for Grace Kelly for the first film, but she had a prior commitment. Susan Hayward, at whom he had stared through an entire party ten years before, was cast as his co-star. When she was mentioned to him, he couldn't remember who she was.

There was one lady blotting out images of all others for him: Kay.

Kay?

Kay Williams Capps de Alzaga Ungue Spreckels. She was divorced from Adolph Spreckels two years earlier, and lived in Bel Air with their children, Adolph III (called Bunker), age five, and Joan (Joanie), age three. Kay had given up her career as model and starlet years before, but was a woman of some substance. At her divorce

hearing she reported a net worth of $550,000. Louella
Parsons reported that each of the children had a million-
dollar trust fund and that Kay had been given an oil well
by their grandmother.

Clark had seen Kay at several parties since their 1944
romance. During her first divorce suit with Spreckels in
1948 (which dissolved in a reconciliation), Clark had
escorted her to dinner with the Langs. Spreckels cited
this "date" in the second divorce suit, which was an ugly
affair exploited in newspapers for more than a year.
Among other things, Kay testified that Adolph was drunk
almost steadily during their first three years of marriage,
and had once buried an ax in the bedroom door. Adolph,
in a cross-complaint, said money was his wife's only passion. He verbally abused her while the divorce was pending, and after it, beat her unconscious with her own shoe.

Clark began dating Kay, whom he called Kathleen, at
about the time he signed with 20th Century-Fox. They
saw each other daily, spending a lot of time with her
children, and a lot of time playing golf in Palm Springs.
He left her reluctantly when he flew to the Far East for
Soldier of Fortune in early November. She was waiting
for him at the airport when he returned in mid-
December. One film and seven months later, they were
married by a justice of peace in Minden, Nevada.

Kay's sister attended the wedding, as did the Menascos.
Mrs. Gable wore a tailored navy-blue suit designed by
Irene; Mr. Gable wore what he usually wore to his wed-
dings: a navy suit and white shirt. Howard Strickling
released the news to the press, out of friendship. Clark
asked him to do it out of habit: "Kathleen and I are
getting married tomorrow," he had said. "Al Menasco
will phone you after the ceremony, when we're safely
away, and then you can tell the reporters."

"There," he seemed to be saying. "Nothing's changed
at all."

50

She called him Pa, and occasionally he called her Ma. The children called him "Dearest Stepfather." They led the early-to-bed, early-to-rise, pastoral existence of two old marrieds from the day, five days after their wedding, they moved to the ranch. Clark gave Kay the option of looking for a new home that wasn't haunted, but Kay didn't mind Carole's ghost. Rather, she heeded Sylvia's mistakes. She made some alterations in the guest house so it could become living quarters for the children and their governess, and then left well enough alone. Clark ordered the only change that was made in the main house; he had his gun cabinet dismantled because Bunker was too curious about the collection. The gun room was converted to a family den. Later, the caretaker's cottage was turned into a guest house but it got so little use it became Jean Garceau's office.

Kay Gable's job was not so much wife as custodian of a national treasure, and she took it very seriously. She wrote in 1960, "Everything I did had just one thought behind it: Pa's happiness and comfort. I keyed my life entirely to his needs."

He needed more than he'd needed in nearly a quarter of a century, because he'd lost his buffer between Camelot and the rest of the world when he lost MGM. The kind of swaddling the studio had provided its human assets nearly crippled many of them. Ursula Theiss recalls that when her late husband, Robert Taylor, left MGM, he was so helpless he didn't know how to call a restaurant for a dinner reservation. "It was like teaching a baby to walk," she says. The success of marriages like hers and Kay Gable's depended on their ability and willingness to be wife, mistress, and mother studio.

Kay took to the tasks without feminist conflict. She wrote, "I believe in any marriage . . . it is up to the wife to give just a little bit more than the husband. After all, she has more to gain from marriage than he." Her goal was to see that her husband lived like the patrician he had become, and that he was never bored.

They were two people who had had enough adventure. Both wanted peace and stability. Kay gave this description of the order of their days to Liza Wilson of *The American Weekly*:

> After breakfast he reads the newspapers and confers with his executive secretary. . . . The children drop in to say good-bye on their way to the school bus. Mr. G. then checks with his two gardeners and spends the rest of the morning with them, plowing, planting, pruning, watering, and painting fences. . . .
>
> We lunch on trays around two o'clock, by the pool, or on the lazy rocking-chair porch. The afternoons, while I am arranging flowers or working on my scrapbooks, he spends in his study making business phone calls, discussing films with his writers and directors, or reading scripts.
>
> At five-thirty we gather with the kids in the den. And while they have their dinner we have our cocktails and nibble on cheese and crackers. While I work on petit point slippers for Clark and the kids . . . they watch television. Usually we have a game of bingo with Joan and Bunker and the nurse before they leave for their cottage. Before we have dinner we walk over to their cottage and listen to their prayers. After dinner we look at fights or special programs on our color TV set. Sometimes, but not often, I can persuade Mr. G. to run one of his old pictures on his projection machine.

She was not about to make any of Sylvia's uneducated errors. She entertained infrequently, and only for a few friends. Though she had a married brother and married sister to whom she was quite close, she did not let their presence in Clark's home become intrusive. When the Gables went out, it was to industry events Kay felt were important to Clark's career, or to parties she felt he would enjoy. Their presence at either was rare enough to be considered by those who shared it a privilege bestowed on them. The honored couple usually left early, went home, and drank champagne together far into the night.

At a dinner at Mervyn LeRoy's three months after the Gables were married, the privilege of their company was extended beyond the guests' wildest hopes. Clark revealed to them the extraordinary, surprising news that Kathleen was pregnant. The sublime happiness of this pending parenthood was short-lived, however. In November, Kay became ill of a viral infection, was given medication that science has since proven harmful to expectant mothers, and, indeed, miscarried.

Clark was able to handle this deep disappointment without the therapy of frenetic activity. He was a mellowed, seasoned man, a professional at living as well as at acting. Fate couldn't stagger him anymore because there wasn't a known emotion he hadn't rehearsed—had he not suffered for Rhett when Scarlett miscarried?—and hadn't felt. The actor and the man could now feed each other so that neither would ever starve.

He didn't work for nearly a year, and didn't seem to care. He and Kay took a super-luxurious yachting trip with a shipping magnate she knew, and when they returned Clark made a full-time job out of teaching her to shoot and fish. He did consult often with George Chasin about his career, and finally let himself be talked into joining Jane Russell and her husband, Bob Waterfield, in an independent film production. They formed a company called Russ-Field Gabco Productions, and set into motion a film which was given the unfortunate but exploitable title of The King and Four Queens. He then went on a diet to take off the weight he had gained in a year of self-indulgence. The world was not ready for a portly Gable in CinemaScope.

The theme of the publicity for King and Four Queens could well have been "Gable talks." It was a part of the new business of movie-making he was in to promote himself with the press, and it was at this time—when he began to speak to reporters—that the legend of Gable's privacy was set in cement. What reporters found when they got the first interviews with the King in twenty years was that he would talk about anything except himself. He told the press it had been MGM's idea to make an elusive male Garbo of him; but Gable face-to-face was more enigmatic than he had been when he was Howard Strickling's closet Charlie McCarthy.

Reporters always wrote that Gable looked great, and that could well have been because they didn't want to risk losing touch with him. Renee Conley, who fitted his costumes for *King,* found him in less than perfect condition. His complexion was gray, she reports, and he shook so badly he had to sit down between fittings. On the way to one of the fittings, he told her, he had gotten a ticket for driving too slowly on the freeway. She thought, from the color of his skin, that he was ill, but she had no idea of what.

Shooting began in May in St. George, Utah. Clark, watching production costs like a mogul, rented a small house for himself and Kay, and worked long, full days without mentioning a five o'clock quitting time. Kay did not appear anywhere near the working location, so as not to be a distraction. She joined local quilting and needlework groups, cooked and mowed the lawn, all of which activities were well covered by the press.

As rooster to four young chicks (Eleanor Parker, Barbara Nichols, Jean Willes, and Sara Shane) he did little but pose with arms akimbo and a leer on his face. The New York *Times* said the film was "a dreary comedown for Hollywood royalty," and *Time* magazine called the film "an amoral and tawdry Western." Only the trade papers were any kinder. *The King and Four Queens* was the only film made by Russ-Field Gabco Productions.

Clark's next film was much worse. In fact, *Band of Angels,* a Civil War story made in Louisiana for Warner Brothers, with Walsh directing again, was probably the nadir of Gable's career. Shortly before he had signed for the film, *Gone With the Wind* was re-released and catapulted him once again to the top of the list of box-office attractions. Apparently paralyzed by the might of Gable's unfailing bankability, Walsh turned everything familiar and appealing about him into a caricature. He even went so far as to set his big love scene with co-star Yvonne DeCarlo against the background of that lightning and thunder reserved for the mating of the gods.

Everyone, by this time, venerated Gable, not only because of his own stature in the industry, but also because he carried to other studios the mystique of MGM. For Hollywood performers who never made it to that hallowed place, a cornerstone of it was a sacred object. Sidney Poitier, Gable's antagonist in the film, says, "I was in awe of him. He was incredibly disciplined, the ultimate professional. He had gone through the years of training actors were no longer getting, and certainly aren't getting now. When we talked at all, it was about acting. Two shy men aren't going to be buddies very easily."

Yvonne DeCarlo kept a respectful distance from Clark when they were not working together, in deference to his rank. He was courteous but indifferent to her until one day she talked "a little brash" to him and broke through his reserve. "It happened accidentally," she says. "We were walking by the honey wagon one day. That was as near to the set as the fans could get, and they were always lined up to watch whoever went in. I said to Clark, 'They take pictures of me zipping up my fly—so to speak—every time I come out of the wagon.' He loved it. After that he felt he could talk frankly and openly and use earthy language. He liked that kind of humor.

"Kay was that kind of person, too, and he got a big kick out of trading quips with her. He'd say, 'You do what I tell you or I'll kick you in the ass.' Then they'd both laugh together and were very pleased with themselves. Their repartee was always a little zany and maybe a little naïve. But they talked to each other in a way that few other people talked to either of them."

Louisiana turned out for Clark and Kay the way Georgia had turned out for Clark and Carole. They were smothered in invitations to country club dinners, to shooting clubs, to parties and balls. Mrs. Gable had lunch with Mrs. Earl Long (the governor's wife) at the governor's mansion. Mrs. Gable gave her husband a birthday party at the Baton Rouge Country Club. Mr. Gable went quail hunting with a local judge. Mrs. Gable was given the keys to Natchez, Mississippi, when she took a side trip there to tour antebellum homes. The Gables were so lionized everywhere they went they didn't even have to be rich, which they were, for despite the box-office failure of Clark's freelance ventures, his money was coming off the top, and turning him into a millionaire.

Clark always kept an eye on both hands of fate, however. Inevitably, as it petted him with one, it delivered a blow with the other. And now, Kay was in poor health. In June, upon returning from Utah with Clark, she was stricken with angina. She was at Cedars of Lebanon for weeks (during which Clark lived in a room adjoining hers), then confined to bed for a month, then confined to the house and limited activities for two more months. She was well enough in October to send Clark on a hunting trip without her, to take a ride in his new Mercedes with the gull-winged doors, and to attend the premiere of *Giant*. By January she was permitted to go to Louisiana with Clark, but tired easily, and was never out of reach of nitroglycerin pills.

The Gables' life settled ever more permanently into a state of posh domesticity. Clark would make a film, and then he and Kay, and her children—when they were not at camp or school—would take a protracted vacation. Kay traveled with her maid, Louisa, and a wardrobe made for her while she watched, at home. Clark worked at home at the role of father, and was the perfect combination of teacher, disciplinarian, and social director. He made *Teacher's Pet*, a popular Perlberg-Seaton comedy with Doris Day, and then went to Honolulu with Kay for two months. He made *Run Silent, Run Deep*, with Burt Lancaster (a World War II submarine film in which he dies heroically), and then went with Kay to New York to promote the film and take in some shows. When that trip ended, he hunted with Kay, and then again hit the road to promote the film—making a sweep across the entire country—and stopped in Washington to call on President Eisenhower.

He was working at his career harder than he had in two decades, driven by a new anxiety. "I've got a family now, and a big responsibility," he told Jean Garceau. He talked about selling the ranch to cut down on living expenses, but admitted, when his bluff was called, that he still didn't mean it.

He kept after Chasin to line up properties for him, and that his agent did. The Perlberg-Seaton comedy did well, so Clark signed for another called *But Not for Me*, and worked for the first time with Walter Lang, Fieldsie's husband. Clark had rekindled his friendship with the Langs and added their son, Richard, who owned his Oscar, to his collection of hunting buddies.

With this Lang film, Clark again became the darling of critics who had been tough on him since he left MGM, and at times suggested the star retire before his legend did. Now *Life* magazine noted, typically, ". . . in his 65th film, he proves that despite his 57 years, he is still the indestructible all-around charmer." Before this comedy, critics had become picky not only about his acting, but also his looks. Now they ceased to mention the obvious: that suddenly he was aging. After *Band of Angels*, he gained weight that he could not seem to shed, or did not try to. He looked bloated. And, as James Agee noticed, "something unfortunate happened to his mouth." His smile showed spaces between his carefully structured teeth (a puzzling thing, but perhaps an attempt at a natural look on the part of his dentist), and his facial expressions seemed to collapse beneath his mustache. Despite it all, Gable was Gable in his posture and his sense of fun, and his fans stayed with him.

When he finished the Lang film, he and Kay went to Palm Springs, where they had bought a contemporary house near the Bermuda Dunes Golf Club. It was the wife of one of the men with whom he played who observed Clark in the midst of what she was sure was a mild heart attack. Other friends dismissed her report of this, but one, Wayne Griffin, knew if it had been a heart attack, it was at least his second. Clark continued to drink and smoke as heavily as he chose, and that, as much as anything, convinced most of his cronies he was in good health. They still did not know him well enough to understand that Gable was going to live until he died. When journalists asked him about a rumor that his doctor ordered him off cigarettes and liquor, he quipped, "Yeah, I heard about it. I was having a highball at the time."

In the late spring of 1959, Clark began studying the script of his eighth freelance film, a romantic comedy by Mel Shavelson called *It Started in Naples*. His co-star was to be the young, voluptuous Sophia Loren. The power of his appeal was still so blinding no one thought it odd that theirs would be a screen romance between a man nearing sixty and a woman of twenty-five. The picture would start in August in Italy, the new European Hollywood, where the Gables would be ensconced in a proper villa outside Rome. They decided to spend the early summer months vacationing with the children in an

Austrian villa, and sailed for Europe as soon as the school term ended.

Before they left, Clark lost another tie to his past. Jean Garceau, feeling that he was well looked after in his new life, retired. She hired a replacement for herself, trained her for two months, and then, for the last time, moved her personal effects from the Gable ranch. Clark stayed in touch with her the way he stayed in touch with Howard Strickling, and Howard and Jean stayed in touch with each other. For Howard and Jean, the well-being of Clark Gable would always be a matter of paramount concern.

In the mail at his Italian villa, Clark received a screenplay to which George Chasin had attached a note of commendation. It was written by Chasin client Arthur Miller, and was called *The Misfits*. Miller's wife, Marilyn Monroe, also a Chasin client, was committed to the project, and John Huston had signed on as director. Clark read the script, was moved by it, but didn't understand it. An almost plotless contemporary western, it centered on three atavistic cowboys who live hand-to-mouth on beans and booze, making an occasional dollar rounding up mustangs for a dog-food manufacturer; and a child-woman they meet on their travels. It was a far more cerebral work than Clark had ever been offered, and he was flattered by it. He told Chasin he would think about it, and they'd discuss it when he got home. The script called for a lot of rugged action, and that challenged him. But "Gay Langland," the aging, rootless cowboy he would play, mystified him. Like producer Frank Taylor, he didn't want to see anyone else in the part, but he didn't quite see himself in it, either. He really planned to make only two more films, and he wanted at least one of them to be great. If he turned down *The Misfits,* he wondered, would he miss the last chance to prove himself an actor? He didn't know what to do. He was also sadly out of shape, thanks to a four-month pasta orgy. He weighed a record 230.

He returned home late in November, anxious to ponder, with friends, the matter of the *Misfits*.

51

"I've never been able to connect stars with parts I write," says Arthur Miller, "but after meeting Gable I could see him as Gay Langland. He had the same sort of lyricism underneath, something one didn't usually think of, watching him. It was his secret charm—tough but responsive to feeling and ideals."

The star and the playwright met through George Chasin at the Beverly Hills Hotel. Says Miller, "Gable was wavering about *The Misfits;* Chasin keeping pressure on him to do it. He didn't understand it because it was a western yet somehow not a western, and he didn't think he understood what I was driving at. After a couple of hours talk he understood perfectly—Gay was just like *him*."

Clark described "Gay" as a man who "had a truck and a lonely dog, that's all. When he wakes up, he scratches himself, looks around, whistles a little, fries a couple of eggs. . . . The boundaries of his world have always been the mountains and plains of Nevada, and he has a real love of women, but no trust in 'em. Between wild horses and wild women—that's how he lives. . . . The world has gone and left this man. Gay never stops saying about his own life, 'It's better than wages.' At one point he says, 'Fellow, when you get through wishing, all there is is a man's work. Everything else is wages.' " When the announcement of his signing for the film was released, he told a reporter who asked what it was about, "It's about people who sell their work, but not their lives."

He did not sign the contract with Seven Arts, the production company, until January, 1960, because the negotiations were so complicated. Clark (and Chasin) smelled trouble on this picture—as who wouldn't, with the temperaments involved—and wanted protection against all contingencies. Montgomery Clift, who would play a psyched-out rodeo performer, and Monroe were known as card-carrying troublemakers. Miller, who had never written a screenplay before, would have to learn as he went. Huston was as spoiled and unpredictable as any of his temperamental stars.

Even if Clark had not had his own misgivings about *Misfits*, he couldn't have escaped shadows of doubt because all his old friends were against his making the film. Strickling, Wallis, Griffin, Mahin—all told him it would be a mistake to get involved. The first three objected to the project in general. Mahin was more specific.

Clark had asked him to read the script, saying he was worried about the end, but didn't know why. Mahin read it and said to him, "You're dead if you shoot this script. Clark, you're a good competent actor, but you're no Spencer Tracy, and people don't come to see you because you're a great actor, you know that. You can hold your own all right, boy, you and I know you can. But you are looking at a mare with the little colt trying to nudge her tit, hungry, and the mare is heaving, and you say, 'the stud'll go over eight hundred pounds, that's ninety dollars; the mare and colt ought to go around ninety'—you'll be dead. You're dead when you *start* to harass the horses. Just for dog food? I understand what Arthur's getting at, and I like a lot of it, but it's a misfit for Clark Gable."

Says Strickling, "Money was his weakness. It's all he wanted. He finally did *The Misfits* because he wanted to be the guy that got more money than anybody else ever got."

He signed a contract that gave him such tight control of the script not a line could be changed without his okay. He was given 10 percent of the gross and guaranteed three-quarters of a million dollars. His nine-to-five day was written in, ironclad. If he worked overtime, it was to be at a rate of $48,000 a week.

Once he was committed to the picture, Clark holed up at the Palm Springs house with Kay, both of them with one goal: to get the star down to 195 pounds; in khakis and a fitted shirt, there'd be no place to hide more than that. He had until March 3 to lose the thirty-five pounds —that was the starting date. He crash-dieted and went at golf as though he were planning to become a pro when he retired. He read the script over and over and over.

When February ended, he was ready to begin work—but *The Misfits* wasn't. An actors' strike had delayed the film Monroe was finishing (*Let's Make Love*, with Yves Montand). When the strike ended, Monroe delayed the picture Monroe was making. In June there was still no new starting date.

One of the handicaps of the late start was that the group would miss any chance of reasonable weather. Nevada burns to an ash and blows away in the summer. Clark was less disturbed at the thought of being grilled alive than the rest of the group. No place on earth ever seemed too hot for him. He and Kay stayed in Palm Springs long after people with normal body temperatures fled it. Clark even played golf in the desert summer. So long as he had iced tea or lemonade on his golf cart, he was fine. Just fine.

The Monroe film wrapped July 1, and a starting date of July 18 was set for *The Misfits*. Clark and Kay had the lovely idea of leaving early and meeting the Menascos in Minden, where they were married, to celebrate their fifth wedding anniversary. They moved into their location living quarters—a large, undistinguished one-story house which adjoined a golf course and had a pool—and were joined by Bunker, Joanie, their governess, and Kay's faithful Louisa. Martin did not travel with his boss. Clark's working group was an entourage of one: Lew Smith, an innocent, childlike man who worshipped him and was listed as the dialogue coach on *The Misfits* payroll.* The star was provided a chauffeured Cadillac to use for transportation to locations, but chose to drive his Mercedes, usually picking up Lew on the way.

Clark was wary of the fey New York "Method" actors he was to work with but had never met. The method actors were snobbish about him, expecting him to be a hyper-masculine lunk. It was with this mutual skepticism that they gathered for the first time at a dinner party at Frank Taylor's rented house. Frank's wife, Nan, an experienced, sophisticated hostess, planned the evening to be casual but elegant. She was apprehensive because it was a high-powered group that gathered, and Monty Clift

---

* Lew Smith was shot and killed in the mid-sixties in a bar in Culver City.

and Kevin McCarthy, who arrived first, had started the evening making arrogant remarks about the King of Hollywood.

The Gables were the last to arrive, and one must guess that was calculated because Clark was never late, and almost always early. Among those present were Huston, Wallach, Clift, and McCarthy, and photographer Henri Cartier-Bresson. They were sitting around drinking, some of them cross-legged on the floor, when Nan escorted the Gables into the living room. One by one, each stood up. It was an unplanned act; something about Clark just automatically brought them to their feet. There was one large wing chair in the room and Clark walked to it and sat down. It was a tufted, beige monstrosity, tacky enough to make Frank Taylor shudder, but with Gable filling it, wing to wing, it became a throne. In short order, everyone in the room was sitting on the floor around the chair—at the feet of the man they had expected to mock.

They talked about the script of the film, agreeing that it was remarkable, tight, and exciting. Clark mentioned his surprise at how well rounded all the characters were; he had thought Miller had written the film for Marilyn and Marilyn alone. (Marilyn had declined her invitation to the dinner, and so, therefore, had Arthur.) Inevitably, Clift and McCarthy talked about their method of acting, how they related to a part, how they got into it. Seeing curiosity on Clark's face, McCarthy asked what he did when he got a new role to play. He said, "I bring to it everything I have been, everything I am, and everything I hope to be."

Frank Taylor felt that from that moment on, Clark was the leader and guiding spirit of his production. He says, "What we originally wanted was his essence—the essence of the movie star named Gable. I didn't expect that there would be so much to him. He was kind of a poet. His sensitivity about everything undid me."

He was the Billy Budd of *The Misfits* from the first day of shooting to the last. On his first day, he had a short scene with John Huston's friend, socialite Marietta Tree, who had come to visit the director and wound up, at Gable's suggestion, with a small part in the film. She had never acted in her life but later said she had not one moment of anxiety. She said, "Gable was so accomplished, I was never nervous. I felt like a very young ballet dancer being wafted across the stage by Nijinsky."

It is well known now that Marilyn Monroe, as an adolescent, kept a photograph of Clark Gable in her room and told her friends he was her father. She was completely unstrung by the thought of performing with him. It is also known that when *The Misfits* began, Marilyn fancied herself in love with Yves Montand, who had rejected her, was on an elevator of drugs to take her up and down, and that her volatile marriage to Arthur Miller was nearing its bitter end. Even the slightest perusal of the millions of words written about this strange, tortured woman leaves the impression that, at best, Miss Monroe was schizophrenic. As she began *The Misfits*, she was as sick as, if not sicker than, she had been in a lifetime of insanity. Clark sensed this about her immediately and handled her as though he were a male nurse, always calming, soothing, reassuring her. She could not sleep at all the night before she was to do her first scene with him. She took an enormous amount of Nembutal, and, of course, couldn't be moved in the morning. She arrived on the set two hours late, and had in tow Arthur Miller, her press agent Rupert Allan, coach Paula Strasberg, plus two hairdressers, a make-up man, body cosmetician, stand-in, masseur, secretary, wardrobe girl, seamstress, and personal maid. Before making any other move, she left this troup, went to the honey wagon, and threw up. Then they glued her together, and she rushed to Clark to apologize for being late. He put his hands on her shoulders, said, "You're not late, Honey," and led her off by the hand. He softly said something to her that made her giggle, and then laugh. He went off her list of problems, and tried to stay off. "Mr. Gable likes me," she shouted at a reporter one day. "Ask him if I'm the temperamental person I'm pictured."

He tried to protect her. Harry Mines, one of the film's publicists, was having trouble getting Marilyn to keep her commitments to the press, which regularly was in and out of the location. "She was a pain in the ass," says Mines. "We had a terrible fight. I went to Frank Taylor and said, 'I hate this dame, and I'm going to walk off the picture. You're flying people in from all over the world to see her, and she plays games with me and I can't produce her.' Gable heard about the trouble and came to see me. He said, 'If I can help you, you call on me at any time. I realize I'm not Marilyn Monroe, but maybe you can bring the people to me and I can keep them entertained until you can go and find her.' "

One day Clark was leaving at about five-thirty and saw Marilyn being made up and coiffed. He asked her why she wasn't going home, and she said she had to pose for a *Life* cover. He said, "You're not going to have pictures taken after a hard day and hard work, I won't allow it." And he had the session changed.

He treated Monty Clift much the same way—as though Clift were a mental patient—but he was also fascinated by his talent and showed up to watch him work even when he wasn't on call himself.

With Wallach, initially he was uneasy. When they first worked together both of them blew their lines over and over. Eventually they learned to respect each other, and then their relationship turned into a Gable-Tracy stand-off. Clark particularly liked to kid Eli about his Actor's Studio background. Once when they were shooting a night scene at high noon, around a fire, with blankets over them—and sweating in the intense heat like visitors to a steam bath—Wallach smelled the first odors from the lunch wagon and said, "What's for lunch?" Clark looked him in the eye and said, "Boiled ham." Eli taunted him with lines like, "Hey, King, can you lower my taxes?"

"Gable never wanted anyone to have the last line," says Sheldon Roskin, another publicist on the film. "He was always ready with that kind of Hollywood repartee —everything was a gag, a punch line. If somebody one-upped him, he'd say, 'Listen, Bub, we've *got* a writer on the payroll.' "

Clark's one really involved relationship with *The Misfits* was with John Huston. Within the acting group there was competition for best actor of the day—that was real, visible, but constructive in that they were goading each other to new heights of perfection. None of them was forming a friendship; they were learning how to work together, feeling each other out. Between Huston and Gable, there was something else, and those who sensed it found it unhealthy. Frank Taylor termed them "virility rivals." They were the two men's men in the group: the hunters, the boozers, the fearless Hemingway figures.

Huston wore the kind of safari clothes Clark collected in his white hunter days. Huston, at fifty-four, was the younger of the two. And Huston was still in a stage of high-living Clark had abandoned when he married Kay. Clark came to *The Misfits* in the height of serenity in his marriage. Huston was carousing, performing (he rode in a chamber of commerce camel race, for instance, challenging ex-jockey and big-time gambler Billy Pearson), and worst of all, to Clark, he was gambling nightly in Reno, dropping thousands of dollars at a clip and bragging about it on the set. Huston proclaimed, "The one great lesson in gambling is that money doesn't mean a goddamn thing." That kind of statement could open a hole in Clark's gut.

Huston was like Will Gable in many ways, and the zest with which he flaunted his masculinity combined with the impossibility of impressing the man revived Clark's darkest doubts about himself. "Gable had a virility complex," says Harry Mines. "No man, no understudy, no stand-in could do anything he couldn't do." He had *had* a "virility complex" and had shelved it. Huston flagged it into the arena again. What the assemblage sensed was that, like the two fastest guns in the West, the two men would inevitably have a showdown.

In the first month of production, this rivalry was covert because Marilyn's vicissitudes caused so much tension on the set. She had only an occasional lucid day. She was always late, she was often missing altogether, and when she worked, she couldn't remember the simplest lines. There were many days when all work ceased because of her.

On one of them, in mid-August, Harry Mines became the first person in the group to know that Kay Gable was pregnant. Clark and Kay had gone antique hunting while Clark was waiting around for action to begin. When they returned to the set, it was swarming with a new group of junketing press Harry Mines was herding. Clark walked over and asked if he could see Harry alone. He recalls, "I said, 'Jesus, something's happened,' and went to talk to him. He said, 'I don't want to have them over to the car. We've been meaning to tell you this but . . . well, one of the things we bought and it's in back of the car—is an antique cradle.' I said, 'Well?' He said, 'I haven't finished the story. Kathleen is pregnant.' And I said, 'Holy Jesus' and he said, 'You're not to tell. This is our story and Kathleen wants to make the announcement.' I said, 'Of course, but how in the hell are we going to keep them from looking in the back of the car?' It aged me for the afternoon, because the car was there, the cradle was there, and the press was there. I think Kay finally gave the story to Hedda Hopper. She was a great friend of Hedda's." (Actually, it was to Louella she gave the news, and not until October, when her doctor told her she was out of danger of miscarrying.)

On August 27 there was no work because Marilyn collapsed and was flown to Los Angeles. On August 29, an announcement was made that she was suffering from acute exhaustion and would be hospitalized for a week's rest. Production was suspended. No one knew when or if it would resume, or whether Marilyn would ever return.

The last lines of dialogue Clark delivered to her, on August 25, were:

"Honey, we all got to go sometime, reason or no reason. Dyin's as natural as livin'; man who's afraid to die is too afraid to live, far as I've ever seen. So there's nothin' to do but forget it, that's all. Seems to me."

52

Miraculously, Marilyn returned and shooting resumed on September 6. Writer James Goode, who chronicled the making of the film, reported, "Last week's enforced vacation has changed the character and attitude of everyone. The rising tension that culminated in Marilyn's exhaustion has been dispelled, the players and the technicians alike seemed to have acquired perspective about the picture and their jobs, and today were quiet and content."

The location of the shooting moved to a dry lake 4,000 feet above sea level, about fifty miles from Reno. The working unit commuted back and forth every day, because the area was pure alkali, which when dry threw a fine dust into the air and when wet was slippery as oil. Clark drove his Mercedes back and forth every day. The morning call was always for nine o'clock and he was usually there at eight forty-five. Shooting never began until at least eleven, and that was not always because of Marilyn. Sometimes it was Huston, hugging the crap tables since the night before, who arrived two hours late. Clark was determined to stay calm and keep his own order. Says Harry Mines, "He sat outside his trailer dressing room, his leather-bound script open to the place, all ready to go, his books and papers all folded neatly, very neatly." Anyone who asked him whether the waiting was driving him mad got the same type of answer: "No, it doesn't drive me mad. Of course it would be better if we did start. But I'm being paid for it, very handsomely." Even if the shooting didn't begin until three, which happened when Marilyn was involved, he quit at five. He said good night, and he went home. Cast, crew, and reporters began to predict that Gable would finally explode. He was determined to fool them and he did. He had a remarkable talent for simultaneous involvement and detachment. Says Harry Mines, "You couldn't get past his dignity and you didn't want to because you'd realize you were somewhere you didn't belong."

Arthur Miller was often as prompt as Clark, and the two of them had what Miller calls "some long, relaxed, feet-up talks on that desert." Miller admired Gable unabashedly. He says, "He must have been at his wits' end when for days he couldn't get to act at all and the weeks and months going by in so strained an atmosphere. Yet he managed never to blow his cool. He seemed not to blame anybody—just wanted to do his job the best he could, and out. He had no pretensions about acting but he studied his words carefully, common-sensed the real-life equivalents of a scene like a peasant piecing together a situation, slowly, cautiously.

"He would ask me bread-and-butter questions, like how tired the character would be now, how sad, how desperate. He'd boast about how, in the old days, he'd finish a picture, go out on a three-day weekend party, arrive back at the studio Monday morning in his tux, and get his first look at the new script while being dressed by his valet an hour before walking onto the set to begin shooting. He was proud of his no-nonsense ability to bull-doze a scene into existence, create some excitement where they had not put any in. Acting was an animal thing with him, proudly so, but he respected intellectuals who could do, create, set something on its feet. Of course, he was on his guard, everyone is on a set.

"I liked him a lot. He was not about to try to prove anything to anybody concerning himself, his fame, his character. If you wanted something of him you could come and ask; if not, that was all right, too. He had tamed his uncertainty to behave in public, yet he wasn't hard, unfeeling. He wanted to live in balance, not in conflict with others. He'd got to solid ground, he thought —or I thought he thought. He was of course more glam-orous than the real Gay, the one I wrote—any actor would be, the acting dimension does this. But the gallant essence, he did not enlarge on or overdo. He was a gent."

Harry Mines thought the reason for Clark's balance was Kay's pregnancy, and once the others knew of it, they agreed. Says Harry, "After he told me about it and we'd all had that time off because of Marilyn, he kind of got a new step, a new manner. He sort of flourished. He kept saying to me, 'Imagine, I'm going to be a father.' His big joke, once everyone knew, was to tell people that his and Kay's combined ages were over one hundred. He kept grinning and saying, 'Must be the altitude.' "

He seemed to be in a retrospective mood. He wanted to talk about his days of struggle in the theater, and he wanted his old friends around him. Over the weeks, he invited the Stricklings to visit him, and Dave Chasen (the restaurateur with whom he hunted), and the Griffins, and the Mahins. With them he was open about his distress at the way the film was going. He told Griffin getting involved with the project had been a mistake, saying, "I don't see how they're going to get a picture out of it, but I'm with it now and I'm going to do the best I can." He added, "It's been hard on me."

When the Mahins arrived, Clark asked John to go with him to the location one morning. "I want to show you how pictures are made today," he said. Mahin recalls that when they got to the set at three minutes to nine (for a nine o'clock call), only the assistant director was there, and the doubles, and the extras—*"five hundred* extras." Clark said to him, "Isn't this great, John? This is the way they make pictures today." Says Mahin, "He was starting to burn, burn, burn. He knows his dialogue, all ready for the scene—big, long scene, four pages— and nobody's there.

"At ten, Eli Wallach comes in, comes right over and says, 'Sorry, Clark, I guess I'm not used to these hours or something, but nobody seems to be around anyway, so I just took advantage of it.'

"At eleven, Thelma Ritter arrived. She said, 'Well, I knew nobody would be here, so I didn't rush.' Finally, Marilyn showed up and somebody got hold of Huston, who was down at a casino trying to get back five grand. At twelve-thirty, Marilyn, the poor little thing, comes out and immediately retires somewhere to throw up.

"Clark said, 'Well, how do you like it? I quit at five o'clock.' And he quit at five o'clock. They got one shot. It was awful. He said, 'I suspected that this was what it was going to be, but it drives me nuts. It's not professional, John, it's stealing. It's stealing the bank's money and United Artist's money.' "

None of the Misfits knew he felt this way. As far as they could tell, he was peaceful in the knowledge he was getting paid overtime, and, additionally, the most patient man alive. They marveled at the fact he never raised his voice, spoke so low sometimes he was barely audible. They didn't hear him the night he ripped into Kay for being careless about her pregnancy; one of their house guests did. The wife of a visiting dignitary had gotten drunk at dinner and fallen on the floor. Clark walked in the room and found Kay trying to lift her and, says the observer, "went right through the roof. He was afraid she was going to lose the baby. They fought and fought, all night. And Kay was crying and crying."

He had gotten similarly angry with Kay in Louisiana when he felt she was taking foolish risks with her health, had sent her to bed in the middle of a tea she was giving for some Southern ladies, and then kicked her, she admitted, in her "most kickable spot" when he found her out of bed, carrying an electric fan to her maid. He couldn't tolerate her taking herself less seriously than he took her. He loved and needed her. And the baby she was carrying was going to give him two new lives: its and his.

He had very definite plans, now, for his future. He

would make his tenth freelance film, as he had told Chasin he would. He was committed to it, in fact: *Diamond Head* was the picture, and he had the same deal on it he had on *The Misfits*. When he finished that one, he would retire and raise his child, whom he hoped would be a son. He would raise it on the ranch, and was having plans drawn up for an additional wing for the house so all the children could live together.

But all the King's plans, and all his common sense, brushed off him like the alkali dust was brushed from his clothes when he stood before the cameras—and the director behind them. For a month commencing in mid-September, every day he worked was brutal physically or emotionally or both. Those were the days of the roping scenes on the dry lake. They involved such action as Clark's lassoing a wild stallion, being dragged behind it, and running behind a truck that, in the film, driven by Wallach, leaves him on the desert. The most dangerous scenes with the horses were done by two stunt men, both of whom were injured, one seriously. Clark had watched them work and was sickened by the risks the men were allowed to take. He watched them knowing his turn was coming, and that he had a choice of refusing to do any of the action shots. If he had been at MGM, there would have been no dilemma; he wouldn't have been permitted to do them. Here he was not even cautioned about the extent of his exertion.

Clift had been wading into his action scenes without hesitation or complaint. He had been kicked, slashed, and rope-burned. Someone had goofed at the start of his roping scenes, neglecting to put gloves on him, and his hands looked like steak tartare. Since hundreds of feet of film had been shot of him without gloves, he couldn't suddenly appear with them, so he worked with his bloody hands clinging to a rope.

Huston's attitude was to take whatever the actors would give. Real blood, real sweat, and real pain photographed just as well as fake.

Will Gable had declared acting was for sissies. Well, Will would have learned a thing or two if he'd been out on the flats of Nevada watching the actors roping the mustangs.

Says Harry Mines, "Gable didn't need to fool around with those horses, but he wanted to. It was a matter of pride for him. We had wonderful stunt men on the picture, but they were not called in because Gable wanted to do it all himself." Huston helped, taking over for the man whose job it was to flail fake stallion's hooves at Clark while he struggled beneath them.

Lying on his side, hanging onto a rope attached to a truck, Gable was pulled four hundred feet through the alkali bed. He ran an equal distance behind a truck, the dust from its turning wheels billowing into his face. He roped a mare, running, pulling, straining—did it all again and again until Huston was satisfied with the shots.

There were long delays between takes and retakes. Sometimes days passed. Huston got bronchitis from the dust and left Nevada in the most crucial part of the shooting. Miller, or one of the cast, would suddenly be dissatisfied with the script, and everything halted while Taylor, Huston, and Miller struggled over the changes. The weather began to go bad, and many days the group sat all day waiting for the sky to clear. And it was cold when the sun didn't shine—desert cold, and windy. Clark sat outside on a director's chair, a sheepskin jacket thrown over his shoulders like a cape, making jokes. Always making jokes. "It reads well, doesn't it?" Miller asked about the stallion fight in the script. "Yeah," said Clark, "I wondered, when I read it, who was going to do it."

One day during a weather watch, he called to Huston a few feet away, "Hey, Chief, I hear some people over in Dayton have a tame bobcat. Let's go take a look at it." They drove off for the sixty-mile ride like a pair of volunteer firemen to a blaze. During another delay, the two men were flown out of Nevada to go duck hunting, but to two different destinations. They were not about to find out who really was the best shot.

Even the torture of *The Misfits* had to end sometime, and on October 18, the group left Nevada for Los Angeles, where the clean-up shots would be done in comfort at Paramount Studios. The ordeal of the film was almost, but not quite over. There remained, on what was supposed to be the last day of shooting (November 2), one more hassle over the script. Arthur Miller felt the need for revisions in an early part of the film, to clarify the relationship between the characters. He handed five new pages of script to Clark, who had to approve them, and Clark let out the one yell all of the cast and crew finally heard. He went to his dressing room and called his agent. "George," he said, "they're trying to screw up this great script and I won't have it." They talked for a few minutes, and then Clark reappeared on the set. He barked, "There'll be a screening tomorrow morning at nine. I want to see everything you have," and stormed off without saying good-bye.

Marilyn stopped him at the door of the sound stage. "It's finished," Clark said to her. She said, "Didn't you get revisions?" He said, "Don't worry, Hon, I'm finished today, and they can't do anything without me."

The next morning, Gable, Chasin, and Taylor silently viewed the unfinished rough cut of the film. When it ended, Clark turned to Taylor, who had been sitting behind him, and said, "Thank you very, very much. I now have two things to be proud of in my career: *Gone With the Wind*, and this."

They did not revise the early scene, but they asked for a retake of the last. On November 4, Clark and Marilyn did one take, and the picture wrapped. Clark hung around the studio awhile, talking to friends and fans, and then drove home. He wasn't feeling well, and thought he might be getting the flu. He'd been thinking of going duck hunting in Stockton on the weekend, or going with Howard Strickling to look at some horses Howard wanted to buy—but he decided to take it easy around the ranch.

He slept late Saturday, and felt better when he got up, but still under par. He worked out his hunting dog for a while, played with Bunker and Joanie, and then decided to change a tire on his jeep. He squatted to get a grip on the tire, lifted it, and got a pain in his chest so acute it dropped him to his knees. Perspiring, he waited for the pain to subside, which it did, and he went back to the house. Kay thought he looked terribly tired and upset and suggested he eat an early dinner and go to bed, which he did. In the middle of the night he awoke with a headache and what he thought was indigestion. He took aspirin and slept fitfully until seven-thirty. He started to dress. As he bent to pull on his khakis he doubled over as though he had been shot. He woke Kay and told her he had a terrible pain in his chest. He said he thought it was indigestion, but the pain was so severe he felt like "a huge hand has crawled inside me and is tearing my rib cage apart." His face was gray, and he was sweating profusely.

Over his protests, Kay called his doctor, Fred Cerini, who called the Encino Fire Department for emergency oxygen, and rushed to the ranch. While the rescue squad administered oxygen, Dr. Cerini called an ambulance. Clark protested; he didn't want to go to a hospital. He wanted everyone to calm down, fearing the panic would upset his pregnant wife. She insisted on riding with him to Presbyterian Hospital, which also upset him. All the way there, he kept apologizing to her.

The tests immediately done at the hospital confirmed the doctor's opinion that Clark had suffered a coronary thrombosis. The back of his heart muscle had been damaged. He was given anticoagulants and sedatives, and oxygen was supplied to him through tubes in his nose. Nurses were ordered around the clock—two per shift, a pacemaker was placed in his room, and a specialist, Dr. George Griffiths, who had been a consultant for President Eisenhower, was brought into the case. Kay stayed in Clark's room, sitting by his side all day, and sleeping on a cot at his feet all night. When the room became overcrowded with people and machinery, she moved to an adjoining room to sleep. Clark's life was in danger, and would be, the doctors knew, for two weeks, no matter how well he recovered initially.

He did make remarkable progress in his recovery. On Tuesday, only forty-eight hours after he was taken to the hospital, he was well enough to fill out an absentee ballot and vote in the national election. Soon he was able to sit up and read, and to look through a few of the thousands of letters, cards, and telegrams that were bringing him good wishes from all over the world. (President Eisenhower wired: "Be a good boy, Clark, and do as the doctors tell you to do. With my best wishes. Ike.") Howard Strickling, the only person other than Kay to see Clark, acted as the funnel for information about him to their friends. The news was that Clark was getting better every day. Late in the week, the doctor let him listen to his baby's heartbeat with a stethoscope, which cheered him very much. Over the weekend, the pacemaker was removed from his room, and that cheered him even more. Howard dropped a note to Adela: "Clark won't be able to do much but read for a while. Kay wants you please to look around for some books he'd enjoy. You know his taste so well."

On the ninth day of Clark's confinement, Kay felt it

safe to leave him for a few hours, and went home to pick up a few things he wanted. When she returned to the hospital he asked her not to leave him again.

The next day Rufus Martin brought Clark some gifts from friends and reported home that Mr. Gable looked like his old self—peaceful and strong and with good color in his face. Late in the day, Minna Wallis phoned Kay and asked her, "Is there anything I can get for Pa, anything he would like?" Kay said she'd go ask him, and returned with the news that he was sitting up and reading, and would love "some of that custard your maid makes." Minna said she'd bring it to the hospital in the morning.

But in the morning, Clark Gable was gone. At ten-ten, the night of November 16, Kay Gable kissed her husband and went to her room to lie down. At ten-fifty Clark turned a page of the magazine he was reading, put back his head, and died. His wife held him for two hours before she was led down the back steps to avoid the waiting reporters.

He once told a reporter his epitaph would read "He was lucky, and he knew it." There is, however, no epitaph on the crypt next to Carole Lombard's where his body was entombed. There is only a plaque reading

Clark Gable
February 1, 1901—November 16, 1960

Kay Gable gave birth to an eight-pound boy (by Caesarean section), whom she named John Clark, on March 20, 1961. On March 25, 1961, Richard Lang went to see the baby and took with him, as his gift, Clark Gable's 1934 Academy Award. Attached to it was a letter which said, ". . . it is only in your possession. The real Oscar is his alone forever from all those people who gave it to him with supreme thanks for giving us a part of himself."

Appendix

When the research for this biography was completed, there remained the task of understanding the man who emerged from it, a task I felt beyond my professional qualifications. I therefore took Clark Gable, by way of my collected knowledge about him, to someone whose profession it is to comprehend human motivations and needs. Dr. Alice Ginott, the noted psychologist, psychoanalyst, columnist, lecturer, writer, and author of How to Help Children Mourn *and the soon-to-be-published* How to Drive Yourself Sane, *joined me in the noble experiment of analyzing Clark Gable through my research, and research of her own. We did this in a series of therapeutic sessions at which I was both reporter and surrogate patient. Dr. Ginott stopped me in the tracks of obvious assumptions about Clark Gable and taught me the great lesson of not making a judgment where there was no evidence for one. I taped our last session and offer, herewith, a small portion of her remarks, having to do primarily with the Gable-Lombard relationship.*

Clark Gable's mother died when he was ten months old. One would think that at ten months a child would be too young to remember, that he would not miss someone he lost at such an early age.

But at that age an infant has already formed a deep attachment to his mother. She had already become a unique person in his life, an exclusively important adult for him. As such, she's not easily forgotten, or easily replaced.

By ten months a mother's face, smell, touch, her whole being are etched in a child's memory. To lose her at this time was a very traumatic event for Clark Gable. Suddenly, the one person he trusted to always be there had disappeared.

At the very beginning of his life anyone is able to

gratify an infant's needs, to feed, hold, and change him. He does not seem to be able to tell the difference. But as soon as a baby begins to discriminate, he starts to place his trust in his mother. She is usually the one person who seems to be there most of the time when he needs her. He becomes dependent on her. He becomes emotionally attached to her. She becomes the most important person in his life. He cries when she leaves and coos happily when she returns. He won't let anyone else satisfy his needs. He won't let others replace her.

It's usually a very happy time for both mother and child because his need of her is reciprocated by her need to be needed. They are interdependent, delighting in each other as they fulfill each other's needs.

But one day when Clark Gable was ten months old he woke up and his mother was not there. Nor did she return the next day or the next. He never saw her again. But he did not forget her either.

How does one explain to an infant that his mother died? He cannot understand what happened. He only knows that the person he needs most is gone. Despite his tears, she does not return. Since he's unable to mourn or rationalize his loss, he ends up feeling unloved and abandoned.

It's sad that despite his stepmother's attempt, Clark Gable could not accept her as a substitute, to form a trusting and loving relationship with her.

Only when Clark Gable met Carole Lombard did he find the woman with whom he could re-create the feeling he experienced with his mother. He fell in love.

It's interesting that when Clark Gable married older women, people commented that he was looking for a mother. But age has very little to do with mothering. Carole Lombard was much younger than he, yet she was able to continue the mothering he was deprived of at such an early age.

Carole Lombard went out of her way to satisfy her husband's needs and wishes. Their life was arranged to meet his demands. She treated him the way a mother takes care of an infant, expecting little from him except the satisfaction of taking care of him, of making him happy. A baby is not aware of his mother's needs. It takes a lot of growing up before a child accepts that his mother is not there only for his benefit, that her needs and wishes have to be considered, too.

It was a good marriage because Clark Gable's and Carole Lombard's needs were reciprocal. She needed to be giving and he needed to be cared for. She took exquisite care of him. She talked about arranging everything, catering to him, making his interests hers. She did not ask him to reciprocate. To become the most important person in his life, to be indispensable to him must have been very gratifying. It must have made her feel very good about herself that she was able to make Clark Gable feel the way no other woman had.

It's interesting how careful she was not to enrage him. Do you remember when she wanted to change the dining room? She did it while he was away because he hated a mess and he hated carpenters. Later she said that before he came home she got a magnifying glass, got down on her hands and knees, and went over every inch of the dining room to make sure that not a speck of dirt was left.

Do you remember the argument they had about it? I'll read: "When she asked him to enlarge the dining room he said absolutely not! Gable was furious, and Carole couldn't understand why he was so angry. She says, 'Listen, you son of a bitch. What the hell is wrong with you; why do you go off your rocker when I merely mention I want something changed?'

" 'I can't stand carpenters, that's why.'

" 'What do you mean by that?'

" 'They're the only workmen who don't clean up when they're through on a job. Painters clean up, plasterers clean up, but not carpenters. I won't have them in the house. I don't want to be here and see the mess they make.' "

It took Clark Gable a long time to find Carole Lombard, a woman with whom he could form the intimacy he must have experienced with his mother. What a tragedy that he lost her, too, after such a short time. It speaks well of human resilience that he lived through the second loss.

1935 CONTRACT (ABRIDGED)

Agreement executed at Culver City, California, July 29, 1935 by and between Metro Goldwyn Mayer Corporation. a New York corporation hereinafter referred to as the Producer, and Clark Gable, hereinafter referred to as the Artist, for and in consideration of the covenants, conditions and agreements hereinafter contained and set forth, the parties hereto have agreed to do hereby as follows:

1) The Producer hereby employs the Artist to render his exclusive services as herein required for and during the term of this Agreement and the Artist hereby accepts such employment and agrees to keep and perform all of the duties, obligations and agreements assumed and entered into by him hereunder.

2) The Artist agrees that throughout the term hereof he will render the services hereinafter specified solely and exclusively for and as requested by the Producer, and he will render his services as an actor in such roles and in such photoplays as the Producer may designate, that he will render his services as a radio performer, not only by broadcasting in person, but also by making electrical transcriptions and/or by any present or future methods or means, that he will render his services as an actor in television production, and that he will render his services in connection with the broadcasting and/or transmission of his likeness and/or voice by means of television, radio and/or otherwise, whether such broadcasting and/or transmission be either directly or indirectly in connection with or independent of photoplays . . . provided however that the Artist may not without his consent be required to render his services permanently as distinguished from services on location outside the United States of America. . . .

3) The Artist further agrees that during the term hereof he will not render his services as an actor or pose, act, appear, write, direct or render any other services in any way connected with motion pictures or photoplays, nor will he render any services of any kind or character whatsoever in any way connected with dramatic, theatrical, musical, vaudeville, radio, television, or other productions, shows performances and/or entertainments, nor will he render any other similar services to or for himself or to or for any person, firm or corporation other than the Producer without the written consent of the Producer. . . . The Artist further agrees that he will not consent to nor permit any other person to advertise, announce or make known directly or indirectly by paid advertisements, press notices or otherwise that he has contracted to do or perform any act or services contrary to the terms of this Agreement. . . .

4) [Paraphrased] The artist gives to the Producer the right to photograph him, record his voice, as the Producer may desire and further gives the Producer rights of every kind to the use of the name of the Artist. "The Producer shall have the right to double or dub the acts, poses and appearances of the Artist and as well the voice of the Artist, and all instrumental, musical and/or other sound effects to be produced by the Artist to such extent as may be desired by the Producer, such doubling or dubbing of the Artist's voice to be in English and/or in any other language or languages designated or desired by the Producer. . . ." Article 4 also prohibits the Artist from letting other people use his name or likeness in any way.

5) The Artist hereby expressly gives and grants to the Producer the right to lend the services of the Artist to any other person or persons in any capacity in which the Artist is required to render his services hereunder, upon the distinct understanding and condition, however, that this contract shall nevertheless continue in full force and effect, and that the Artist shall not be required to do any act or perform any services contrary to the provisions of this Agreement. . . . In the event that the Artist is required to render services for any other person or persons as

here and above provided, he agrees to render the same to the best of his ability. . . .

6) [Paraphrased] The company may take out insurance on the Artist and the Artist shall have no right or title to it.

7) In the event that by reason of mental or physical disability or otherwise the Artist shall be incapacitated from fully performing the terms hereof or complying with each and all of his obligations hereunder, or in the event that he suffers any facial or physical disfigurement materially detracting from his appearance on the screen or interfering with his ability to perform properly his required services hereunder, or in the event that his present facial or physical appearance be materially altered or changed, or in the event that he suffer any impairment of his voice, then this Agreement shall be suspended during the period of such disability or incapacity [etc.] . . . and no compensation may be paid the Artist during the period of such suspension. . . . It is further agreed that if the Artist alleges that he is incapacitated by illness or other disability or incapacity from the full and faithful performance of this Agreement, the Producer shall have the right at its option to have medical examinations of the Artist made by such physician or physicians as the Producer may designate. Should the Producer have any medical examination of the Artist made as aforesaid, the Artist at his option may have his own physician present at such examination.

8) [Paraphrased] In the event that at any time during the term hereof the Producer or anyone the Artist is loaned to should be hampered by fire, strike or labor conditions or Acts of God, so that the majority of motion picture theatres in the United States shall be closed, the obligations of each of the parties under this Agreement may be suspended. If such suspension should continue for a period of six weeks during any year, the Artist or the Producer may elect to terminate the Artist's employment hereunder.

9) It is agreed that if at the time of the expiration of the Agreement, the Artist is engaged in the production of a photoplay or photoplays or in the rendition of any of his other required services, then and in that event the Artist's employment hereunder at the option

of the Producer may be continued and extended at the same rate of salary and upon the same conditions as shall be operative hereunder immediately prior to the time of such expiration. . . .

10) It is distinctly understood and agreed by and between the parties hereto that the services to be rendered by the Artist under the terms hereof and the rights and privileges granted to the Producer by the Artist under the terms hereof are of a special, unique, unusual, extraordinary and intellectual character which gives them a peculiar value, the loss of which cannot be reasonably or adequately compensated in the damages in an action at law, and that a breach by the Artist of any of the provisions contained in this Agreement will cause the Producer irreparable injury and damage. The Artist hereby expressly agrees that the Producer shall be entitled to injunctive and other equitable relief to prevent a breach of this Agreement by the Artist. This provision however shall not be construed as a waiver of any other rights that the Producer may have in the premises for damages or otherwise. . . . [Paraphrase]: If at the time of such failure, refusal or neglect the Artist shall have been cast to portray a role in a photoplay or shall have been directed to render any other of his required services hereunder, then and in either of said events the Producer shall have the right to refuse to pay the Artist any compensation during the time which would have been reasonably required to complete the portrayal of said role and/or during the time which would have been reasonably required to render such other services, and in either of such events the Producer shall also have the right to extend the year concerned of the term of his Agreement and all of the provisions hereof for a like period of time. . . .

11) No waiver by the Producer of any breach of any covenant or provision of this Agreement shall be deemed to be a waiver of any preceding or succeeding breach of the same. . . .

12) All notices which the Producer is required or may desire to serve upon the Artist under or in connection with this Agreement may be served by addressing the same to the Artist at such address. . . .

13) Nothing in this contract contained shall be construed

so as to require the commission of any acts contrary to law, and wherever there is any conflict between any provision of this contract and any material statute, law or ordinance contrary to which the parties have no legal right to contract, the latter shall prevail. . . .

14) The Artist shall provide at his own expense such modern wardrobe and wearing apparel as may be necessary for any and all roles to be portrayed by the Artist hereunder, it being agreed however that should so called character or period costumes be required the Producer shall supply the same. The costumes, apparel and other articles furnished or paid for by the Producer pursuant to the terms of this Agreement or otherwise shall be and remain the property of the Producer and shall be returned promptly to it.

15) Subject to the provisions of Paragraph 2 hereof that the service of the Artist may not be required permanently, outside the United States of America without his consent, it is understood that the services of the Artist hereunder are to be rendered at such place or places as may from time to time be designated by the Producer. When the Artist is required to render his services on location outside of a radius of 25 miles from any studio used as a base for the production of any photoplay . . . the Producer agrees to furnish the necessary and reasonable first class lodging and transportation if available required for the Artist during and on account of the rendition of such services.

16) The Producer agrees to give the Artist credit as a "star" or "co star" on the screen and in advertising and paid publicity issued by the Producer in connection with photoplays in which the Artist appears for the Producer. . . . The Producer further agrees that in giving the Artist credit as aforesaid the name of no other member of the cast shall appear in type larger than that used to display the Artist's name. Nothing contained in this Paragraph shall be construed so as to prevent so called teaser and/or special advertising, publicity and/or exploitation relating to the story upon which each respective photoplay is based. . . . [No] casual or inadvertent failure to comply with the

provisions of this Paragraph shall constitute a breach
of this Agreement.

17) The term of employment hereunder shall be deemed
to have commenced on December 13, 1934 and shall
continue for a period of seven years. . . .

18) The Producer agrees that during each year of the
term hereof compensation will be paid to the Artist
for a period or aggregate of periods of not less than
forty weeks. . . . Any compensation due the Artist
hereunder shall be payable on Saturday of each week
for services rendered up to and including the Wednesday preceding. During any period or periods in which
the Artist is not entitled to compensation hereunder
he shall be deemed to be laid off without pay, and
during such periods of course the Artist shall not have
the right to render his services for any person, firm or
corporation other than the Producer without the written consent of the Producer first had and obtained.
The Artist agrees that of the layoffs without pay of
the Artist pursuant to this Paragraph at least six
weeks thereof will be consecutive during each year of
the term hereof. The Producer further agrees to give
the Artist at least one week's advance written notice
of the commencement date of each such six consecutive weeks layoff and each such layoff shall com-
mence on the date thus designated, provided
however that if on such date the Artist's services are
being rendered in connection with any matter or thing
not then completed, the commencement of such
layoff at the Producer's option may be postponed until
the completion of such of the Artist's required services
as the Producer may desire in connection with such
matter or thing. Notwithstanding anything else where
contained herein the Producer agrees that a period of
not less than one week during which the Artist shall
be required to render any services hereunder shall
intervene between the completion of the ordinary as
distinguished from retakes, added scenes and/or
changes, photographing of the Artist's role in any
photoplay hereunder in the commencement of the
photographing of his role in the next photoplay.

19) The Producer agrees that during each year of the
term hereof during which the Artist commences and
completes the roles assigned to him including all re-

takes, added scenes and/or changes desired by the
Producer in connection therewith in more than 3 photoplays, it will pay him in addition to the compensation provided for in Paragraph 18 hereof the sum of
$25,000 for each such photoplay in excess of 3, to
be payable in the manner hereinafter provided: upon
the completion of each excess photoplay concerned if
the Artist fully and completely keeps and performs
all of his obligations and agreements hereunder and
if as to the year concerned of the term hereof the artist is ready willing and able to render his services
hereunder throughout the year, then whether or not
an aggregate of $50,000 would be payable pursuant
to the first sentence of this Paragraph 19, the Producer agrees that an aggregate of not less than
$50,000 including payments made pursuant to the first
sentence of this Paragraph 19 will actually be paid by
it during each year of the term hereof in the manner
hereinafter provided. . . . [Money to go in Bank of
America National Trust and Savings Association as
a trustee.] . . . Should the Producer suffer any loss,
cost, expense and/or damage by reason of any
breach by the Artist . . . [notice will be given the
Artist that the Producer has suffered such losses; ar-
bitrators may make an independent investigation,
which Producer and Artist will abide by.]

20) [Deals with previous contracts]
21) In the event of the merger or consolidation of the
Producer with any other corporation or corporations
or in the event of the sale or transfer by the Producer
of a major portion of its assets . . . the Artist shall
continue to perform his duties according to the
terms and tenor hereof to and for such successor in
interest and/or assignee and/or transferee.

EXCERPTS FROM THE GRAPHOLOGICAL ANALYSIS, CHARTING AND MICROSCOPIC EVALUATION OF TWO SPECIMENS OF THE HANDWRITING OF CLARK GABLE WRITTEN AT AGES 23 AND 41 BY DANIEL S. ANTHONY

Clark Gable's handwriting at age twenty-three expresses individuality, versatility, artistry and vague self-reproach for not being the person he consciously thinks and feels he ought to be. It shows him to be living in a state of emotional flux and psychosexual irresolution. He must have blamed himself continuously for feeling more prissy and demanding than most persons recognized in him.

His writing in this conflicted period indicates that he had to be much closer and more intimate with his mother and women than with his father and men. If he had no mother or father around him during his formative years, then he chose mother figures rather than typical father figures in his search for surcease from the miseries of growing up and being what conventional society and his friends expected of him. His script at this period illustrates so many of these feelings of uncertainty, self-abnegation, and real self-doubt about what actually gave him joy and happiness.

A case in point would be the adaptation of the name Billy instead of Clark. "Bill" was male and manly; "Clark" was associated with the sissy way he often felt in his internalized comparisons of himself with the masculine prototypes and tough fellows whom he wanted to emulate. His written "Billy" is not only significantly larger than "Clark," but also graphically articulated with far more dynamic expression. This larger, more self-confidently defined "Billy" shows his greater desire at this stage of his life to come across as the masculine Bill prototype. Comparing the height, breadth, and dynamism of stroke quality between the Billy and the Clark Gable, one readily discerns the inferior quality, movement, and personality projection in the latter.

At age twenty-three his heart, head, gut, and his very

life are in limbo. He is searching for a real identity, a reason to feel important, a key to an ambitious drive in an otherwise ambivalent and unhappy life. And up to this 1924 specimen of his writing, the resolutions to his problems seem to have evaded him.

At age forty-one, these five lines we have from which to judge his progress toward his chosen goals give us more nuances and qualitative subtleties about his changing habits, thoughts, and feelings. His 1942 script projects quite clearly his own concept of: "I've come a long way, baby." The larger size, the more consistently defiant backhand or left-leaning strokes, express quite adamantly his growth in ego strength and self-assurance as well as a modicum of self-acceptance and self-actualization.

He has begun to shore up his weak foundations and truly believe in the masculine image he presents to the world, but why does he still write the girlish backhand, the mama's boy script, the lonely and introspective projections of an essentially unfulfilled dreamer? Because, so long as he lived (I am suggesting from this 1942 specimen alone), he always wanted to become a more accepted intellectual, a creative genius or poet-philosopher-artist type genius, and not the cocksure sex symbol with which he had become identified.

He *was* now intellectually sharp enough and sufficiently shrewd and conniving to play his King's roles to the hilt and remain cock of the walk, while biding time for a stroke of delayed genius with which he might smite his movie world.

His 1942 script corroborates his acceptance of his playboy, sex idol, roustabout, love 'em and leave 'em male dominant role. Unfortunately, his "feminine," soft, tender writing proves also that he became and remained a Don Juan character in real life because his libidinous motivations confused him about who he really was. Since he could not figure himself out, he must have had to use alcohol as an opiate to convince him he was the man everyone else knew he had to be. Or, in order to live with himself, he needed the help of alcohol to maintain the illusion of his masculine kingly world status while really wanting always to relax into the sensuous world of poetic dreams and total irresponsibility.

(Daniel S. Anthony, who submitted a lengthy analysis of

Clark Gable's handwriting to this author, is America's foremost college instructor in handwriting forensic expertise
and the psychology of handwriting. He and his wife,
Florence, conduct a seven-semester graphology program at
the New School for Social Research in New York City.
He also directs a consultation service used by the legal,
medical, and psychological professions, and by business
and industry. He and his wife are partners in the New
Jersey firm of Daniel S. Anthony Associates.)

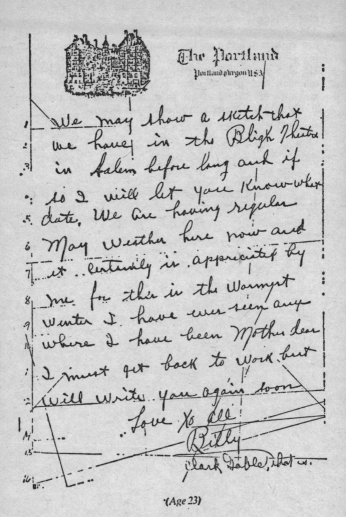

The Portland
Portland, Oregon U.S.A.

We may show a sketch that
we have in the Bligh Theatre
in Salem before long and if
so I will let you know what
date. We are having regular
May weather here now and
it certainly is appreciated by
me for this is the warmest
winter I have ever seen any
where I have been Mother dear
I must get back to work but
will write you again soon
Love to all
Billy
Clark Gable, that is.

(Age 23)

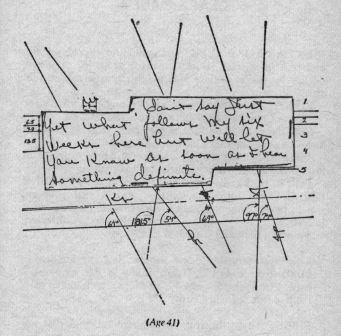

don't say just
Yet what follows my six
weeks here but will let
you know as soon as I hear
something definite.

(Age 41)

LAST WILL AND TESTAMENT
of
CLARK GABLE

I, CLARK GABLE, being of sound and disposing mind, and free from fraud, duress, menace or undue influence, do hereby make, declare and publish this, my Last Will and Testament.

FIRST: I hereby expressly revoke any and all former Wills and Codicils thereto heretofore made by me.

SECOND: I hereby declare that I am married to Kathleen G. Gable and that I have no children.

THIRD: I direct that all of my just debts, expenses of last illness and expenses of burial be first paid.

FOURTH: I give, devise and bequeath to JOSEPHINE DILLON, my former wife, that certain real property situate in the County of Los Angeles, State of California, known as 12746 Landale, North Hollywood, California, and more particularly described as follows:

The West fifty (50) feet of the East on hundred (100) feet of Lot 9, Tract 5588, as per map recorded in Book 59, page 49, of Maps, in the office of the Recorder of said County.

FIFTH: All of the rest, residue and remainder of my estate, real, personal or mixed, I give, devise and bequeath to my beloved wife, KATHLEEN G. GABLE.

SIXTH: I direct that all succession, inheritance or other death taxes or duties (by whatever name called) imposed upon or in relation to any property owned by me at the time of my death or required to be included in my gross estate under the provisions of any tax law shall be paid out of the residue of my estate without any charge therefor against any specific bequest or devise hereunder or against any assets not included in my probate estate.

SEVENTH: I hereby generally and expressly disinherit each and all persons whomsoever claiming to be and who may be my heirs at law, and each and all persons whomsoever who, if I died intestate, would be entitled to any part of my estate, except those herein provided for. If any devisee, legatee or beneficiary under this Will, or any person claiming under or through any devisee, legatee or beneficiary, or any other person who, if I died wholly or partially intestate, would be entitled to share in my estate, shall in any manner whatsoever, directly or indirectly, contest this Will or attack or oppose, or in any manner seek to impair or invalidate any provision hereof, or shall endeavor to succeed to any part of my estate otherwise than through this Will, then in each of the above mentioned cases I hereby bequeath to such person or persons the sum of One ($1.00) Dollars only, and all other bequests, devises and interest in this Will given to such person or persons shall be forfeited and become a part of the residue of my estate.

EIGHTH: I hereby appoint my beloved wife, KATHLEEN G. GABLE, to serve as executrix of my estate, without bond.

IN WITNESS WHEREOF, I have hereunto set my hand this—————day of————————, 1955.

————————————————

The foregoing instrument, consisting of three pages, including the page signed by the testator, was on the date hereof by the said CLARK GABLE, subscribed, published and declared to be his Last Will and Testament in the presence of us, and each of us, who at his request and in his presence, and in the presence of each other, have signed the same as witnesses thereto.

————————————Residing at————————
————————————Residing at————————
————————————Residing at————————

Index

411

SPELLBINDING BIOGRAPHIES OF SUPERSTARS

_____ 80353 APPLE TO THE CORE: The Unmaking of The Beatles, McCabe and Schonfeld $1.95

_____ 80889 CAGNEY BY CAGNEY, James Cagney $1.95

_____ 48355 CLEMENTE! Kai Wagenheim $1.45

_____ 80746 FONZ: The Henry Winkler Story, Charles E. Pike $1.50

_____ 80365 GROUCHO, HARPO, CHICO AND SOMETIMES ZEPPO, Joe Adamson $2.50

_____ 80917 JACK BENNY, Irving Fein $1.95

_____ 80228 JUDY GARLAND: A Biography, Anne Edwards $1.95

_____ 80209 KATHARINE HEPBURN, Gary Carey $1.95

_____ 78946 LIZA! James Robert Parish $1.50

_____ 78568 MY WAY OF LIFE, Joan Crawford $1.50

_____ 80211 SHOOTING STAR: A Biography of John Wayne, Maurice Zolotow $1.95

_____ 81394 VALENTINO, Irving Schulman $1.95

_____ 80496 YES, I CAN, Sammy Davis Jr. $2.75

Available at bookstores everywhere, or order direct from the publisher.

SBS 7-77

POCKET BOOKS
Department RK
1230 Avenue of the Americas
New York, N.Y. 10020

Please send me the books I have checked above. I am enclosing $_____ (please add 50¢ to cover postage and handling). Send check or money order—no cash or C.O.D.'s please.

NAME_____

ADDRESS_____

CITY_____ STATE/ZIP_____

SBS 7-77